Modern Standard Arabic
An Arabic Reading **Book**

Tarek Mahfouz

Written by:
Tarek Mahfouz

Edited by:
John Palmer

Cover Design:
Leo Alvarado

ISBN: 978-1-304-92494-0

First printing:
March 2014

Printed in the United States of America

TABLE OF CONTENTS

Introduction
The purpose of this book is to shed a new light on Modern Standard Arabic, which has not been adequately covered in teaching Arabic as a foreign language. This is MSA in Conversation.

How to use this book
This book is organized into more than sixty lessons. Most of the lessons are centered on topical dialogues, each designed to highlight specific vocabulary in context. Vocabulary sections and questions in English follow each dialogue. There is a fully vocalized text and a translated text at the end of the book to remove any ambiguities in the Arabic texts or to help you understand the lessons.

There are also grammar lessons in the book, but they are not exhaustive: the goal of this book is to increase your vocabulary rather than improve your Arabic grammar.

The main feature of this book is dialogue written mostly in Modern Standard Arabic. These conversations are between individuals in a certain situations or discussing particular topics. Conversations are better to introduce new vocabulary than presenting words in a list, and this is one of the main goals of learning a language: to use words in sentences. This way you will be acquiring new words and understanding how to use them in context.

MSA in conversation
Is MSA used only in written texts and not spoken?
Not necessarily. MSA is the language used in many spoken situations. Although each Arab country has it is own dialect, the widespread usage of satellite TV and the internet means there is demand for mutual understanding among Arabs. Their common language is MSA, which means that all Arabs can understand each other. There is a growing number of non-Arabs who are interested in the Arab world, most of whom only study MSA in their home countries.

An increasing awareness of this group's existence puts pressure on the media to use MSA. This version of Arabic is the one usually taught in foreign language schools. It is most apparent in any type of spoken materials that are used all over the Arab world: TV interviews, video games, education software, classroom teaching and public speaking.

Regardless of the situation, Arabs do not speak one form of the language exclusively in conversation, whether MSA or colloquial. Instead, they alternate between the two (especially when it comes to words related to religion or social situations, where MSA is used). Spoken Arabic tends to be mainly colloquial, and written texts are mainly MSA, but not consistently. There are many mutual words between MSA and colloquial Arabic. It is possible to trace many colloquial words to its MSA/FusHA origin if the Arabic words are not imported from other languages.

Conversations in Arabic progress differently to English conversations, and responses do not always parallel those in English. This is because of an abundance of well-wishing, niceties, and greetings that require certain, fixed words and phrases in response. These are expected responses and could be uttered anywhere in the conversation but must be as a specific response to hearing certain information. The situations where these phrases are used range from someone travelling to talking to someone who has just finished praying. It is important to know what to say in these situations and how to respond, as an Arab could find it offensive if these phrases are not used when expected.

Questions about the dialogues and vocabulary sections
After the dialogues there are questions written in English. These have two potential functions. They could test your understanding of the Arabic conversation or they could be used to aid your understanding of the conversations' progression, as the order of questions matches the development of the dialogues.

As well as asking questions in English, the vocabulary sections, which follow each dialogue, help you to understand new words and idioms.

Reading section:
The supplementary reading section is a short, fully vocalized and translated text that can help you practice reading. You can use it as such, or you can test your reading by reading it back to your instructor. You can also use it to learn grammar rules, especially to determine why certain words are in certain cases. You can also use it as the basis of a Q and A.

Hand-written notes
The ability to read hand-written text is important. I included some hand-written materials in some lessons.

Grammar
The grammar in the book is chosen to cover topics that are either not covered in a typical Arabic grammar book (such as the correct usage of the two words that mean "never") or not adequately covered in Arabic textbooks, such as verb forms and examples of tanween.

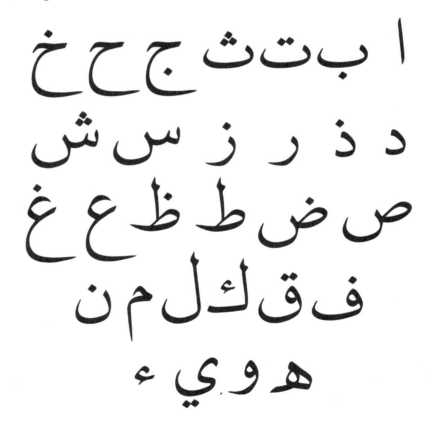

عَلَامَات التَّرْقِيْم

Punctuation marks

Punctuation is relatively new to the Arabic language and, as you see, most of the punctuation marks are taken from Western scripts. The question mark faces to the right because the writing is right-to-left. The comma and semicolon face upward so that they are not confused with the "waaw". The quotation marks are written like two pairs of smaller parentheses and are written on the line, not breaching it.

Arabic does not have an apostrophe. Until now, you would have seen different shapes for quotation marks and for parentheses. Note that the Qur'an itself does not have any punctuation marks.

؟	(( ))	؛	،	"	: :	◆
Question mark	Quotation marks	Semicolon	Comma	Quotation marks	Colon	Period
علامة الاستفهام	القوسان	الفاصلة المنقوطة	الفاصلة	التنصيص	النقطتان	النقطة
—	( )	•••	=	✕	[ ]	/	!
Hyphen	Parentheses	Ellipsis	Relational sign	No apostrophe	Square brackets	Back slash	Exclamation point
شرطة	القوسان	علامة الحذف	علامة التبعية		القوسان المستطيلان	الإشارة المائلة المعاكسة	علامة التأثر

Even though the Qur'an does not have any punctuation marks, it has many instructions written in a very small font over the verses. These give the reciter certain directions for correct recitation, and so are similar to punctuation marks. These indicators are beyond the scope of this book, but are easy to learn and can be found near the end of any copy of the Qur'an, although they themselves are not part of the Koran. Above are some examples of these recitation marks.

These are the arabic numbers from one to nine:

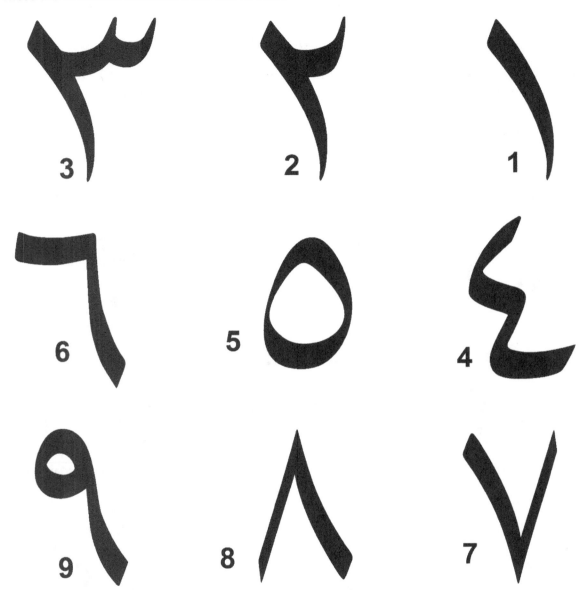

The objective of this introduction is to be able to name and locate the Arab countries first in English, then in Arabic. Most of the place names are very close to their English counterparts (with the exception of Egypt). The second goal is to be able to locate the Arab countries on a map and to know which country borders which other countries. In general, most Arab countries are large and easily identified. Some countries, however, are more difficult to identify. These are the countries in the 'fertile crescent' or 'al-hilal al-khaSeeb': Iraq, Syria, Jordan, Palestine and Lebanon, and also the smaller countries of the Gulf region: United Arab Emirates and Qatar. Some parts of the Arab world are grouped together, for example, the Gulf region or the Saharan countries, Morocco, Tunisia and Algeria called 'al-maghreb'.

The Arab world is going through a period of great change. The case of Sudan is one example, where the people of the South voted to secede from the Arab north. There are similar divisions in countries such as Yemen, Libya, Syria and Iraq, all of which could see changes to the geography of the region.

السكان	الدولة	السكان	الدولة
٢٨,٢٢١,٠٠٠	العراق	٢٤,٨٠٧,٠٠٠	المملكة العربية السعودية
٣,٣١١,٠٠٠	سلطنة عُمان	٦,١٩٨,٠٠٠	الأردن
٣,٩٠٧,٠٠٠	فلسطين	٤,٦٢١,٠٠٠	الإمارات العربية المتحدة
٨٢٤,٠٠٠	قطر	٧١٨,٠٠٠	مملكة البحرين
٢,٥٩٦,٠٠٠	الكويت	١٠,٣٨٣,٠٠٠	تونس
٣,٩٧١,٠٠٠	لبنان	٣٣,٧٦٩,٠٠٠	الجزائر
٦,١٧٣,٠٠٠	ليبيا	٧٣١,٠٠٠	جزر القمر
٨١,٧١٣,٠٠٠	مصر	٥٠٦,٠٠٠	جيبوتي
٣٤,٣٤٣,٠٠٠	المغرب	٤٠,٢١٨,٠٠٠	السودان
٣,٣٦٤,٠٠٠	موريتانيا	١٩,٧٤٧,٠٠٠	سوريا
٢٣,٠١٣,٠٠٠	الجمهورية اليمنية	٩,٥٥٨,٠٠٠	الصومال

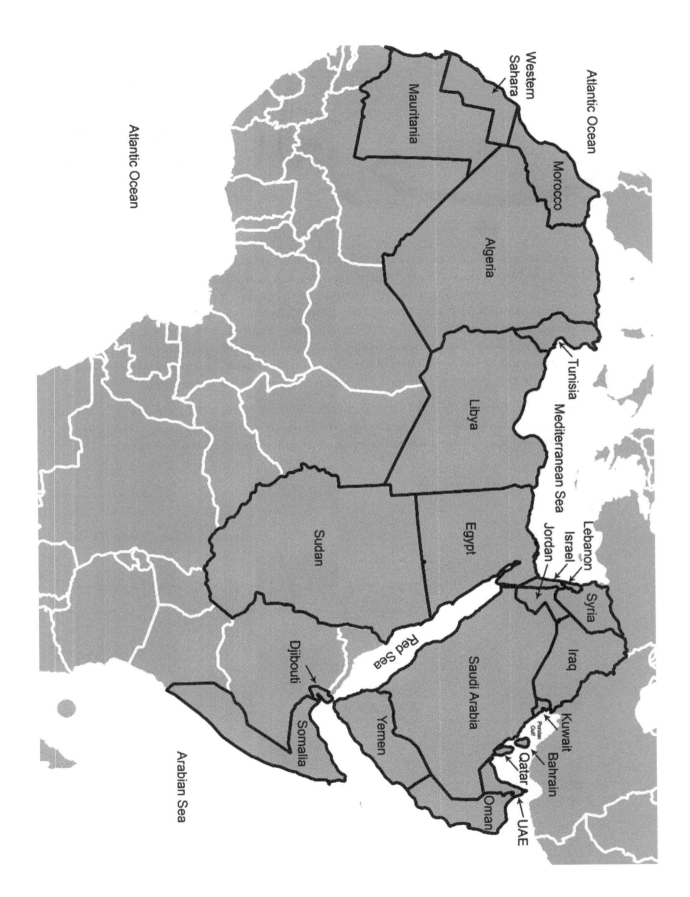

This is a list of the Arab countries with their respective capitals. (Number 1, for instance, says Saudi Arabia - Al-Rhyiad.)

1. اَلْسَعُوْدِيْةٌ-اَلْرِيَاضُ

2. مِصْرُ -اَلْقَاهِرَةٌ

3. اَلْبَحْرَيْنُ-المَنَامَةُ

4. قَطَرُ-اَلْدَّوْحَةُ

5. عُمَاْنُ-مَسْقَط

6. اليَمَنُ-صَنْعَاءُ

7. سُوْرِيَا -دِمَشْق

8. اَلْأُرْدُن -عَمَّان

9. فِلِسْطِيْنُ -اَلْقُدْسُ

10. لُبْنَاْنُ -بَيْرُوْتُ

11. اَلْعِرَاْق-بَغْدَادُ

12. اَلْكُوَيْتُ. الكويت

13. لِيْبِياْ -طَرَابُلُس

14. تُوْنِس -تونس

15. اَلْجَزَأِئِر-الجزائر

16. اَلْمَغْرِب-الرَبَأْط

17. مُورِيتَأْنِياْ -نَوَأْكشُوط

18. جِيْبُوْتِيْ -جيبوتي

19. اَلْسُوْدَأْن-الخَرْطُوْم

20. اَلْصُوْمَأْل -مَقَدِيِشُوْ

21. -اَلْاِمَاْرَأْت- أبو ظبي

11

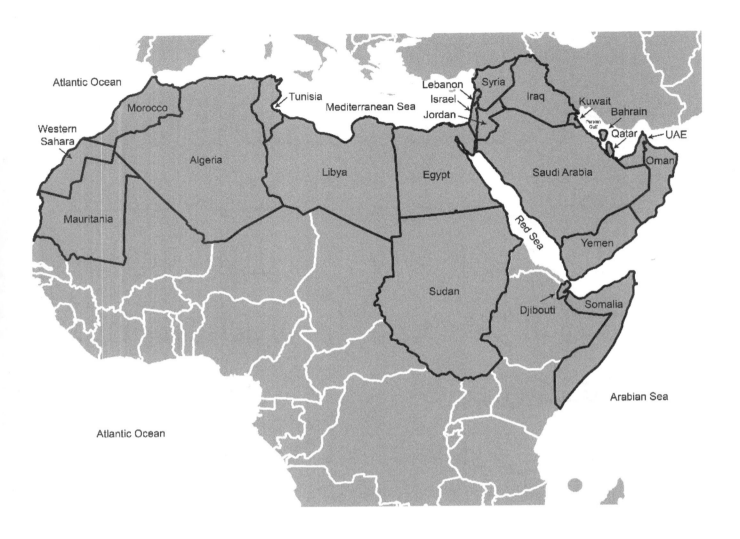

On the blank map overleaf, write the names of the Arab countries and the surrounding bodies of water. Please note that in maps produced in the Arab world, you will not find the state of Israel: it will be presented as the state of Palestine. Sometimes Arab maps are presented slightly differently to Western maps. Further, the name of the Persian Gulf will be called the Arabian Gulf, and Morocco will occupy the space of the Western Sahara. Note: On some of these maps, you can see Greater Sudan. In 2011, this country split into two smaller countries when the South voted for independence. South Sudan is not an Arab country, but its northern neighbor is.

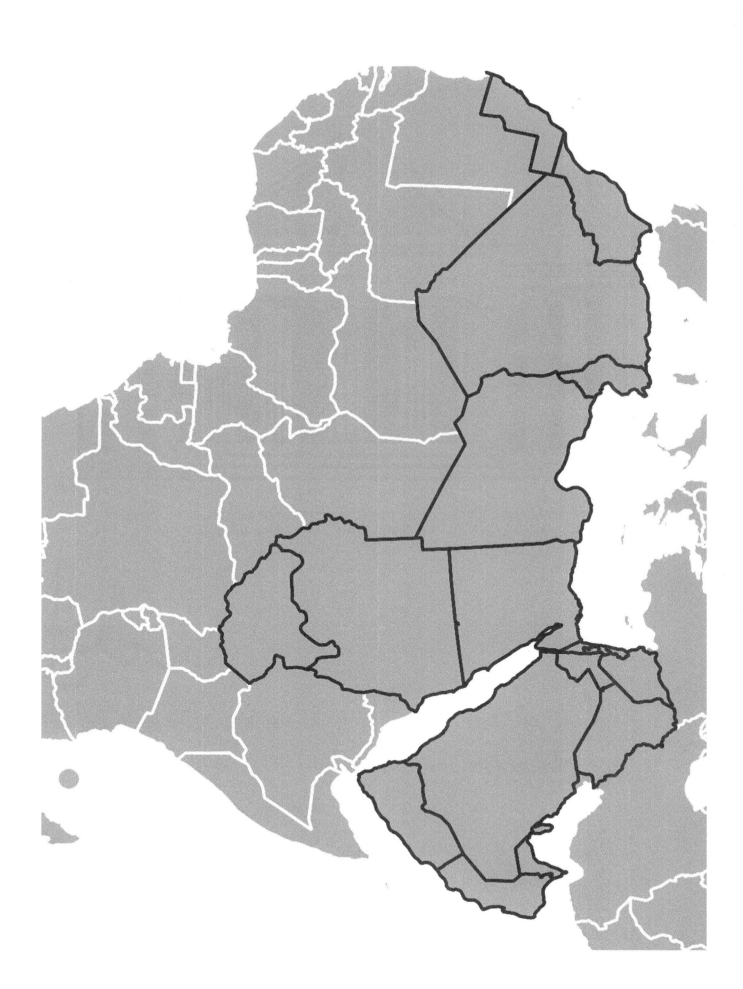

حَفلَةُ تَعَارُفِ طُلابِ القِسْمِ العَرَبِيِّ بِالجَامِعَةِ الامْرِيكِيَة

This is a conversation taking place in the Arabic department of an American University. The students are describing where they are from and why they chose to study Arabic.

علي: اسْمِي عَلِّيٌّ، وَانَا مِنْ وِلايَةِ نورث دَاكُوتَا.

محمد: أهْلاً وَسَهْلاً يَاأُسْتَاذ عَلي، انَا مُحَمَّدٌ مِنْ بِرُوكلِين، مِنْ وِلايَةِ نيويُورك.

عمر: اسْمِي عُمَر وَأَنَا ايضاً مِنْ نِيويُورك.

دافيد: اهْلاً وَسَهْلاً بِكُم، اسْمِي دافِيد، مِنْ نِيوجِيرسِي، انَا طَالِبٌ جَدِيدٌ في قِسْمِ اللغَةِ العَرَبِيَّةِ.

14

مها: اسْمِي مَهَا، وَانَا ايْضاً طَالِبَةٌ جَدِيدَةٌ في القِسْمِ، مَنْ مِنكُمْ يَتَكَلَّمُ اللُّغَةَ العَرَبِيَةَ؟

علي: انَا اتَكَلَّمُ وَاقْرَا وَاكْتُبُ اللُّغَةَ العَرَبِيَةَ.

مها: أيْنَ دَرَسْتَ اللُّغَةَ العَرَبِيَةَ؟

علي: دَرَسْتُهَا في جَامِعَةِ نُورثِ كَارُولِينَا،

طارق: مَسَاءُ الخَيرِ، انَا طَارِقٌ، انَا اسْتَاذكُمْ لِلُّغَةِ العَرَبِيَةِ.

الجميع: اهْلاً يَا أسْتَاذ طَارِق،

طارق: لِمَاذا تُرِيدُونَ تَعَلُّمَ اللُّغَةِ العَرَبِيَةِ؟

علي: ارِيدُ تَعَلُّمَ العَرَبِيَةِ لِاسْتَطِيعَ التَحَدُّثَ مَعَ عَائِلَتِي في الازدُنِ.

محمد: وَانَا اتَعَلَمُهَا لِلحُصُولِ عَلَى عَمَلٍ في الامَمِ المُتَّحِدَةِ.

علي: وانَا اتَعَلَمُهَا لِاسْتَطِيعَ قِرَاءَةَ القِران.

طارق: بَارَكَ اللهُ فِيكَ.

عمر: انَا اتَعَلَمُهَا لِانِّي احِبُّ تَعَلُّمَ اللُّغَاتِ.

دافيد: وَانَا احْتَاجُهَا لِعَمَلِي في وَزَارَةِ الخَارجِيَةِ.

مها: وانَا اتَعَلَمُهَا لِانَّ صَدِيقِي عَرَبِيٌ.

طارق: جَيِّدٌ جِداً، حَظاً سَعيداً لَكمْ جَمِيعاً.

الجميع: شُكْراً.

الكلماتُ الجديدة

معناها	الكلمة
Introductory party	حَفلَةُ تَعارُفٍ
Arabic section	القِسْمِ العَرَبيِّ
State	وِلايَةٍ
Speak , read, and write	اتَكَلَّمُ وَاقْرَا وَاكْتُبُ
Talking	التَحَدُّثَ
To obtain	لِلحُصُولِ عَلَى
Reading the Koran	قِرَاءَةَ القرانِ
God bless you	بَارَكَ اللهُ فِيكَ
I love learning languages	احِبُّ تَعَلَّمَ اللُّغَاتِ
Ministry of Foreign Affairs	وَزَارَةِ الخَارِجيةِ
Good luck	حَظاً سَعيداً

أسئلة:

1. Which student is from North Dakota?

2. Which borough of New York City is Mohammed from?

3. How many of the students are from New York?

4. What is the name of the student from New Jersey, and is he a new or a returning student?

5. How many female students are there in the class?

6. Where did Ali study Arabic in the states?

7. What is the professor's name?

8. Why does Ali want to learn Arabic?

9. Which student's family lives in Jordan?

10. Which student wants to learn Arabic in order to get a job?

11. Is Ali able to read the Qur'an?

12. Which student likes to learn languages?

13. In which branch of the government does David work?

14. Who wants to learn Arabic to be able to communicate with his Arab friend?

To get accustomed to hand-written Arabic, read the various hand-written notes in this book, such as this one:

الصّديق

لم أعد أرى الصديق الوفي بحق، ولم أعد أرى معاني
الصداقة تتجلى في أحد من البشر هذه الأيام،
النبل والوفاء والإخلاص والتضحية والحب
بكل معانيه، كل هذه المعاني اختفت تماما
من البشر، ولم يعد هناك الصديق الوفي، نعم
لقد صدق من قال: المستحيلات ثلاثة: الغول
والعنقاء والخل الوفي.

حقا كانت أقصى أمنياتي أن أجد هذا الصديق
الصدوق ولكن للأسف ...
هي حقا أزمة بكل المقاييس ألا تجد في حياتك
صديقا وفيا مخلصا.

لقد حرت صراحة في هذا الأمر، لماذا لا يوجد
خل وفي في هذه الدنيا.

17

In this dialogue, you will be introduced to the common Arabic greeting, *salaam alikum*, meaning 'peace be upon you'.

Some countries in the Arab world take the definite article 'al' before their names, such as Saudi Arabia and the United Arab Emirates. You can see these examples in the dialogue.

مُحَمَّدٌ: السَّلاَمُ عَلَيْكُمْ وَرَحْمَةُ اللَّه وَبَرَكاتُه

(The) Peace be upon you, Allah's mercy, and his blessing.

حَسَنٌ: وَعَلَيْكُمُ السَّلاَمُ وَرَحْمَةُ اللَّه وَبَرَكاتُهُ

And (the) peace be upon you and Allah's mercy and his blessing.

مُحَمَّدٌ: أَنَا مُحَمَّدٌ مِنَ السَّعُوْدِيَّة

I am Mohammed from (the) Saudi Arabia.

حَسَنٌ: وَأَنَا حَسَنٌ مِنَ الإِمَأْرَأْت

And I am Hassan from (the) Emirates.

مُحَمَّدٌ: هَلْ أَنْتَ طَالِبٌ جَدِيدٌ؟ Are you a new student?

حَسَنٌ: نَعَمْ. أَنَا طَالِبٌ جَدِيدٌ، Yes I am a new student.

مُحَمَّدٌ: مَرْحَبًا بِكَ فِيْ الْجَامِعَةِ الْأَمْرِيكِيَّةُ Welcome to the American University.

The dialogue	الحِوَار
The peace	السَّلامُ
On you	عَلَيْكُمْ
and	وَ
Mercy	رَحْمَةُ
Allah, God's name in Islam	اللَّه
Blessings	بَرَكَاتُ
His, his blessings	ـه بَرَكَاتُهُ
I am	أَنَا
From	مِنَ
Is (it good?) Are (you happy?) Do (they smoke?)	هَلْ
You are	أَنْتَ
Student	طَالِبٌ
New	جَدِيدٌ
Yes	نَعَمْ
welcome	مَرْحَبًا

With/by you	بكَ = بِ كَ
In; at	في
The university	الْجَامِعَة
The American	الْأَمْريكية

اِقْرَأ

يَحْتَفِلُ النَّاطِقُونَ بِاللُّغَةِ الْعَرَبِيَّةِ بِالْيَوْمِ الْعَالَمِيِّ لِلُغَةِ الضَّادِ الَّذي يُوافِقُ الـ 18 مِنْ ديسَمْبَرَ مِنْ كُلِّ عَامٍ، وَهُوَ التَّاريخُ الَّذي أَقَرَّتْ فيهِ الْجَمْعِيَّةُ الْعامَّةُ لِلْأُمَمِ الْمُتَّحِدَةِ إِدْخَالَ اللُّغَةِ الْعَرَبِيَّةِ ضِمْنَ اللُّغاتِ الرَّسْمِيَّةِ وَجَعْلَها لُغَةَ عَمَلٍ في الْأُمَمِ الْمُتَّحِدَةِ.

فَعِنْدَ إِنْشَاءِ الْأُمَمِ الْمُتَّحِدَةِ عامَ 1945، اعْتَمَدَتِ الْمُنَظَّمَةُ الدُّوَلِيَّةُ خَمْسَ لُغاتٍ حَيَّةٍ هِيَ الْإِسْبانِيَّةُ وَالْإِنْجِليزِيَّةُ وَالرُّوسِيَّةُ وَالصِّينِيَّةُ وَالْفَرَنْسِيَّةُ، بِحَيْثُ تَكُونُ لُغاتِ تَوْثيقِ الْمَحاضِرِ الرَّسْمِيَّةِ وَأَوْراقِ الْعَمَلِ أَثْناءَ الاجْتِماعاتِ، وَتُعْتَمَدُ في التَّرْجَمَةِ الْحَيَّةِ الْمُباشِرَةِ أَثْناءَ الْمُؤْتَمَراتِ تَحَدُّثًا وَكِتابَةً.

وَيَعُودُ الْفَضْلُ في إِدْراجِ الْعَرَبِيَّةِ لِتَكُونَ لُغَةً سادِسَةً بِجانِبِ تِلْكَ اللُّغاتِ إِلَى اقْتِراحٍ تَقَدَّمَتْ بِهِ السُّعُودِيَّةُ وَالْمَغْرِبُ أَثْناءَ انْعِقادِ الدَّوْرَةِ الـ 190 لِلْمَجْلِسِ التَّنْفيذِيِّ لِلْيُونِسْكُو عامَ 1973.

The Arabic speaking world celebrates the international day of the language of 'Daad', which falls on the 18th December each year. This is the date when the General Assembly of the United Nations decided to include Arabic among the official languages of the United Nations, making it a language of business in the United Nations. At the establishment of the United Nations in 1945, the organization adopted five official languages: Spanish, English, French, Russian and Chinese. These languages were to be the languages in which working papers and official sessions were documented, and they would be adopted in simultaneous translation, used in conferences in both reading and writing. The inclusion of Arabic as the sixth language in addition to the original five languages was achieved due to the much-appreciated proposal from Saudi Arabia and Morocco during the Executive Council of UNESCO's 190 Session in 1973.

هارب أم مهاجر

لم أكن أتوقع يومًا أن أعيش في بلدي وكأنني غريب ، لا أهل لي ، لا وطن لي ..

أشعر ببرد شديد هنا في بلدي ، ليس هذا مناخها وليس هذا طقسها الذي اعتدنا عليه .

لم أكد أعرف حبيبي من عدوي ، الظلم تفشى بين الناس ، انعدمت الأخلاق على الإطلاق ..

لم يعد لي في بلدي حضن دافئ يؤويني ، فأنا أشعر ببرد الغربة في بلدي ، فلا أجد وظيفة ولا زوجة ولا صاحب ولا حتى أصل .

ها أنا قد عزمت الرحيل --- رحيل بلا عودة سأذهب إلى أيّ بلد آخر وأجعل منه موطنا وملاذًا ... لست مهاجرًا بل هاربًا .

21

أَنْوَاعُ التَنوينِ (الضَّمُ -الكَسْرُ -الفَتْحُ)	

This dialogue exposes you to words that carry the tanween sign. The conversation is between two female friends. One girl tells the other about her vacation. There are three types of tanween: Dum, kasr and fatH. Dum means two dummah, FatH means two fatHa and kasr means two kasra.

Depending on the word إعراب, you choose which tanween should be placed on the last letter of the noun. (Remember tanween is only used with nouns.) Notice that tanween fatHa is placed on the penultimate letter after an alif is added to the word (except when a noun ends in taa marbouTah or hamzah).

الحِوَار

سارة: أهلاً فَاطِمَةُ، كَيفَ حَالُكِ؟

فاطمة: بِخَيرٍ.

سارة: كَيفَ الأَجَازَةُ مَعَكِ؟

فاطمة: رَائِعَةٌ!!

سارة: الَى أَينَ ذَهَبْتِ؟

فاطمة: الَى بَلَدٍ جَمِيلٍ.

سارة: مَا اسْمُ هَذا البَلَدِ؟

فاطمة: ذَهَبْتُ الَى المَغرِبِ.

سارة: لابُدَ أنَّها كَانت رِحْلَةً مُمتِعَةً.

فاطمة: المَغرِبُ بَلَدٌ جَمِيلٌ يَاسَارة.

سارة: حَقًّا!! المَغرِبُ بَلَدٌ رَائِعٌ.

فاطمة: طَبعًا.

سارة: لابُدَ أنْ أذهَبَ هُنَاكَ يَومًا.

فاطمة: حَتمًا، ان شَاءَ اللهُ، نُسَافِرُ مَعًا.

سارة: الَى المَغرِبِ سَوِيًا، طَبْعًا.

23

الكلمات الجديدة

معناها	الكلمة
Types	أنْوَاعُ
Adding two vowels marks to an indefinite noun, it is considered a iᵉrab sign	التَنوينِ
Pleasant trip	رِحْلَةٌ مُمتِعَة
Together	سَوِيًّا
Hi	أهلاً
How are you doing	كيفَ حَالُكِ
How was your vacation?	كَيفَ الأَجَازَةُ مَعَكِ؟
Good	بِخَيرٍ
Holiday	الأَجَازَةُ
Wonderful	رَائِعَة
Country	بَلَدٍ
Beautiful	جَميلٍ
Name	اسْمُ
Must	لابُدَ
It is	أنَّها
It was	كَانت
Trip	رِحْلَة

Fun, enjoyable	مُمتِعَة
Really	حَقًّا
Of course	طَبَعًا
One day	يَومًا

أسئلة:

1. Which girl has just returned from her vacation?
2. How was her vacation?
3. Did she enjoy her vacation?
4. Which country did she visit?
5. Does her description of her vacation make her friend want to go there?
6. If she does visit, would she go alone?
7. Start a similar conversation with your classmate. Ask him where he went on his vacation, let him describe it and ask him some questions about it.
8. Why do we call Morocco 'al-Maghreb'?

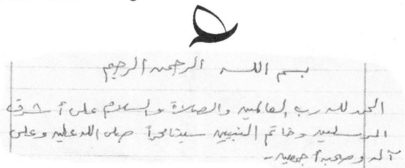

An introduction to a written letter

It is not unusual for an Arab Muslim to start writing a letter with an introduction like the one illustrated above, especially if it is between devoted Muslims:

By the name of Allah, the Most Compassionate, the Most Merciful (should be written in the center of the line on the first space available for writing).

Praise be to Allah, the lord of the two worlds (the humans and the genies), and pray for and peace be upon the most honorable of messengers, and the last of the prophets, our master Muhammad. May Allah bless him, his family and his companions all.

نَعِيمًا

الحِوارُ

مُنَىْ: لَقَد حَلَقَت ذقنك يَا طارق، نعيمًا.

طارق: أنعَمَ اللهُ عَلَيكِ يَا مُنى، شُكرًا لَكِ.

مُنى: عَفوًا يَاطَارِق.

طارق: هَلْ صَلَّيتِ العَصْرَ؟

27

مُنى: نَعَم، حَمْدًا لله.

طارق: حَرَمًا.

مُنى: جَمْعًا ان شَاءَ الله.

جَرسُ البَابِ يَدُق

أحْمَد: أهْلاً وَسَهْلاً يَا أُمِّي.

مُنَى: مَرْحَبًا يَا أُمِّي، جِئْتِ فِي مَوعِدِكِ، سَنَأكُلُ سَوِيًّا طَعَامَ الغَدَاءِ، أعدَدتُ شَيئًا لَذِيذًا.

الأم: أهْلاً بِكُم جَمِيعًا، كُلُوا أنتُمْ، هَنِيئًا مَرِيئًا.

مُنى: صَبْرًا، دَقَائِق وَأُحضِرُ لَكُم الغَدَاءَ.

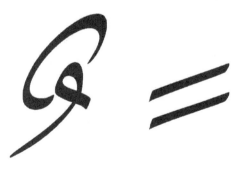

In this lesson, you will encounter several words that have tanween fatHa. Many Arabic words carry this type of tanween when they denote well wishing. It is written as two fatHas on top of each other. When the word is in the case of نَصْب , it is usually written on the last letter of the word after an alif has been prefixed, unless the word ends in hamzah ء or the feminine sign taa marbouta ــة is present - in these case no alif should be added.

الكلمات الجديدة

معناها	الكلمة
Indeed	لَقَد
You shaved	حَلَقت
Your Chin (in English, we say, "you shaved your beard", but in Arabic, you would say, "you shaved your chin")	ذقنك

نعيمًا

Bliss, comfort, happiness. 'Naɛimn'. Arabs say this in greeting, usually said to someone in relation to cleansing: after someone has taken a shower, cut their hair, had a shave etc. Usually this is also said by the barber when he has finished cutting his customer's hair. In the Arab world, the barber will replace your towel more than once during the haircut, so saying 'na3imn' indicates he has finished. Whenever someone says 'naɛimn', respond using the phrase below.

God has blessed you	أنعَمَ اللهُ عَلَيكِ

عَفوًا

Pardon me (pardon me/ excuse me in Arabic actually means "forgiving") 'Afwan' is said most commonly in response to 'shukran', thank you. It literally means 'not worthy of thanks', but is an idiomatic phrase rather than one close to this literal meaning.

I prayed	صَلَّيتِ

حَرَمًا

Sanctuary (this is a greeting that Muslims say when they see that somebody has just finished praying and means that both parties will pray together in the sacred sanctuary in Mecca) This is said when you are performing a group prayer, or by someone who has just seen you finish praying. People will be kneeling (the last position of praying) when they say 'Haramen'. This will be the first word after the prayer has finished, and is said simultaneously with a handshake.

You say this to the person on your right then the person on your left. How do you know that a Muslim has finished praying? There are different prayer positions. The last movement is with the head: it is an acknowledgement to the angels on the left and on the right who write your good deeds and your bad deeds.

These two angels must be greeted upon finishing every prayer. If you are not praying with him and you see him do this, he has finished his prayer. However, he might do some supplementary prayers. He will have finished his prayer when his lips have stopped moving. At this point you can say to him, 'Haramen'.

Together (this is the proper response to the greeting above)	جَمْعًا
The doorbell is ringing	جَرَسُ البَابِ يَدُقّ
You came at the right time (this expression actually means "you came at (the time) of your appointment")	جِئْتِ فِي مَوعِدِكِ
Savory/ Delicious	لَذِيذًا
Welcome to you all	أَهْلاً بِكُم جَمِيعًا
You (pl.) eat (as in the imperative, "you go ahead and eat")	كُلُوا أنتُمْ
Bon Appetite/ Enjoy your meal (this expression literally means "wholesome and healthful")	هَنِيئًا مَرِيئًا

أَسئِلة:

1. What are the names of the parties involved in the conversation?

2. What is the first observation that one of the parties makes upon seeing the other person?

3. Which prayer is mentioned in this conversation?

4. What is Ahmed's relationship to the people he is visiting?

5. Which meal are they about to eat and was it prepared or not?

6. Which greeting will you say to someone who has just finished having a shower?

7. How do you know when a barber has finished cutting your hair?

8. Which greeting do you say to someone who has just finished praying?

9. How do you know that someone has just finished praying to greet him?

الرَّئيس

أزمة حقيقية فعلا تعيشها مصر هذه الأيام، المصريون لا يستطيعون إلى الآن - بعد مرور ثلاث سنوات - أن يختاروا رئيساً لهم، المصريون منقسمون إلى شقين، أحدهم يؤيد قائد الجيش وآخرون يؤيدون الرئيس السابق الذى عزل مؤخراً.

فَقَط

In this lesson, we will have a few examples of how to use the word "only" in Arabic فَقَط (faqaT). We will be translating sentences into Arabic that contain the word "faqaT", which can mean "only", "just", or "nearly".

I will only drink this coffee	سَأَشْرَبُ هَذِهِ القَهْوَةِ فَقَطْ
Give me only one piece of cake .	أَعْطِنِي قَطْعَةً وَاحِدَةً مِنَ الكَعْكَةِ فَقَطْ
I will only say one word.	سَأَقُولُ كَلِمَةً وَاحِدَةً فَقَطْ
Meet me just once.	قَابِلِنِي مَرَّةً وَاحِدَةً فَقَطْ

Only you and I will go out together .	سَنَخْرُجُ مَعًا، فَقَطْ أَنَا وَأَنْتَ
There is only one way to the hospital.	يُوجَدُ طَرِيقٌ وَاحِدٌ فَقَطْ الَى الْمُسْتَشْفَى
This bathroom is for women only .	هَذا الْحَمَّامُ خَاصٌّ فَقَطْ بِالنِّسَاءِ
This elevator is for workers only .	هَذا الْمِصْعَدُ خَاصٌّ بِالعَامِلِين فَقَطْ
This game is for smart (people) only.	هَذِهِ اللَّعْبَةُ لِلأذكِيَاءِ فَقَطْ
This job is available for men only .	هَذِهِ الوَظِيفَةُ مُتَاحَةٌ لِلرِّجَالِ فَقَطْ
You have only chance to win .	أَمَامَكَ فُرْصَةٌ وَاحِدَةٌ فَقَطْ لِلفَوزِ

رَشَّحَتِ الْجَمْعِيَّةُ الْعَرَبِيَّةُ السُّعُودِيَّةُ لِلثَّقَافَةِ وَالْفُنُونِ فِيلْمَ "وَجْدَة" لِلْمُخْرِجَةِ هَيْفَاء الْمَنْصُور لِلْمُشَارَكَةِ فِي مُسَابَقَةِ الأُوسْكَارِ عَنْ فِئَةِ الأَفْلامِ الأَجْنَبِيَّةِ، وَأَقَرَّتْ أَكَادِيمِيَّةُ الْعُلُومِ وَالْفُنُونِ الأَمِيرْكِيَّةُ دُخُولَ الْفِيلْمِ ضِمْنَ التَّرْشِيحَاتِ الأَوَّلِيَّةِ لأُوسْكَارِ أَفْضَلِ فِيلْمٍ أَجْنَبِيٍّ لِعَامِ 2013، لِيُصْبِحَ أَوَّلَ فِيلْمٍ سُعُودِيٍّ يُشَارِكُ فِي أَبْرَزِ تَظَاهُرَةٍ سِينِمَائِيَّةٍ عَالَمِيَّةٍ.

The Saudi Arabian society for Culture and Art nominated the movie 'Wajda' by director Iiaifa al Mansour, to participate in the Foreign Film Category of the Oscars. The inclusion of the movie is also endorsed by the Academy of Sciences and Arts for its entry into the International film awards ceremony.

وَبَدَأَ الْفِيلْمُ عُرُوضَهُ التِّجَارِيَّةَ فِي الصَّالَاتِ الأَمِيرْكِيَّةِ أَمْسِ الْجُمْعَةَ بَعْدَ عَرْضِهِ بِالْقَاعَاتِ الأُورُوبِّيَّةِ، وَكَانَ قَدْ حَقَّقَ نَجَاحَاتٍ مُهِمَّةً فِي مِهْرَجَانَاتٍ عَالَمِيَّةٍ، أَهَمُّهَا الْبُنْدُقِيَّةِ وَبِرْلِين، وَنَالَ الْعَامَ الْمَاضِيَ جَائِزَتَيْ أَفْضَلِ فِيلْمٍ (الْمُهْرُ الذَّهَبِيُّ) وَأَفْضَلِ مُمَثِّلَةٍ (الطِّفْلَةُ وَعْدُ مُحَمَّدٍ) بِمِهْرَجَانِ دُبَي كَمَا حَازَ أَيْضًا جَائِزَةَ الْجُمْهُورِ فِي مِهْرَجَانِ فرِيبُورغ السُّوِيسْرِيِّ وَجَائِزَةَ "فَرَنْسَا ثَقَافَةُ سِينِمَا" (فِئَةِ الأكْتِشَافِ) مِنْ مِهْرَجَانِ كَانْ.

The movie started its commercial showing in American movie theatres yesterday Friday, after having been shown in European movie theatres and achieving great success at International festivals such as Venice and Berlin. Last year, he won two awards; one for best film (Golden Colt), and one for best Actress (the child Waag Muhammad) at the Dubai Festival. They also earned the Audience Award at the Fribourg Festival in Switzerland, as well as French Cultural Cinema in the discovery category at Cannes Film Festival.

فَقَطْ

في مَدْرَسَةِ تَعْلِيمِ اللُّغَاتِ

مَدْرَسَةُ اللُّغَةِ العَرَبِيَّةِ

Arabic Language School

Here is a conversation between an American student who has come to Egypt to study Arabic and receptionist at the language school. You will exposed to vocabulary relating to enrolling in an Arabic language center, and the necessary information to begin your study.

الحِوَارُ

صَبَاحُ الخَيْرِ.

صَبَاحُ النُّورِ يَا فَنْدِم.

انَا اِسْمِي تُوم. انَا طَالِبٌ اَجْنَبِي مِنْ اَمرِيكَا. المُدِيرَةُ مَوْجُودَةٌ لَو سَمَحْتِي؟

لَا، انَا آسِفٌ..هِيَ لَيْسَتْ مَوجُودَةً. أَيُّ خِدمَةٍ؟

لَو سَمَحْتِي، كَمْ دَورَةٌ لِتَعْلِيمِ اللُّغَةِ العَرَبِيَةِ بِالمَرْكَزِ؟ خَمْسُ دَوَرَاتٍ؟

لَا، عِنْدَنَا عَشْرُ دَوَرَاتٍ.

كَمْ أُسْبُوعًا مُدَّةُ الدَّورَةِ؟

مُدَّةُ الدَّورَةِ بَيْنَ خَمْسَةِ أَسَابِيعٍ وتِسْعَةِ أَسَابِيعٍ.

وَكَمْ سَاعَةً فِي الدَّوْرَةِ؟

اللَّهْجَةُ العَامِيَّةُ أَرْبَعُونَ سَاعَةً وَاللُّغَةُ الفُصْحَى خَمْسُونَ سَاعَةً.

هَلْ رَقَمُ الهَاتِفِ 2432185 هُوَ رَقَمُكُمُ الوَحِيدُ، أَمْ عِنْدَكُمْ رَقَمٌ آخَرُ؟

عِنْدَنَا رَقَمٌ آخَرُ وَهُوَ 2432186

شُكْرًا، الفُ شُكْرٍ

العَفْوُ، لَكِنْ لَابُدَّ مِنِ اخْتِبَارٍ لِتَحْدِيدِ المُسْتَوى.

حَقًّا! أَنَا مُبْتَدِئٌ فِي اللُّغَةِ العَرَبِيَّةِ، كَمْ مُسْتَوَىً فِي اللُّغَةِ العَرَبِيَّةِ لَدَيْكُمْ؟

إِنَّهُم أَرْبَعَةُ مُسْتَوَيَاتٍ، مُبْتَدِئٌ، مُتَوَسِّطٌ، مُتَقَدِّمٌ وَفَائِقٌ وَكُلُّ مُسْتَوَى ثَلَاثُ دَوْرَاتٍ، عَدَا الفَائِقِ فَهُوَ دَوْرَةٌ وَاحِدَةٌ.

لَمْ أَدْرُسِ اللُّغَةَ مِنْ فَضْلِكِ سَجِّلِي اسْمِي فِي أَوَّلِ دَوْرَةٍ فِي المُسْتَوى المُبْتَدِئِ اِذَنْ، فَأَنَا العَرَبِيَّةَ مِنْ قَبْلٍ.

حَاضِرٌ يَاأُسْتَاذ.

مَا جِنْسِيَةُ مُعَلِّمِ اللُّغَةِ العَرَبِيَّةِ؟

إِنَّهُ مِصْرِيٌّ، وَاللُّغَةُ العَرَبِيَّةُ لُغَتُهُ الأُمُّ.

رَائِعٌ سَأَتَعَلَّمُ اللُّغَةَ مِنْ أَهْلِهَا، ذَلِكَ مُهِمٌّ جِدًّا، أَنَا مُهْتَمٌّ بِالمُحَادَثَةِ كَثِيرًا.

يُوجَدُ دَوْرَاتٌ خَاصَّةٌ وَمُكَثَّفَةٌ لِلْمُحَادَثَةِ وَقَوَاعِدِ النَّحْوِ وَتَحْسِينِ الخَطِّ بَدْءًا مِنَ المُسْتَوى المُتَوَسِّطِ.

هَلْ هِيَ غَالِيَةُ الثَّمَنِ؟

لَا، إِنَّهَا مَعْقُولَةُ التَّكلِفَةِ.

اِنْ شَاءَ اللهُ.

إِنْ شَاءَ اللهُ.

حَظًّا سَعِيدًا وَأَتَمَنَّى لَكَ النَّجَاحَ وَالتَّوْفِيقِ.

شُكْرًا يَاآنِسَة.

فِي خِدْمَتِكَ دَائِمًا.

الْكَلِمَاتُ الْجَدِيدَة

مَعْنَاهَا	الْكَلِمَة
At a language teaching school	فِي مَدْرَسَةِ تَعْلِيمِ اللُّغَاتِ
Foreigner	أَجْنَبِي
How many Arabic courses does the center teach?	كَمْ دَوْرَةٍ لِتَعْلِيمِ اللُّغَةِ الْعَرَبِيَّةِ بِالْمَرْكَزِ
Course duration	مُدَّةُ الدَّوْرَةِ
Colloquial	اللَّهْجَةُ الْعَامِيَّةُ
The classical language	اللُّغَةُ الْفُصْحَى
Your only phone number	رَقَمُكُمُ الْوَحِيدُ
Level determination test	اِخْتِبَارٍ لِتَحْدِيدِ الْمُسْتَوى
Beginner	مُبْتَدِئٌ

How many course levels do you have in Arabic?	كَمْ مُسْتَوىً فِي اللُّغَةِ العَرَبِيَّةِ لَدَيكُمْ؟
Four levels	أَرْبَعَةُ مُسْتَوَياتٍ،
Intermediate	مُتَوَسِّطٌ
Advanced	مُتَقَدِّمٌ
Fluent	فَائِقٌ
Register my name	سَجِّلِي اِسْمِي
I have not studied Arabic before	فَأَنَا لَمْ أَدرُسِ اللُّغَةَ العَرَبِيَّةَ مَنْ قَبْلِ
What is the nationality of the Arabic language teacher?	مَا جِنسِيَّةُ مُعَلِّمِ اللُّغَةِ العَرَبِيَّةِ؟
He is Egyptian and Arabic is his mother tongue	اِنَّهُ مَصْرِيٌّ، وَاللُّغَةُ العَرَبِيَّةُ لُغَتُهُ الأُمُّ
Wonderful , I will learn the language from a native speaker	رائِع سَأتعلم اللُّغَةَ مِنْ أَهلِهَا
I am very interested in conversational (Arabic)	أَنَا مُهْتَمٌّ بِالمُحَادَثَةِ كَثِيرًا
Special and intensive courses	دَوَراتٌ خَاصَّةٌ وَمُكَثَفَةٌ
And the rules of grammar	وَقَواعِدِ النَّحْو
And improving your handwriting	وَتَحْسِينِ الخَطِّ
In starting from the intermediate level	بِدْءًا مِنَ المُسْتَوَى المُتَوَسِّطِ.
Is it expensive?	هَلْ هِيَ غَالِيَةُ الثَمَنِ؟
No, it is reasonably priced	لا، إِنَّهَا مَعقُولَةُ التَكْلِفَةِ.
God willing	إن شَاءَ اللهُ.
Good luck, I wish you success	حَظًّا سَعِيدًا وَأَتَمَنَّى لَكَ النَّجاحَ وَالتَّوفِيقِ.
Always at your service	فِي خِدْمَتِكَ دَائِمًا.

أسئلة:

1. What is the name of the student? Which country does he come from?

2. Whom has he requested to see?

3. How many Arabic courses does the school offer? How many did he think they offer?

4. What is the average duration of the courses?

5. Are all courses the same length?

6. Which courses offer the longer instruction hours? Colloquial or fusHa?

7. How many phone numbers does the school have?

8. Must new students take a test to determine their level of Arabic?

9. What is this student's level?

10. How many levels of Arabic does the school offer?

11. How many courses is the intermediate level?

12. Do they offer courses for fluent foreign speakers?

13. Which course did the student register for?

14. Did the student study Arabic prior to his application to the school?

15. What is the nationality of his Arabic instructor?

16. Which form of the language (reading / speaking / writing) is the student most interested in?

17. Did the school offer a conversational course? Which level does this course begin at?

18. Are the courses at this school expensive?

أَنْطَلَقَتْ بِالْمَرْكَزِ الْإِسْلَامِيِّ فِي رِيبِكَا بِكْرُوَاتْيَا الْمُسَابَقَةُ السَّنَوِيَّةُ لِلشَّيْخِ جَاسِم بْن مُحَمَّد بْن ثَانِي لِلْقُرْآنِ الْكَرِيمِ الْمُخَصَّصَةُ لِغَيْرِ النَّاطِقِينَ بِاللُّغَةِ الْعَرَبِيَّةِ، وَذَلِكَ بِمُشَارَكَةِ مِائَةِ مُتَسَابِقٍ وَمُتَسَابِقَةٍ. وَتَهْدِفُ الْمُسَابَقَةُ الَّتِي تُعَدُّ الْأُولَى مِنْ نَوْعِهَا عَلَى مُسْتَوَى الْعَالَمِ، إِلَى خِدْمَةِ الْقُرْآنِ الْكَرِيمِ وَتَعْزِيزِ عَلَاقَةِ الْمُسْلِمِينَ بِهِ.

وَسَيَتَبَارَى الْمُتَسَابِقُونَ -وَكُلُّهُمْ مِمَّنْ تَجَاوَزَتْ أَعْمَارُهُمْ 14 عَامًا- عَلَى مَدَى أَرْبَعَةِ أَيَّامٍ فِي حِفْظِ الْفَاتِحَةِ وَبَعْضِ قِصَارِ سُوَرِ الْقُرْآنِ الْكَرِيمِ، فَضْلًا عَنْ تَفْسِيرِ بَعْضِ الْكَلِمَاتِ وَحِفْظِ بَعْضِ الْأَحَادِيثِ، عَلَى أَنْ يَحْصُلَ الْعَشَرَةُ الْأَوَائِلُ مِنْهُمْ عَلَى جَوَائِزَ قَيِّمَةٍ، وَتُمْنَحَ لِلْبَاقِينَ جَوَائِزُ رَمْزِيَّةٌ.

وَتَجْرِي الْمُسَابَقَةُ بِالتَّعَاوُنِ مَعَ الْجَمْعِيَّةِ الْإِسْلَامِيَّةِ بِكْرُوَاتْيَا وَيُشَارِكُ فِيهَا مُتَسَابِقُونَ مِنَ الْبُوسْنَةِ وَالْهِرْسَكِ وَسْلُوفِينْيَا وَمَقْدُونْيَا، فِي حِينِ تَتَوَلَّى الْجِهَةُ الْقَطَرِيَّةُ الْمُنَظِّمَةُ جَمِيعَ الِاسْتِعْدَادَاتِ الْمَادِيَّةِ وَالْأَدَبِيَّةِ لِهَذِهِ الْمُسَابَقَةِ.

The annual competition of the noble Koran dedicated to non-Arabic speakers under the sponsorship of Sheikh Jassim bin Mohamed bin Thani, was launched at the Islamic Centre in Rijeka, Croatia. One hundred contesters participate. The competition, which is considered the first competition of its kind in the world, aims to serve the noble Koran and to strengthen the Muslims' relationship with it.

All contestants – who are all over the age of 14 years – compete over four days in: memorization of the fatHa (the opening of the Koran), memorization of some short Suras of the noble Koran; in addition to this, the interpretation of some words and memorization of some hadith (sayings of the Prophet Mohammed).

The first ten contenders will receive valuable prizes and the rest receive simple prizes. The competition is conducted in collaboration with the Islamic Society of Croatia and the participants come from Bosnia and Herzegovina, Slovenia and Macedonia. The country hosting the competition is responsible for financial and literary preparations for the competition.

الجار والمجرور

The prepositional phrase

The prepositional phrase is called Al-Jar and (wa) Al-Majrour in Arabic. Al-Jar refers to the particle (the preposition) that causes a change in case of the noun that follows it. Al-Majrour is a noun that follows the Al-Jar preposition. Al-Majrour nouns should have a kasra below their last letter if it is singular, broken plural or sound feminine plural; or 'yaa' if it is dual, sound masculine plural or one of the five nouns. Prepositional phrases begin with a preposition and end with a noun, pronoun or gerund. These are the "objects" of the preposition. Not all prepositions in English match their apparent counterparts in Arabic, as you can see in the examples below.

Prepositions in any language do not have consistent, concrete meanings. In English, "on" can mean 'on top of', a switch being 'on' or someone being 'on time'. "At" usually means 'at a place', but can also be used to mean 'at a given time'. The same is true in Arabic. In this case, "min" usually means 'from'. See examples below to learn how 'min' is used in different contexts.

If you have a preposition with a word or an idiom, and you are unsure of how to use it, Google it to see how the word can be used in context. This may give you a better idea of how to use the word.

We obtained silk from silkworm.	نحصل عَلَى الحرير مِنَ دودة القـز
I left the house.	خرجت مِنَ المنزل
The apple fell from the tree.	سَقَطَت التفاحة مِنَ الشجرة
I asked my brother for help.	طَلَبت المُساعدة مِنَ أخِي
I took the book from Ali.	أخذت الكتاب مِنَ علي
I ate at the most famous store in Egypt.	أكلت مِنَ أكْثر المحْلات شهرة في مصر.
My mother is one of the most precious people in my heart.	أمي مِنَ أغلى الناس عَلَى قلبي

Libya is located near Egypt.	تقع ليبيا بالقرب مِنَ مصر
The ball was kicked out of the stadium.	خرجت الكرة مِنَ الملعب
I took the information from the book.	اخذت المعلومة مِنَ الكتاب
I avoided the situation (or 'escaped from').	هربت مِنَ الموقف
Do not run away from responsibility.	لا تهرب مِنَ المسئولية
My father returned from abroad after many years.	عاد ابي مِنَ الخارج بعد سنوات طويلة
The player returned from injury after a long struggle.	عاد اللاعب مِنَ الاصابة بعد كفاح طويل
The rain came down from the sky.	نزل المطر مِنَ السماء.
Fish comes from the sea.	يأتي السمك مِنَ البحر
The train gets to Alexandria from Cairo in three hours. (Literally, 'the train cut the distance…' This idiomatic expression applies to any distance covered.)	يقطع القطار المسافة مِنَ القاهرة إلَىٰ الإسكندرية في ثلاث ساعات
Her shoes are made of leather. (Notice the words 'leather' and 'skin' are the same in Arabic(.	تصنع الأحذية مِنَ الجلد
Gold is extracted from the mines.	يستخرج الذهب مِنَ المناجم
The boy is tired of running.	تعب الولد مِنَ الجري
Read more books because it is useful.	أكثر مِنَ قراءة الكتب فإنها مفيدة
We take honey from bees.	نأخذ العسل مِنَ النـحل

إلى

The cows went to the field. ('Went' is usually 'walked' in Arabic)	سارت الماشية إلَى الحقل.
The criminal is taken to jail.	يساق المجرم إلَى السجن
The absentee returns home. (Regarding someone who has been away for a long time(.	يعود الغائب إلَى الوطن
I looked at the beautiful flower.	نظرت إلَى الوردة الجميلة
The traveler returned to his homeland.	عاد المسافر إلَى وطنه
We listened to the conversation.	أصغينا إلَى الحديث
I go to the store in the morning with my sister.	أذهب إلَى المدرسة صباحا مع أختي
Amir went to the hospital.	ذهب أمـيـر إلَى المستشفى
The farmer goes to the field in the morning.	يذهب الفلاح صباحا إلَى الحقل
The human body requires lots of nutrition. (In Arabic the word 'elements' is used here(.	يحتاج الجسم إلَى عناصر كثيرة
My mother listened to the music.	امي تستمع إلَى الموسيقى
Ahmed goes to the club.	يذهب أحمد إلَى النادي
I listened attentively to the teacher's explanation.	استمع إلَى شرح المعلم باهتمام
I would love to go to the parks in Easter. (Easter in Arabic is called 'the smelling of the breeze.')	أحب أن أذهب إلَى الحدائق في شم النسيم
We should cooperate with anyone who requires our cooperation.	يجب ان نتعاون مع كل مِنَ يحتاج إلَى معاونتنا
In the evening, the family went to the theatre.	في المساء ذهبت الأسرة إلَى المسرح
I arrived home late. (In Arabic, 'late' is literally, 'in a late hour(.'	وصلت إلَى المنزل في ساعة متأخرة
Mohammed joined the team.	انضم مُحمد إلَى الفريق

The player hit the ball towards the goal.	سدد اللاعب الكرة إلَى المرمى
Pay attention to the dangers of the road.	انتبه إلَى أخطار الطريق
The student went quickly to the exam.	ذهب الطالب إلَى الامتحان مسرعا
I arrived at work on time. ('On time' in Arabic is 'in the appointed time.')	وصلت إلَى العمل في الموعد
The girl looked at her face in the mirror.	تنظر البنت إلى وجهها في المرآه
We travelled during the summer vacation to MaTrouH.	نسافر في عطلة الصيف إلَى مطروح

My mother got off the couch.	قَامَت أمي عَنْ الأريكة
The soldier is getting off his horse.	ينزل الجندي عَنْ الحصان.
The fear is leaving the child.	يذهب الخوف عَنْ الطفل
The patient kept himself from food.	امتنع المريض عَنْ الطعام
The wise person avoids bad company.	-العاقل يبتعد عَنْ اصحاب السوء
Do not walk in the middle of the road. ('Stay away' is used when telling someone not to do something(.	ابتعد عَنْ السير في وسط الطــريق
We asked our father the cause of his sadness.	ســألنا أبى عَنْ سبب حزنه
Amir is looking for his shoes.	يبحث أمير عَنْ الحذاء
My father asked me for the time of the exam.	سألني ابي عَنْ موعد الامتحان
Do not talk about somebody behind his back.	لا تتحدث عَنْ أحد في ظهره
The lawyer defended his client.	دافع المحامي عَنْ موكله
The father separated from the mother.	انفصل الاب عَنْ الام
The citizen reported the accident.	ابلغ المواطن عَنْ الحادث
Stay away from products with an unknown origin.	ابتعد عَنْ المنتج مجهول المصدر

The child enquired about the reason for learning.	استفسر الطفل عَنْ سبب التعلم
The players defended their team.	دافع اللاعبين عَنْ فريقهم
No one likes to be away from his or her homeland.	لا يرغب أحد في الابتعاد عَنْ وطنه
Do not back away from doing good.	لا تتراجع عَنْ فعل الخير
Do not betray your principles.	لا تتخل عَنْ مبادئك
The teacher said of the student, "he is a hardworking student".	قال المدرس عَنْ الطالب " انه طالب مجتهد "
The mother ordered her son not to stray from the sidewalk.	أمرت الام ابنها بالا يبتعد عَنْ الرصيف
My father talked to me about the subject.	تحدث الي ابي عَنْ الموضوع
You should talk to the children about the facts of life.	يجب التحدث إلَى الابناء عَنْ امور الحياة

Wood floats on water.	يطفو الخشب عَلَىْ الماء
Fruit falls to the ground.	يسقط الثمر عَلَىْ الأرض
The patient did not become strong enough to walk.	أصبح المريض لا يقوى عَلَىْ المشي
There is a guard on each door of the garden.	عَلَىْ كل باب للبستان حارس
The teacher is commending his pupils.	يثني المعلم عَلَىْ تلميذه
The father is angry with his son.	غضب الاب عَلَىْ ابنه
The chicken is sitting on the eggs.	ترقد الدجاجة عَلَىْ البيض
Do not rely on anyone but yourself.	لا تعتمد عَلَىْ غير نفسك
I always walk on the sidewalk.	أسـير عَلَىْ الرصيف دائمـــا
I answered all the questions in the exam.	أجبت عَلَىْ أسئلة الامتحان كلهــا
Wood floats on water.	يطفو الخشب عَلَىْ سطح الماء

The book is on the desk.	الكتاب عَلَىْ المكتب
We rode on the back of the horse.	ركبنا عَلَىْ ظهر الحصان
The thief took the money.	استولى السارق عَلَىْ المال
We boarded the plane.	ركبنا عَلَىْ متن الطائرة
The father is used to teaching his children.	اعتاد الاب عَلَىْ المذاكرة لأبنائه
The coach depended on the player in the game.	اعتمد المدرب عَلَىْ الاعب في المباراة
In the twentieth century, man took his first step on the (surface of the) moon.	في القرن العشرين خطي الانسان خطوته الاولى عَلَىْ سطح القمر
The flower fell on the ground.	وقعت الوردة عَلَىْ الارض
The father entered the room where his son was.	دخل الاب عَلَىْ ابنه في الغرفة

The dog is barking in the garden.	ينبح الكلب في البستان.
The criminal went to jail.	دخل المجرم في السجن
I saw the bird in a cage.	رأيت الطائر في القفص
Put the example in a sentence	ادخل المثال في جملة
The train from Alexandria returned at exactly two o'clock.	يعود قطار الاسكندرية في تمام الثانية
The stars are gleaming in the sky.	تتلألأ النجوم في السماء
The female mouse is hiding in the room.	الفأرة مختبئة في الحجرة
I looked at the useful book.	نظرت في كتاب مفيد
I ran in a big square.	جريت في ميدان فسيح

Read books that are more scientific.	أكثر مِنَ القراءة في الكتب العلمية
Compete amongst each other in doing good.	تنافسوا في العمل الصالح
I put the picture in a wonderful frame.	وضعت الصورة في إطار بديع
There are blooming flowers in the garden.	في البستان زهور متفتحة
I saw a horse in field.	رأيت في الحقل حصاناً
I hate walking in crowded areas .	أكره السير في المناطق المزدحمة.
There are gleaming stars in the sky.	في السماء نجوم لامعة
I see thick dust in the air.	أرى في الجو غباراً كثيفاً
The teacher asked us to write on the topic of 'loving Egypt.'	طلب منا المعلم كتابة موضوع في حب مصر
The man is diving into the water.	يغوص الرجل في الماء
The lightening is flashing in the sky.	يلمع البرق في السماء
The people sprint in the road.	انتشر الناس في الطريق
I put the ink in the inkwell.	وضعت المداد في الدواة
I strive because of my desire to succeed.	اجتهدت رغبةً في النجاح
I gave you the money because I want to help you. ('… my desire to help you' is the literal translation(.	أعطيتك المال رغبةً في مساعدتك.
I sit attentively in the classroom.	أنا أجلس في الفصل منتبهـــا
My friend is in the hospital. (In Arabic, you say, 'lying in the hospital'	صديقي يرقد في المستشفى
Do your best in your studies	اجتهد في مذاكرتك

I peel the fruit with the knife.	قشرت الفاكهة بالسكين
A man will prevail with science.	بالعلم يسود المرء
The carpenter cut the wood with the saw.	يقطع النجار الخشب بالمنشار
I sharpen the pencil with the pencil sharpener.	بريت القلم بالبراية
The fire burned the boy's hand.	أحرق الولد يده بالنار
Do not play with fire!	لا تلعب بالنار
The father got some help from his son trimming the plants. ('Cutting' is used in Arabic).	استعان الاب بابنه في قص الزرع
The police officer caught up with the thief.	لحق الشرطي بالسارق
My brother hit me with a stick.	ضربني اخي بالعصا
My mother advised me to study.	نصحتني امي بالمذاكرة
The student only read the lesson (he did not complete the exercise.(	اكتفى الطالب بقراءةِ الدرس
The ball hit the post.	ا صطدمت الكرة بالقائم
The son contacted his mother to reassure her.	اتصل الابن بأمه ليطمئنها
The child played with the ball.	لعب الطفل بالكرة
The son sat next to his sick father.	جلس الابن بجوار الاب المريض
I wrote with the pen.	كتبت بالقلم
Be patient until you overcome the difficulties .	تحلَّ بالصبر حَتَّى تتغلب عَلَى المصاعب
The male teacher was inflicted with a headache so he did not complete the class. (This is a literal translation(.	أصيبَ المعلم بصداع فلم يكمل الحصة
The student was happy with his success.	فرح الطالب بنجاحه

Talk to the people gently. ('In a gentle persuasion' is literal.)	تحدث للناس بالحسنى
Go in peace.	اذهبوا بسلام

ك

The son tried to wear his clothes like his father.	حاول الابن ان يلبس كأبيه
Be strong like a lion.	كن قويا كالأسد
You must be like a mountain when facing problems.	لابد ان تكون كالجبل فِي مواجهة مشاكلك
Be who you are in any situation you face.	كن كما أنت فِي اي موقف تواجهه
The year passed by like the wind; we did not feel it, it passed so quickly.	مرت السنة كالريح فلم نشعر بها
Science is like water and air.	العلم كالماء والهواء
The player is as fast as a jaguar.	اللاعب سريع كالفهد
The waters of the River Nile is like chains of gold.	ماء النيل كسلاسل الذهب
The player kicked the ball like a missile.	سدد لاعب الكرة كالقذيفة
The pounced on the ball like a jaguar.	انقض اللاعب عَلَىٰ الكرة كالفهد
The face of the believer is lit like the moon.	وجه المؤمن مضيء كالقمر
Time is like a sword: if you do not use it, it will be used against you. (The word 'cut' is used here again: 'if you don't cut it, it will cut you.')	الوقت كالسيف ان لم تقطعه قطعك
Mothers are like schools: if they are prepared well, they will prepare a nation with a good foundation.	الام كالمدرسة ان اعددتها اعددت شعب طيب الاعراق
Do not be proud like a peacock.	لا تباهِ بنفسك كالطاووس

Do not be like an ostrich by running away from your problems. (This is like the English phrase, 'don't stick your head in the ground')	لاتكن كالنعام تهرب مِنَ المشاكل
Age (or life) is like a train: it doesn't wait for anyone	العمر كالقطار لا ينتظر أحد
Be like the seed: wherever it is dropped, it grows	كن كالبذرة اينما سقطت اينعت
Don't complain too much like a child	لاتكن كالطفل كثير الشكوى

I bought a lock for the safe	اشتريت قفلاً للخزانة
The garden has two doors. On each door there's a guard	للبستان بابان وعَلَىٰ كل باب حارس
I bought a saddle for the horse	اشتريت سرجاً للحصان
I brought the food for the dog	احضرت الاكل للكلب
The mother prepared the food for her children	حضرت الام الغذاء لأبنائها
I went to fetch the bowl	ذهبت لإحضار الكرة
I stood waiting for my brother	وقفت انتظارا لأخي
I prepared for the exam by studying	استعددت للامتحانات بالمذاكرة
Mohammed travelled to complete his treatment abroad	سافر محمد لاستكمال علاجه بالخارج
The teacher explained the lesson to the students	شرح المعلم الدرس للطلاب
The lawyer revealed the truth to the people	كشف المحامي الحقيقة للناس
I called my mother to check on her	اتصلت بأمي للاطمئنان عليها
The doctor came to check the patient	جاء الطبيب للكشف عَلَىٰ المريض
The people from the neighborhood handed the thief over to the police	سلمت الاهالي السارق للشرطة
I arrived at Alexandria at exactly two o'clock	وصلت للإسكندرية فِي تمام الثانية

My love for science / knowledge has no boundaries	حبي للعلم ليس له حدود
My brother is the closest person to my heart	اخي هو أقرب شخص لقلبي
Firemen were successful in their attempt to control the fire	-نجحت محاولات المطافئ للسيطرة عَلَىْ الحريق
My father went to the police station to file an incident of theft report.	توجه ابي الي القسم للإبلاغ عَنْ حادث السرقة
The teacher assigned students to supervise their colleagues	قام المعلم بتكليف تلاميذ للإشراف عَلَىْ زملائهم

The preposition Hatta has an ambiguous meaning. It could mean either 'as far as' or 'even'. As you can see in the example, it could mean 'I ate the fish as far as its tail' or 'I ate the fish, even its tail.'

I ate the fish up to its tail. This is could also be translated as, 'I ate fish, even its tail'	اكلت السمكة حَتَّىْ ذيلها
I studied the book right through to the end	ذاكرت الكتاب حَتَّىْ اخره
I ate the dish all the way to its last bite	اكلت الطبق حَتَّىْ اخر قطمة
I read the newspaper from front to back / through to the last page.	اقرأ الصحيفة حَتَّىْ اخر صفحة
I read the article to the last line	قرات المقال حَتَّىْ اخر سطر
I watched the game to the end	شاهدت المباراة حَتَّىْ نهايتها
I watched the movie to the end	شاهدت الفِيلم حَتَّىْ نهايته
I ran in the marathon / race to the end	جريت حَتَّىْ اخر السباق
Muslims fast during Ramadan until sunset	يصوم المسلمون في رمضان حَتَّىْ المغرب
I exercised until the end of the exercise	تمرنت حَتَّىْ اخر التمرين
I was patient until the end of the year	صبرت حَتَّىْ نهاية العام

I studied the curriculum to its end	ذاكرت المنهج حَتَّىٰ نهايته
I drove the car from Cairo to Alexandria	قدت السيارة مِنَ القاهرة حَتَّىٰ الاسكندرية
I listened to the teacher until the end of the lecture	استمعت المعلم حَتَّىٰ نهاية المحاضرة
I spoke with my father until the early morning	تكلمت مع ابي حَتَّىٰ مطلع الصبح
I played the game until its end	لعبت المباراة حَتَّىٰ اخرها
I walked to the end of the road	مشيت حَتَّىٰ نهاية الطريق
I sat in class until the end	جلست حَتَّىٰ انتهاء الحصة
I waited until the end of the exams to travel	انتظرت حَتَّىٰ نهاية الامتحانات لكي اسافر
The distance from Cairo to Aswan is long	المسافة مِنَ القاهرة حَتَّىٰ اسوان كبيرة
I travelled until the end of the holiday	سافرت حَتَّىٰ نهاية الاجازة
I studied from the beginning of the day to its end (dawn till dusk)	ذاكرت مِنَ اول اليوم حَتَّىٰ اخره

In the next part of the book, we will learn how to use prepositions in sentences. For every preposition, you will find ten examples. You will also find vocabulary at the section for new words.

مِنْ

- نَظَرَ خَالِدٌ مِنَ النَّافِذَةِ.

- أَخَذْتُ الكِتَابَ مِنْ صَدِيقِي.

- سَافَرْتُ مِنَ المَدِينَةِ يَوْمَ الثُّلَاثَاءِ.

- سَمِعَ أَحْمَدُ نَصِيحَةً مِنْ وَالِدِهِ.

- لَقَدْ عُدْتُ يَاأُمِّي مِنَ المَدْرَسَةِ.

- تَعِبَ زِيَادٌ مِنَ الرَّكْضِ.

- هَرَبَتْ سِنْدِرِيلَّا مِنَ القَصْرِ مُسْرِعَةً قَبْلَ مُنْتَصَفِ اللَّيلِ.

- سَمِعَ مَازِنٌ خَبَراً سَعِيداً مِنْ مُدَرِّبِ الفَرِيقِ.

- رَائِحَةُ الطَّعَامِ الشَّهِي تَأْتِي مِنَ المَطْبَخِ.

- نَبِيلٌ تِلْمِيذٌ مِنْ تَلَامِيذِ المَدْرَسَةِ الجُدُدُ.

إلى:

وَصَلَتْ هِنْدُ إلى القَرْيَةِ صَبَاحاً.

جَلَسَتْ هِنْدُ مَعَ جَدِّهَا إلى العَصْرِ.

عَادَ زَيْدٌ إلى المَنْزِلِ.

سَافَرَ أَيْمَنُ مِنَ القَرْيَةِ إلى المَدِينَةِ.

أَرْسَلَتْ هِبَةُ رِسَالَةً إلى صَدِيقَتِهَا فِي الهِند.

تَعَالَ مَعِي إلى المَكْتَبَةِ القَرِيبَةِ.

مَرِضَ وَالِدُ أَمِيرٍ فَذَهَبَ إلى الطَّبِيبِ.

ذَهَبَ أَمِيرٌ بِسُرْعَةٍ إلى وَالِدِهِ.

ذَهَبَ التَّلَامِيذُ فِي رِحْلَةٍ مُفِيدَةٍ إلى المُتْحَفِ.

جَلَسَتْ سَارَةُ تُشَاهِدُ الفِيلْمَ إلى النِهَايَةِ.

عَنْ:

كَتَبْتُ مَقَالاً عَنِ النَّجَاحِ وَالتَّفَوُّقِ.

سَأَلَنِي المُعَلِّمُ عَنْ مَوْضُوعٍ هَامٍ.

تَحَدَّثَ عَنْ آجَازَةِ الصَّيْفِ لِزُمَلَائِكَ.

يُدَافِعُ المُحَامِي عَنِ المُتَّهَمِ.

مَاذَا قَرَأْتَ عَنِ اليَابَانِ؟

يَبْحَثُ أَمِيرٌ عَنْ قَمِيصٍ مُنَاسِبٍ.

رَفَعْتُ الغِطَاءَ عَنِ القِدْرِ لِأُضِيفَ المِلْحَ.

سَأُحَدِّثُكَ عَنْ وَصْفَةِ طَعَامٍ شهيةٍ.

إِعْتَذَرَ أَحْمَدُ عَنْ مُقَابَلَةِ صَدِيقِهِ اليَوْمَ.

مَرْيَمُ تَسْأَلُ المُعَلِّمَةَ عَنْ دَرَجَةِ الاخْتِبَارِ.

عَلى:

سَارَ يُوسُفُ عَلَى الجِسْرِ.

وَقَفَ أَمِيرٌ عَلَى الجَبَلِ.

جَلَسْتُ عَلَى المَقْعَدِ.

أَصْبَحْتُ عَجُوزاً لَأَقْوَى عَلَى السَّيْرِ.

أَقْبَلَ الوَلَدُ عَلَى الطَّعَامِ بِشَرَاهَةٍ.

أَشْكُرُ اللهَ عَلَى النِّعَمِ.

اِنْسَكَبَ الحِبْرُ عَلَى الثَّوْبِ الرَّائِعِ.

أَشْكُرُكَ عَلَى حُضُورِكَ لِتَهْنِئَتِي.

هَلْ وَقَفْتَ عَلَى السَّجَادِ بِحِذَاءٍ مُتَّسِخٍ؟

سَأُعَاقِبُكَ عَلَى العَمَلِ السَّيِّئِ.

فِي:

يَنْبَحُ الكَلْبُ فِي الحَدِيقَةِ.

دَخَلَ المُجْرِمُ فِي السِّجْنِ.

خَالِدٌ فِي البَيْتِ.

أَقَمْتُ فِي المَدِينَةِ سَبْعَ سَنَوَاتٍ.

يَغُوصُ السَّبَّاحُ فِي المَاءِ.

وَضَعْتُ الطَّعَامَ فِي الطَّبَقِ.

تَلْمَعُ النُّجُومُ فِي السَّمَاءِ.

فِي المَكْتَبَةِ كُتُبٌ كَثِيرَةٌ وَمُفِيدَةٌ.

يَضَعُ وَالِدِي نُقُودَهُ فِي البَنْكِ.

تَحْتَفِظُ هِنْدُ بِالخَاتَمِ فِي عُلْبَةٍ أَنِيقَةٍ.

الكاف:

صَرَخَ زِيَادٌ كَأَسَدٍ مُتَوَحِّشٍ.

كَانَتْ سُعَادُ جَمِيلَةً كَالزَّهْرَةِ النَّدِيَّةِ.

عَيْنَاهَا زَرْقَاءُ كَزُرْقَةِ البَحْرِ.

مَازِنٌ بَطِيءٌ كَالسُّلَحْفَاةِ.

صَوْتُكَ عَذْبٌ كَالبُلْبُلِ.

أَمِيرٌ يَسْبَحُ كَسَمَكَةٍ فِي المَاءِ.

مَنْزِلُ خَالِدٍ أَنِيقٌ كَمَنْزِلِ أَمِيرٍ.

ثَوْبُ سَارَةَ طَوِيلٌ كَثَوْبِ هِنْدٍ.

شَعْرُ هِنْدٍ نَاعِمٌ كَالحَرِيرِ.

حَدِيثُكَ كَحَدِيثِ وَالِدِي تَمَاماً.

الباء:

أَمْسَكَتْ سَارَةُ بِيَدِ العَجُوزِ.

مَرَرْتُ بِمَنْزِلِ أَحْمَدَ.

أَكَلْتُ الطَّعَامَ بِالمِلْعَقَةِ.

خُذْ هَذِهِ الحَلْوَى بِدُولَارٍ وَاحِدٍ.

ضَرَبَ الرَّجُلُ اللِّصَّ بِقَسْوَةٍ.

ذَهَبَ زَيْدٌ إِلَى مَنْزِلِهِ بِسَلَامٍ.

تَمَّتِ المُسَابَقَةُ بِقَرَارٍ مِنْ مُدِيرِ المَدْرَسَةِ.

قَشَرْتُ الفَاكِهَةَ بِالسِّكِّينِ.

وَصَلَتْ سُعَادٌ بِاللَّيْلِ.

اِحْتَضَنْتُ وَالِدِي بِسَعَادَةٍ.

اللام:

هَذَا القَلَمُ لِسَمِيرٍ.

عَادَتْ هِنْدُ لِلْبَيْتِ مُتَأَخِّرَةً.

الجَائِزَةُ لِلْمُجْتَهِدِ.

العِقَابُ لِلسَّارِقِ.

اِشْتَرَتْ سَارَةُ قُفْلاً لِلْخِزَانَةِ.

أَعْطَى المُعَلِّمُ الوَرَقَةَ لِلتِّلْمِيذِ.

قَرَأْتُ الدَرْسَ لِرِفَاقِي بِالمَدْرَسَةِ.

أَعَدَّتِ الأُمُّ طَعَاماً شَهِيّاً لِلصِّغَارِ.

أَعْطِ النُّقُودَ لِلْبَائِعِ.

اِنْتَقَلَ مَازِنٌ لِمَنْزِلٍ جَدِيدٍ.

حتى:

سَارَ أَحْمَدُ حَتَّى الرَّبْوَةِ.

سَهِرَتْ هِنْدُ حَتَّى الصَّبَاحِ.

شَاهَدَتْ هِنْدُ الفِيلْمَ حَتَّى النِّهَايَةِ.

أَكَلْتُ السَّمَكَةَ حَتَّى الذيلِ.

وَصَلَ الحُجَّاجُ حَتَّى عَرَفَةَ.

أَكَلَ الوَلَدُ الطَّعَامَ حَتَّى الشَّبَعِ.

سَارَتْ هِنْدٌ وَسَارَةٌ حَتَّى مَنْزِلِ أَمِيرَةٍ.

اِنْطَلَقتُ بِسَيَارَتِي حَتَّى المَتْجَرِ القَرِيبِ.

مَشَيْنَا كَثِيراً حَتَّى المَسَاءِ.

زَرَعْتُ الحَدِيقةَ حَتَّى السُّورِ.

In this lesson, we will be studying nine interrogative words: how, when, who, what (In Arabic, there are two words for "what", one for asking questions about nouns such as "what is your name", and the other for verbs such as when we ask "what do you want?" or "what did he say?"), a particle "hal" which is used for questions that have a yes or no answer, where, how many, which/what/who. We will translate each of the following examples that contain interrogative words, but will not list them in the same order as they are in Arabic.

(kayfa) How? 1. How are you? 2. How come you finished answering quickly? 3. How did you draw this painting? 4. How did you prepare this delicious food ? 5. How do you write "apple"? 6. How was your day?	كَيْفَ الحَالُ؟ كَيْفَ تكتُبُ (تُفَّاحة)؟ كَيْفَ كَان يَومُكَ؟ كَيْفَ رَسَمْتَ هَذِه اللوحَة؟ كَيْفَ انتَهيتَ مِن الاجابةِ بسُرعةٍ؟ كَيْفَ أعدَدْتَ هَذا الطَّعامَ الشَهيَّ؟	كَيْفَ	1
(mata)When? 1. Take the book and return it whenever you want (in Arabic, you can use the same word [mata] to say both 'when' and 'whenever' 2. When did the game end ? 3. When does Linda go to school ? 4. When does she come home ? 5. When is the doctor's appointment? 6. When were you as lazy as that ? 7. When will we go to visit our maternal aunt ?	مَتَى تذهَبُ لِيندا الى المدرَسةِ؟ مَتَى تعودُ الى المنزلِ؟ مَتَى موعدُ الطبيبِ؟ مَتَى سَنذهبُ لِزيارةِ خَالتِي؟ مَتَى كُنتَ كسولاً هَكذا؟ مَتَى انتهَت المباراةُ؟	مَتَى	2

	خُذ الكتابَ وأعِدهُ مَتَى تُحِب. (استخدامها هنا بمعنى وقتما وليس سؤال)	
(man) Who/whom? 1. Who are you? (In Arabic, in the present tense, although the verb 'to be' is not written, it is nevertheless implied.) 2. Who is giving me the answer for this question? 3. Who is the star of this movie? (sometimes in Arabic, instead of saying the "star" of a movie, we say the "hero" of the movie 4. Who is this young woman? 5. Who told you this news? 6. Who took the pen from the drawer? 7. Who won the race?	مَن أنتَ؟ مَن تَكون هذه الفتاةُ؟ مَن يُجيبُني على هذا السُّؤالِ؟ مَن أخذَ القلمَ مِن الدُّرجِ؟ مَن أخبرَكُم بهذا الخبرِ؟ مَن الفائِزُ في السِّباقِ؟ مَن بَطلُ هَذا الفيلمِ؟	مَنْ 3
What? Maa (the "what" for nouns) 1. What is the best music you have heard? 2. What is the most delicious food you have eaten? 3. What is your father's job? 4. What is your favorite sport? 5. What is your level in Arabic? 6. What is your name? 7. What is your opinion regarding this topic?	مَااسْمُكَ؟ مَاعملُ والدِكَ؟ مَا رِيَاضتُكَ المفضلةُ؟ مَاأشهَى طعامٍ أكلتَهُ؟ مَاأفضلُ موسيقى سَمِعتَها؟ مَادرجةُ اجادتكَ للغةِ العربيةِ؟ مَارأيُكَ في هَذا الموضوعِ؟	مَا 4
Madha (the "what" for verbs) 1. What did Adam buy? 2. What did Thomas say to his father? 3. What did you do today? 4. What did you for dinner? 5. What do you want? 6. What were you doing?	مَاذَا تُريدُ؟ مَاذَا تُحِبُ على العشاءِ؟ مَاذَا قالَ توماسُ لوالِده؟ مَاذَا أكلتَ على العشاءِ؟	مَاذَا 5

7. What would you like for dinner?	مَاذَا فَعلتَ اليومَ؟ مَاذَا كُنتَ تَفعلُ؟ مَاذَا اشترَى ادمُ؟		
Hal? (used in questions the answers of which will be yes or no) 1. Are you an Arab? / Do you speak the Arabic language? 2. Did Diana go with you? 3. Did Susan help her mother? 4. Did you exercise today? 5. Is this shoe new? 6. Was John in the garden?	هَل أنت عَرَبيٌّ؟ – هَل تتكلمُ اللغةَ العربيةَ؟ هَل ساعَدَتْ سُوزانْ أمَّها؟ هَل كان جون بالحديقةِ؟ هَل ذَهَبتْ ديانا معكُم؟ هَل هذا الحذاءُ جديدٌ؟ هَل تمرَّنْتَ اليَّومَ في النَّادي؟	هَل	6
(ayna) Where? 1. Where are you traveling this summer 2. Where did John go? 3. Where did you put the key? 4. Where do the fish live? 5. Where is my new shoe? 6. Where is the United States? 7. Where was Linda?	أَيْنَ الولاياتِ المتحدةِ؟ أَيْنَ وَضعْتَ المِفتاحَ؟ أَيْنَ ذهبَ جون؟ أَيْنَ حِذائي الجَديد؟ أَيْنَ كانتْ ليندا؟ أَيْنَ يعيشُ السمكُ؟ أَيْنَ تُسافرون هذا الصيفِ؟	أَيْنَ	7
(kam) How many? 1. How many apples did John eat? 2. How many kilometers did the car traverse? 3. How many kilometers does Mike weigh? 4. How many times did you jump rope? 5. How much is the watch? 6. How much is this delicious desert? 7. How much time elapsed while you were playing? (please notice that the "waaw" here doesn't mean "and", but means "while") 8. What time is it?	كَمْ السَّاعةُ؟ - بِكَمْ السَّاعةُ؟ كَمْ مِنَ الوقتِ مَضَى وأنتُم تلعَبون؟ كَمْ تفاحةً أكلَ جون؟ بِكَمْ هَذِه الحلوى اللذيذة؟ كَمْ كيلومتراً قَطَعَت السيارةُ؟ كَمْ كيلوجراماً يَزنُ مايك؟ كَمْ مرةً قفزتَ بالحبلِ؟	كَمْ	8

(ay) (Second Party) who or which?	أيُّ نَوعٍ مِن الرجــالِ أنتَ؟	9
1. Which article did you read?	أيُّ فستانٍ أعجَبَكَ؟	
2. Which dress did you like?	أيُّ مقالٍ قرأتَ؟	أَيُّ
3. Which friend do you like more?	أيُّ صديقٍ تُحبُّه أكثَر؟	
4. Which one of you can tell me the answer to the question?	أيُّ طريقٍ تمشي الى البيتِ؟	
5. Which one of you is Adam?	أيُّكم ادم؟	
6. Which road are you walking to the house?	أيُّكم يخبرُني بإجابة السؤالِ؟	
7. Which type of a man are you?		

أَعْلَنَتْ مَحَطَّةٌ تِلِفِزْيُونِيَّةٌ بريطانِيَّةٌ أنَّها سَتَبُثُّ أذانَ الفَجرِ بِصُورَةٍ حَيَّةٍ طَوالَ شَهرِ رَمَضانَ الكَريمِ لِإعْطاءِ صَوتٍ للأقَلِّيَّةِ المُسْلِمَةِ البالِغ عَدَدُها 2.8 مِلْيُون، وَهِيَ الخُطْوَةُ الَّتِي رَحَّبَ بها مَجْلِسُ مُسْلِمِي بريطانيا.

A British Television Station announced that it would broadcast Fajr (one of five prescribed Muslim prayers that is performed everyday) throughout the holy month of Ramadan, to give voice to the 2.8 million Muslim minority, in a move that was welcomed by the Muslim Council of Britain.

وَأكَّدَتِ القَناةُ الرّابِعَةُ -وَهِيَ قَناةٌ عامَّةٌ أُنشِئَتْ لِجَذْبِ اهتِمام جُمْهُورِ الأقَلِّيَّاتِ- أمْسِ أنَّها سَتَكُونُ أوَّلَ قَناةٍ رَئِيسِيَّةٍ في بريطانيا تَبُثُّ الأذانَ "في الثالِثَةِ مِن صَباحِ كُلِّ يَوْمٍ" طَوالَ شَهرِ رَمَضانَ ابتِداءً مِنْ 9 يُولْيُو/تَمّوزَ.

Channel Four - a public channel created to attract the attention of minority public - confirmed that this would be the first major channel in Britain to broadcast the Call to Prayer at four o' clock every day, during the month of Ramadan starting from July 9th.

وَقالَ مُدِيرُ البَرامِجِ الواقِعِيَّةِ في القَناةِ رالِف لي إنَّهُ يَأمُلُ إعْطاءَ صَوتٍ لِجُمْهُورِ الأقَلِّيَّةِ المُسْلِمَةِ مِمَّنْ يَلْتَزِمُونَ بِالْقانُونِ، مُشِيرًا إلى أنَّ أذانَ الصَّلاةِ يَدْفَعُ المُسْلِمِينَ إلى لَحَظاتِ هُدُوءٍ لِلْعِبادَةِ، وَتَمَنَّى أَنْ يَلْفِتَ أيْضًا انْتِباهَ المُشاهِدِينَ الآخَرِينَ إلى مُلاحَظَةِ هذا الحَدَثِ.

The director of Reality TV shows, Ralph Lee, says he hopes to give voice to the Muslim minority audience who obide by the law, pointing out that Muslim Call to Prayer provides them with quiet moments to worship. He also wished to draw the attention of other viewers to observe this event.

مِهرَجَانُ الكَشَّافَةُ وَالمُرشِدَاتُ العَرَبِيُّ

البِلادُ العَرَبِيةُ وَعَواصِمِهَا

مِنْ أَيِّ بَلَدٍ أَنْتَ؟ وَمَا جِنسِيَتُكَ؟

P.S. all words after أَنَا are names. Every name represent the most popular name in its country.

الحوار

رَئِيسَةُ المِهرَجَانِ: أَهلاً بَكُمْ جَمِيعاً فِي **طَرَابُلُس**، عَاصِمَةِ **لِيبِيَا** وَأَهلاً بكُمْ فِي مِهرَجَانِ الكَشَّافةِ وَالمُرشِدَاتِ العَرَبِيِّ لِطُلَّابٍ وَطَالِبَاتِ المَدَارِسِ الثَّانَوِيَّةِ.

Welcome to you all in Tripoli, the capital of Libya and welcome in the Arabic festival the scouts and (female) guides (female scoutmasters) for the students of the high schools.

والانَ يَتَقَدَّمُ رُؤَسَاءُ الفِرَقِ الكَشفِيَّةِ لِلتَعرِيفِ بِأنفُسِهِم ونَبدأ بِالدُّولِ العَرَبِيَةِ فِي **قَارَةِ افريقِيا**.

Now, the scout team leaders step forward to introduce themselves and we begin with the Arabic countries in the African continent.

الأوَّلُ: أَنَا سُندُسُ مِنْ **تُونُس** عَاصِمَةِ **تُونُس**.

الثَّانِي: وَأَنَا هَيثَمٌ مِنَ **القَاهِرَةِ** عَاصِمَةِ **مِصرَ**.

الثَّالِثُ: وَأَنَا بَكَّارٌ مِنَ **الخُرطُوم** عَاصِمَةِ **السُّودَانِ**.

الرَّابِعُ: أَنَا شَيمَاءُ مِن **طَرَابُلُس** عَاصِمَةِ **لِيبِيَا**.

الخَامِسُ: وأَنَا حُورِيَةُ مِنَ **الرَّبَاطِ** عَاصِمَةِ **المَغرِبِ**.

السَّادِسَ: أَنَا عَبدُ اللهِ مِن **جِيبُوتِي** عَاصِمَةِ **جِيبُوتِي**.

السَّابِع: وَأَنَا عَبدُ الرَّحمنِ مِن **نَوَاكشُوط** عَاصِمَةِ **مُورِيتَانِيَا**.

الثَّامِنَ: أَنَا لَطِيفَةٌ مِنَ **الجَزَائِرِ** عَاصِمَةِ **الجَزَائِرِ**.

التَّاسِعَ: وَأَنَا نُورَةٌ مِن **مَقْدِيشُو** عَاصِمَةِ الصُّومَالِ.

الْعَاشِرُ: أَنَا جَمِيلَةُ مِنْ **مُورُونِي** عَاصِمَةِ جُزُرِ القَمَرِ.

رَئِيسَةُ اتِّحَادِ الكَشَّافَةِ العَرَبِيِّ: والْآنَ يَتَقَدَّمُ رُؤَسَاءُ الفِرَقِ الكَشْفِيَّةِ مِنَ الدُّوَلِ العَرَبِيَّةِ فِي **قَارَةِ اسْيَا** لِلتَّعْرِيفِ بِأَنْفُسِهِمْ.

الأَوَّلُ: أَنَا فَيْصَلٌ مِنَ **الرِّيَاضِ** عَاصِمَةِ المَمْلَكَةِ العَرَبِيَّةِ السُّعُودِيَّةِ.

الثَّانِي: أَنَا بَاسِلٌ مِن **دِمَشْقٍ** عَاصِمَةِ سُورِيَا.

الثَّالِثُ: وَأَنَا عَمَّارُ مِنْ **القُدْسِ** عَاصِمَةِ فِلَسْطِينِ.

الرَّابِعُ: أَنَا سُهَيْلَةُ مِنَ **عَمَّانَ** عَاصِمَةِ الأُرْدُنِ.

الخَامِسُ: وَأَنَا جُومَانَةُ مِنْ **بَيْرُوتٍ** عَاصِمَةِ لُبْنَانَ.

السَّادِسُ: وَأَنَا جَوهَرَةٌ مِنَ **المَنَامَةِ** عَاصِمَةِ البَحْرَيْنِ.

السَّابِعُ: أَنَا عَدنَانُ مِنْ **بَغْدَادَ** عَاصِمَةِ العِرَاقِ.

الثَّامِنُ: وَأَنَا نَاصِرٌ مِن **الكُوَيْتِ** عَاصِمَةِ الكُوَيْتِ.

التَّاسِعُ: أَنَا سُلْطَانُ مِنْ **مَسْقَطٍ** عَاصِمَةِ عُمَانِ.

الْعَاشِرُ: وَأَنَا حَمَدٌ مِنَ **الدَّوْحَةِ** عَاصِمَةِ قَطَرٍ.

الحَادِيَ عَشَرَ: أَنَا خَلْفَانُ مِنْ **أَبِي ظَبْيٍ** عَاصِمَةِ الامَارَاتِ.

الثَّانِيَ عَشَرَ: وَأَنَا سَعِيدٌ مِنْ **صَنعَاءَ** عَاصِمَةِ اليَمَنِ.

رَئِيسَةُ اتِّحَادِ الكَشَّافَةِ وَالمُرْشِدَاتِ:

أَهْلاً بِكُمْ جَمِيعاً مِنْ كُلِّ الدُوَلِ العَرَبِيَةِ، سَنُقِيمُ مُعَسْكَراً كَبِيراً، وَسَنُخَيِّمُ فِيهِ، وَتَتَعَارَفُ جَمِيعُ الفِرَقِ مِنْ جَمِيعِ البِلادِ العَرَبِيَةِ.

Write in the right-hand column the correct country of the following capitals

	مُورُونِي		تُونُس
	الرِّيَاضِ		القَاهِرَةِ
	دِمَشْقِ		الخُرطُومِ
	القُدْسِ		طَرَابْلُس
	عَمَّانَ		الرِّبَاطِ
	بَيْرُوتِ		جِيبُوتِي
	المَنَامَةِ		نَوَاكْشُوط
	بَغْدَادِ		الجَزَائِرِ
	الكُوَيْتِ		مَقْدِيشُو

	مَسْقَطٍ
	الدَّوْحَةِ
	أبي ظَبْيٍّ
	صَنعَاءَ

The Arab world covers parts of Africa and Asia. Write the names of Arab countries under these continents.

قَارَةِ اسْيَا	قَارَةِ افرِيقِيا

الكلماتُ الجديدة

معناها	الكلمة
Festival	مِهرَجَانٌ
Scouts	الكَشَّافَة
Female Guides	المُرشِدَاتُ
Chairperson	رئيسَة
Advance	يَتَقَدَّمُ

To introduce themselves	لِلتَعرِيفِ بأنفُسِهِم
Continent	قَارَة
camp	مُعسْكَرًا
We will Camp	سَنُخَيِّمُ

الشُّرْطَةُ الدِّينِيَّةُ

The religious police of a certain Arabic country arrested a teenager while he was trying to give a pet as a gift to a girl he loved.

هَيْئَةُ الأَمْرِ بِالمَعْرُوفِ وَالنَّهْيِ عَنِ المُنْكَرِ

أَلْقَتْ الشُّرْطَةُ الدِّينِيَّةُ السُّعُودِيَّةُ القَبْضَ عَلَى مُرَاهِقٍ أَثْنَاءَ مُحَاوَلَتِهِ تَقْدِيمَ هَدِيَّةٍ لِحَبِيبَتِهِ كَانَتْ عِبَارَةً عَنْ قِطَّةٍ جَمِيلَةٍ، حَسْبَ مَا نَقَلَتْهُ وَسَائِلُ إِعْلَامٍ سُعُودِيَّةٍ يَوْمَ الجُمُعَةِ المَاضِي.

وَضَبَطَتْ هَيْئَةُ الأَمْرِ بِالمَعْرُوفِ وَالنَّهْيِ عَنِ المُنْكَرِ (الشُّرْطَةُ الدِّينِيَّةُ) بِمُحَافَظَةِ عُنَيْزَةَ، شَمَالَ الرِّيَاضِ مُرَاهِقًا يَحْمِلُ جِنْسِيَّةً عَرَبِيَّةً، عِنْدَ مُحَاوَلَتِهِ إِهْدَاءَ حَبِيبَتِهِ قِطَّةً جَمِيلَةً تَبْلُغُ قِيمَتُهَا 600 رِيَالٍ، تَعْبِيرًا عَنْ حُبِّهِ لَهَا.

وَشَاهَدَ رِجَالُ الهَيْئَةِ الشَّابَّ يَقِفُ بِجِوَارِ بَوَّابَةِ مَدْرَسَةٍ ثَانَوِيَّةٍ لِلبَنَاتِ، فَانْتَهَرُوهُ وَحَاوَلُوا مَنْعَهُ، الا أَنَّهُ حَاوَلَ مَرَّةً أُخْرَى مِنَ البَابِ الآخَرِ، فَتَمَّ القَبْضُ عَلَيْهِ وَإِحَالَتُهُ إِلَى شُرْطَةِ

مُحَافَظَةِ عنيزَةٍ، وَمِنْ ثَمَّ تَحْوِيلُهُ إِلَى دَارِ المُلَاحَظَةِ بِمَدِينَةِ بُرِيدَةٍ، شَمَالَ الرِّيَاضِ، فِيْمَا سَلَّمَ رِجَالُ الهَيْئَةِ القِطَّةَ إِلَى وَالِدِهِ.

الكلماتُ الجديدة

معناها	الكلمة
Religious Police	الشُّرْطَةُ الدِّينِيَة
Arrested	أَلْقَتِ القَبْضَ
Religious Police, literal translation: Commission for the Promotion of Virtue and the Prevention of Vice	هَيْئَةُ الأَمْرِ بِالمَعْرُوفِ وَالنَّهِي عَنِ المُنْكَرِ
Teenager	مُرَاهِقٍ
According	حَسْبَ
Reported	نَقَلَتْهُ
Media	وَسَائِلُ إِعْلَامٍ
Capture	ضَبَطَتْ
Nationality	جِنْسِيَةً
Carrying the Nationality- when they talk about foreign nationalities, we say that he is "carrying" the nationality	يَحْمِلُ جِنْسِيَةً

Expressing	تَعْبِيرًا
Gate	بَوَابَة
High School for Girls	مَدْرَسَةٍ ثَانَوِيَةٍ لِلبَنَاتِ
Scolded him	انتَهَرُوهُ
Referred him to	إِحَالَتَهُ
To transfer him	تَحْوِيلُهُ
House	دَارٍ
Observation	المُلاحَظَة
Observation House- the name of the juvenile detention center in certain Arabic countries	دَارِ المُلاحَظَة
Deliver, handover	سَلَّمَ

أسئلة:

1. What is the name of the religious police in this text?
2. To what country do the religious police belong?
3. What is the nationality of the teenager?
4. On which day was this story reported in the media?
5. In which governorate did this incident take place?
6. What type of pet was it? How much did it cost?
7. How do you say "juvenile detention center" in Arabic?
8. What happened to the pet?

1. ﴿وَلْتَكُنْ مِنكُمْ أُمَّةٌ يَدْعُونَ إِلَى الْخَيْرِ وَيَأْمُرُونَ بِالْمَعْرُوفِ وَيَنْهَوْنَ عَنِ الْمُنكَرِ وَأُولَئِكَ هُمُ الْمُفْلِحُونَ﴾

2. ﴿كُنتُمْ خَيْرَ أُمَّةٍ أُخْرِجَتْ لِلنَّاسِ تَأْمُرُونَ بِالْمَعْرُوفِ وَتَنْهَوْنَ عَنِ الْمُنكَرِ وَتُؤْمِنُونَ بِاللَّهِ وَلَوْ آمَنَ أَهْلُ الْكِتَابِ لَكَانَ خَيْرًا لَّهُم مِّنْهُمُ الْمُؤْمِنُونَ وَأَكْثَرُهُمُ الْفَاسِقُونَ﴾

3. ﴿وَالْمُؤْمِنُونَ وَالْمُؤْمِنَاتُ بَعْضُهُمْ أَوْلِيَاءُ بَعْضٍ يَأْمُرُونَ بِالْمَعْرُوفِ وَيَنْهَوْنَ عَنِ الْمُنكَرِ وَيُقِيمُونَ الصَّلَاةَ وَيُؤْتُونَ الزَّكَاةَ وَيُطِيعُونَ اللهَ وَرَسُولَهُ أُولَئِكَ سَيَرْحَمُهُمُ اللهُ إِنَّ اللهَ عَزِيزٌ حَكِيمٌ﴾

The religious police take their name from the Quran. There are three verses in which Allah tells believers to form a group (in the first verse) that will instruct and promote good actions and forbid bad actions. The second verse talks about true believers, the Muslims are the best people ever to have existed and how Islam is a nation, the best nation that exists; a nation that enjoins in good and forbids bad actions. The third verse demonstrates how the group promotes good forbids evil. This is where the name of the religious police comes from.

The Future of the Religious Police

Most citizens regard the religious police as overbearing and intrusive. An article like the one above will further damage the image of the religious police.

Historically, people were so obedient and appreciative in their dealings with the religious police, but this behavior is drastically changing: people are starting to respond violently to the religious police's intrusions into their lives. There are still communities that respect the religious police, but most people do not. The consensus is that the religious police must reform themselves or risk losing all authority and becoming obsolete.

يَشْكُو الْعَالَمُ مُنْذُ سَنَوَاتٍ مِنَ ارْتِفَاعِ أَسْعَارِ الْغِذَاءِ، وَتَزَايُدِ عَدَدِ الْجَوْعَى لِيَتَجَاوَزَ مِلْيَارَ إِنْسَانٍ، وَتَضَاعُفِ أَعْدَادِ الْمَرْضَى بِالسَّرَطَانَاتِ نَتِيجَةً لِلْغِذَاءِ الْمُسَمَّمِ، وَانْتِشَارِ الْمَخَاوِفِ مِنَ الْمُنْتَجَاتِ الزِّرَاعِيَّةِ الْمُسْتَنْبَتَةِ مِنَ الْبُذُورِ الْمُهَجَّنَةِ وِرَاثِيًّا، وَأَضْرَارِ الِاسْتِخْدَامِ الْمُفْرِطِ لِلْأَسْمِدَةِ وَالْمُبِيدَاتِ الْكِيمِيَائِيَّةِ عَلَى صِحَّةِ الْبَشَرِ، وَعَلَى التَّوَازُنِ الْبِيئِيِّ.

The world has complained for years about the rising food prices, and the number of hungry people has grown to more than a billion people. The number of cancer patients has doubled as a result of poisoned food, and the fears of genetically modified and hybrid seeds in agricultural products has spread. The excessive use of fertilizers and chemical pesticides has damaged human health and the ecological balance.

, and the damage from the excessive use of fertilizers and chemical pesticides on human health and ecological balance has worsened.

أشهرُ معالمُ بلدي

This lesson takes place in an Arabic lesson. The students are native Arabs but they have forgotten their ancestors' language. Students introduce themselves by indicating their nationality, where they live, and what are the most famous monuments in their native country. Students' names represent their country's most popular name.

الحوار

مَرْحَباً بِكُم فِي الحِصَّةِ الاولى مِنْ فَصْلِ تَعْلِيمِ اللُّغَةِ العَرَبِيَةِ لِلأَجَانِب، أُرِيدُ مِنْ كُلِّ وَاحِدٍ مِنكُم أَنْ يَتَحَدَثَ عَنْ نَفسِه، مِنْ ايِّ بَلَدٍ هُوَ، جِنسِيَتِه وَفِي ايِّ مَدِينَةٍ يَعِيشُ، وَاشهَرُ مَعَالِمِ بَلَدِه، التَّرتِيبُ سَيَكُونُ حَسَبَ الحُرُوف الهِجَائِيَة، تَفَضَل يَا أُسْتَاذ احمَد.....

أحمد: أنَا مِصريُ، وَأعِيشُ فِي مَدِينَةِ الاسكَنَدَرِيَةِ، اشهَرُ مَعَالِمِ بَلَدِي الاهرَامَاتُ وَأَبُو الهَولِ والاثَارِ الفِرعَونِيَةِ.

بشير: أنَا سودَانيٌّ، وَأعِيشُ فِي مَدِينَةِ أُمّ دِرمَانٍ، اشهَرُ مَعَالِمِ بَلَدِي جَبَلُ مَرَّة وَهوَ جَبَلٌ بُركَانيٌّ مُتَعَدِد القِمَمِ، تَتخلَلُهُ الشَّلالاتُ والبحَيرَاتُ والنَبَاتَاتُ النَّادِرةُ والطَّبِيعَةُ التِي تُبهِرُ السَّائِحِينَ.

تغريد: أنَا لِيبِيةٌ، وَأعِيشُ فِي مَدِينَةِ بَنِي غَازِي، اشهَرُ مَعَالِمِ بَلَدِي كَاتدرَائِيَة بَنِي غَازِي مِنْ أكبَرِ الكَاتدرَائِيَاتِ العَرَبِيَةِ، وقَلعَةُ طرَابُلُس والتِي تُعرَفُ بالسَرَاي الحَمرَاءِ.

رقية: وَأنَا تُونِسِيةٌ، وأعِيشُ فِي مَدِينَةِ صَفَاقِس، أشهَرُ مَعَالِم بَلَدِي الخضرَاءُ جَامِعُ الزَّيتُونةِ التُّحفَةُ المِعمَارِيةُ، وَمَدِينَةِ القِيرَوان التَّي بَنَاهَا عُقبَة ابنِ نَافِعٍ.

ثابت: أنَا مَغرِبيٌّ، وَأعِيشُ فِي مَدِينَةِ الرِّبَاطِ، أشهَرُ مَعَالِمِ بَلَدِي مَسجِدُ صَومَعَةِ حَسَّان، والاثَارُ والعِمَارَةُ الاسلامِيَةِ.

جمال: أنَا جِيبُوتيٌّ، وَأعِيشُ فِي مَدِينَةِ أبخ، أشهَرُ مَعَالِمِ بَلَدِي بُحَيرةُ عَسَلٍ التِي يُغطِيهَا المِلحُ وَسِيَاحةُ الغَطسِ عَلَى سَوَاحِلِ خَلِيجِ عَدَن.

حسن: وَأَنَا مُورِيتَانِيٌّ، وَأَعِيشُ فِي مَدِينَةِ نَوَاذِيبُو، أَشْهَرُ مَعَالِمِ بَلَدِي حُفْرَةُ الرِّيشَاتِ واسمُهَا عينُ الصَّحرَاءِ لهَا شَكلٌ دَائِرِيٌّ مُمَيَّزٌ وَيُمْكِنُ رُؤْيَتَهَا مِنَ الفَضَاءِ.

خالد: أَنَا جَزَائِرِي، وَأَعِيشُ فِي مَدِينَةِ وَهرَانِ، أَشْهَرُ مَعَالِمِ بَلَدِي

جِبَالُ الهَقَّارِ فِي الصَّحرَاءِ، ومَمَرُّ الأَسْكَرَام الذي يُمْكِنُ مِنهُ مَشَاهَدَةُ أَجْمَلِ شُرُوقٍ وَغُرُوبٍ لِلشَمسِ فِي العَالَمِ كُلِّهِ.

دلال: أَنَا صُومَالِيَةٌ، وَأَعِيشُ فِي مَدِينَةِ مَرْكًا، أَشْهَرُ مَعَالِمِ بَلَدِي قَلْعَةُ تَالِيح وَهِيَ أَهَمُّ وَأَبرَزُ آثَارِ دَولَةِ الدَّرَاوِيشِ.

ذكي: أَنَا كُومُورِي مِن (الكُومور) جُزُرِ القُمَرِ القاف مضمومة، وَأَعِيشُ فِي مَدِينَةِ مُوتسَامُودُو، أَشْهَرُ مَعَالِمِ بَلَدِي الطَّبِيعَةُ الخَلَابَةُ، وَبُرْكَانُ كَارْتَالا الذي يُعَدُّ مِنْ انشَطِ البَرَاكِينِ فِي العَالَمِ وَفُوَهَتُهُ أَكبَرُ فُوَهَةِ بُرْكَانٍ فِي العَالَمِ.

رامي: أَنَا سوري وأعيش فِي مَدِينَةِ حَلَبٍ، أَشْهَرُ مَعَالِمِ بَلَدِي الجَامِعُ الأَمَوِيُّ وَالعِمَارَةُ العُثْمَانِيَةُ.

زهرة: أَنَا سُعُودِيَةٌ، وَأَعِيشُ فِي مَدِينَةِ جَدَّةٍ، أَشْهَرُ مَعَالِمِ بَلَدِي

الكَعبَةُ المُشَرَّفَةُ التي يَحِجُّ النَّاسُ اِلَيهَا فِي كُلِّ عَامٍ.

سُهيل: أَنَا فِلَسْطِينِي، وَأَعِيشُ فِي مَدِينَةِ غَزَّةَ، أَشْهَرُ مَعَالِمِ بَلَدِي

المَسجِدُ الأَقصَى وَمَسجِدُ قُبَّةِ الصَّخرَةِ.

شادي: أَنَا أُردُنِيٌّ، وَأَعِيشُ فِي مَدِينَةِ الزَّرقَاءِ، أَشْهَرُ مَعَالِمِ بَلَدِي مَدِينَةُ البَترَاءِ مِنْ أَشْهَرِ المَعَالِمِ الأَثرِيَةِ فِي الأُردُنِ، وَهِيَ مَدِينَةٌ مَحفُورَةٌ فِي الصُّخُورِ.

صوفيا: أَنَا لُبْنَانِيَةٌ، وَأَعيشُ في مَدِينَةِ طَرَابلس، أَشْهَرُ مَعَالِمِ بَلَدِي مَغَارَةُ جعِيتَا وَالقِلَاع التاريخية العَدِيدَةِ.

ضِيف: أَنَا بَحرِيني، وَأَعيشُ في مَدِينَةِ المُحَرَّق، أَشْهَرُ مَعَالِمِ بَلَدِي قَلَعَةُ البَحرَين، وَقَلَعَةُ عَرَادٍ.

طاهر: أَنَا عِرَاقِيٌّ، وَأَعيشُ في مَدِينَةِ البَصْرَةِ، أَشْهَرُ مَعَالِمِ بَلَدِي حَدَائِقُ بَابِلٍ المُعَلَّقَةِ وَأَسَدُ بَابِلٍ وَالكَثِيرِ مِنَ العِمَارَةِ العَبَّاسِيَةِ.

ظافر: أَنَا كُوِيتي، وَأَعيشُ في مَدِينَةِ الأَحمَدِي، أَشْهَرُ مَعَالِمِ بَلَدِي بَوَابَاتُ سُورِ الكُوَيتِ القَدِيم وَالقَصْرُ الأَحمَرُ في مَنطِقَةِ الجَهْرَاءِ وَسُمِّيَ بِهَذَا الاسْمِ لِأَنَّهُ بُنِيَ مِنَ الطِّينِ وَاللَبِنِ الأَحمَرِ.

عامر: أَنَا عُمَانِيٌّ، وَأَعيشُ في مَدِينَةِ صَلَالَةِ، أَشْهَرُ مَعَالِمِ بَلَدِي مَحمِيَةُ مَنطِقَةِ هَانُون أَو حَانُون، وَهِيَ مَحمِيَةٌ طَبيعِيَةٌ لِأَشجَارِ اللِّبَانِ وَمُسَجَلَةٌ في قَائِمَةِ التُّرَاثِ العَالَمِي، وَ بَيتُ المِقحِم مِنَ المَعَالِمِ التَارِيخِيَةِ الأَثرِيَةِ العَرِيقَةِ.

غالي: أَنَا قَطَرِي، وَأَعيشُ في مَدِينَةِ الوَكرَة، أَشْهَرُ مَعَالِمِ بَلَدِي قَلَعَةُ الكُوتِ، وَسُوقُ وَاقِفٍ مِنْ أَشْهَرِ الأَسْوَاقِ وَأَقدَمِهَا، عَلَى مُستَوَى الخَلِيجِ العَرَبِي وَلَهُ شُهْرَةٌ كَبِيرَة.

فاروق: أَنَا امَارَاتِي، وَأَعيشُ في مَدِينَةِ دُبَي، أَشْهَرُ مَعَالِمِ بَلَدِي قَصْرُ الحِصْنِ وَقَرْيَة حَتَّا التُّرَاثِيَةُ.

قمر: أَنَا يَمَنِي، وَأَعيشُ في مَدِينَةِ عَدَنْ، أَشْهَرُ مَعَالِمِ بَلَدِي مَدِينَةُ بَرَاقِشِ الأَثرِيَةِ، وَمَسجِدُ المِحْضَارِ.

الكلمات الجديدة

معناها	الكلمة
The first period	الحِصَّةِ الاولَى
The classroom	فَصْلِ
For foreigners	لِلأَجَانِبِ
Talking about himself	يَتَحَدَّثَ عَنْ نَفْسِهِ
The most famous landmark in his country	اشْهَرُ مَعَالِمِ بَلَدِه
The order (sequence)	التَرْتِيبُ
According	حَسَبَ
The alphabet	الحُرُوفِ الهِجَائِيَةِ
Go ahead (literally, 'be kind enough [to sit down]')	تَفَضَل
Monuments	الاثَار
Pharaonic	الفِرعَونيَةِ
Mountain	جَبَلُ
Volcanic	بُركانيٌّ
Multi / multiple	مُتَعَدِد

Summit	القِمَمِ
Appear throughout	تَتخلَّلُهُ
Waterfalls	الشَّلالاتُ
Lakes	البحَيرَاتُ
Plants	النَبَاتَاتُ
Rare	النَّادِرَةُ
Nature	الطَّبِيعَة
Dazzle	تُبهِرُ
Tourist	السَّائحِينَ
Cathedral	كَاتِدرَائِيَة
Citadel	قَلعَة
Government house / palace	السَرَاي
Is known	تُعرَفُ
Mosque	جَامِعُ
Masterpiece	التُّحفَة
Architecture	المِعمَارِية
Was built by	بَنَاهَا
Hermitage	صَومَعَةِ
Islamic architecture	العِمارَةُ الاسلامِيَة

Lake	بُحَيرَة
The salt	المِلحُ
Diving	الغَطسِ
Tourism	سِيَاحة
Coasts	سَوَاحِل
Gulf	خَلِيجٍ
Hole	حُفرَة
The space	الفَضَاءِ
To see	رُؤْيَتَهَا
Passage	مَمَرُ
Viewing	مَشَاهَدَة
Prettier	أجَمَلِ
Sunrise	شِرُوقٍ
Sunset	غُرُوبٍ
The world	العَالَم

Here is a table with the names of Arab cities. Write the correct country that the city is located in.

	مَرْكَا		عَدَنْ
	وَهرَانِ		دُبِي
	نَوَاذِيبُو		الوَكَرَةِ
	أبخ		صَلالَةٍ
	الرِّبَاطِ		الأَحمَدِي
	صَفَاقِس		البَصْرَةِ
	بَنِي غَازِي		المِحَرِّق
	أُمَّ دِرْمَانِ		طَرَابلس
	الاسْكَندَرِيَةِ		الزَّرقَاء
			غَزَّةَ
			جَدَّةٍ
			حَلَبٍ
			مُوتسَامُودُو

This table contains different landmarks. Name the country in which the landmark is located. You could research these landmarks on the internet by typing their names in Arabic. You will find information in English about them.

	قَلعَةُ عَرَادٍ
	قَلعَةُ البَحرَينِ
	مَغارَةُ جعيتَا
	مَدِينَةُ البَتراءِ
	مَسجِدُ قُبَّةِ الصَخرَةِ
	المَسجِدُ الأقصَى
	الكَعبَةُ
	الجَامِعُ الأَمَوِيُّ
	بُركَانُ كَارتَالا
	قَلعَةُ تَاليح
	مَمَرُ الأسكرَام
	جِبَالُ الهَقَارِ

	حُفْرَةُ الرِّيشَاتِ
	بُحَيْرَةُ عَسَلٍ
	مَسْجِدُ صَوْمَعَةِ حَسَّان
	مَدِينَةِ القَيرَوان
	جَامِعُ الزَّيْتُونةِ
	السَّرَاي الحَمرَاءِ
	قَلْعَةُ طَرَابلُس
	كَاتِدرَائِيَةُ بَنِي غَازِي
	جَبَلُ مَرَّة
	الاثَارِ الفِرعَونِيَةِ
	أَبُو الهَولِ
	الاهرَامَاتُ
	حَدَائِقُ بَابِلِ المُعَلَّقَةِ
	أَسَدُ بَابِلٍ

	بَوَابَاتُ سُورِ الكُوَيتِ القَدِيمِ
	القَصْرُ الأَحْمَرُ
	مَحمِيَةُ مَنطِقَةِ هَانُون
	بَيتُ المِقحِمِ
	قَلعَةُ الكُوتِ
	سُوقُ وَاقِفٍ
	قَصْرُ الحِصْنِ
	قَرْيَةُ حَتَّا التُرَاثِيَة
	مَدِينَةُ بَرَاقِشِ الأَثَرِيَةِ
	مَسجِدُ المِحْضَار

جِيبُوتِي بَلَدٌ أَفْرِيقِيٌّ وعَرَبِيٌّ يَقَعُ عَلَى الشَّاطِئِ الشَّرْقِيِّ لِأَفْرِيقيا، يَفْصِلُهُ عَنِ الجَزِيرَةِ العَرَبِيَّةِ مَضِيقُ بَابِ المَنْدَبِ، وتَبْلُغُ مِسَاحَتُهُ 23 أَلْفَ كِيلُومتْرٍ مُرَبَّعٍ، وَعَدَدُ سُكَّانِه أَقَلَّ مِنْ مِلْيُونِ نَسَمَةٍ، وجَمِيعُهُمْ مُسْلِمُونَ.

Djibouti, an Arab country in Africa, is located on the Eastern shore of Africa. It is separated from the Arabian Peninsula by the Strait of Bab el Mandeb (the Gate of Grief), and covers an area of 23 thousand square kilmoters. It has a population of less than a million people, all of whom are Muslims.

يَتَكَوَّنُ النَّسِيجُ المُجْتَمَعِيُّ مِنَ القَوْمِيَّتَيْنِ الصُّومَالِيَّةِ والعَفَرِيَّةِ إِلَى جَانِبِ الجَالِيَةِ العَرَبِيَّةِ المُنْحَدِرَةِ مِنْ شَمَالِ اليَمَنِ المُجَاوِرِ. وَقَدْ خَضَعَتْ جِيبُوتِي لِلِاسْتِعْمَارِ الفَرَنْسِيِّ مُدَّةً تَزِيدُ عَلَى قَرْنٍ مِنْ الزَّمَنِ قَبْلَ أَنْ تَنَالَ اسْتِقْلَالَهَا يَوْمَ 27 يُولِيُو/تَمُّوز 1977.

The social fabric consists of the Somali nation-and العفرية along with Afro-Arab community north of neighboring Yemen. Djibouti has undergone the French colonization for more than a century before that impair its independence on July 27 / July 1977.

وَتَكْمُنُ الأَهَمِّيَّةُ الإِسْتِرَاتِيجِيَّةُ لِجِيبُوتِي فِي مَوْقِعِهَا الجُغْرَافِيِّ المُتَمَيِّزِ، الَّذِي ازْدَادَتْ أَهَمِّيَّتُهُ مُنْذُ افْتِتَاحِ قَنَاةِ السُّوَيْسِ، إِذْ صَارَتْ بِمَثَابَةِ مِينَاءِ عُبُورٍ "تَرَانْزِيت" لِلمِنْطَقَةِ، خُصُوصًا لِإِثْيُوبْيَا الَّتِي تَسْتَوْرِدُ 80% مِن احْتِيَاجَاتِهَا مِنَ السِّلَعِ والمُنْتَجَاتِ عَبْرَ مِينَاءِ جِيبُوتِي.

The strategic importance of Djibouti lies in its distinguished geographical location, which has increased in importance since the opening of Suez Canal. It became a port of transit for the region, especially for Ethiopia, which imports 80% of its products and goods through the port of Djibouti.

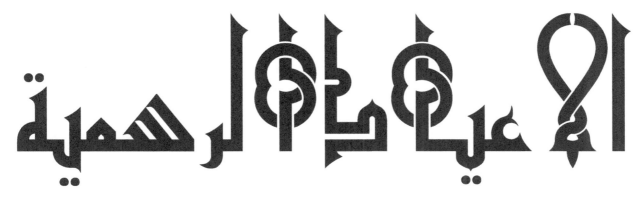

الأعياد الرسمية

The objective of this lesson is to introduce you to U.S. official holidays in Arabic in the form of a conversation between Mohammed and John. Both of them are employees in an American government entity working in an Arab country.

الحِوارُ

هَذَا حِوارٌ بَيْنَ مُحَمَدٍ وَجُون، كِلاهُمَا مُوَظَفانِ في هَيْئَةٍ حُكُومِيَةٍ امْرِيكِيَةٍ تَعْمَلُ في بَلَدٍ عَرَبِي.

محمد: صَبَاحُ الخَيرِ يَا جُون.

جون: صَبَاحُ النُّورِ يَا مُحَمَّد.

محمد: سَمِعْتُ انَّ غَداً اجَازَةٌ، لِمَاذَا؟

جون: لانَّ غَداً عِيدُ الاسْتِقلالِ، وَهُوَ واحِدٌ مِنْ الاعْيَادِ الرَّسْمِيَةِ السَّنَوِيَةِ التِّي يَحْتَفِلُ بِهَا الشَّعْبُ الامْرِيكِي.

محمد: هَذَا رَائِعٌ، انا وَانتَ سَنَحْصُلُ عَلَى ايَّام عُطلَةٍ اكثَرَ بِسَبَبِ الاحتِفَالِ بِأعيَادِ البَلَدَينِ مَعاً.

جون: نَعَمْ.

محمد: وَمَا هِيَ الاعْيَادُ الأخُرَى التِّي تَحْتَفِلُونَ بِهَا؟

جون: مِثلُكُمْ نَحتَفِلُ بِعِيدِ رَأسِ السَّنَةِ، كَمَا نَحْتَفِلُ بِعِيدِ مِيلادِ مَارتِين لُوثرْ كِينج، وَعِيدِ مِيلادِ واشِنطُون.

محمد: كَمْ يَوماً تَحتَفِلُونَ في كُلِّ مُنَاسَبَةٍ؟

جون: يَومٌ وَاحِدٌ فَقَط، لا نَحْتَفِلُ بِأكثرَ مِنْ ذلِكَ.

محمد: وَمَا هِيَ الأعْيَادُ الأُخرَى الَّتي تَحْتَفِلُونَ بِهَا؟

جون: نَحتفِلُ ايْضاً بِيَومِ الشُّهَدَاءِ وَبِعيدِ العُمَّالِ، وَيَومِ كُولُومبُوس، كَمَا نَحتَفِلُ بِيَومِ المُحَارِبِينَ القدَامَى، وَعِيدِ الشُّكرِ.

محمد: اه، هذَا العِيدُ الذي تأكُلونَ فِيهِ الدِّيكَ الرُّومِي.

جون: نَعَمْ.

محمد: انَا أُحِبُّ الاعْيَادَ الَّتي يُحْتَفَلُ بِهَا بِأكْلِ اطعِمَةٍ خَاصَةٍ، هَلْ هَذِهِ هي كُلُّ الاعْيَادِ الَّتِي تَحْتَفِلُونَ بِهَا؟

جون: لاَ، نَحْتَفِلُ مِثلُكُمْ ايْضاً بِعِيدِ مِيلادِ المَسِيحِ وبِعيدِ العُمَّالِ.

محمد: اعْتَقِدُ انَّ عِيْدَ العُمَّالِ عِيْدٌ عَالَمِي يُحتفَلُ بِهِ في جَمِيعِ انحَاءِ العَالَمِ.

جون: نَعَمْ، وَانتَ مَا هُوَ العِيدُ المُفَضَّلُ لَدَيْكَ؟

محمد: عِيْدُ مِيلادِي.

جون: هَا هَا هَا.

83

الكلماتُ الجديدة

معناها	الكلمة
Official holidays	الاعيادُ الرَّسميَّةُ
Governmental Organization	هَيئَةٍ حُكوميةٍ
Vacation	اجازَةٌ
Independence Day	عيدُ الاسْتِقلالِ
Wonderful	رائِعٌ
Holiday	عُطلَةٍ
New Year's Eve	رأسِ السَّنَةِ
Martin Luther King Jr. Day	عيدِ ميلادِ مَارتِين لُوثْر كِين
Presidents' Day (in Arabic, this is called Washington's Birthday)	عيدِ ميلادِ وَاشنطُون
We do not celebrate more than that, (These are the only holidays that we observe.)	لان هَحْتَفِلُ بِأكثرِ مِنْ ذلِكَ
Martyrs' Day	يَومِ الشُّهَداءِ
Columbus Day	يَومِ كُولُومبُوس
Veterans Day	يَومِ المُحارِبينَ القدَامَى
The Thanksgiving	عيدِ الشُّكرِ
Turkey	الدِّيكَ الرُّومِي

The birthday of Christ (Christmas Day)	عِيدِ مِيلادِ المَسِيحِ
The Labor Day	عِيدُ العُمَّالِ
International Holiday	عِيدٌ عَالَمِي
My Birthday	عِيدُ مِيلادِي

أسْئِلَة:

1. In the timeline of this dialogue, when is Independence Day?

2. Why does Mohammed conclude that he and John will have more days off?

3. Which holidays do Arabs and Americans share?

4. Why Mohammed is surprised that American holidays are just one day and why?

5. Which holiday is a universal holiday?

6. What is Mohammed's favorite holiday?

قَالَ الرَّئِيسُ التَّنْفِيذِيُّ لِلْخُطُوطِ الْجَوِّيَّةِ الْقَطَرِيَّةِ إِنَّ مَنْعَ طَائِرَةِ بوينغ 787 دريملاينر مِنَ التَّحْلِيقِ أَضَاعَ عَلَى الشَّرِكَةِ إِيرَادَاتٍ بَلَغَتْ 200 مِلْيُون دولار حَتَّى أَبْرِيل/نِيسَان 2013.

وَتَقُولُ الْخُطُوطُ الْقَطَرِيَّةُ إِنَّهَا سَتَحْصُلُ عَلَى تَعْوِيضٍ مِنْ بوينغ، بِسَبَبِ مَنْعِ تَحْلِيقِ طَائِرَتِهَا بِنَاءً عَلَى أَوَامِرَ مِنَ السُّلُطَاتِ الْأَمِيرِكِيَّةِ نَتِيجَةَ مَخَاوِفَ تَتَعَلَّقُ بِالسَّلَامَةِ.

The Chief Executive Officer of Qatar Airways says that the prevention of Boeing 787 Dreamliner aircraft from flying made the company miss revenue amounting to $200 million dollars until April 2013.
Qatar Airways says that it will get compensation from Boeing due to the prevention of these airplanes from flying on orders from the US authority as a result of safety concerns.

وَقَدْ مُنِعَتْ طَائِرَاتُ دريملاينر الْخَمْسُونَ الْمُسْتَخْدَمَةُ فِي الْعَالَمِ مِنَ الْقِيَامِ بِرَحَلَاتٍ بَعْدَ حَوَادِثَ فِي الْبَطَّارِيَّاتِ حَصَلَتْ فِي اثْنَتَيْنِ مِنْهَا. ثُمَّ أَعْطَتْ السُّلُطَاتُ الْأَمِيرِكِيَّةُ الْإِذْنَ بِإِعَادَةِ تَشْغِيلِ هَذِهِ الطَّائِرَاتِ فِي نِهَايَةِ الشَّهْرِ الْمَاضِي.

The fifty Dreamliner airplanes that are used in the world were prevented from flying after incidents in batteries affected two of the aircraft. Following this, the U.S. authorities gave permission to restart the operation of these airplanes at the end of last month.

أَهْرَامَاتُ اَلْجِيزَةِ

This is a conversation between a cab driver and a tourist in Egypt. The tourist wants to go to the Pyramids.

السائح: صَبَاحُ الخَير.

سائق التاكسي: صَبَاحُ الخَير.

السائح: أريدُ الذهَابَ اَلَى الأهرَامَاتِ مِنْ فَضلِك.

سائق التاكسي: تَفضَّل يَاسَيِدي.

السائح: مِصْرُ بَلدٌ رَائِعٌ حَقاً.

سائق التاكسي: أهرَامَاتُ الجِيزَةِ مِنْ أهَمِّ المَعَالِمِ السِيَاحِيةِ والتاريخِيةِ، أبُو الهَوْلِ يَقِفُ الَى جِوَارِ الأهْرَامَاتِ.

السائح: رُكوبُ الخَيلِ يُمَكِنُنِي مِن اكتِشَافِ هَذا المكانِ المُذهِلِ، حَضَارَةُ الفَرَاعِنَةِ عَرِيقَةٌ ومُذهِلَةٌ.

سائق التاكسي: المكَانُ جَمِيلٌ ويُمَكِّنَكَ مِن التِقاطِ صُورٍ جَمِيلةٍ للذِكرَى.

السائح: الكَامِيرَا أحْمِلُهَا مَعِي فِي كُلِّ وَقتٍ، فأنا مِن هُوَاةِ التَصويرِ، الوَقتُ يَنفَذ، اليَومُ يَمْضِي بِسُرعَةٍ، أسْرِع قلِيلاً إذا كُلَّ الوَقتِ لِيَفعَلوا كُلَّ مَا يَرغَبُونَ وَيكتشِفونَ كُلَّ شيءٍ.

السائق: التَاكسِي وَصَلَ أمَامَ مَكانِ التذاكِرِ، الجَوُ يُناسِبُ التَصويرَ، يَومُكَ سَعِيدٌ، رِحْلَةٌ مُمتِعَة.

الكَلِماتُ الجَدِيدَة

الكلمة	معناها
وصف الاماكن السياحية	Description of tourist sites
أهرامات الجيزة	Pyramids of Giza
أهَمِّ المَعَالِمِ السِيَاحِيةِ	Top landmarks

Sphinx	أبُو الهَوْلِ
Horseback riding	رُكوبُ الخَيلِ
Discovery	اكتِشَاف
This place is amazing	هَذا المَكانِ المُذهِلِ
Civilization	حَضَارَةٌ
Ancient	عَريقَة
Time is running out	الوَقتُ يَنفَذ
The day passes quickly	اليَّومُ يَمْضي بِسُرعَةٍ
Box office	مَكانِ التذاكِرِ
The weather is good for taking pictures	الجَوُ يُناسِبُ التَصويرَ
Your day is happy (a greeting)	يَومُكَ سَعيدٌ
Pleasant trip	رِحْلَةٌ مُمتِعَة

أسئلة:

1. Where does the tourist want to go?
2. Besides looking at the Pyramids, what other activities can a tourist do here?
3. Where is the Sphinx located?
4. Is the tourist an amateur or a professional photographer?
5. Is it light enough on this day to take pictures?
6. Does the tourist have plenty of time for sightseeing?
7. Is the driver driving fast enough for the tourist?
8. Is the driver nice to the tourist?
9. Where is the tourist dropped off?

اكْتَشَفَ بَاحِثُونَ مِنْ جَامِعَةِ تَل أَبِيب آثَارًا عُمْرَانِيَّةً وَكُنُوزًا نَادِرَةً فِي مَنْطِقَةِ آرْسُوف التَّارِيخِيَّةِ دَاخِلَ الْخَطِّ الْأَخْضَرِ تَعُودُ لِفَتَرَاتِ الْحُكْمِ الْبِيزَنْطِيِّ وَالْإِسْلَامِيِّ. وَتُعْتَبَرُ آرْسُوفُ، الْمُجَاوِرَةُ لِقَرْيَةٍ فِلَسْطِينِيَّةٍ مَهْجُورَةٍ مُنْذُ نَكْبَةِ 48 تُدْعَى إِجْلِيلَ، مِنْ أَهَمِّ مُدُنِ فِلَسْطِينَ مُنْذُ أَنْ بُنِيَّتْ عَلَى أَيْدِي الْفِينِيقِيِّينَ فِي الْقَرْنِ الرَّابِعِ قَبْلَ الْمِيلَادِ.

Research from the University of Tel Aviv discovered urban artefacts and rare treasures in the historical area of Asuf, inside the Green Line, dating back to the Islamic and Byzantine eras. Asuf, is adjacent to an abandoned Palestinian village from the catastrophe of '48 called Ijlil, which is one of the most important Palestinian cities since it was built by the Phoenicians in the fourth century BC.

In the Arabic world, the '48 war between Arabs and Israelis, which ended in the occupation of historical Palestine, is referred to as 'nakbah', which means catastrophe. There is a similar word naksaah, meaning 'setback' or 'relapse', and infers the Arab defeat at the hands of the Israeli's in 1967. By calling the first defeat a 'catastrophe', and the second a 'relapse', Arabs felt that the loss of Palestine is not irreversible, aiming in the future to reclaim their land.

وَعَثَرَ عُلَمَاءُ الْآثَارِ فِي آرْسُوفَ عَلَى مُنْشَآتٍ لِإِعْدَادِ الْمَحَاصِيلِ الزِّرَاعِيَّةِ وَمَعَاصِرَ وَأَدَوَاتٍ مَنْزِلِيَّةٍ مِنَ الْقَرْنِ الْخَامِسِ حَتَّى السَّابِعِ الْمِيلَادِي. كَمَا تَمَّ اكْتِشَافُ آبَارٍ اسْتُخْدِمَتْ لِلْقُمَامَةِ مِنَ الْفَتْرَةِ الْبِيزَنْطِيَّةِ يَبْلُغُ قِطْرُ أَكْبَرِهَا 30 مِتْرًا وَفِيهَا أَدَوَاتٌ فَخَّارِيَّةٌ وَزُجَاجِيَّةٌ وَعِظَامٌ حَيَوَانِيَّةٌ.

In Asuf, archaeologists found facilities for the preparation of agricultural crops as well as household items from the 5th-17th century. Also, wells used for rubbish in the Byzantine period, the largest one with a diameter of 30 meters, were discovered containing pottery, glass tools and animal bones.

أَبَدًا: لِلنَفِي فِي زَمَنِ المُستَقبَلِ.	قَطُّ: لِلنَفِي فِي الزَّمَنِ المَاضِي.

There are two words in Arabic that mean 'never': 'qat' and 'abadan'. 'Qat' is used in the past tense, for example, "I never said that!" 'Abdan' is used in the future tense: "Promise you will never leave me."

Read the following sentences where both 'qat' and 'abadan' are used.

I have not stolen anything from you.	مَا سَرَقْتُ مِنْكَ شيء قَطُّ
I never said that.	ما قُلْتُ هَذَا قَطُّ.
Promise me you'll never leave me (Future Tense)	عِدني أَلا تَتْرُكَنِي أَبَدًا.
I have never tasted such delicious food like this	مَاذُقْتُ طَعَامًا لَذِيذًا مِثْلَ هَذا قَطُّ.
I will never forgive you	لَنْ أَسَامِحَكَ أَبَدًا.
never will I have never apologized to anyone, and I	لَمْ أَعْتَذِرْ لِأَحَدٍ قَطِّ، وَلَنْ أَعْتَذِرَ أَبَدًا

90

I have never seen such beauty.	مَا رَأَيْتُ فِي جَمَالِهَا قَطُّ.
I have never dated a young man.	لَمْ أُوَاعِدْ شَابًّا قَطُّ.
I will never get married.	أَنَا لَن أَتَزَوَجَ أَبَدًا.
I have never asked for help.	لَمْ أَطْلُبْ الْمُسَاعَدَةَ قَطُّ.
I have never failed before, and I never will.	لَمْ أَرْسُبْ مِنْ قَبْلُ قَطُّ، وَلَنْ أَرْسُبَ أَبَدًا.

اِقْرَأْ

أَقَرَّ مَجْلِسُ الْوُزَرَاءِ الْإِمَارَاتِيُّ أَمْسِ الْأَحَدَ قَانُونًا لِلْخِدْمَةِ الْوَطَنِيَّةِ وَالِاحْتِيَاطِيَّةِ، يَجْعَلُ الْخِدْمَةَ الْعَسْكَرِيَّةَ إِجْبَارِيَّةً عَلَى الذُّكُورِ وَاخْتِيَارِيَّةً لِلْإِنَاثِ، وَيَهْدِفُ الْقَانُونُ إِلَى تَعْزِيزِ قُوَّةِ الدِّفَاعِ الْوَطَنِيَّةِ.

وَسَتَشْمَلُ الْخِدْمَةُ الْوَطَنِيَّةُ تَمَارِينَ عَسْكَرِيَّةً وَأَمْنِيَّةً لِلْمُجَنَّدِينَ فِي الْقُوَّاتِ الْمُسَلَّحَةِ، عَلَى أَنْ تَكُونَ مُدَّتُهَا تِسْعَةَ أَشْهُرٍ لِخِرِّيجِي الثَّانَوِيَّةِ وَسَنَتَيْنِ لِلَّذِينَ لَمْ يَتَجَاوَزُوا الْمَرْحَلَةَ الثَّانَوِيَّةَ.

The UAE cabinet approved on Sunday a law for national service and the military reserve. It will make military service compulsory for males and optional for females, and the law aims to strengthen the national defense force.

The national service will include security and military exercises for recruits in the armed forces to be nine-months. It will be two years for high school graduates and for those who did not go beyond high school.

في حَديقة الحَيَوان

This is a conversation between a mother and her children during their time at the zoo.

الأم: نَحْنُ الانَ فِي حَديقَةِ الحَيَوانِ يا أولاد

توم: رَائِعْ يا أُمِّي، حَديقَةُ الحَيَوانِ كَبيرَةٌ جِداً!!!

الأم: تَعَالوا نَبدَأ مِن قَفَصِ القُرُودِ.

جاك: ذَيلُ القِرْدِ طَويلٌ جِداً ياأُمِّي.

93

الأم: نَعَمْ يا جَاك، ذيلُ القِرْد طَويلٌ لأنهُ يَتَسَلْقُ أشْجَارَ الحَديقَةِ.

توم: انظُري ياأُمِّي كَيْفَ تَأْخُذُ القُرُودُ المَوزَ مِنْ زُوَّارِ الحَديقةِ.

جاك: توم توم...دَعْكَ مِنْ قَفَصِ القُرُودِ، وَانظُرْ الَى قَفَصِ الأُسُودِ.

توم: الأَسَدُ مَلِكُ الغَابَةِ بِلاشَكٍ.

جاك: يَا الَهِي، أنْيَابُ الأَسَدِ كَبيرَةٌ جِداً.

الأم: أنْيَابُ الأَسَدِ كَبيرَةٌ لأنهُ مِنَ الحَيَوانَاتِ اكِلَةِ اللُّحُومِ ويُمَزِّقُ بأنْيَابِهِ الفَريسَةَ.

جاك: زَئِيرُ الأَسَدِ قَوِيٌّ ومُخيفٌ.

الأم: ذَلِكَ لأنَّ قَلْبَ الأَسَدِ قَوِيٌّ وَجَريءٌ لا يَخَافُ، وَيُطَارِدُ فَريسَتَهُ بإصْرَارٍ.

الأم: دَعُونَا الانَ نَرْتَاحُ قَليلاً ونشتَري شيئاً مِنْ بَائِعِ العَصيرِ.

جاك وتوم مُبتَسِمَين: قِطْعَةُ الحَلْوَى لَذيذةٌ، شُكْراً ياأُمِّي الجَميلَة.

الكَلِماتُ الجَديدة

الكلمة	معناها
حَديقَةِ الحَيَوان	Zoo

Boys	أولاد
Wonderful	رَائِعْ
Come	تَعَالوا
We start	نَبَدَأ
Cage	قَفَصٍ
Monkeys	القُرُودِ
Tail	ذَيلُ
Very	جداً
Because he	لأنهُ
Climbs	يَتَسَلَّقُ
Trees	أشْجَارَ
Garden	الحَدِيقَةِ
Look	انظُرِي
Take	تَأخُذ
Bananas	المَوزَ
Visitors	زُوَارِ
Don't bother with, never mind	دَعْكَ
The lions	الأُسُودِ

Undoubtedly	بِلاشَكٍ
Oh my God	يَا اِلَهِي
Canines	أَنْيَابٌ
Meat eaters	اكِلَةِ اللَّحُومِ
Rip	يُمَزِّقُ
Prey	الفَرِيسَةَ
Roar	زَئِيرٌ
Frightening	مُخِيفٌ
That	ذَلِكَ
Bold / Brave	جَرِيءٌ
chase	يُطَارِدُ
Determinedly	بِاصْرَارٍ
Let us	دَعُونَا
W rest	نَرْتَاحُ
We buy	نَشتَرِي
Something	شَيئاً
Vendor	بَائِعٍ
Juice	العَصِير

Smiling	مُبتَسِمَين
Piece	قِطْعَة
Candy	الحَلْوَى
Delicious	لَذيذةٌ
Beautiful	الجَميلَة

أسئلة:

1. What animals did they see first?

2. What was Jack's observation regarding the monkey's tail?

3. What was the mother's response to this observation?

4. What type of food are the visitors to the zoo feeding the monkeys?

5. What is the next animal they visited?

6. What did Tom call the lion?

7. Which animal has long canines?

8. Which carnivores did the family visit at the zoo?

9. How did Jack describe the roaring of the lion?

10. What did the family have to eat at the end of their visit?

فِي مِتْرُو الأَنْفَاقِ بِلَنْدَنْ

كُلُّ - بَعْضُ - مُعْظَمُ - عِدَّةُ

In this lesson, we will introduce you to four words (all, some, most, and several). Please note that these words always appear in the IDafa construction. The following is a dialogue between an American tourist and an Englishman in which the tourist is asking the Englishman for directions. You will see these four words appear in the dialogue.

السائح: مِنْ فَضْلِكَ كَيْفَ أَصِلُ اِلَى بَوَابَةِ لانكِسْتِر؟، كُلُّ الرُّكَابِ رِكِبُوا قِطَارَ المِتْرُو وَأَنَا لاأَزَالُ تَائِهاً!!

الرجل الانجليزي: مُعْظَمُ الرُّكَابِ يَعْرِفُونَ وِجْهَتَهُمْ، مِنْ أَيِّ بَلَدٍ أَنْتَ تَبْدُو سَائِحاً؟

السائح: أَنَا مِنْ أَمْرِيكَا، أَهْلاً بِكَ، لَقَدْ رَأَيْتُ عِدَّةَ لَوْحَاتٍ ارْشَادِيَةٍ وَمَازِلْتُ أَجْهَلُ الطَّرِيقَ اِلَى البَوَابَةِ؟!!

الرجل الانجليزي: أَمْرِيكَا!! زُرْتُ مُعْظَمَ دُوَلِ العَالَمِ، وَلَمْ أَزُرْ أَمْرِيكَا بَعْدُ، بَعْضُ الارْشَادَاتِ مُضَلِّلَةٌ حَقاً، وَسَوْفَ يُغَيِّرُونَهَا قَرِيباً جِداً، هُنَاكَ عِدَّةُ بَوَابَاتٍ كَمَا تَعْلَمُ، لَكِنْ، يَجِبُ انْ تَأْخُذَ الطَّرِيقَ الصَّحِيحَ، خُذْ خَطَّ العَاصِمَةِ اِلَى شَارِعِ لِيفِرْبُول ثُمَّ بَدِّلْ اِلَى الخَطِّ المَرْكَزِي.

السائح: شُكْراً لَكَ، بَعْضُ النَّاسِ يُحِبُّونَ مُسَاعَدَةَ الاخَرِينَ حَقاً.

الرجل الانجليزي: اذَا ارَدْتَ بَعْضَ الحَلْوَى قَبْلَ انْ تَسْتَقِلَّ القِطَارَ، هُنَاكَ كُشْكُ فِي الزَاوِيَةِ، كَمَا يُمْكِنُكَ تَغيِيرَ بَعْضِ العُمْلاتِ، انهُ يَبِيعُ أَيْضاً كُلَّ الصُّحُفِ والمَجَلاتِ العَالَمِيَةِ.

السائح: كُلُّ الشُّكرِ لكَ، علَى كُلِّ هَذَا الكَرَمِ،

مُعظَمُ مَنْ قَابَلتُهُم لَمْ يَمْلِكُوا بَعْض هَذَا الكَرَمِ، فقَد سَألتُ عِدَّةَ أشخَاصٍ فترَكوْنِي وَانصَرَفُوا.

الرجل الانجليزي: لاشُكرَ أبَداً، أتَمَنَّى انْ تَقضِي عِدَّةَ ايَّامٍ اخرَى فِي لَندَن فَهيَ مَدِينَةٌ رَائِعَةٌ وَبهَا عِدَّةُ أمَاكِنِ لِلتَّسَوقِ الجَيِّدِ.

الكلماتُ الجديدة

معناها	الكلمة
Subway / underground / tube	مِترُو الأنْفَاق
All	كُلُّ
Some	بَعْضٌ
Most	مُعْظَمٌ
Several	عِدَّةٌ
Lost	تَائِهاً

Their destination	وِجْهَتَهُمْ
Directional signs	لَوْحَاتٍ اِرْشَادِيَةٍ
Misleading	مُضَلِّلة
Central	المَرْكَزي
Booth	كُشْكُ
Candy / sweets	الحَلْوَى
Currencies	العُمْلاتِ
They left me	فتَرَكوْني
They departed	انْصَرَفُوا

أسئلة:

1. Where does the tourist want to go?

2. Did the Englishman ask him about his country of origin?

3. Are the direction- signs in the London subways system confusing or are they clearly written?

4. Did the English man visit America, or not yet?

5. Does the tourist think that all English people are helpful, or not?

6. If the tourist wanted to buy some sweets, where can he buy them?

7. Where can the tourist exchange currencies?

8. Which subway line should the tourist take to get to his destination?

9. Why did the British man invite the tourist to spend a few extra days in London?

10. Why does the tourist think the British man that helped him is different than most of the people whom he asked for help?

11. If the tourist wanted to buy foreign newspapers, where can he buy them?

انْطَلَقَتْ في إمارَة عَجْمانَ، إحْدَى الْإماراتِ السَّبْعِ الْمُكَوّنَةِ لِدَوْلَةِ الْإماراتِ الْعَرَبِيَّةِ الْمُتَّحِدَةِ، دَعواتٌ لِلسِّياحَةِ بَيْنَ مَعالِمَ مِنَ الْقَرْنِ الثَّامِنَ عَشَرَ.

The emirate of Ajman, one of the seven emirates comprising the United Arab Emirates (UAE), calls for tourism to its eighteenth century landmarks.

وَرَغْمَ أَنَّ عَجْمانَ هِيَ صُغْرَى الْإماراتِ السَّبْعِ، فَإِنَّها تُخَطِّطُ لِاسْتِقْطابِ أَعْدادٍ كَبِيرَةٍ مِنَ السُّيّاحِ الْأُورُوبِّيِّنَ الْقادِمِينَ لِدُوَلِ الْخَلِيجِ، مُعْلِنَةً عَنْ تَقْدِيمِ وَجْبَةٍ سِياحِيَّةٍ مُتَكامِلَةٍ لِكُلِّ سائِحٍ. تَبْدَأُ بِجَوْلَةٍ في التَّارِيخِ، ثُمَّ الْانْطِلاقُ لِلْمُتْعَةِ في الصَّحْراءِ وَالسِّياحَةِ الْاسْتِجْمامِيَّةِ وَالدِّينِيَّةِ.

Although Ajman is the smallest of seven Emirates, it plans to attract large numbers of European tourists coming to the Gulf States, stating that it will provide an integrated touristic experience for every visitor starting with a tour into history, and then going on to have some fun in the desert, with both recreational and religious tourism.

As you begin to acquire a stronger knowledge of the Arabic language, and you are beginning to translate more and more, you will find that many expressions in Arabic are very different to in English. For example, in the above text, you will see the phrase 'complete meal' is used to mean 'a full experience', where nothing is left to be desired. Bear in mind that it is the same for Arabic speakers when learning English. This is one reason why it is very difficult for an Arab to achieve full fluency in English, and vice versa, in both phonetics and vocabulary.

وَتَفْخَرُ الْإمارَةُ بِامْتِلاكِها حِصْنَ عَجْمانَ، الَّذِي تَعْتَبِرُهُ أَهَمَّ مَعْلَمٍ أَثَرِيٍّ يُمْكِنُ أَنْ يَزُورَهُ السَّائِحُ، وَيُرْجِعُ عُلَماءُ آثارٍ تارِيخَ إنْشاءِ هَذا الْحِصْنِ إلَى الْقَرْنِ الثَّامِنَ عَشَرَ، وَقَدِ اسْتُعْمِلَتْ في بِنائِهِ الْمَوادُّ الْمَحَلِّيَّةُ كَحِجارَةِ الْبَحْرِ الْمَرْجانِيَّةِ وَتَمَّ تَسْقِيفُهُ بِجُذُوعِ أَشْجارٍ، وَقَدْ تَعَرَّضَ الْحِصْنُ عامَ 1820 لِقَصْفِ السُّفُنِ الْحَرْبِيَّةِ الْبَرِيطانِيَّةِ.

The Emirate prides itself of its possession of Fort Ajman, which is considered the most important archaeological landmark that a tourist can visit. The archaeologists date the establishment of this fort to the eighteenth century. Local materials such as sea reef stones were used in the building, and tree trunks were used for the roof. The fort was subjected to bombing from British warships in 1820.

دِرَاسَةٌ جَدِيدَةٌ

كشَفَتْ دِرَاسَةٌ جَدِيدَةٌ نَشَرَتها صَحِيفَةُ دِيلي اكسبرِيس اليَومَ الخَمِيسَ أنَّ البِرِيطَانِيينَ يَكذِبُونَ في شهرِ يَناير أكثرَ مِنْ أيِّ وقتٍ آخَرَ مِنَ العَامِ.

ووَجَدَت الدِراسَةُ أنَّ الكَذِبَ حَولَ قَرَارَاتِ السَّنةِ الجَدِيدَةِ والمُبَالَغةِ بِشَأنِ تأثيرِ الحِمِيَاتِ الغِذائِيَةِ وعَدَدِ هَدَايَا عيدِ المِيلادِ والتبَاهِي بِكمِيَاتِ المَشرُوبَاتِ المُستَهلَكَةِ خِلالَ مَوسِمِ الأعيَادِ، تُضِيفُ نَحْوَ 217 كَذبَةٍ إلَى أكَاذِيبِ هَذا الشَّهرِ. وقَالَتْ إنَّ الكَثِيرَ مِنَ البِريطَانِيينَ يَستَخدِمُونَ صَبَاحَاتِ الشِّتَاءِ البَارِدَةِ في شهرِ يَناير كَذَرِيعةٍ للتَغَيُّبِ عَنِ العَمَلِ بِدَاعِي المَرَضِ، فِيمَا يَلجَأُ نِصفُهُم تَقرِيباً للتَهَرُّبِ مِنَ المُنَاسَبَاتِ العَائِلِيَةِ بِذَرائِعَ وَاهِيَةٍ.

وأَضَافَتْ الدِّرَاسَةُ أنَّ البِريطَانِيينَ يَكذِبُونَ سَبْعَ مَرَّاتٍ في اليَومِ خِلالَ شَهْرِ يَناير بِالمُقارَنَةِ مَعَ أربَعِ كَذبَاتٍ في بَقِيَةِ أشهُرِ السَّنةِ، لَكِنَّ نِصفَهُم اعْتَرَفُوا بِأنَّ أكَاذِيبَهُم سُرعَانَ مَا تُكتَشَفُ وَفي هَذا الشَّهرِ تَحدِيداً، وأَشَارَتْ إلَى أنَّ المَالَ يُشَكِّلُ وَاحِداً مِنْ أكْثَرِ الأُمُورِ المُثِيرَةِ لأكَاذِيبِ البِريطَانِيينَ خِلالَ شَهْرِ

يَنَايِر، وَيَلْجَأُ الكَثِيرُ مِنهُم إِلَى إِخفَاءِ مِقدَارِ الدِيُونِ التِّي تَرَاكَمَتْ عَلَيهِم بِفِعلِ الإِنفَاقِ عَلَى عِيدِ المِيلادِ.

وَقَالَتِ الدِّرَاسَةُ إِنَّ رُبعَ البِريطَانِيينَ يَكذِبُونَ بِشَأنِ حَجمِ الأَموَالِ التِّي يُنفِقُونَهَا خِلالَ مَوسِمِ تَخفِيضَاتِ الأَسعَارِ فِي يَنَايِر، فِيمَا يَكذِبُ خُمسُهُم بِشَأنِ الأَمَاكِنِ التِّي قَضُوا فِيهَا احتِفَالاتِ رَأسِ السَّنَةِ المِيلادِيَةِ وَيَتَظَاهَرُونَ بِأَنَّهُم أَمضُوهَا بِحَفَلاتٍ رَاقِيَةٍ، فِي حِينِ أَنَّهُم كَانُوا فِي وَاقِعِ الأَمرِ دَاخِلَ مَنَازِلِهِم يُشَاهِدُونَ التِلفِزيون. وَأَضَافَتْ أَنَّ مِنْ بَينِ الأَسبَابِ الأُخرَى المُثِيرَةِ لِلكَذِبِ، حِمَايَةُ مَشَاعِرِ الآخَرِينَ أَو عَدَمِ الرَّغبَةِ بِخِذلانِهِم، وَاعتَرَفَ مَا يَقرُبُ مِن نِصفِ البِريطَانِيينَ بِأَنَّهُم كَسَرُوا قَرَارَاتِ السَّنَةِ الجَدِيدَةِ وَكَذَبُوا بِشَأنِهَا، فِيمَا أَقرَّ وَاحِدٌ مِنْ كُلِّ سِتَةٍ مِنهُم بِأَنَّهُ كَذَبَ حَتَّى عَلَى شَرِيكَةِ حَيَاتِهِ حَولَ حَقِيقَةِ مَا حَصَلَ بِحَفلَةِ عِيدِ المِيلادِ.

أَسئِلة:

True or False

1. The article is based on a new study.
2. It was originally published in the London Times.
3. It appeared last week on Thursday.
4. It was concerned with the habits of the British people.
5. It was concerned with families.
6. It was concerned with the month of January.
7. People are modest about their New Year's resolutions.
8. They exaggerate how effective their diet has been.
9. They exaggerate the quality of their Christmas presents.
10. They exaggerate how many good meals they have eaten.

11. The average person lies 217 times in December.
12. People call in sick more in January.
13. Part of this is attributed to cold winter mornings.
14. A third of people lie to avoid family events.
15. They usually pretend serious illness.
16. The average person lies 4 times a day in January.
17. This is more than double the number than the rest of the year.
18. People acknowledged that half of their lies were found out.
19. The thing that is lied about most is sex.
20. Many people lie about the amount of debt they have.
21. The debt comes mainly from holidays abroad.
22. A quarter of British people lie about how much they spend in the sales.
23. A fifth of people lie about where they spent Christmas.
24. A quarter of them lie about where they spent New Year's Eve.
25. They claim to have been at an exciting party.
26. They have really been at the pub with friends.
27. A major reason for lying is protecting other people's feelings.
28. Another reason is to want to seem more important.
29. Half of British people admitted to breaking their New Year's resolutions.
30. A quarter of people lied to their partners about what happened at Christmas parties.

الْآنَ وَقَدْ خَارَتْ قُوَاهُ وَاحْدَوْدَبَ ظَهْرُهُ وَتَثَاقَلَتْ مِشْيَتُهُ، هَا هُوَ إِسْمَائِيتِيْش بْنُ حَامِدٍ أَخِيرًا يَرَى بِأُمِّ عَيْنَيْهِ صَرْحًا أَضْخَمَ وَأَجْمَلَ مِنْ كُلِّ مَا تَصَوَّرَهُ عِنْدَمَا قَدَّمَ قَبْلَ ثَلَاثِينَ عَامًا هُوَ وَبَعْضُ مُسْلِمِي يُوغُسْلَافْيَا السَّابِقَةِ طَلَبًا لِبِنَاءِ مَسْجِدٍ فِي بَلْدَةِ رِييكَا الْكُرُواتِيَّةِ لِتَأْدِيَةِ ثَانِي أَرْكَانِ الْإِسْلَامِ.

لَكِنْ بَعْدَ حُصُولِهِمْ عَلَى الْإِذْنِ عَامَ 1989، وَقَبْلَ أَنْ يَتَمَكَّنُوا مِنْ مُبَاشَرَةِ الْبِنَاءِ، عَصَفَتْ بِالْمِنْطَقَةِ تَقَلُّبَاتٌ جِذْرِيَّةٌ زَلْزَلَتْ كُلَّ شَيْءٍ إِلَّا تَصْمِيمَ هَؤُلَاءِ الْقَوْمِ عَلَى إِنْجَازِ مَشْرُوعِهِمْ، فَلَمْ

يُثْنِهِمْ تَفَكُّكُ الدَّوْلَةِ الَّتِي مَنَحَتْهُمُ الإِذْنَ، وَلَا مُعَارَضَةُ سَاكِنِي الْمَنْطِقَةِ الْعَنِيفَةِ أَحْيَانًا، وَلَا قِلَّةُ ذَاتِ الْيَدِ عَنِ الِاسْتِمْرَارِ فِي سَعْيِهِمْ لِتَحْقِيقِ حُلْمِهِمْ.

Now that his strength is sapped, his back is hunched and his gait has become slow, here he is, Asmaúic bin Hamed. He finally sees with his own eyes the largest and most beautiful edifice, prettier than anything he could have imagined when he applied thirty years ago with some Muslims in the former Yugoslavia to build a mosque in the town of Rijeka, Croatia, in order to perform the second pillar of Islam.

But after getting permission in 1989, and before they could begin building, the region was devastated by a seismic changes, which upended everything except the resolve of these people to finish their project. They were not affected by the disintegration of the state, which gave them permission, nor by the opposition from the local people of the area who were sometimes violent, nor by the lack of money to continue in their quest to achieve their dream.

لِقَاءٌ وَالْحَدِيْثُ عَنْ خِطْبَةٍ وَزَوَاج

This conversation is written in a Saudi dialect. It occurs between Fahd and Faisl, where one man proposes to the other's sister. You will be learning vocabulary relating to marriage, weddings and friendship in a Saudi dialect. The most obvious difference in this dialect is the letter 'qaaf' - it is often replaced by the 'jiim.'

الحِوَار

فَهَد: هَلا فِيصَلْ، كيف حَالك؟

فيصل: هَلا فَهَدْ، بِخير الحَمد لله.

فهد: وِيْن كِنْتْ؟ صَارْ لِي سَاعَة انْطِرْك جِدَّام البِيْت.

فيصل: وَالله اسِفْ يَاخُوي، مُو جصْدِي، اِعْذِرْني.

فَهَد: مَاعَلِيه، مَسمُوح، بَسْ لِيش مِجَفِّل الجَوَال؟ أدِج عَلِيك مَاترد !!!

فيصل: مَا عِنْدِي بَطَّارِيَه.

فهد: زين لاتحَاتِي، عِنْدِي شَاحِنْ بِالسَّيَارَة.

فيصل: ايش فِيك؟ لِيه مِعَصّب؟ ايش فِيه؟

فهد: أجول، تَرى مَايصِير نِتكَلَّم بِالطَّرِيج، تَعَالْ بِالسَّيَارَة أبِيك بِمَوضُوع.

فهد وفيصل بالسيارة

فيصل: الحِين اِنْت تَدرِي انِّي أبِي أتزَوَج وأدَور عَرُوسٍ زِينَة، وجِلْتْ مَافِي الاَّ بِنْت عَمِّي العَنُود، مِنِّي وفِيني، هَاه ايْش رأيك يَاوِلْد عَمِّي؟

فهد: هاهاها، الحِيْنْ مِن صِدْجِك انْتْ تِتْكَلَّم ؟!! رُوح حَج عَمَّك، أنَا مَالِي دَخَلْ؟ الله يَجطَع ابلِيسِك.

فيصل: انْتْ وِلْد عَمِّي واخُوي، ابِي رَايِك.

فهد: والله، انْت رَجَالٍ والنَّعَم فِيه، ومتيَسِرْ، وفُوج (فوق) هَذا وِلْد عَمْهَا وأوْلَى بْهَا.

فيصل: الله يبَشْرَك بِالخِير، زِيْن بَكَلَّم عَمِّي اليُوم اخْطِب بِنْت عَمِّي الجُمَرْ (القمَرْ)، تهَبّل والله.

فهد: اجول، اسْتِحِي عَلَى وَجْهِك، تَرَاك مَصَّخْتهَا.

فيصل: هه، جَصْدِي بِنْتْ عَمِّي الغَالِي يَالغَالِي، فَدِيتْهَا، بَرُوح ابَشِّر ابَشّر الأهَلْ.

فهد: زِيْنْ بَرُوح، يَالله مَعَ السَّلامَة.

فيصل: مَعَ السَّلامَة، فَمَان الله.

فهد: فَمَان الله.

الكلمات الجديدة

معناها	الكلمة
Wedding and marriage	خِطْبَةٍ وَزَوَاج
Hello	هَلا
Where have you been?	وِيْن كِنْتْ؟
I waited for you	انْطِرْك
In front of	جِدَّام
I did not mean it	مُو جِصْدِي
Never mind	مَاعَلِيه
Permissible / allowable	مَسمُوح
Why did you turn off your cell phone?	لِيش مِجَفِّل الجَوَال
I called you but you did not answer	أدِج عَلِيك مَاترد
I don't have any battery (my battery ran out)	مَا عِنْدِي بَطَّارَيه
Fine, don't worry about it	زين لاتحَاتِي
I have a charger in my car	عِنْدِي شَاحِنْ بِالسِّيَارَة
What is wrong with you?	ايش فِيك
Why are you nervous?	لِيه مِعَصِّب
I am saying	أجول

It is not a good idea to talk in the street	تَرى مَايصِير نِتكَلَّم بِالطُّريج
I need you / I want to talk to you about something	أبِيك بِمَوضُوع
Nice bride	عَرُوسٍ زِينَة
And I said that there's no one but my female cousin	وجِلْتْ مَافِي الًّا بِنْت عَمِّي
She is one of us	مِنِّي وفِينِي
Okay, what is your opinion, my cousin?	هَاه ايْش رأيك يَاوِلْد عَمِّي
I cannot believe you said that!	الحِينْ مِن صِدْجِك انْتْ تِتْكَلَّم
Go to your uncle	رُوح حَج عَمِّك
This is not my business	أنَا مَالِي دَخَلْ
May God destroy your devil	الله يَجطَع ابلِيسِك
I need your opinion	ابِي رَايِك
You are a man who has all good qualities	انْتْ رَجَالٍ والنِّعَم فِيه
And financially secure	ومتيَسِرْ،
And above all,	وفُوج
you are her cousin and you deserve her more than anyone else	هَذا وِلْد عَمْهَا وأولَى بْهَا.
May Allah give you a good omen	الله يَبَشِّرَك بِالخِير
Excellent, I'll talk to my uncle today	زِيْن بَكَلِّم عَمِّي اليُوم
The moon	الجُمَرْ
drives me crazy, by Allah	تهَبِّل والله
I would say	اجول

Behave yourself	اسْتِحِي عَلَى وَجْهِك
You just defamed her	تَرَاك مَصَّخْتها
What I meant is, my precious female cousin, oh precious	جَصْدِي بِنْت عَمِّي الغَالِي يَالغَالِي
I would sacrifice myself for her	فَدِيتْهَا
I am going to tell the family the good news	بَرُوح ابَشِّر الأهَلْ.
In Allah's safety / prediction	فَمَان الله

أَسْئِلَة:

1. What is the relationship between Fahd and Faisl?

2. How long is Fahd waiting for Faisl?

3. Where is Fahd waiting for Faisl?

4. Did Faisl apologize for being late?

5. Did Fahd try to call Faisl on his cell phone? Why was he unable to answer?

6. Where is Fahd's phone charger?

7. How does Fahd seem to Faisl?

8. Where does Fahd suggest they go to talk?

9. Why is Faisl thinking about marrying his friend's sister? What is her name?

10. What is Fahd's reaction to Faisl?

11. Fahd is unable to make a decision regarding his friend. He tells him to ask someone else – who is this person?

12. Does Fahd believe Faisl is worthy of his sister?

13. What qualities does Fahd find in Faisl?

14. When does Faisl intend officially to express his desire for this engagement?

15. How does Fahd react when Faisl starts talking flatteringly about his sister?

16. Where does Faisl go after the conversation with Fahd?

هل القاهرة مدينة امنة

The following is a conversation between Jack and Khalid regarding how safe Egypt is after the revolution. Jack has some concerns regarding the security of his family who he wants to bring to Cairo for vacation. Khalid tries to assuage his feelings about the security situation and tells him some precautions he might take to have a safe and enjoyable stay in Cairo.

الحوار

جاك: هَلْ تَعْتَقِدُ يَاخَالِد أَنَّهُ مِنَ المُنَاسِبِ أَنْ أُحْضِرَ عَائِلَتِي لِأَجَازَةٍ قَصِيرَةٍ مَعِي هُنَا فِي القَاهِرَةِ حَتَّى أَنْتَهِي مِنْ عَمَلِي؟

خالد: نَعَمْ، جاك، طَبْعاً.

جاك: أَنَا قَلِقٌ جِداً، أَنْتَ تَعْلَمُ أَنَّهُ بَعْدَ الثَّوْرَةِ المِصْرِيَةِ، وانعِدَامِ وجُودِ البُولِيسِ (الشُّرْطَةُ) بِشَكْلٍ فَعَّالٍ، وُخُرُوجِ المَساجِينِ ومُسَجَّلِي الخَطَرِ مِنَ السُّجُونِ، وَرُبَّمَا مُتَطَرِّفِينَ وارْهَابِيِّينَ، أَنَا قَلِقٌ.

خالد: مَعَكَ حَقٌّ أَنْ تَقْلَقَ، الوَضْعُ اخْتَلَفَ، لَكِنْ لاتَخَفْ، انَّ المِصْرِيِينَ قَامُوا بِدَوْرِ الشُّرْطَةِ أَثْنَاءَ الثَّوْرَةِ، كَانُوا يَنْزِلُونَ جَمَاعَاتٍ لِحِمَايَةِ الشَّوَارِعِ وَالبُيُوتِ والمَحَلَّاتِ، وَكَانُوا مُسِكُونَ بِالحَرَامِيَةِ (اللُّصُوصِ)، وَأَعَادَ النَّاسُ الكَثِيرَ مِنَ المَسْرُوقَاتِ، الانَ الوَضْعُ مُسْتَقِرٌّ أَكْثَرَ، المِصْرِيُّونَ شَعْبٌ وَدُودٌ بِطَبْعِه وَمُسَالِمٌ.

جاك: اذَن، الوَضْعُ امِنٌ.

خالد: أَنَا لَا أَنْصَحُكَ بِالذَّهَابِ اِلَى سَيْنَاءٍ أو شَرْمِ الشَّيْخِ فَالوَضْعُ هُنَاكَ غَيْرُ مُسْتَقِرٍ، لَكِنَّ القَاهِرَةَ امِنَةٌ، وَسَتَظَلُّ امِنَةً دَائِماً، انَّ مِصْرَ سَتَظَلُّ امِنَةً دَائِماً بِحِفْظِ الله ، هَلْ رَأَيْتَ شَعْباً فِي العَالَمِ يُحَافِظُ عَلَى الأَمْنِ دُونَ بُولِيسٍ أو شُرْطَةٍ؟

جاك: أَعْتَقَدُ أَنَّنِي سَأُحْضِرُ عَائِلَتِي هُنَا مُدَّةَ أُسْبُوعٍ حَتَّى أُنْهِيَ عَمَلِي.

خالد: اذَا التَزَمْتَ قَوَاعِدَ بَسِيطَةً لِسَلَامَتِكَ كُلُّ شَيْءٍ سَيَكُونُ رَائِعاً، لَأتُسَافِر عَلى الطُرقِ السَرِيعَةِ لَيلاً، لَأتَحْمِل مَعَكَ مَبَالِغَ كَبِيرَةً مِنَ المَالِ، احذر الشَّحاتِينَ المُتَسَوِلِينَ، وَابتَعِد عَنهُم، فَأكثَرُهُم حَرَامِية (لُصُوصٌ)، وَاحْرِص عَلى شَحْنِ المُوبَايلِ (الهَاتِف المَحمُول) بالطَّاقَةِ وَدَائِماً يَكُونُ مَعَكَ، وهَذِهِ أمُورٌ تَتَبَعُهَا حَتَّى فِي بَلَدِكَ، لاتَخَفْ لاتَزَالُ مِصْرُ امِنَةً.

الكلمَاتُ الجَديدة

معناها	الكلمة
Is Cairo a safe city?	هَلْ القَاهِرَةُ مَدِينَةٌ امِنَة
Do you believe?	تَعْتَقِدُ
For a short vacation	لأجَازَةٍ قَصِيرَةٍ
Worrying	قَلِقٌ
The revolution	الثَّورَة
The police	الشُّرطَة
An effective form	شَكلٍ فَعَّالٍ
The prisoners	المساجين
Armed and danger (literally, 'he is registered as a dangerous criminal')	مُسَجَّلِي الخَطَر
Extremists	مُتَطَرِفينَ

Terrorists	ارْهَابِيِينَ
You are right	مَعَكَ حَقٌّ
Walk down the street	يَنْزِلُونَ
To protect the streets	لِحِمَايَةِ الشَّوَارِعِ
Thieves	اللُّصُوصِ
Loot	المَسْرُوقَاتِ
The situation is stable	الوَضْعُ مُسْتَقِرٌّ
Friendly people	شَعْبٌ وَدُودٌ
By his nature	بِطَبْعِه
Peaceful	مُسَالِمٌ
In Allah's protection	بِحِفْظِ الله
Committed	التَزَمْتَ
Simple rules	قَوَاعِدَ بَسِيطَةً
Don't carry	لاَتَحْمِل
Beggars	المُتَسَوِلِينَ
Charging the cell-phone	شَحْنِ المُوبَايِل

أسْئِلة:

1. Why is it that Jack does not think Egypt is safe?

2. Who played the role of the police in the absence of the actual police?

3. How is the situation in Sinai and Sharm-Al-Sheikh?

4. In the absence of the police, who protected the houses and the shops?

5. Why does Khalid think Cairo is safe and that it will remain safe?

6. For how long does Jack want to bring his family to Cairo?

7. Why did Khalid warn Jack about beggars?

8. What did Khalid advise Jack to do about his cell phone?

9. What caused the security in Egypt to be unstable?

أَكَّدَ السَّفِيرُ الْأَلْمَانِيُّ بِالْقَاهِرَةِ مِيشَائِيل بُوك أَنَّ أَغْلَبِيَّةَ أَعْضَاءِ جَمَاعَةِ الْإِخْوَانِ الْمُسْلِمِينَ سِلْمِيُّونَ، وَقَالَ "بوك" خِلَالَ مُؤْتَمَرٍ صَحَفِيٍّ الْيَوْمَ الْإِثْنَيْنِ "يُوجَدُ بِلَا شَكٍّ دَاخِلَ قِوَى الْإِسْلَامِ السِّيَاسِيِّ بَعْضُ الْأَطْرَافِ الَّتِي تَدْعُو لِلْعُنْفِ وَلِكِنَّنَا نَرَى أَنَّ أَغْلَبِيَّةَ الْإِخْوَانِ سِلْمِيُّونَ، وَلَا بُدَّ مِنْ تَقْدِيمِ مَنْ يُحَرِّضُ عَلَى الْعُنْفِ إِلَى الْمُحَاكَمَةِ."

The German Ambassador in Cairo Michael Bock stressed that the majority of the Muslim Brotherhood members are peaceful. Bock said, during a news conference today, Monday, 'without a doubt, there are forces within political Islam that call for violence. But we see that the majority of The Brotherhood are peaceful, and anybody who advocates violence should be brought to trial.'

وَأَشَارَ السَّفِيرُ إِلَى إِدَانَةِ الِاتِّحَادِ الْأُورُوبِّيِّ الْوَاضِحَةِ لِكُلِّ مَنْ يَدْعُو لِلْعُنْفِ أَوْ يَحُثُّ عَلَى الْكَرَاهِيَّةِ، وَكَذَلِكَ إِدَانَةِ وَزِيرِ الْخَارِجِيَّةِ الْأَلْمَانِيِّ لِلِاعْتِدَاءِ عَلَى أَفْرَادِ الْأَمْنِ فِي سِينَاءَ. وَاعْتَبَرَ "بوك" أَنَّ قُوَّاتِ الْأَمْنِ فِي مِصْرَ اسْتَخْدَمَتِ الْعُنْفَ الْمُفْرِطَ فِي فَضِّ اعْتِصَامِ رَابِعَةَ الْعَدَوِيَّةِ وَهُوَ مَا أَدَّى إِلَى سُقُوطِ أَلْفِ ضَحِيَّةٍ، بِحَسَبِ قَوْلِهِ.

The ambassador pointed to the clear condemnation of the European Union for whoever advocates violence or urged hatred. Also, the German foreign Minister condemned the assault of security personnel in Sinai. He said that security forces in Egypt used excessive violence to break up the sit-in Raba al-adaweya, which led to the fall of a thousand victims, according to him.

اِقْرَأْ

تَصَدَّتْ قُوَّاتُ الْأَمْنِ الْمِصرِيَّةُ لِمُظَاهَرَةٍ طُلَّابِيَّةٍ بِجَامِعَةِ الْمَنْصُورَةِ خَرَجَتْ ضِمْنَ مُظَاهَرَاتٍ شَهِدَهَا عَدَدٌ مِنَ الْجَامِعَاتِ أَمْسِ الِاثْنَيْنِ، وَذَلِكَ ضِمْنَ فَعَّالِيَّاتِ أُسْبُوعِ "التَّصْعِيدِ الثَّوْرِيِّ" الَّذِي دَعَا إِلَيْهِ التَّحَالُفُ الْوَطَنِيُّ لِدَعْمِ الشَّرْعِيَّةِ وَرَفْضِ الِانْقِلَابِ، وَيَنْتَهِي بِحُلُولِ الذِّكْرَى الثَّالِثَةِ لِثَوْرَةِ 25 يَنَايِر.

وَبَثَّ نَاشِطُونَ صُوَرًا أَظْهَرَتِ اقْتِحَامَ قُوَّاتِ الْأَمْنِ حَرَمَ جَامِعَةِ الْمَنْصُورَةِ بِالْمُدَرَّعَاتِ، وَاعْتِقَالَ عَدَدٍ مِنَ الطُّلَّابِ بَعْدَ تَفْرِيقِ مُظَاهَرَةٍ رَافِضَةٍ لِلِانْقِلَابِ.

Egyptian security forces responded to a student demonstration at the University of Mansoura. The demonstrations began as part of other demonstrations yesterday (Monday) during activities week; this week was named the "Revolutionary Escalation". It was called for by the National Alliance to support the legitimacy of the deposed President and to reject the coup. It ends on the third anniversary of the revolution of January 25.

Activists transmitted pictures showing security forces storming the campus of Mansoura University with armored vehicles, and arresting some students after dispersing a protest against the coup.

أُخْرَى	آخَر
أُخْرَى مَعَ شيء مُؤَنَّث	آخَرْ مَعَ شيء مُذَكَّرٍ

In this lesson we will be using the Arabic word for 'last', 'final', 'terminal', 'other' and 'another'. As you can see from the above, if this word is used with a feminine object, it will be suffixed with an alif maqsura, and the vowel will change. Please read the sentences below, which will demonstrate the usage of this word, and read the translations to confirm their meanings.

(1) خُذ هَذَا الْهَاتِف فَعِنْدِي هَاتِف آخَر.

(2) هَذِهِ سَيَّارَتُنَا وَلَنَا سَيَّارَة أُخْرَى فِي الجَرَاج.

(3) الَتَقَيْتُ عَمِّي وَمَعَهُ رَجُلٌ آخَرُ لا أَعْرِفُهُ.

(4) غَابَتْ اليومَ هَالَة وَطَالِبَةٌ أُخْرَى.

(5) هُنَاكَ رَجُلٌ أُخْرَى فِي حَيَاةِ مَنْ أُحِبُّ.

(6) سَأحفَظ اليومَ سورةَ البَقَرْة وسورةً أُخْرَى.

(7) عندي خَاتَمٌ أَنِيقٌ وَسَأَشْتَرِي خَاتَمًا آخَرَ أَجْمَل.

(8) فَازَ هِشَام وَفَائِزٌ آخَرُ فِي المُسَابَقَةِ الثَّقَافِيَة.

(9) هَاتِي تُفَّاحَةً أُخْرَى يا أُمِّي.

(10) أُرِيْدُ دُوْلَارًا آخَرَ، فَهَذِهِ النُّقُودُ لاتَكْفِي.

119

الكلماتُ الجديدة

معناها	الكلمة
Take this pill, I have another pill	خُذ هَذَا القَلَم فَعِنْدِي قَلَمٌ آخَرْ.
This our car, and we have another car in the garage	هَذِهِ سَيَّارَتُنَا وَلَنَا سَيَّارَةٌ أُخْرَى فِي الجَرَاجِ.
I met my paternal uncle, and he was with another man who I don't know	التَقَيْتُ عَمِّي وَمَعَهُ رَجُلٌ آخَرُ لا أَعْرِفُهُ.
Reem and another female student were absent today	غَابَتْ اليومَ رِيمٌ وَطَالِبَةٌ أُخْرَى.
There is another girl in the life of whom I love	هُنَاكَ فَتَاةٌ أُخْرَى فِي حَيَاةِ مَنْ أُحِبُّ.
Today I will memorize Surat and alWaqaa, and another Sura	سَأحْفَظ اليومَ سورةَ الوَاقِعَة وسورةً أُخْرَى
I have an elegant ring and I will buy another, more beautiful ring	عندِي خَاتَمٌ أَنِيقٌ وَسَأشْتَرِي خَاتَمًا آخَرَ أَجْمَل
Sayeed and another person won the culture competition	فَازَ سَعِيدٌ وَفَائِزٌ آخَرُ فِي المُسَابَقَةِ الثَّقَافِيَةِ
Give me another orange, mother	هَاتِي بُرْتَقَالَةً أُخْرَى يا أُمِّي.
I want another pound – this money is not enough	أُرِيدُ جُنَيْهًا آخَرَ، فَهَذِهِ النُّقُودُ لاتَكْفِي.

قَالَ وَزِيرُ الطَّاقَةِ وَالْمَنَاجِمِ الْجَزَائِرِيُّ فِي مُؤْتَمَرٍ صَحَفِيٍّ أَمْسِ الْأَحَد إِنَّ بِلَادَهُ تَعْتَزِمُ إِنْشَاءَ أَوَّلِ مَحَطَّةٍ نَوَوِيَّةٍ لَهَا عَامَ 2025 لِمُوَاجَهَةِ الطَّلَبِ الْمُتَنَامِي عَلَى الْكَهْرَبَاءِ. وَأَضَافَ أَنَّ مَعْهَدَ الْهَنْدَسَةِ النَّوَوِيَّةِ الَّذِي تَمَّ إِنْشَاؤُهُ مُؤَخَّرًا سَيُشْرِفُ عَلَى تَكْوِينِ الْمُهَنْدِسِينَ وَالتِّقْنِيِّينَ الَّذِينَ سَيُكَلَّفُونَ بِتَشْغِيلِ الْمَحَطَّةِ النَّوَوِيَّةِ.

The Algerian Minister of Energy and Mines said at a news conference yesterday, Sunday, that his country intends to build its first nuclear plant in 2025 to meet growing demands for electricity. He added that the Nuclear Engineering Institution, which was created recently, would oversee the gathering of engineers and technicians, who will be assigned to operate this nuclear plant.

وَقَرَّرَتِ الْجَزَائِرُ اللُّجُوءَ جُزْئِيًّا إِلَى الطَّاقَةِ النَّوَوِيَّةِ لِإِنْتَاجِ الْكَهْرَبَاءِ حِرْصًا مِنْهَا عَلَى خَفْضِ فَاتُورَةِ إِنْتَاجِ الطَّاقَةِ فِي بَلَدٍ تَزَايَدَ اسْتِهْلَاكُ الْكَهْرَبَاءِ فِيهِ خِلَالَ السَّنَوَاتِ الْأَخِيرَةِ بِنِسْبَةٍ تَتَرَاوَحُ بَيْنَ 15 و20%.

Algeria decided to partially resort to nuclear energy to produce electricity keen to reduce the bill for energy production in the country increased electricity consumption which in recent years by between 15 and 20%.

Algeria decided to partially resort to nuclear energy to produce electricity in order to reduce the energy production costs in a country where electricity consumption increased in the last few years by between 15 and 20%.

فِعْلُ الأَمْرِ

Arabic verbs have three tenses: past, present and imperative. (Future tense verbs are formed simply by adding 'siin' or 'saufa' before the present verb.) Please note that the 'siin' is for near future verbs, whilst 'saufa' is used for the more distant future – this is to be decided by speaker or writer.

In considering the imperative as a tense, you must understand that Arabs see commands as something to be done in a specific time frame: usually in the immediate future, but not necessarily. Because of this, it is considered part of the future tense. Imperative verbs are said to the second person ('you'), so the creation of future verbs using the 'siin' and 'saufa' comes when the first or third person is being addressed.

The past tense in Arabic does not include the perfect aspect as we have in English: the perfect aspect ('I have eaten...') could suggest that the action has not yet been completed. In Arabic, the action of the verb when in the past tense will necessarily be completed. Thus, 'I ate...' as in the English imperfect aspect.

The past tense in Arabic, as noted, concerns actions that took place before the time of speaking or writing. Actions reported in the English present tense occur at the time of articulation; because of the use of 'siin' and 'saufa' in the Arabic present tense, actions can happen during or after the time of articulation.

This lesson will introduce the formation of imperative verbs. Below you can see a table that has the three tenses of verbs in Arabic. The past tense is on the first column on the right, the present tense is next to it in the middle, and imperative verbs are on the left.

الأَمْرُ	المضارع	الماضي	الأَمْرُ	المضارع	الماضي
اِسْمَعْ	يَسْمَعُ	سَمِعَ	اِقْتُلْ	يَقْتُلُ	قَتَلَ

122

اِرْفَعْ	يَرْفَعُ	رَفَعَ	اِذْهَب	يَذْهَبُ	ذَهَب
اِدْرُسْ	يَدْرُسُ	دَرَسَ	اِجْلِسْ	يَجْلِسُ	جَلَسَ
اِعْلَمْ	يَعْلَمُ	عَلِمَ	اِفْهَمْ	يَفْهَمُ	فَهِم
اِشْرَبْ	يَشْرَبُ	شَرِبَ	اِحْفَظْ	يَحْفَظُ	حَفِظَ
اِحْلِقْ	يَحْلِقُ	حَلَقَ	اِسْجُدْ	يَسْجُدُ	سَجَدَ
اِكْسِرْ	يَكْسِرُ	كَسَرَ	اِرْكَعْ	يَرْكَعُ	رَكَعَ
اِغْسِلْ	يَغْسِلُ	غَسَلَ	اِشْكُرْ	يَشْكُرُ	شَكَرَ
اِفْتَحْ	يَفْتَحُ	فَتَحَ	اِطْبُخْ	يَطْبُخُ	طَبَخَ
اِضْرِبْ	يَضْرِبُ	ضَرَبَ	اِقْطَعْ	يَقْطَعُ	قَطَعَ
اُكْتُبْ	يَكْتُبُ	كَتَبَ	اِجْمَعْ	يَجْمَعُ	جَمَعَ
اِسْأَلْ	يَسْأَلُ	سَأَلَ	اِعْبُدْ	يَعْبُدُ	عَبَدَ
اِمْنَعْ	يَمْنَعُ	مَنَعَ	اِنْزِلْ	يَنْزِلُ	نَزَلَ
اِضْحَكْ	يَضْحَكُ	ضَحِكَ	اِعْرَفْ	يَعْرِفُ	عَرَفَ
اِرْكَبْ	يَرْكَبُ	رَكِبَ	كُلْ	يَأْكُلُ	أَكَلَ
خُذْ	يَأْخُذُ	أَخَذَ	اِفْعَلْ	يَفْعَلُ	فَعَلَ

Here two sentences are introduced. The first is in the present tense, the second in the imperative. See how the verb and the sentence construction changes from the present tense to the imperative:

'Mohammed is writing his lessons.'

'Write your lessons, Mohammed.'

Please note that when you use the imperative case, precede the sentence by saying, 'yaa'.

In English, you either garner the person's attention by using the name first ('Mohammed, write the lesson'); or you write the imperative form and then the name – 'Write the lesson, Mohammed.' In Arabic, you never put the name at the end of the sentence. Remember this when you translate from English into Arabic.

Mohammed is writing the lesson.	يَكْتُبُ مُحَمَّدٌ الدَّرْسَ.
Mohammed, write the lesson.	اِكْتُبْ يَامُحَمَّدُ الدَّرْسَ.
The pupil understands the lesson.	يَفْهَمُ التِّلْمِيذُ الدَّرْسَ.
Understand the lesson.	اِفْهَمْ الدَّرْسَ.
Khalid is listening to the song.	يَسْمَعُ خَالِدٌ الأُغْنِيَةَ.
Khalid, listen to the song.	يَاخَالِدُ، اِسْمَعْ الأُغْنِيَةَ.
The believer thanks Allah.	يَشْكُرُ المُؤْمِنُ الله.
Thank Allah.	اِشْكُرْ اللهَ.
Adel goes to visit his grandfather on Friday.	يَذْهَبُ عَادِلُ لِزِيَارَةِ جَدِّهِ يَومَ الجُمُعَةِ.
Adel, visit your grandfather on Friday.	اِذْهَبْ يَاعَادِلُ لِزِيَارَةِ جَدَّكَ يَومَ الجُمُعَةِ.
Haitham washes his face every morning.	يَغْسِلَ هَيْثَمُ وَجْهَهُ كُلَّ صَبَاحٍ.
Haitham, wash your face every morning.	يَا هَيْثَمُ، اِغْسِلْ وَجْهَكَ كُلَّ صَبَاحٍ.
The Muslim worships Allah.	يَعبُدُ المُسْلِمُ اللهَ.

Worship Allah.	اعْبُدْ اللهَ.
The son discussed the matter with his father.	يُنَاقِشُ الابْنُ المَوضُوعَ مَعَ وَالِدِهِ.
Discuss the matter with your father.	نَاقِشْ المَوضُوعَ مَعَ وَالِدِكَ.
The baby drinks the milk. ('Baby' in Arabic literally means, 'he who suckles a lot.')	يَشْرَبُ الرَّضِيعُ الحَلِيبَ.
Drink milk.	اشْرَبْ الحَلِيبَ.
Reem wears the coat.	تَلْبَسُ رِيْمُ المِعْطَفَ.
Wear the coat.	البَسِي المِعْطَفَ.
Muslims fast during Ramadan.	يَصُومُ المُسْلِمُ رَمَضَانَ.
Fast during Ramadan.	صُمْ رَمَضَانَ.
The man entered the room.	يَدْخُلُ الرَّجُلُ الَى الغُرْفَةِ.
Enter the room.	ادْخُلْ الغُرْفَةَ.
Reem goes to work every day.	تَخْرُجُ رِيْمُ الَى العَمَلِ كُلَّ يَومٍ.
Go to work every day.	اخْرُجِي الَى العَمَلِ كُلَّ يَومٍ.

The basic form of the verb in English is called the infinitive. This is the root verb with 'to' in front of it, and the form written in dictionaries. We write 'to' in front of it to show that there are no persons involved, which changes the nature of the verb. In Arabic, rather than using the infinitive form, verbs are listed in the third person masculine singular as their basic form. This is how you find verbs in Arabic dictionaries. The reason is that in this form the verb has the least number of letters (the original letters). If you were to list verbs in the same way as in English, they would become nouns!

Here is a list of the verbs we used in this lesson.

معناها	الكلمة
To eat	أَكَلَ
To sit	جَلَسَ
To collect	جَمَعَ
To memorize	حَفِظَ
To shave	حَلَقَ
To study	دَرَسَ
To go	ذَهَبَ
To raise	رَفَعَ
To kneel	رَكَعَ
To prostrate	سَجَدَ
To hear	سَمِعَ

Drink	شَرِبَ
To thank	شَكَرَ
To hit	ضَرَبَ
To cook	طَبَخَ
To worship	عَبَدَ
To know	عَرَفَ
To learn	عَلِمَ
To wash	غَسَلَ
To open	فَتَحَ
To do	فَعَلَ
To understand	فَهِمَ
To kill	قَتَلَ
To cut	قَطَعَ
To break	كَسَرَ
To descend	نَزَلَ

قَالَتْ رَئِيسَةُ لِيتْوانْيَا الَّتِي تَتَوَلَّى بِلَادُهَا رِئَاسَةَ الِاتِّحَادِ الْأُورُوبِّيِّ الْيَوْمَ الِاثْنَيْنِ إِنَّ تَوَسُّعَ الِاسْتِيطَانِ فِي الْأَرَاضِي الْفِلَسْطِينِيَّةِ الْمُحْتَلَّةِ يُعَرْقِلُ الْمُفَاوَضَاتِ الَّتِي اسْتُؤْنِفَتْ قَبْلَ حَوَالَيْ ثَلَاثَةِ أَشْهُرٍ.

The Lithuanian President, whose country holds the Presidency of the European Union, said today, Monday, that settlement expansion in the occupied Palestinian territories is hampering the negotiations, which resumed about three months ago.

وَيَقُولُ مُفَاوِضُونَ فِلَسْطِينِيُّونَ وَتَقَارِيرُ إِعْلَامِيَّةٌ إِسْرَائِيلِيَّةٌ إِنَّ الْمُفَاوَضَاتِ أَصْبَحَتْ مُهَدَّدَةً بِالِانْهِيَارِ، بِسَبَبِ الِاسْتِيطَانِ خَاصَّةً.

Palestinian negotiators and Israeli media report that negotiations are threatened with collapse, in most part due to a settlement.

Put a line under the المُضاف and two lines under the المُضاف اليه on the sentences below.

All these sentences are fully translated, but not in the same order in which they are listed in Arabic. Write the number next to the English section that corresponds to the correct Arabic sentence.

1. وَقَفَ التِلْمِيْذُ عَلَى مَنَصَةِ المَسْرَحِ.

2. وَسَائِلُ المَوَاصَلاتِ مُتَنَوِّعَةٌ.

3. عَرَضْتُ صَحِيْفَةَ ۞ الفَصْلِ أَمَامَ الْمُعَلِمِ

4. تَقِفُ الطُّيُوْرُ عَلَى غُصُوْنِ الأَشْجَارِ

5. أمتعةُ السفرِ جاهزةٌ

6. الإسلامُ دينُ العدلِ

7. ارتفعَ صَوْتُ المؤذنِ

8. حَبلُ الكِذبِ قصيرٌ

9. -نَهرُ النيلِ من أعظمِ الانهارِ

10. وقفَ جَميعُ التَلاميذِ في الطَابورِ

11. نُحِبُّ كلَّ إنسانٍ كريمٍ

12. اتجَهتْ بَعضُ دُولِ العَالمِ الى العوَّلمَةِ

129

1. The pupil stands on the stage platform.	-وسائلُ المواصلاتِ متنوعةٌ.
2. The means of transportation are varied.	-عرَضْتُ صحيفةَ الفصلِ أمامَ المعلمِ
3. The classroom newspaper were displayed in front of the teacher.	-تقِفُ الطيورُ على غصونِ الأشجارِ
4. The birds perch on three branches.	-أمتعةُ السفرِ جاهزةٌ
5. The travel luggage is ready.	-الإسلامُ دينُ العدلِ
6. Islam is a religion of justice.	-ارتفعَ صوتُ المؤذنِ
7. The voice of the muezzin has risen.	-حبلُ الكذبِ قصيرٌ
8. The ropes of lying are short (this is an Arabic proverb which means that you can only go so far with lying)	-نهرُ النيلِ من اعظمِ الانهارِ
9. The Nile River is one of the greatest rivers.	- وقفَ جميعُ التلاميذِ في الطابورِ
10. All pupils stand in the queue	- نُحِبُ كلَ انسانٍ كريمٍ
11. Love every kind person.	- اتجَهتْ بعضُ دولِ العالمِ الى العولمةِ

الأَسْمَاءُ المَوْصُولَةُ

Relative pronouns

In this lesson, we will learn about relative pronouns in Arabic. There are relative pronouns for masculine singular, feminine singular, dual masculine, feminine dual, masculine plural and feminine plural. We will see all of them used in sentences. The Arabic name for relative pronouns is written above in bold.

In English, 'that' is used when the sub-clause is restrictive – this means that it is necessary to the meaning of the initial noun. 'Which' is used when the sub-clause is not necessary to the meaning of the sentence. Arabic does not have this distinction. There are also 'who' whom' and 'whose' in English. Nowadays people only use 'whom' when it is preceded by a preposition. 'Whose' is used in conjunction with possessive nouns. 'Who' is used for all other relative persons pronouns.

In this table, we will demonstrate the usage of relative pronouns in pairs (masculine and feminine for singular, dual and plural).

التِّي	الذِّي
اِسْمٌ مَوْصُولٌ لِلْمُفْرَدِ المُؤَنَّث	اِسْمٌ مَوْصُولٌ لِلْمُفْرَدِ المُذَكَّرِ

The comb, which is on the table, is for my mother.	المِشْطُ الذِّي عَلَى الطَّاوَلَةِ لِأُمِّي.
Here is the pen that you were looking for.	هَاهُوَ القَلَمُ الذِّي تَبْحَثُ عَنْهُ.
Look at the portrait that I painted for the exhibition.	اِنْظُرْ اِلَى اللَّوْحَةِ التِّي رَسَمْتُهَا لِلْمَعْرَضِ.

The cake that my mother made is very delicious.	الكَعْكُ الَّذِي صَنَعَتْهُ أُمِّي لَذِيذٌ جِدّاً.
Come and look at the car that my father bought for me.	تَعَالْ وَشَاهِدْ السَّيَّارَةَ الَّتِي اشْتَرَاهَا لِي وَالِدِي.
The girl who is standing beside the red door is waiting for you.	الفَتَاةُ الَّتِي تَقِفُ بِجِوَارِ السَّيَّارَةِ الحَمْرَاءِ تَنْتَظِرُك.
Who is the young man who you greeted?	مَنْ هَذَا الشَّابُ الَّذِي سَلَّمْتَ عَلَيْهِ.
The exercise that come after these are very easy.	التَّمَارِينُ الَّتِي بَعْدَ هَذَا التَّمْرِينِ سَهْلَةٌ جِدًا.
The people caught the thief who stole the woman's bag.	أَمْسَكَ النَّاسُ بِاللِّصِّ الَّذِي سَرَقَ حَقِيبَةَ السَّيِّدَةِ.
Are these papers that on the desk for you, Tarek? No, they are for my sister, Mona.	أَتِلْكَ الأَوْرَاقُ الَّتِي عَلَى المَكْتَبِ لَكَ يَا طَارِق؟ لا. هِيَ لِأُخْتِي مُنَى.

اللَّتَان	اللَّذَان
اِسْمٌ مَوْصُولٌ لِلْمُثَنَّى المُؤَنَّث	اِسْمٌ مَوْصُولٌ لِلْمُثَنَّى المُذَكَّر

The two cats, who my grandmother is looking after for me, are beautiful.	القِطَّتَان اللَّتَان تَرْعَاهُمَا جَدَّتِي جَمِيلَتَان.
The two games that my father bought are very entertaining.	اللُّعْبَتَان اللَّتَان اِشْتَرَاهُمَا وَالِدِي مُسَلِّيَتَان.
The two pupils, who were absent yesterday, came today.	التِّلْمِيذَان اللَّذَان تَغَيَّبَا بِالأَمْسِ حَضَرَا اليَوْمَ.
The two male doctors who treated my wife are clever.	الطَّبِيبَان اللَّذَان عَالَجَا زَوْجَتِي مَاهِرَان.
Here are the two pens that you are looking for.	هَاهُمَا القَلَمَان اللَّذَان تَبْحَثُ عَنْهُمَا.

I asked my son to eat the apples that are on the dish.	طَلَبْتُ مِنْ اِبْنِي أَنْ يَأْكُلَ التُّفَاحَتَانِ اللَّتَانِ فِي الطَّبَقِ.

اللَّاتِي	الَّذِين
اِسْمٌ مَوْصُولٌ لِلْجَمْعِ المُؤَنَّثِ	اِسْمٌ مَوْصُولٌ لِلْجَمْعِ المُذَكَّرِ

I saw the thieves who robbed our neighbor's house.	رَأَيْتُ اللُّصُوصَ الَّذِينَ سَرَقُوا بَيْتَ جَارِنَا.
All the girls who attended the party are hard workers.	جَمِيعُ الفَتَيَاتِ اللَّاتِي حَضَرْنَ الحَفْلَ مُجْتَهِدَاتٌ.
I met the guests who came to congratulate me.	قَابَلْتُ الضُّيُوفَ الَّذِينَ حَضَرُوا لِتَهْنِئَتِي.
The female teacher rewarded the girls who won the contest.	كَافَأَت المُعَلِّمَةُ الفَتَيَاتِ اللَّاتِي فُزْنَ فِي المُسَابَقَةِ.
The passengers who left the airport lounge are now travelling to Kuwait.	الرُّكَّابُ الَّذِينَ غَادَرُوا صَالَةَ المَطَارِ الانَ مُسَافِرُونَ إِلَى الكُوَيْتِ.
Mothers who discuss different matters with their children are intelligent.	الأُمَّهَاتُ اللَّاتِي يُنَاقِشْنَ أَوْلَادَهُنَّ فِي مُخْتَلَفِ الأُمُورِ ذَكِيَاتٌ.

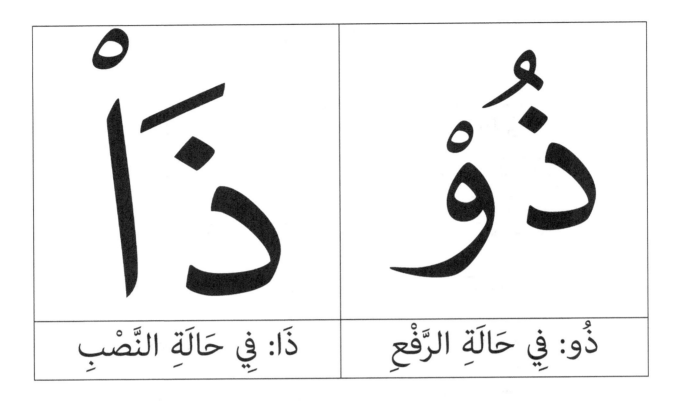

| ذَا: فِي حَالَةِ النَّصْبِ | ذُو: فِي حَالَةِ الرَّفْعِ |

'Zu' means 'possessor of', 'owner of', 'holder of', 'endowed with' or 'having'. For instance, when you say, 'Where is the man with a white shirt?' you use 'zu'. In the case of رفع, the word is written with 'dhaal' and in the case of نصب, write it with 'zaa alif'. Please read the following examples to see how these words are used. 'Zu' is one of the five nouns.

I have a shoe with a colored stripe	عندي حِذَاءٌ ذُو شَرَيْطٍ مُلَوَّنٍ .
This dress has large patterns	هذا فُسْتَانٌ ذُو نُقُوشٍ كَبِيرَةٍ.
I bought a notebook that has lined paper	اِشْتَرَيْتُ دفتراً ذَا وَرَقٍ مُسَطَّرٍ.
Where is the young man with blond hair?	أَيْنَ الشَّابُ ذُو الشَّعْرِ الأَشْقَرِ؟
I saw a beggar on the street with tattered clothes.	رَأَيْتُ فِي الشَّارِعِ مُتَسَوِّلاً ذَا ثِيَابٍ رَثَّةٍ.
This house has a large garden	هَذَا بَيْتٌ ذُو حَدِيقَةٍ كَبِيرَةٍ.
I saw the house that has cramped rooms	بِعْتُ مَنْزِلاً ذَا غُرَفٍ ضَيِّقَةٍ.

Where did I put the tablecloth with the prominent embroidering?	أَيْنَ وَضَعْتَ المَفْرَشَ ذَا التَطْرِيزِ البَارِزِ؟
Who is this man with a thick moustache?	مَنْ هُوَ الرَّجُلُ ذُو الشَّارِبِ الكَثِيفِ؟
I heard a singer with a beautiful voice	سَمِعْتُ مُطْرِبًا ذَا صَوتٍ جَمِيلٍ .
This festival is very popular	هَذَا المِهْرَجَانُ ذُو شَعْبِيَةٍ كَبِيرَةٍ.

الكلماتُ الجديدة

معناها	الكلمة
Nominative	حَالَةِ الرَّفْعِ
Accusative	حَالَةِ النَّصْبِ
The sentence	الجُمَلَ
The blank	الفَرَاغِ
The stripe	شَرَيْطٍ
Colored	مُلَوَنٍ
Dress	فُسْتَانٌ
Pattern	نُقُوشٍ
Notebook	دفتراً

Lined (paper)	مُسَطَّر
Blond	الأَشْقَرِ
Hair	الشَّعْرِ
Beggar	مُتَسَوِّلاً
Clothes	ثِيَابٍ
Tattered	رَثَّةٍ
Garden	حَدِيقَةٍ
I sold	بِعْتُ
A house	مَنْزِلاً
Rooms	غُرَفٍ
Narrow / Tight / Cramped	ضَيِّقَةٍ
Tablecloth	المَفْرَشَ
Embroidering	التَطْرِيزِ
Prominent	البَارِزِ
The moustache	الشَّارِبِ
Thick	الكَثِيفِ
A singer	مُطْرِبًا
The festival	المِهْرَجَانُ
Popular	شَعْبِيةٍ

| إعْرَأُبْ | Inflection |

The word Iɛrab is the verbal noun of the verb aɛraba, أعْرَب , which means to clarify or to express clearly.

We have studied the three vowels signs in Arabic: fatHa, Dumma and kasra, and also the vowelless sign "sukuun". These are sounds that are written as diacritical symbols above or below the appropriate Arabic letter. In most cases, when they are written on internal letters of words, these vowels are rigid and cannot be altered; but when they are written on the last letter, they are subject to change. A word can have on its last letter any of the four aforementioned sings. The determining factor in placing a particular sign on a word is its grammatical function, and this is the most important topic in Arabic grammar – determining the function of a word and placing the appropriate sign on its last letter. This process is called "Iɛrab".

Thus, Iɛrab changes symbols on the end of Arabic words to correspond to its grammatical function. This could be as simple as placing a short vowel on the last letter of the word or it could be more complicated, as in the case of eliding letters (replacing them or changing the vowels on the internal letters of the word). By doing that the function and the meaning of the word is clarified, hence the name for this process, Iعrab.

In it is simplest form, a singular or broken plural word can have a short vowel or a 'sukuun' on its last letter as you see below:

Depending on its grammatical purpose, the last letter of the word 'al-kitab', 'the book', can take one of three vowels or a sukuun on it is last letter, 'baa'. Therefore, 'al-kitab' could be pronounced as 'al-kitabu', 'alkitaba' or 'al-kitabi'. The 'sukuun' as an I3rab symbol comes only with verbs, but it is possible that you pronounce a noun with a 'sukuun' as if there an actual 'sukuun' written on it.

When speaking Arabic correctly you need to say the word in its correct Iعrab form. This means saying the last letter of the word with the correct short vowel, which is not an easy task if you are talking without time to think about it ("on the fly"). If you do not know how to say the last letter correctly vowelized, then say it with a 'sukuun'.

The advantage of Iعrab

Iعrab has several benefits:

1. To know the correct pronunciation of words. When there is disagreement on how to pronounce a word, performing Iعrab or syntax analysis is the way to determine the grammatical function of the word and consequently its vowels and tashkeel, and therefore how to pronounce it accordingly.

2. Signs of Iɛrab serve to dispel excess words in a sentence, as you will study later. One word with the correct vowel symbols can sufficiently carry the meaning without adding more words to further clarification.
3. Identify the grammatical function of words regardless of their placement in sentences, as you will see later in the lesson.
4. Enable writers, poets and the like to express their creative side by manipulating words.
5. Clarify the meaning of words.

This lesson introduces you to the concept of cases. As many people do not know about the concept of cases, not even in English, the purpose of this lesson is to focus on why we learn language construction. As we go along in detail, you will understand what you need to focus on and memorize.

Cases in English grammar

In English grammar, the case of a noun or pronoun is a change in form that indicates its grammatical function in a phrase, clause, or sentence. Cases help us to identify the grammatical role of a noun or pronoun in a sentence. A pronoun replaces a name (i.e. instead of a name, you can say **I, you, he, she.**)

So by using certain words in English, we are indicating a certain function in grammar. In English, it is broken down to the **Subjective case, Objective case, and Possessive case.**

Examples: a noun may play the role of:

1. Subject
   a. "I kicked the ball" – you can see here that the pronoun "I" is used as a subject. Therefore, it is known as a subjective case.
2. Direct Object
   a. "John kicked *me*" – the "me" here is the object of the verb, i.e. the verb is doing something to "me". Therefore, it is in the objective case.
3. Possessor
   a. "*My* ball" – We used the word "my" to indicate possession of the said thing. This is known as the possessive case.

The 4 cases in Arabic

We also have cases in Arabic. They are known in Arabic grammar books written for non-Arabs as the Nominative case, Accusative case, and Genitive case. The Nominative case is similar to the English Subjective case; the Accusative case is similar to the Objective case; and the Genitive case is similar to the Possessive case (see below).

- Nominative
  - The case of a noun that is functioning as the subject of a sentence or clause, generally a noun doing something.

  - The Arabic case name of the Nominative Case is " "
  - In its simplest form, a Dumma is drawn on the last letter of the word,

- Accusative
  - The case that identifies the object of a verb or other word i.e. the one receiving the action.

  - The Arabic case name of the Accusative case is " "
  - In its simplest form, a fatHa is drawn on the last letter of the word,

- Genitive
  - The case that identifies the effect of a preposition, or being part of a construct phrase, so for the most part, it acts as a possessive case in English. It acts as possession.

  - The Arabic case name of the Genitive case is " "
  - In its simplest form, a kasra is drawn on the last letter of the word,

Also:
- Jussive

140

- o The case that identifies the effect of certain particles that precede verbs, or the case of an imperative verbs. There are several signs for jussive; one of them is the sukuun.

- o The Arabic case name of the jussive form case is " جَزْم ا "
- o In its simplest form, a sukuun is drawn on the last letter of the word,

The above categorization is the simplest form of cases in Arabic. A word can have many other functions in a sentence other than what is listed above. A word can be in the case of رفع in thirteen cases. In the case of نصب in eighteen and in the case of جر in six. Also, cases in Arabic don't exactly match those in English, so calling Nominative رفع, Accusative نصب and Genitive جر doesn't give you the what these Arabic cases exactly comprise, but at this stage of Arabic study it is a good starting point.

Iعrab means "expressing clearly", and it is important because by changing the vowel signs/letters in words we can understand what parts of the sentence affect other parts of sentences. In English, word order helps us define what the sentence is saying.

For Example:

   "Ali hit Tariq"

In this sentence, we can see that Ali was the source of the verb "hit" and Tariq received the action. So Ali was the subject and Tariq was the object. If we swap the word order to "Tariq hit Ali", it changes the situation completely.

Now in Arabic, this is slightly different. Word order is not necessarily required in order to see what is going on in the sentence.

Tariq is the subject of the verb

Ali is the subject of the verb

Tariq is the object of the verb

" Tariq hit Ali "

Tariq is the object of the verb

"Ali hit Tariq"

Simple Example:

The top phrase states, "Daraba Aliun tariqan". Daraba is an action verb that means 'to hit' or 'to strike'. We also have Aliun with a dummatain, indicating the subject, and tariqan with a fatHatain, indicating the object.

In the right-hand phrase, the same sentence has swapped the Aliun with Alian and tariqan with tariqun, swapping the fatHatain and dummatain around.

The word order in the two phrases are the same: "Daraba, Ali then Tariq". However, the first one means "Ali hit Tariq" and the second one means, "Tariq hit Ali". Iɛrab, which is the changing of vowel signs/letters in words, is the reason for this through the collective use of letters, tanween, or even vowels. It helps us understand what is going on in the sentence.

Different إعْرَاب

Many Iɛrab can be used in different ways. The following are the signs and forms that you will most likely encounter. You should know this at beginning of your Arabic study.

With Tanween	**With Tanween**
When the word is indefinite, the Iɛrab signs will be in tanween. Here we have Kitab, which means "a book". In the top part, we have Kitab-un and on the bottom, we have fi-kitab-in. The top part is in the nominative case so Kitab-un is not the object, but the subject. The bottom part is in the genitive case. Because we have the kasratain on the Kitab, we know that "Book" is being affected by the preposition "Fi". This is an example that tanween is used to indicate the noun. Thus, "in the book".	"a book" in the nominative case With tanween "a book" in the genitve case 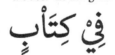

142

With short vowels	With short vowels
Definite words will take the short vowels Iɛrab. Here we have the word "the man". At the top, it is read "al rajulu", so with the dumma it indicates that 'man' is in the Nominative Case. Other cases are illustrated.	الرَجُلُ The man in the nominative case مِنَ الرَجُلِ The man in the genetive case إنَّ الرَجُلَ The man in the accusative case

With Extra Letters	With extra letters
Extra letters can be used to indicate the inflection taking place. Here in the "Muslim-una" and "Muslim-ina", both mean plural male Muslims. The first one is in the nominative case (subject) and the second one is in the genitive case (possessive). In this example, these extra letters "una" and "ina" determine the case of the noun.	"Muslims" in nominative case مُسْلِمُونَ "Muslims" in genetive case مِنَ الـمُسْلِمِينَ

There are more examples of different I'ɛrabs. The ones given above are to give you an idea of the importance of I'ɛrab and that we need to do it correctly.

Not all Arabic words are subject to changing case endings – there are words whose last letter will always be pronounced the same, no matter what its grammatical function. Some of these words are:

- Pronouns
- Interrogatives
- Demonstratives
- Compound numbers
- Relative pronouns

In conclusion:

1. We understand what "cases" are in English.
2. We understand what cases are used in Arabic (Nominative, Accusative, Genitive) and how they relate to the English cases (Subjective, Objective, Possessive)
3. We understand the meaning and importance of Iɛrab.
4. We understand how cases are represented in Arabic. (tanween, short vowels, extra letters)

ظَرْفِ المَكَانِ (أَمَامَ-خَلْفَ)

This lesson is about adverb of place (zarf al-makaan), i.e. front/back.

أَمَامَ

Why do you sit in front of the television all day?	لِمَاذا تَجْلِسُ أَمَامَ التِلِفِزيُون طُوَالَ اليَوم؟
Do not sit in front of your colleague. You are tall and he is short.	لا تَجْلِسْ أَمَامَ زَمِيلِكَ، أَنْتَ طَوِيلٌ، وَهُوَ قَصِيرٌ.
My apartment in Alexandria is directly in front of the sea.	شَقَتِي في الاسْكِنْدَرِيَةِ أَمَامَ البَحْرِ مُبَاشَرَةً.
It is impolite to smoke in front of your father .	لَيسَ مِنَ الأَدَبِ أَنْ تُدَخِنَ أَمَامَ وَالِدَكَ.
My house is nearby. It is in front of the school .	منزِلِي قَرِيبٌ، إِنَّهُ أَمَامَ المَدْرَسَةِ.
I saw you playing in front of your house.	رَأَيْتُكَ تَلْعَبُ أَمَامَ مَنْزِلِكَ.
You have a long road ahead of you until you get to the city .	أَمَامَكَ طَرِيقٌ طَوِيلٌ حَتَّى المَدِينَةِ.
The board is in front of the students.	السُّبُورَةُ أَمَامَ الطُّلاب.
Eat from the food that is in front of you.	كُلْ مِنَ الطَّعَامِ الذي أَمَامَكَ.

خَلْفْ

I left the past behind me.	تَرَكْتُ المَاضِي خَلْفِي.
Sit behind your colleague. You are tall and he is short.	اجْلِسْ خَلْفَ زَمِيلِكَ، أَنْتَ طَوِيلٌ، وَهُوَ قَصِيرٌ.
I put my car behind the ambulance.	وَضَعْتُ سَيَارَتِي خَلْفَ سَيَارَةِ الاسعَافِ.

I walk quickly behind the manager so he will not see me come in late.	مَرَرْتُ مُسْرِعًا خَلْفَ المُدِيرِ حَتى لايَرَانِي مُتَأَخِرًا.
I ran after the thief. I did not catch him.	جَرَيْتُ خَلْفَ اللِّصِ، وَلَمْ أَلْحَقْ بِهِ.
The mini-bus driver surprised me from behind the truck.	سَائِقُ المِيكرُوباص فَاجَأَنِي مِنْ خَلْفِ الشَّاحِنَةِ.
Please drive/ go behind this car.	مِنْ فَضْلِكِ، سِرْ خَلْفَ هَذِهِ السَيَّارَةِ.
The board is behind the teacher.	السُّبُورَةُ خَلْفَ المُعَلِّمِ.
I put the chair behind the door so no one can open it.	وَضَعْتُ الكُرسِيَ خَلْفَ البَابِ، كَي لايَفْتَحَ أَحَدٌ.

إِسْمُ إِشَارَةٍ لِلْبَعِيدِ (ذَلِكَ، تِلْكَ)	There are two demonstrative pronouns for distant objects: a masculine (zelaka) and a feminine (telka).	
ذَلِكَ: لِلْمُفْرَدِ الْمُذَكَرِ	Zelaka is for singular masculine.	
تِلْكَ: لِلْمُفْرَدِ الْمُؤَنَّثِ	Telka is for singular feminine.	

This table contains the demonstrative pronouns. Here they are used with different nouns.

ذَلِكَ قَلَمٌ.	ذَلِكَ أَبٌ.	تِلْكَ أُمٌّ.
ذَلِكَ قَفَصٌ لِلطُّيُورِ.	تِلْكَ أَنْفٌ.	تِلْكَ مِلْعَقَةٌ.
تِلْكَ نَافِذَةٌ.	ذَلِكَ اِبرِيقٌ.	ذَلِكَ قَمِيصٌ.
تِلْكَ شَجَرَةٌ كَبِيرَةٌ.	ذَلِكَ كَلْبٌ.	تِلْكَ قِطَّةٌ.
تِلْكَ مُمَرِّضَةٌ.	ذَلِكَ مُؤَذِّنٌ.	ذَلِكَ مَطْعَمٌ مُمْتَازٌ.
ذَلِكَ مَالٌ وَفِيرٌ.	تِلْكَ نُقُودٌ كَثِيرَة.	ذَلِكَ سَرِيرٌ وَثِيرٌ.

الكلماتُ الجديدة

معناها	الكلمة
Demonstrative pronoun	اِسْمُ إِشَارَةٍ
Cage	قَفَصٌ
For the Birds	لِلطُّيُورِ
Pitcher	اِبرِيقٌ
Crier	مُؤَذِّنٌ
Money	مَالٌ
Abundant	وَفِيرٌ
Spoon	مِلْعَقَةٌ
Nose	أَنْفٌ
Shirt	قَمِيصٌ
Window	نَافِذَةٌ
Tree	شَجَرَةٌ
Excellent	مُمْتَازٌ
Restaurant	مَطْعَمٌ

اَلْهِوَايَات

The objective of this lesson is to introduce you to vocabulary related to hobbies through a conversation between students and their teacher .

أنَا أهوَى الكُمبيوتَر وَالانتَرنِتَ وَمَواقِعَ التَّوَاصُلِ الاجتِمَاعِيِّ وَأنتَ ما هوايتك؟

My hobbies are *working with* computers, internet-*surfing*, and social networking. And you? What are your hobbies?

المعلم: سَتُقَامُ مُسَابَقَةٌ أدَبِيةٌ فِي الكِتَابَةِ وَالشِّعْرِ وَالقِصَّةِ القَصِيرَةِ.

حسن: رَائِعٌ، أنَا أهوَى الكِتَابَةَ وَالقِرَاءَةَ، وَأعتَقِدُ أنِّي سَأكتُبُ قِصَّةً، فَأنَا أهوَى كِتَابَةَ القِصَصِ البُوليسِيَةِ.

المُعلِّم: رَائِعٌ يَاحَسَن، سَتُوَزَعُ جَوَائِزٌ فِي اليَومِ التَّرفِيهِيِّ الذي سَيُقَامُ الأسبُوعَ القَادِمَ، وَسَيُقَامُ مَعرِضٌ لِلأعْمَالِ اليَدَوِيةِ مِن صُنْعِ الطُّلابِ، وَسَتَكُونُ هُنَاكَ حَفلَةٌ مُوسِيقِيةٌ لِهُوَاةِ سَمَاعِ الأغاني.

هيثم: حَقاً يَاأُستَاذ؟ هَل يَعنِي ذَلِكَ أنَّهُ سَتُقَامُ مُسَابَقَاتٌ وَمَرَحٌ؟ هَل يُمكِنُني المُشَارَكَةُ بَالعَزفِ وَالغِنَاءِ فَأنَا أهوَى المُوسِيقَى.

المعلم: طَبعاً يُمكِنُكَ ذَلِكَ يَاهيثم، وَطَبعاً سَتَتِمُ مُسَابَقَاتٌ لِمَنْ يَهوَى الرِّيَاضَةَ وَالمَشْيَ السَّرِيعَ وَالجَرْيَ وَلَعِبَ الشَّطرَنج وَالدُومِينُو وَالوَرَقَ (الكُوتشِينَة) وَالرَّسمَ وَالتَّصوِيرَ الفوتوغرَافِي، وَسَنعرِضُ فِيلْماً وَثَائِقِياً عَنِ الحَضَارَةِ الفِرعَونِيةِ لِهُوَاةِ مُشَاهَدَةِ الأفلامِ الوَثَائِقِيةِ.

وائل: أنا أهوى جَمعَ الطَّوابعِ البَريدِيةِ وَجَمعَ العُمْلاتِ القَديمَةِ، هَل بِامكَانِي أنْ أعرِضَ مَجمُوعَتي.

المعلم: نَعَمْ يَاوَائِل بِالطَّبعِ، جَمِيعُ الهوَايَاتِ مَطلُوبَةٌ وَمَأجمَلَ أنْ تَستَغِلُوا وَقتَ الفَرَاغِ !!

لَميَاءُ: اذن، سَأحضِرُ أعمَالِي فَأنَ أهوَيَ الخِيَاطَةَ وَالترِيكُو وَالكرُوشِيه وَالتَّفصِيلَ.

رنا: وَمَا رَأْيُكُم أنْ أحضِرَأنَا بَعضاً مِنَ الأطعِمَةِ المُمَيَزَةِ، فَأنَا أهوَى الطَّبخَ وِاعدَادَ المأكولاتِ.

المعلم: كُلُّهَا أفكَارٌ جَمِيلَةٌ.

المُشرِفَةُ: بَعدَ اذنِكَ يَاأستَاذُ سَتُقَامُ رِحلَةٌ اْلى شَرمِ الشَّيخِ في أجَازَةِ مُنتَصَفِ العَامِ، مَن يُرِيدُ الاشتِرَاكَ؟

وَائِل: أنَا أهوَى السَّفَرَ وَالرَّحَلاتِ، بِإمكاننا تأجِيرُ قَارَبٍ ومُمَارَسةُ السِّبَاحَةِ وَالغَطسِ ورُبَّمَا الصَّيدِ، وبِإمكاننا رُكُوبُ الخَيلِ لَدَى بَدوِ سِيْنَاءَ وَاقَامَةُ مُعسْكَرٍ في الصَّحَرَاءِ وَتَسَلُّقِ الجِبَالِ.

رنَا: أمَّا أنَا فَأهوَى التَّسَوُّقَ في شَرمِ الشَّيخِ وَزِيَارَةَ الأمَاكِنِ الأثَرِيَةِ كَعُيُونِ مُوسَى، وَأهوَى الاستِجمَامَ في المُنتَجَعَاتِ الصِّحِيةِ لِلحُصُولِ عَلَى جَلسَاتِ السَّاوُنَا وَالجَاكُوزِي وَالمَسَاجِ.

هيثم: كُنتُ أتَمَنَّى لَو كَانَت رِحلَةً نِيلِيَةً اِلَى الأقصُرِ وأسوَانِ، لِمُمَارَسَةِ هِوَايَتِي في التَّجدِيفِ بِنَهرِ النَّيلِ.

المعلم: كُلُّ الأنشِطَةِ وَالهوَايَاتِ مُفِيدَةٌ وَتَشغَلُ وَقتَ الفَرَاغِ.

الكلمات الجديدة

معناها	الكلمة
Hobbies	الهِوَايَاتُ
Social networking site	مَواقِعَ التَّوَاصُلِ الاجتِمَاعيِّ
Contest	مُسَابَقَة
Poetry	الشِّعْرِ
Detective stories	القِصَصِ البُولِيسِيَةِ
Recreational	التَّرْفِيهيِّ
Handicrafts	لِلأَعْمَالِ اليَدَوِيَةِ
For amateurs	لِهُوَاةِ
Competitions	مُسَابَقَاتٌ
Fun	مَرَحٌ
Play music	عَزَفِ
Brisk walking	المَشْيَ السَّرِيعَ
Chess	الشَّطرَنج
Dominoes	دُومِينُو
Playing cards	الكُوتشِينَة

Documentary film	فِيلْماً وَثَائِقِياً
Postage stamps	الطَّوَابِعِ البَرِيدِيَةِ
Old coins	العُمْلاتِ القَدِيمَةِ
My collection	مَجمُوعَتِي
Sowing	الخِيَاطَة
Knitting	التِريكُو
Crochet	الكرُوشِيه
Preparing gourmet food	الأطعِمَةِ المُميَزَةِ
Tailoring	التَّفصِيلَ
Food preparation	إعدَادَ المأكولاتِ
A trip will take place	سَتُقَامُ رِحلَةٌ
Boat rental	تأجِيرُ قَارَبِ
Practice	مُمَارَسَةٌ
Swimming and diving	السِّبَاحَةِ وَالغَطسِ
Hunting	الصَّيدِ
Horse riding	رُكُوبُ الخَيلِ
Sinai Bedouins	بَدوِ سِينَاءَ
Camp	مُعسْكَرِ
Mountain climbing	تَسَلُّقَ الجِبَالِ
Shopping	التَّسَوُّقَ

Archaeological places	الأَمَاكِنِ الأَثَرِيَةِ
Moses springs	عُيُونِ مُوسَى
Recreation	الاستِجمَامَ
Spas	المُنتَجَعَاتِ الصِّحِيةِ
Nile cruise	رِحلَةً نِيلِيَة
Rowing	التَّجدِيفِ
Occupying leisure time	شَغَلُ وَقْتَ الفَرَاغَ

أسئلة:

1. The teacher announced a literary competition in writing poetry and what else?

2. Why does Hassan think he is a good fit for the writing competition?

3. When will the rewards be distributed?

4. Besides the literary part of the competition, what else will there be?

5. Will Haithem take part in the musical portion of the competition?

6. Which student likes to display his collection of postal stamps and old coins?

7. Which student will bring her knitting and crochet work to the competition?

8. Which student will bring a distinguished food?

9. When will the trip to Sharm al-Sheikh take place?

10. What types of activities can students participate in while in Sharm al-Sheikh?

11. If the trip was to Luxor and Aswan instead of Sharm al-Sheikh, what kinds of activities will there be?

هَذَا الْكِتَابُ يُنَاقِشُ جُذُورَ الْخَلَلِ فِي نُظُمِ الزِّرَاعَةِ الْحَدِيثَةِ، وَالْمَآسِيَ الَّتِي جَلَبَتْهَا عَلَى نُظُمِ الزِّرَاعَةِ التَّقْلِيدِيَّةِ، فِي آسْيَا وَأَفْرِيقْيَا وَأَمِيرْكَا اللَّاتِينِيَّةِ، كَمَا يَرْصُدُ نِضَالَ الْفَلَّاحِينَ الْمُثَابِرِينَ دِفَاعًا عَنْ تَطْوِيرِ الزِّرَاعَةِ الْمُتَوَارَثَةِ، مِنْ أَجْلِ تَوْفِيرِ احْتِيَاجَاتِ الْبَشَرِ وَالْحَيَوَانَاتِ مِنَ الْغِذَاءِ.

This book discusses the roots of the imbalance in modern farming systems, and the tragedies brought about on the traditional farming systems in Asia, Africa and Latin America. It also observes the struggle of the hardworking farmers who defend the development of inherited (traditional) agricultural methods, in order to provide food for the needs of human and animals.

وَالْمُؤَلِّفُ "وَالدن بيللو" أُسْتَاذُ عِلْمِ اجْتِمَاعٍ بِجَامِعَةِ الْفِلِبّينِ، وَأَحَدُ الْقِيَادَاتِ الْبَارِزَةِ فِي الْحَرَكَاتِ الْعَالَمِيَّةِ الْمُنَاهِضَةِ لِلْعَوْلَمَةِ، وَلَهُ الْعَدِيدُ مِنَ الدِّرَاسَاتِ بِشَأْنِ أَزْمَةِ الْغِذَاءِ، وَالْأَزْمَةِ الْمَالِيَّةِ.

Author Walden Bello, Professor of Sociology at the University of the Philippines and one of the leading figures in the global movements of anti-globalization, has also written many studies on the food and financial crises.

الأدوات المدرسية

المسطرة هي أهم الأدوات المدرسية، حيث يستعملها كل الطلاب في المدارس.

وهناك أدوات مدرسية متعددة كالمثلث والمنقلة والاسطوانة الصغيرة، والممحاة وغيرها من الأدوات.

القلم الرصاص، والقلم الجاف، والأقلام الملونة، كلها أدوات يستعملها الطلاب في مدارسهم.

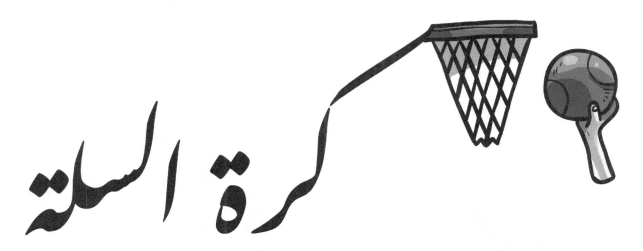

كرة السلة

الحوار

جنيفر :السَّلامُ عَلَيْكُمْ وَرَحْمَةُ اللَّهِ وَبَركاتُه

مُحَمَّدٌ :وَعَلَيْكُمُ السَّلاَمُ وَرَحْمَةُ اللَّهِ وَبَركاتُهُ

جنيفر :مَتَى تَذْهَبُ إِلى النَّادِي؟

مُحَمَّدٌ :أَذْهَبُ إِلَيْهِ فِي السَّاعَةِ الثَّالِثَةِ عَصْرًا .

جنيفر :وَمَتَى تَعودُ إِلَى البَيْتِ؟

مُحَمَّدٌ :أَعودُ فِي السَّابِعَةِ مَسَاءً.

جنيفر :ماذا تَلْعَبُ فِي النَّادِي؟

مُحَمَّدٌ :أَلْعَبُ كُرَةَ السَّلَةِ.

جنيفر :كَمْ يَوْماً تَتَدَرَّبُ فِي الأَسْبُوعِ؟

155

مُحَمَّدٌ: أَتَدَرَّبُ فِي الْأُسْبُوعِ ثَلاثَةُ أَيَّامٍ .

جنيفر: وَكَمْ سَاعَةَ تَتَدَرَّبُ فِي الْيَوْمِ الْوَاحِدِ؟

مُحَمَّدٌ: أَتَدَرَّبُ فِي الْيَوْمِ أَرْبَعَ سَاعَاتٍ.

الكَلِمَاتُ الجَدِيدَة

معناها	الكلمة
The club	النَّادِي
Basketball (the word basketball in Arabic is written using the IDafa construction, so the first word is "ball" and the second word is "the basket" and this applies to the names of every sport with a ball)	كُرَةُ السَّلَةِ
You train	تَتَدَرَّبُ
Your trainer/ Your coach	مُدَرِّبَكَ
Your trainer who is training you	مُدَرِّبِكَ الذي يُدَرِّبُكَ
An hour (this word is also sometimes used to say "watch/clock"	سَاعَةً
A week	الْأُسْبُوع
You play	تَلْعَبُ

Evening	مَسَاءً
Seventh	السَّابِعَةِ
The house	البَيْتِ
To	إِلَى
You return/ come back	تَعُودُ
When	مَتَى
Afternoon	عَصْرًا
O'clock	السَّاعَةِ
You go	تَذْهَبُ

أسئلة:

1. مَتَى تَذْهَبُ إِلَى النَّادِي؟.......................

2. مَتَى تَعُودُ إِلَى البَيْتِ؟.......................

3. ماذا تَلْعَبُ في النَّادِي؟.......................

4. لماذا اخترت ذلك النادي؟.......................

5. كَمْ يَوْماً تَتَدَرَّبُ في الأسْبُوعِ؟.......................

6. كَمْ رِيَاضَةً تُمَارِسُهَا في النَّادِي؟.......................

7. كَمْ سَاعَةً تَتَدَرَّبُ في اليَوْمِ الوَاحِدِ؟.......................

8. مَا اسمُ مُدَرِّبِكَ الذي يُدَرِّبُكَ؟.......................

9. مَأ اِسم نادِيْك؟ ....

10.ما اسمك؟ ....

11.مَأ هِيْ رِيَاضَتَك المُفَضَلة؟ ....

اِقْرَأْ

أَصْبَحَ الرَّسَّامُ وَالْخَطَّاطُ الْفِلَسْطِينِيُّ جَمِيل الْعَنْبَتاوِي يُعْرَفُ بِعَمِيدِ رَسَّامِي الْمَسَاجِدِ الْفِلَسْطِينِيَّةِ بِفَضْلِ حِرَفِيَّتِهِ النَّادِرَةِ وَمَسِيرَتِه الطَّوِيلَةِ الَّتِي بَرَعَ خِلَالَهَا فِي تَزْيِينِ الْعَشَرَاتِ مِنْ بُيُوتِ الله بِالْآيَاتِ الْقُرْآنِيَّةِ وَالزَّرْكَشَاتِ الْإِسْلَامِيَّةِ.

يَرْسُمُ الْعَنبتاوي فِي الْمَدَارِسِ وَصَالُونَاتِ الْمَنَازِلِ وَغَيْرِهَا، لِيَقْرِنَ الْإِبْدَاع الْفَنِّيَّ بِكَسْبِ قُوتِهِ، وَتَبْقَى أَحَبُّ الْأَعْمَالِ الْفَنِّيَّةِ إِلَى قَلْبِهِ مَا يُنْجِزُهُ فِي بُيُوتِ الله، فَهِيَ تَبْعَثُ فِيهِ الْفَرَحَ وَتُشَكِّلُ تَحَدِّيًا جَدِيدًا فِي كُلِّ مَرَّةٍ يَضَعُ فِيهَا تَصَوُّرًا لِزَخْرَفَةِ جُدْرَانِ الْمَسْجِدِ وَقُبَّتِهِ وَيَبْدَأُ مَرْحَلَةَ الْإِنْجَازِ.

The Palestinian painter and calligrapher Jameal Anabtawi became known as a dean of calligraphy for Palestinian mosques. Thanks to his rare professionalism and long career, he excelled in decorating houses of God with Koranic verses and Islamic ornamentation.

Anabtawi paints in schools, houses and salons (rooms set aside for receiving guests of the house) so he can pair artistic creativity with making a living. His best-loved works of art are what he accomplishes in the houses of God. It makes him happy and he looks forward to new challenges every time he envisions decorating the walls of mosques and its dome: this is when the stage of realizing his vision starts.

159

النِّسْبة

The grammatical objective of this lesson is to introduce to the concept of 'nisba'. 'Nisba' means attribution or ascription - a cause by association. The grammatical term means 'relative' or 'relational adjective'. This means you are describing somebody who belongs to a certain group of people, or a particular field, i.e. Moroccan, American, medical, commercial. 'Nisba' can be built from nouns using several methods. The most prevalent way is for a kasra to be placed under the last letter of the noun, and then add to it 'yaa' with a shaddah.

This dialogue is between three people. They are talking about other people's nationalities, religions and occupations. They also talk about which field their jobs are in and their physical features. Throughout this discussion, they use the 'nisba'. Usually when you talk about these topics in Arabic, you will use the 'nisba'.

أَنَا مَغْرِبِيٌّ مِنَ المَغْرِب، وَبِالتَّحْدِيدِ رِبَاطِيٌّ مِنَ العَاصِمَةِ الرَّبَاطِ، وَأَنْتَ، مِنْ أَيْنَ تَكُونُ؟
I am Moroccan from Morocco and, to be exact, Rabati, from the capital Rabat. And you? Where are you from?

حَامِد: هَذا الرَّجُلُ ذُو الشَّعرِ الذَّهَبِي عِرَاقِيُّ الجِنسِيَةِ وَهُوَ يَعْمَلُ فِي المَجَالِ الطِّبِّي وَيَعْتَنِقُ الدِّينَ الاسلامِيَ.

حَسَن: هَلْ هُوَ بَغْدَادِيٌّ؟

حَامِد: نَعَم، إنَّهُ مِنْ بَغْدَاد العَاصِمَة.

حَسَن: حَقاً!! حَسِبتُهُ سُورِيَا مِنْ سُورِيَا وَبِالتَّحْدِيدِ حَلَبِياً مِنْ مَدِينَةِ حَلَبٍ أَوْ دِمَشْقِياً مِنْ مَدِينَةِ دِمَشْقِ العَاصِمَةِ.

حَامِد: أَتَعْلَمُ أَنَّ مَذهَبَهُ شِيعِيٌّ؟

160

حَسَن: حَقاً !! حَسِبْتُهُ سُنِياً مِنْ أَهْلِ السُّنَّةِ.

حَامِد: لا، اِنَّهُ مِنَ الشِّيْعَةِ.

حَسَن: أَتَذكُرُ تِلْكَ المُوظَفَةَ الجَدِيدَةَ التي جَاءَتْ أَوَلَ أَمْسٍ؟

حَامِد: لا، مَنْ هِيَ؟

حَسَن: كَارُول، الفَتَاةُ ذَاتُ الشَّعْرِ الكِسْتِنَائيُّ، والعَيْنَيْنِ السَّمَاوِيَتَيْنِ؟

حَامِد: نَعَمْ، تَذكَّرْتُهَا.

حَسَن: اِنَّهَا مَسِيحِيةُ الدِّيَانَةِ، وَهِيَ لُبْنَانِيَةٌ، بَيْرُوتِيةٌ مِنَ العَاصِمَةِ بَيْرُوتٍ، وهِيَ تَعْمَلُ في القِسْمِ التَّسْوِيقي.

حَامِد: صَحِيحٌ !! كُنْتُ أَتمنَّى لَو كَانَتْ في الفَرْعِ الادَارِي، فَالفَرْعُ التِّجَارِيُّ أَصْبَحَ مُكتَظاً.

حَسَن: لَقَدْ كَانَتْ تَعْمَلُ في المَجَالِ السِّيَاحِي في لُبْنَان، وَلَدَيْهَا الكَثِيرُ مِنَ العلاقَاتِ العَامَةِ فَتَمَ تَرْشِيحُهَا للقِسْمِ التِسْوِيقِي.

كارول: صَبَاحُ الخَيْرِ .هَلْ رَأى أَحَدُكُم السَّيدَ ...!!!. حَقِيقَةً لأذكُرُ اِسْمَهُ.... !!!

حسن: صِفِيه لَنَا.

كارول: حَسَناً، اِنَّهُ شَابٌ قَمْحِيُّ اللَّونِ، رَمَادِيُّ الشَّعْرِ، اِيْطَاليُّ الجِنسِيَةِ، يَهُودِيُّ الدِّيَانَةِ.

حَامِد: أَنْتِ تَقصِدِينَ دِيفِيد فَهُوَ الوحِيدُ بَهَذِه المُوَاصَفَاتِ، اِنَّهُ مِيلانيٌّ مِنْ مَدِينَةِ مِيلان في شَمَالِ ايطَالِيَا، وَهُوَ مَسؤُولٌ عَنِ القِسْمِ الصَّناعِيِّ بالمُؤَسَّسَةِ.

كارول: شُكراً لَكَ، نَعَمْ اِنَّهُ دِيفِيد، وَأَنْتَ عَرِّفنِي بِنَفسِكَ.

حَامِد: أَنَا حَامِدٌ مَسؤُولُ الانْتَاجِ الزِرَاعِي والحَيَوَانِي بالمُؤَسَسَةِ، وَأَنَا مِصْرِيٌّ.

كارول: هل أنتَ مِنَ القاهِرَةِ؟

حسن: نَعَمْ، أَنَا قَاهِرِيٌّ مِنَ القَاهِرَةِ.

كارول: حَسِبْتُكَ خَلِيجِياً مِنْ أَهْلِ الخَلِيجِ، وَبِالتَحْدِيدِ سُعُودِياً.

حسن: لِمَاذا؟

كارول: شَارِبُكَ وَشَعرُكَ الكَثِيفُ الأَسْوَدُ النَّاعِمُ وَبَشَرَتُكَ الرَّمليَةُ بِلَوْنِ رِمَالِ الصَّحَرَاءِ كُلُّهَا تُوحِي بِذَلِكَ.

حامد: أَنَا مِصرِيٌّ، وَعَرَبِيٌّ أفخَرُ بِعُرُوبَتِي، أَتَعْلَمِينَ؟ حَسِبْتُكِ أوروبِيَةً أوْ رُوسِيَةً حَتَّى تَحَدَّثتِ بِالعَرَبِيَةِ، أَعَرِّفُكِ بِحَسَنٍ، مَسْؤُوْلُ القِسْمِ الرِّيَاضِيِّ وِنَادِي المُؤَسَسَةِ، وَهُوَ اماَرَاتِيٌّ.

حَسَن: أَنَا ظِبِيَانِيٌّ مِنْ أبِي ظَبْي العَاصِمَةِ، أَهلاً بِكِ يَاكَارُول.

كارول: أَهْلاً بِكُمْ جَمِيْعاً.

حسن: أَهْلاً بِكِ، وَتَشَرَّفْنَا بِمَعْرِفَتِكِ.

الكلماتُ الجديدة

معناها	الكلمة
Nisba- relative or relational adjective, i.e. Moroccan, American, Christian etc....	النِّسْبَة
Moroccan	مَغْرِبِيٌّ
Rabati (from Rabat, the capital of Morocco)	رِبَاطِيٌّ
Golden	الذَّهبِي
Iraqi	عِرَاقِيٌّ
Citizenship	الجِنسِيَةِ

Medical	الطِّبِّي
Islamic	الاسْلامِي
Baghdadi (someone from Baghdad, the capital of Iraq)	بَغْدَادِيٌّ
Syrian	سُورِياً
Aleppian (somebody from Aleppo, a city in Syria)	حَلَبِياً
Damascene (somebody from Damascus, the capital of Syria)	دِمَشْقِياً
Shiite	شِيعِيٌّ
Sunni	سُنِياً
Maroon, Chestnut, Auburn (the color, mostly used to describe hair color)	الكِسْتِنائِيُّ
Sky blue eyes (notice that the color blue was not mentioned, except implicitly in the Nisba, by combining the word "eye" and "sky", the eyes are blue)	العَينَينِ السَّماوِيَتَينِ
Christian/ Christianity (feminine form)	مَسِيْحِية
Religion	الدِّيَانَة
Lebanese (feminine form)	لُبْنَانِية
Beiruti (somebody from Beirut)	بَيْرُوتِية
Marketing Department	القِسْمِ التَّسْوِيقِي
Fact/True/ Truth	حَقِيقَة
Describe him	صِفِيه
A tan young man	شَابٌّ قَمْحِيُ اللَّونِ
Gray	رَمَادِيٌ
Italian	ايْطَالِيٌ

163

Jewish	يَهُودِيٌ
You mean	أنْتِ تَقصِدِينَ
Only	الوحِيدُ
Specifications	المُواصَفَاتِ
Milani	مِيلانِيٌّ
Responsible/ Official	مَسؤولٌ
Industrial	الصِّنَاعِيِّ
Foundation	بالمُؤسَسَةِ
Introduce me	عَرِّفني
Introduce yourself to me	عَرِّفني بِنَفسِكَ
Agriculture/ Animal- like	الزراعِي وَالحَيَوَانِي
Egyptian	مِصرِيٌّ
Cairenes (somebody from Cairo)	قَاهِرِيٌّ
Gulfi (somebody from the Gulf)	خَلِيجِياً
Saudi	سُعُودِياً
Your moustache	شَارِبُكَ
Thick	الكَثِيفُ
Soft	النَّاعِمُ
Your sand-colored skin	وَبَشرَتُكَ الرَّملِية
Desert sand	رِمَال الصَّحَراءِ
To suggest that	تُوحِي بِذَلِكَ
I am proud of my Arabic character	أفخَرُ بِعَرُوبَتِي

Do you know?	أَتَعْلَمِينَ
I thought you… (were American, for example)	حَسِبْتُكِ
I thought you were European or Russian	حَسِبْتُكِ أوروبِيَةً أوْ رُوسِيَةً
Until you spoke in Arabic	حَتَّى تَحَدَّثْتِ بِالعَرَبِيَةِ
Emirati (someone from the United Arab Emirates)	اَمَارَاتيٌّ
Dhubiani (someone from Abu Dhabi)	ظِبيانيٌّ
And we are honored to meet you	وَتَشَرَّفْنَا بِمَعْرِفَتِكِ

أسئلة:

1. Write the male names of the people involved in this conversation.
2. What is the nationality of the blond person?
3. In which field does he work and what is his religion?
4. Is he a shi'a or a Sunni?
5. What is the name of the new female employee?
6. What is the color of her hair and eyes?
7. What is her religion and nationality?
8. In which department does she work and why?
9. When she was in her country, in which field did she work?
10. She was looking for a young man. What is his name, nationality, and religion?
11. Who is Egyptian and why did they think he was a Saudi?
12. What is the nationality of the head of the athletics department?

Please read the following aloud (to your teacher, if you can).

يَزُورُ وَزِيرُ الْخَارِجِيَّةِ الْأَمِيرِكِي جُون كِيرِي الْقَاهِرَةَ الْيَوْمَ قَبْلَ يَوْمٍ مِنْ مُحَاكَمَةِ الرَّئِيسِ الْمَعْزُولِ مُحَمَّد مُرْسِي وَهِيَ الزِّيَارَةُ الْأُوْلَى لَهُ مُنْذُ انْقِلابِ 3 يُولْيُو/ تَمُوز الْمَاضِي، بَيْنَما أَعْلَنَ الرَّئِيسُ الْمِصْرِيُّ الْمُؤَقَّتُ حِرْصَ بِلادِهِ عَلَى عَلاَقَتِهَا بِوَاشُنْطُن الَّتِي تَوَتَّرَتْ بَعْدَ تَعْلِيقِ الْأَخِيرَةِ بَعْضَ مُسَاعَدَاتِهَا الْعَسْكَرِيَّةِ لِمِصْرَ.

American Secretary of State John Kerry is visiting Cairo today the day before the trial of the deposed President Mohammed Morsi. It is his first visit since the coup of last July 3rd.

Egypt's interim President announced his country's desire for a relationship with Washington, which was strained after the recent suspension of military aid to Egypt.

تَأَخَّرْتُ قَرْزًا

خَرَجْتُ في الصَّباحِ السَّاعةَ السَّابِعةَ إلى عَمَلي ،
رَكِبْتُ سَيّارَتي الفِضِّيَّةَ اللَّوْنِ ، وبَدَأْتُ أَسيرُ
في شَوارِعِ المَدينةِ ، الطَّريقُ كانَ مُزْدَحِمًا جِدًّا
ومَلِيءٌ بِالنَّاسِ والسَّيّاراتِ ، حاوَلْتُ الوُصولَ
إلى مَكْتَبي مُبَكِّرًا لَكِنْ لِلأَسَفِ وَصَلْتُ مُتَأَخِّرًا
خَمْسَ دَقائِقَ ، لَمْ أَعْتَدْ أَبَدًا التَّأَخُّرَ عَنْ عَمَلي
أَوْ أَيِّ مَوْعِدٍ لي .

أَخْبَرَتْني سِكرِتيرَتي أَنَّ هُناكَ مَوْعِدًا يَنْتَظِرُني
السَّاعةَ التَّاسِعةَ بِالضَّبْطِ ، وَلَمَّا هَمَمْتُ بِالذَّهابِ
إلى الاجْتِماعِ وَقَعَتِ القَهْوةُ على مَلابِسي ،
فَذَهَبْتُ مُسْرِعًا إلى الحَمَّامِ أُنَظِّفُها وأُجَفِّفُها ،
فَأَخَذَ مِنّي ذلك وَقْتًا طَويلًا وَما كادَ لي أَنَّهُ أَتَأَخَّرُ
عَنْ أَيِّ مَوْعِدٍ أَبَدًا .

166

صَحْرَاءُ سِينَاءَ

أوتوبيس سِيَاحِي

A bus broke down while traveling in the middle of a desert, so they used a satellite phone to request spare parts from a nearby city and after the arrival of the parts, a mechanic fixed it and the bus continued its trip.

تَعَطَّلَ الأوتوبيس السِّيَاحِي خِلالَ سَيرِهِ وَسَطَ صَحْرَاءِ سِينَاءَ بِالقُرب مِنْ دِيرِ سَانت كَاترين مُتَجِهًا الَى دَهَبٍ ، مِمَّا اسْتَلزَمَ طَلَبَ قِطَعِ غِيَارٍ لَهَا مِنْ مَدِينَةِ دَهَبٍ، عَنْ طَرِيقِ هَاتِفِ الثُّرَيَا بِتَكلِفَةٍ تَصِلُ إِلَى أَرْبَعَةِ آلافِ جُنيهٍ،وَتَطَلَّبَ ايصَالِ القِطْعَةِ إِلَى سَانتْ كَاترين مَبْلَغًا تَجَاوَزَ قِيمَةَ قِطَعِ الغِيَارِ، إِلاَّ أَنَّ القَائِمِينَ عَلَى الرِّحْلَةِ كَانُوا مُضطَرِينَ لِتَأمِينِهَا لِضَمَانِ مُوَاصَلَةِ سَيرِ الرِّحْلَةِ لا سِيَّمَا بَعْدَ أَنْ عَرْقَلَتْ تِلَكَ الحَافِلَةَ الرِّحْلَةُ أَكْثَرَ مِنْ مَرَّةٍ نَتِيجَةَ غَوصِهَا فِي الرِّمَالِ حَيثُ إِنَّهَا كَانَتْ تَسِيرُ بِدُونِ دَبل.

167

وَبَعْدَ وُصُولِ قِطَعِ الغِيَارِ إِلَى سَانت كَاترين قَاطِعَةً مَسَافَةً تَتَجَاوَزُ 200 كم لِيَبْدَأَ الميكَانِيكِيُّ المُنْتَدَبُ مَهَامَ عَمَلِهِ فِي تَرْكِيبِ القِطعَةِ فِي أَسْرَعِ وَقتٍ مَعَ غُرُوبِ الشَّمْسِ لِيُعْلِنَ قُبَيلَ بُزُوغِ الشَّمْسِ صَبَاحًا انتِهَاءَ المُهِمَّةِ بِنَجَاحٍ بَعْدَ تَرْكِيبِ القِطعَةِ الجَدِيدَةِ لِتُوَاصِلَ الحَافِلَةُ سَيرَهَا مُتَوَغِّلَةً فِي عُمْقِ الصَّحْرَاءِ الَى مَدِينَةِ دَهَبٍ.

الكلماتُ الجديدة

معناها	الكلمة
Breakdown	تَعَطَّلَ
Tourist Bus (notice that we used the nisba of tourist, which is touristic)	الأوتوبيس السِّيَاحِي
Its driving	سَيرِهِ
Heading	مُتَّجِهًا
Required	استَلزَمَ
Spare parts	قِطَعِ غِيَارٍ
Satellite handheld phone	هَاتِفِ الثُّرَيَا
Cost	بِتَكلِفَةٍ
Piece/ Part	القِطْعَة

Amount	مَبْلَغًا
Exceed	تَجَاوَزَ
Value	قِيمَة
Caretakers	القَائِمِينَ
Forced/ Obligated	مُضْطَرِينَ
Ensure	تَأْمِينِ
Guarantee	ضَمَان
Continue	مُوَاصَلَة
Especially	لا سِّيمَا
Obstructed	عَرْقَلَتْ
Bus	الحَافِلَة
Diving/ Submerge	غَوص
sand	الرِّمَالِ
The bus is traveling without a spare tire.	تَسِيرُ بِدُونِ دَبل
Distance	مَسَافَة
The mechanic	المِيكَانِيكِيُّ
Representative/delegate	المُنْتَدَبُ
Asks	مَهَام
Installation	تَرْكِيب
Soon	أسْرَعِ وَقتٍ
Sunset	غُرُوبِ الشَّمْسِ
Right before	قُبَيلَ

Sunrise	بُزُوغِ الشَّمْسِ
Mission is accomplished	انتِهَاءَ المُهِمَّةِ
Go deep into...	مُتَوَغِّلَة
Breakdown	عُمْقِ الصَّحْرَاءِ

أسئلة:

Please answer the following questions

1. What is the name of the desert this bus was traveling through and where was it going?

2. From which city did they request the spare parts, and how much did it cost?

3. Were the spare parts' transportation cost more than the cost of the spare parts?

4. Was it the first time that the bus had broken down?

5. How many kilometers did the spare parts have to travel to reach the bus?

6. When did the mechanic start working on the bus and when did he finish?

7. Where was the bus heading?

أَشَادَ الرَّئِيسُ الفَرَنْسِيُّ فرانْسوا هُولاند بِالْعَلَاقَاتِ الَّتِي تَرْبِطُ بِلَادَهُ بِدَوْلَةِ قَطَر وَوَصَفَهَا بِأَنَّهَا مُمْتَازَةٌ، مُشَدِّدًا عَلَى وُجُودِ "احْتِرَامٍ مُتَبَادَلٍ وَتَفَاهُمٍ" بَيْنَ الْبَلَدَيْنِ. وَكَانَ هُولاند يَتَحَدَّثُ أَثْنَاءَ لِقَائِهِ الْجَالِيَةَ الْفَرَنْسِيَّةَ فِي قَطَر بُعَيْدَ وُصُولِهِ إِلَى الدَّوْحَةِ يَوْمَ السَّبْتِ فِي زِيَارَةٍ رَسْمِيَّةٍ لِقَطَر.

French President Francois Hollande praised relations between his country and Qatar and described it as excellent. He stressed the existence of "mutual respect and understanding" between the two countries. Hollande was quoted during a meeting with the French community in Qatar, shortly after his arrival in Doha on Saturday, during an official visit to Qatar.

تَحْذِير

للمُسَافِرِينَ الَي البَحْرَينِ مِنْ وَزَارَةِ الخَارِجِيَةِ الامْرِيكِيَةِ

Ashura is an important religious festival celebrated by many across Bahrain. As a part of this festival, religious observations, processions and events will take place throughout Bahrain between 14 and 30 November. Although these processions and events are expected to be peaceful, there is a possibility that there might be anti-government protests, which could involve clashes with the police. If this occurs, appropriate measures should be taken to avoid these areas. If you encounter a large public gathering or demonstration, depart the vicinity immediately.

171

أسئلة:

1. مَا هُوَ عَاشُورَاءُ؟

2. هَلْ هَذِهِ المُنَاسَبَةُ ذَاتُ طَابَعٍ دِينِي؟

3. مَا مَظَاهِرُ الاحتِفَالِ بِهَذِهِ المُنَاسَبَةِ فِي البَحرَينِ؟

4. مَا الوَقتُ الذي يَحتَفِلُ بِهِ النَّاسُ فِي البَحرَينِ بِمُنَاسَبَةِ عَاشُورَاءَ؟

5. هَلْ يُتَوَقَّعُ أَنْ تَكُونَ الاحتِفَالاتُ والتَّجَمُّعَاتُ بِهَذِهِ المُنَاسَبَةِ سِلمِيَةً وَامِنَةً؟

6. هَلْ يُتَوَقَّعُ أَنْ يَكُونَ هُنَاكَ احتِجَاجَاتٌ مُنَاهِضَةٌ لِلحُكُومَةِ أَثنَاءَ الاحتِفَالِ بِمُنَاسَبَةِ عَاشُورَاءَ؟

7. هَلْ مِنَ المُمكِنِ أَن تَحْدُثَ اشتِبَاكَاتٌ بَينَ المُحتَفِلِينَ والشُّرطَةِ؟

8. اذَا لَم تَكُنِ الاحتِفَالاتُ امِنَةً فِي بَعضِ الأَمَاكِنِ، فَمَا العَمَلُ حِينَئِذٍ؟

9. بِمَاذَا تَنصَحُ وَزَارَةُ الخَارِجِيَةِ الامرِيكِيَةِ رَعَايَاهَا المُسَافِرِينَ الَى البَحرَينِ، اذَا صَادَفُوا مُظَاهَرَةً أو تَجَمُّعاً كَبِيراً؟

1. هَلْ يُعَدُّ ذَلِكَ تحذِيراً مِنْ وَزَارَةِ الخَارِجِيَةِ الامرِيكِيَةِ الَى الأَمرِيكِيين المُسَافِرِينَ الَى البَحرَينِ؟

الكلماتُ الجديدة

معناها	الكلمة
Warning	تَحْذيرٌ
Religious nature	طَابَعٍ دِيني
Signs of festivities	مَظَاهِرُ الاحتِفَال
Appropriate	المُنَاسَبَةِ
Expected	يُتَوَقَعُ
Peaceful	سِلمِيَة
Safe	امِنَة
Protests	احتِجَاجَاتٌ
Anti-government	مُنَاهِضَةٌ لِلحُكُومَةِ
Clashes	اشتِبَاكَاتٌ
Revelers	المُحتَفِلينَ
Police	الشُّرطَة
Then	حِينَئِذٍ
They encountered	صَادَفُوا
Rally, gathering	تَجَمعاً
Demonstration	مُظَاهَرَةً

اقرأ

كَشَفَ الرَّئِيسُ الْأَمِيرِكِيُّ بَارَاك أُوبَامَا عَنْ تَبَادُلِهِ رَسَائِلَ مَعَ نَظِيرِهِ الْإِيرَانِيِّ، وَأَعْلَنَ فِي مُقَابَلَةٍ بَثَّتْهَا قَنَاةُ أَي بِي سِي نِيوز أَنَّهُ حَذَّرَ الرَّئِيسَ رُوحَانِي مِنْ أَنَّ تَمَهُّلَ وَاشِنْطُن بِشَأْنِ تَوْجِيهِ ضَرْبَةٍ عَسْكَرِيَّةٍ إِلَى سُورِيَا لَا يُؤَثِّرُ عَلَى التَّهْدِيدَاتِ الْأَمِيرِكِيَّةِ بِاسْتِخْدَامِ الْقُوَّةِ لِمَنْعِ إِيرَانَ مِنْ تَصْنِيعِ أَسْلِحَةٍ نَوَوِيَّةٍ.

American President Barack Obama revealed that he exchanged letters with his Iranian counterpart, announcing in an interview with news channel ABC that he warned President Hassan Rohani that the delay of Washington's decision over military strikes against Syria does not affect the American threats to use force to prevent Iran from manufacturing nuclear weapons.

وَأَبْدَى اعْتِقَادَهُ بِأَنَّ أَزْمَةَ الْأَسْلِحَةِ الْكِيمِيَائِيَّةِ السُّورِيَّةِ أَظْهَرَتْ أَنَّ الدِّبْلُومَاسِيَّةَ يُمْكِنُ أَنْ تُؤْتِيَ بِنَتَائِجَ إِيجَابِيَّةٍ إِذَا مَا اقْتَرَنَتْ بِتَهْدِيدَاتٍ عَسْكَرِيَّةٍ. وَقَالَ أُوبَامَا إِنَّهُ اتَّصَلَ بِرُوحَانِي "كَمَا اتَّصَلَ بِي هُوَ أَيْضًا. لَقَدْ تَوَاصَلْنَا مُبَاشَرَةً"، لَافِتًا إِلَى أَنَّ تَوَاصُلَهُمَا كَانَ عَبْرَ رَسَائِلَ.

He emphasized his belief that the Syrian chemical weapons crisis showed that diplomacy could yield positive results if combined with military threats. Obama said he contacted Rohani, "as he also contacted me. We communicated directly." He pointed out that their contact was through letters.

حِوارُ الحُرُوفِ
الْ الشَّمْسِيَةُ والْ القَمَرِية

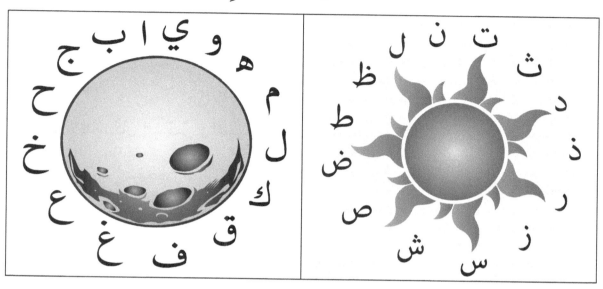

يُحْكَى أَنَّهُ فِي قَدِيمِ الزَّمَانِ: بَيْنَما الحُرُوفُ الهِجَائِيَةُ يَلْهُونَ وَيَلْعَبُونَ، مَرَّتْ بِهِمْ الْ التَّعْرِيفِ وَقَالَتَ:

مَرْحَباً، أَنَا الْ التَّعْرِيفِ، مَارَأَيُكُم أَنْ أَدْخُلَ عَلَى كُلِّ حَرْفٍ مِنْكُمْ فَأُعَرِّفَهُ.

تَجَمَّعَت الحُرُوفُ الهِجَائِيَةُ العَرَبِيَةُ، ثُمَّ انْقَسَمَتْ الَى قِسْمَيْنِ حَوْلَ الَ التَّعْرِيفِ.

القِسْمُ الأَوَّلُ وَيَضُمُّ الحُرُوفَ: أ، ب، ج، ح، خ، ع، غ، ف، ق، ك، م، هـ، و، ي.

المُكَوَّنَةُ لِجُمْلَةٍ: (جُحَا غَبِي فَكَ مُخَهُ وَقَعَ).

القِسْمُ الثَّانِي وَيَضُّمُ الحُرُوفَ: ت، ث، د، ذ، ر، ز، س، ش، ص، ض، ط، ظ، ل، ن.

اخْتَارَت حُرُوفُ القِسْمِ الأَوَّلِ حَرْفَ القَافِ لِيَتَكَلَّمَ بِاسْمِهَا، فَقَالَ:

نَحْنُ مُوَافِقُونَ عَلَى طَلَبِ الِ التَّعْرِيفِ، بِشَرْطِ أَنْ تُكْتَبَ وَتُنْطَقَ، وَأَنْ يَكُونَ الحَرْفُ الذي يَلِيهَا مُتَحَرِكاً غَيْرَ مُشَدَّدٍ.

175

أمَّا القِسْمُ الثَّانِي فَقَد اخْتَارَتْ حُرُوفُهُ حَرْفَ الشِّينِ لِيَتكلَّم باسْمِهَا، فقَالَ:

نَحْنُ أيضاً مُوافِقون عَلَى طلَبِ الـ التَّعريفِ، بِشَرْطِ أَنْ تُكْتَبَ ولاتنطق، وَأَنْ يَكونَ الحَرْفُ الذِي يَليهَا مُشَدَّداً.

قَالَت الُ التَّعْريفِ: انَا مُوافِقَةٌ عَلَى شِرُوطِكُمَا وَلَكِن لابُد ان نَجِدَ اسماً لِكُلِّ مَجمُوعَةٍ مِنكُم لِنُمَيِّزَهَا.

في هَذِه الأثْنَاء، كَانَ الشَّمْسُ والقَمَرُ يَسْتَمعَانِ لِهَذا الحِوَارِ الدَّائرِ،

قَالَت الشَّمْسُ: أتَسْمَحُونَ لَنَا أن نُسَاعِدَكُم في حَلِّ هَذِه المُشكِلَةِ.

قَالَت الحُرُوفُ: نَعَمْ، تفَضَّلُوا.

قالَ القَمَرُ: نُسَمِّي الَ المَجْمُوعَةِ الأُولَى، (اللَّامَ القَمَريَّةِ).

قَالَت الشَّمْسُ: نُسَمِّي الَ المَجْمُوعَةِ الثَّانِيَةِ، (اللَّامَ الشَّمْسِيَةِ).

ضَحِكَ الجَميعُ وَوَافقوا عَلَى هَذا الحَلِّ الجَميلِ.

الكلماتُ الجديدة

الكلمة	معناها
يُحْكَى أنَّهُ في قَديمِ الزَّمَانِ	Once upon a time

While	بَيْنَما
Alphabets	الحُرُوفُ الهِجَائِيَّة
Having fun	يَلْهُونَ
Section	القِسْمِ
Passed by them	مَرَّتْ بِهِمْ
Insert	أَدْخُلَ
Change it into definite (noun)	أُعَرِّفَهُ
gathered	تَجَمَّعَت
Divided	انْقَسَمَتْ
Which make up the sentence.	المُكَوِّنَةُ لِجُمْلَة
To speak on its behalf	لِيَتَكَلَّمَ بِاسْمِهَا
Agree	مُوَافِقُونَ
Provided that	بِشَرْطِ
Written and pronounced	تُكتَبَ وَتُنْطَقَ
Followed by	يَليهَا
Vowelled.	مُتَحَرِكاً
Does not carry a shadda.	غَيْرَ مُشَدَّدٍ
We distinguished	مُمَيِّزَهَا
In the meantime,	في هَذِه الأثْنَاء
Debate	الحِوَارِ الدَّائِرِ

أسئلة:

1. How do you say in Arabic "once upon a time"?

2. What were the alphabet letters doing when the definite article passed by them?

3. What is the name of the definite article in Arabic?

4. How does the definite article explain her job to the Arabic alphabet letters?

5. Into how many groups were the letters split?

6. Arab students, when they are faced with memorizing a large group of letters that have a grammatical function, such as the moon letters, they memorize them by arranging the letters to form a sentence. What is the sentence that contains all the moon letters and what is the sentence that contains all the sun letters?

7. Which letter represents the moon letters?

8. Under what conditions do the moon letters agree to the definite article's request?

9. Which letter represents the sun letters?

10. Under what conditions do the sun letters agree to the definite article's request?

11. There was still an issue that was not yet resolved. What is the issue, who helped them to resolve this problem, and how?

12. What were the names that were given to these groups of letters?

13. Which group of letters have a shadda following the definite article?

اللّامُ القَمَرِيَّةُ وَاللّامُ الشَّمْسِيَّةُ

اسْتَخْرِجِ اللّامَ الشَّمْسِيَةَ وَاللّامَ القَمَرِيَةَ مِنَ الحِوَارِ، وَتَذَكَّرْ أَنَّ:

اللّامُ القَمَرِيَّةُ تُكْتَبُ وَتُنْطَقُ، وَيَكونُ الحَرْفُ الذي يَليهَا مُتَحَرِّكاً غَيْرَ مُشَدَّدٍ. وأَحَدُ الحُرُوفِ المُكَوِّنَةُ لِجُمْلَةِ (جُحَا غَبِي فَكَ مُخَّهُ وَقَعَ).

اللّامُ الشَّمْسِيَّةُ تُكْتَبُ وَلاتُنْطَقُ، وَيَكونُ الحَرْفُ الذي يَليهَا مُشَدَّداً.

أحمد: مَاذَا تُحِبّينَ أَنْ تَفْعَلي في وَقْتِ فَرَاغِكِ يَا رِيمُ؟

ريم: أُحِبُّ الذَّهَابَ الَى النَّادي وَمُمَارَسَةَ الرِّيَاضَةِ.

أحمد: أَيُّ رِيَاضَةٍ تُمارِسينَ؟

ريم: أُمَارِسُ السِّبَاحَةَ، وَكُرَةَ الطَّائِرَةِ، وَالجُمْبَازَ في صَالَةِ الأَلعَابِ، وَأَنْتَ مَاذَا تَفْعَلُ في وَقْتِ فَرَاغِكَ؟

أحمد: أَنَا أَلْعَبُ كُرَةَ القَدَمِ في النَّادي، وَأُمَارِسُ الرَّسْمَ وَالقِرَاءَةَ وَكِتَابَةَ المَقَالاتِ في المَكْتَبَةِ القَريبَةِ.

ريم: رَائِع!! هَلْ تَعْلَمُ أَنَّ وَالِدَةَ صَديقَتي هِيَ الأَمينَةُ المَسؤُولَةُ عَنِ الأَقسَامِ العِلْمِيَةِ وَالثَّقَافِيَةِ وَجَميعِ الأَنشِطَةِ في المَكْتَبَةِ؟

أحمد: حَقًّا!!!! أَلَمْ يَكُنْ الرَّجُلُ العَجُوزُ هُوَ الأَمينُ؟

179

ريم: لا، لَقَدْ كَانَ فِي مَكَانِهَا مُؤَقَّتًا حَتَّى تَعُودُ مِنَ السَّفَرِ، لَقَدْ سَافَرَتْ لِقَضَاءِ الأَجَازَةِ مَعَ زَوجَهَا بِالخَارِجِ.

أحمد: نَعَمْ، نَعَمْ، لَقَدْ تَذَكَّرْتُهَا، انَّهَا المَرْأَةُ النَّحِيلَةُ ذَاتُ النَّظَّارَةِ الكَبِيرَةِ، وَذَاتُ الشَّعْرِ الأَشْقَرِ الطَّوِيلِ.

ريم: نَعَمْ، انَّهَا هِيَ بِلاشَكٍ أَيُّهَا الذَّكِيُّ، يَاصَاحِبَ الذَّاكِرَةِ الجَيِّدَةِ.

أحمد: شُكْرًا عَلَى المَدِيحِ يَاأُخْتِي الغَالِيَة.

ريم: أَحْمَد، خُذْنِي مَعَكَ فِي المَرَّةِ القَادِمَةِ لأُسَلِّمَ عَلَيْهَا.

أحمد: لَو سَمَحَتْ الظُّرُوفُ، فِي نِهَايَةِ الأُسْبُوعِ سَآخُذُكِ مَعِي.

ريم: شُكْرًا لَكَ يَاأَخِي العَزِيز.

الكَلِمَاتُ الجَدِيدَة

الكَلِمَة	مَعْنَاها
اللاَّمُ القَمَرِيَّةُ وَاللاَّمُ الشَّمْسِيَّةُ	The moon 'laam' and the sun 'laam' (or 'lunar laam' and 'solar laam')

Your spare time	وَقْتِ فَرَاغِكِ
Practicing sport	مُمَارَسَةَ الرِّيَاضَةِ
Swimming	السِّبَاحَةَ
Volleyball	كُرَةَ الطَّائِرَةِ
Gymnastics	وَالجُمْبَازُ
Gym	صَالَةِ الأَلْعَابِ
Soccer	كُرَةَ القَدَمِ
Drawing	الرَّسْمَ
Reading	القِرَاءَةَ
Writing articles	كِتَابَةَ المَقَالاتِ
The secretary responsible for the scientific and culture departments and all activities in the library	الأَمِينَةُ المَسؤُولَةُ عَنِ الأَقْسَامِ العِلْمِيَةِ وَالثَّقَافِيَةِ وَجَمِيعِ الأَنْشِطَةِ فِي المَكْتَبَةِ
Temporarily	مُؤَقَّتًا
Thin	النَّحِيلَةُ
Long blond hair	الشَّعْرِ الأَشْقَرِ الطَّوِيلِ
Oh you who has a good memory	يَاصَاحِبَ الذَّاكِرَةِ الجَيِّدَةِ
Praise	المَدِيحِ
If circumstances permit	سَمَحَتْ الظُّرُوفُ

قَالَتْ شَرِكَةُ "مِصْرَ الْعَالَمِيَّةُ لِلسِّينَمَا" إِنَّهُ تَقَرَّرَ إِطْلَاقُ اسْمِ مُؤَسِّسِهَا الْمُخْرِجِ الْمِصْرِيِّ الرَّاحِلِ يُوسُف شَاهِين (1926-2008) عَلَى إِحْدَى الْقَاعَاتِ الْأَثَرِيَّةِ بِمُجَمَّعِ سِينَمَا الْأُقْصُرِ بِالْعَاصِمَةِ الْفَرَنْسِيَّةِ بَارِيسَ.

The company Egypt International Cinema has decided to name its founder, the late Egyptian director Youssef Chahine (1926-2008) on one of the archaeological halls of the Luxor Cinema Complex in the French capital Paris.

وَكَشَفَتِ الشَّرِكَةُ فِي بَيَانٍ لَهَا عَنْ هَذَا التَّكْرِيمِ الدَّوْلِيِّ الَّذِي يُضَافُ لِسِلْسِلَةِ تَكْرِيمَاتٍ حَظِيَ بِهَا مُؤَسِّسُهَا الرَّاحِلُ الَّذِي حَصَلَ عَلَى عِدَّةِ جَوَائِزَ عَالَمِيَّةٍ، وَتَمَّ إِطْلَاقُ اسْمِهِ عَلَى شَوَارِعَ عِدَّةٍ فِي مُخْتَلَفِ بُلْدَانِ الْعَالَمِ.

The company said in a statement about this international recognition, which is added to a series of honors won by the late founder who has won several international awards, his name, has been launched on the streets of several in countries around the world.

وَيُعَدُّ الْمُجَمَّعُ الْفَرَنْسِيُّ مِنْ بَيْنِ أَكْبَرِ مُجَمَّعَاتِ الْعَرْضِ السِّينَمَائِيِّ فِي بَارِيسَ، وَتَمَّ تَشْيِيدُهُ عَامَ 1921 وَتَقَرَّرَ إِغْلَاقُهُ عَامَ 1983، وَمِنَ الْمُقَرَّرِ إِعَادَةُ افْتِتَاحِهِ يَوْمَ 17 أَبْرِيل/ نِيسَان الْجَارِي بِعَرْضِ فِيلْمِ "الْمَصِير" لِيُوسُف شَاهِين الَّذِي أُنْتَجَ عَامَ 1997.

The French complex is considered among the largest French cinema complexes in Paris. It was built in 1921, and decided to close in 1983. It is scheduled to reopen on the 17th April this month, for the purpose of showing the movie 'Destiny' by Youssef Chahine, which was produced in 1997.

الانتِخَابَاتُ مَعْرَكَةٌ يَحْسِمُهَا صُنْدُوقُ الانتِخَابِ

Election battle resolved by the ballot box

Some people are talking about elections. New vocabulary will be about choosing candidates and the election process in the Arab world.

الحِوَار

خالد: هَلْ سَتَذْهَبُ مَعَنَا يَا أمِير؟ سَنَذْهَبُ للإدلاءِ بِأصْوَاتِنَا فِي انتِخَابَاتِ الرِّئَاسَةِ؟

أمير: لا لَنْ أذْهَبَ، أنَا غَيْرُ مُقْتَنِعٍ بِنَزَاهَةِ هَذِهِ الانتِخَابَاتِ.

خالد: لا يَا أمِير، يَجِبُ أنْ نُشَارِك، فَالاقْتِرَاعُ العَامُ حَقٌّ لِكُلِّ فَرْدٍ بَالِغٍ سِنَ الرُّشْدِ، يَحْمِلُ الجِنسِيَةَ المِصْرِيَةَ، انَّهَا حُرِّيَةُ التَّعْبِيرِ عَنِ الرأيِ والدِيمُوقرَاطِيَةِ، انَّ المُشَارَكَةَ فِي الحَيَاةِ السِّيَاسِيَةِ أفضَلُ لِلمُجتَمَعِ.

أمير: اذن، أيُّ مُرَشَحٍ أختَارُ؟

183

خالد: اِخْتَرْ مَنْ تَقْتَنِعُ بِبَرْنَامَجِهِ الانْتِخَابِي، يُمْكِنُكَ مُشَاهَدَةُ المُنَاظَرَاتِ الانْتِخَابِيَةِ التي تُذَاعُ في التِّلِيفِزْيُون، واخْتَرْ مَنْ تَشْعُرُ بِجِدِيَتِهِ وَفَعَالِيَةِ مُقْتَرَحَاتِهِ وَأفكَارِهِ فَصَوتُكَ أَمَانَةٌ.

أمير: إذا لَمْ يَنْجَحْ مَنْ رَشَحْتُهُ لِلفَوزِ، سَيُصِيبُنِي الاحْبَاطُ

خالد: وَلِمَاذا تَحْزَنُ؟ يَجِبُ أَنْ تَتَقَبَلَ فَوزَ مُرَشَحِكَ أو خَسَارَتَهُ بِرُوحٍ رِيَاضِيَةٍ، فَالذي يَحْكُمُ هُوَ صُنْدُوقُ الانْتِخَابِ، وَرَأيُ الأَغْلَبِيَةِ يَفُوزُ، والأَقَلِيَةُ تَخْسَرُ.

نَادية: خَالِد، أُرِيدُ الذَهَابَ مَعَكُمْ، كَيْفَ أعرِفُ لَجْنَتِي الانْتِخَابِيَةَ؟

خالد: ادخُلِي الَى الانترَنَت مِنَ اللابتوب أو الكُمبيُوتر الخاص بِكِ الَى المَوقِع الرَّسمِي لِلَجنَةِ الانتِخَابِ، وأدخِلِي رَقَمَكِ القَومِي، وَسَتَعرِفِينَ مَكَانَ لَجنَتِكِ.

نَادِيَة: سَمِعتُ أنَّهُ يُمكِنُنِي مَعرِفَةُ لَجنَتِي باستِخْدامِ المُوبَايلِ مِنْ خِلالِ رَقمِ خَطٍّ سَاخِنٍ.

خالد: نَعَم، صَحِيحٌ يَا نَادِيَة.

أمير: سَأقِفُ في طَابُورٍ طَويلٍ لِأَتَمَكَنَ مِن دُخُولِ اللَّجنَةِ والانتِخابِ.

خالد: نَعَمْ يَا أَمِير، الزِّحَامُ شَدِيدٌ، لَكِنْ هُنَاكَ أوقَاتٌ يَقِلُّ فِيهَا الزِّحَامُ.

أمير: أَنَا مُحْتَارٌ، المُرَشَحُونَ كَثِيرُون.

نادية: بَعْضُ المُرَشَحِينَ يَنتَمُونَ لِأحزَابٍ وَتَيَّارَاتٍ سِيَاسِيَةٍ مُخْتَلِفَةٍ، انظُرْ أيَّ حِزبٍ أو اتِجَاهٍ سِيَاسِي تُفَضِّلُ.

أمير: أَنَا أُفَضِّلُ حِزبَ الكَنَبَةِ.

نادية: هاهاها، وَمَا هُوَ حِزبُ الكَنَبَةِ؟

خالد: هاهاها، يَا نَادِيَة، أمِيرٌ لا يُرِيدُ المُشَارَكَةَ في الانتِخَابِ، وَيَقصِدُ أنَّهُ سَيَكتَفِي بِمُتَابَعَةِ الانتِخَابِ أمَامَ التِّليفزيون جَالِساً عَلَى كَنَبَةٍ مُرِيحَةٍ.

نادِيَة: أميرٌ مِنَ الأغلَبِيةِ الصَّامِتَةِ.

الكلماتُ الجديدة

معناها	الكلمة
The elections	الانتِخَابَاتِ
Battle	مَعْرَكَة
Will be resolved	يَحْسِمُهَا
Ballet box	صُندُوقُ الانتِخَابِ
Cast our vote	للإدلاءِ بِأَصْوَاتِنَا
Presidency	الرِّئَاسَةِ
I am convinced	مُقتَنِعٍ
Integrity	نَزَاهَةِ
General election	الاقتِرَاعُ العَام
Right	حَقٌّ
An adult	فَرْدٍ بَالِغٍ
Puberty	سِنَ الرُّشْدِ
Hold Egyptian citizenship	يَحمِلُ الجِنسِيَةَ المِصْرِيَةَ
Freedom of expression	حُرِّيَةُ التَّعْبِيرِ

Choose	اِخْتَرْ
Convinced	تَقْتَنِعُ
Run on a ticket (manifesto)	بِبَرْنَامَجِهِ الاِنتِخَابِي
Debates	المُنَاظَرَات
Broadcast	تُذَاعُ
His seriousness	بِجِدِّيَتِه
Effectiveness	فَعَالِيَة
His proposals	مُقتَرَحَاتِه
His ideas	أفكَارِه
Your voice is trust (i.e. your vote is a voice which secures you trust in society)	فَصَوتُكَ أمَانَة
Frustration	الاحْبَاطُ
Take it sportingly	بِرُوحٍ رِيَاضِيةٍ
The majority	الأغَلَبِيَة
The minority	الأقَلِيَة
My election committee /Polling booth	لَجْنَتِي الانْتِخَابِيَّة
Your national number	رَقَمِكِ القَومِي
A hotline	خَطِ سَاخِنٍ
Correct / true	صَحِيحٌ
Political ideologue	وَتَيَارَاتٍ سِيَاسِيةٍ
Couch	الكَنَبَة
He doesn't want to participate	لا يُرِيدُ المُشَارَكَة
It would be enough for him	سَيَكتَفِي

To follow up	مُتَابَعَةٍ
Comfortable	مُرِيحَةٍ
The silent majority	الأغْلَبِيَّةِ الصَّامِتَةِ

أسئلة:

1. Name the people involved in this conversation. Which are male and which are female?
2. Who will vote and who will not?
3. What type of election is it?
4. What reasons are given for not voting?
5. Who is illegible to vote?
6. What reasons are given for voting?
7. How do people decide whom to vote for according to this conversation?
8. Will anyone be upset if his chosen candidate does not succeed in the election?
9. How do his friends help him overcome the feared disappointment of his choice?
10. How does a voter find his polling station?
11. Do you need your national security number to vote?
12. Can you use your national security number to find your nearest polling station?
13. Can you find your nearest polling station with your cell phone?
14. Is there a hotline that you can use to find your nearest polling station?
15. Is there usually a long line of people waiting to vote at a polling station?
16. Are there a lot candidates running in this election?
17. One of the friends said he is a member of the Couch Party. What does he mean?

رَجَّحَ وَزِيرُ التَّنْمِيَةِ الرِّيفِيَّةِ الْمُورِيتانِيُّ مُحَمَّد الْمُخْتَار وَلَد مُبَارَك أَنْ تَتَمَكَّنَ بِلادُهُ مِنْ إِنْتَاج أَكْثَرَ مِنْ 65% مِنْ حاجاتِهَا الْغِذائِيَّةِ هَذِهِ السَّنَةَ.

The Mauritanian Minister of Rural Development Mohamed Mokhtar Walad Mubarak anticipated that his country could produce more than 65% of the food it needs this year

وَعَزَا الْوَزِيرُ التَّطَوُّرَ فِي الْإِنْتَاجِ الزِّرَاعِيِّ فِي بِلَادِهِ إِلَى التَّنْظِيمَاتِ وَالتَّحْسِينَاتِ الزِّرَاعِيَّةِ الْجَدِيدَةِ الَّتِي اتَّبَعَتْهَا وَزَارَةُ الزِّرَاعَةِ، وَالَّتِي مِنْ شَأْنِهَا أَنْ تُمَكِّنَ مِنْ زِيَادَةِ إِنْتَاجِ مُورِيتَانِيَا مِنَ الْحُبُوبِ، فِيمَا يُعْتَبَرُ خُطْوَةً "نَوْعِيَّةً غَيْرَ مَسْبُوقَةٍ" فِي الْبِلَادِ.

The Minister attributed the development in his country's agricultural production to the regulations and new agricultural improvements that the Ministry of Agriculture followed, enabling Mauritania to increase its production of grain, regarded as an unprecedented measure within the country.

وَأَوْضَحَ وَلَد مُبَارَك فِي كَلِمَةٍ بَثَّتْهَا الْإِذَاعَةُ الْمُورِيتَانِيَّةُ أَنَّ الْحُكُومَةَ خَطَّطَتْ لِإِنْتَاجِيَّةٍ قَوِيَّةٍ لِتَغْطِيَةِ 66% مِنْ حَاجَةِ الْبِلَادِ مِنَ الْمُنْتَجَاتِ الزِّرَاعِيَّةِ مِنَ الْحُبُوبِ، خَاصَّةً الْأُرْزَ وَالْقَمْحَ.

Walad Mubarak pointed out in a speech that was broadcast by Mauritanian radio, that the government claimed a strong productivity that covers 66% of the country's need of agriculture grain products, particularly rice and wheat.

أَنَا أُحِبُّ الْكُشَرِي

سُوزَانُ وَصَفَاءُ فِي الْقَاهِرَةِ، يَتَجَوَّلَانِ فِيْ وَسَطِ الْبَلَدِ (وَسَطِ الْمَدِينَةِ).

This topic is about koshery. This is an Egyptian dish but you can eat it across the Arab world. The vocabulary in this section is about eating koshery.

سوزان: لَقَدْ تَسَوَّقْنَا الْانَ بِمَا فِيهِ الْكِفَايَةِ، وَاشْتَرَيْتُ الْهَدَايَا لِلْعَائِلَةِ فِي أَمْرِيكَا.

صفاء: انَّ الأشْيَاءَ الفِرْعَونِيَةَ وَالتَمَاثِيلَ الصَّغِيرَةَ وَالحَقَائِبَ وَاوْرَاقَ البَرْدِيِّ المُلَوَنَةَ تُعَدُّ هَدَايَا مِثَالِيَةً لِلأَصْدِقَاءِ وَالأَقرِبَاءِ.

سوزان: أنَا جَائِعَةٌ جِداً، وَلاَ أَصْبِرُ عَلَى الطَّعَامِ (بَطْنِي تُصَوصِو).

صفاء: هَا هُوَ مَحَلُّ أَبُو طَارِقٍ لِلكُشَرِي، أَكلَةٌ مِصْرِيَةٌ أَصِيلَةٌ، وَأَكثرُ المَحَلاتِ شُهْرَةً بِإعْدَادِ الكُشَرِي الشَهِي سَتأَكلِين أَصَابِعَكِ وَرَاءَهُ.

صفاء: يَا جَرْسُون مِنْ فَضْلِكَ أَرِيدُ طَبَقَيْنِ كَبِيرَيْنِ مِنَ الكُشَرِي.

سوزان: مِمَ يَتَكَوَّنُ طَبَقُ الكُشَرِي؟

صفاء للجرسون: أَرْزٌ وَمَكرُونَةٌ وَعَدْسٌ أَسْوَدٌ (عَدْسٌ بِجَبَّةٍ) وَالحُمُّصُ، مُكَوِّنَاتٌ سَاخِنَةٌ وَعَلَيهَا اِضَافَاتُ الدَّقَةِ بِالثَّوْمِ وَهِيَ مَزِيجُ الخَلِّ بِالثَّوْمِ، وَاِضَافَاتٌ مِنَ الصَّلصَةِ أَو الشَّطَةِ الحَرَّاقَةِ (المُشَطشَطَةِ) أَو إِضَافَاتٍ مِنَ البَصَلِ المَبْشُورِ المَقلِّي المُقَرْمَشِ .

بَعْدَ الغَدَاءِ فِي مَطْعَمِ أَبُو طَارِقٍ لِلكُشَرِي:

سوزان: مممم ...أَكلْتُ كَثِيراً حَتَّى انِّي أَعْتَقِدُ انَّ بَطْنِي سَيَنْفَجِرُ، هههه، أَشْعُرُ بِالشَّطَةِ فِي فَمِي، اِنَّ فَمِي يَحْتَرِقُ!!!

صفاء: الانَ وَقْتُ طَبَقِ الرِزِ بِالحَلِيبِ، انَّهُ طَبَقُ الحُلْوُ هُنَا، سَيُهَدِّئُ الحَرِيقَ فِي فَمِكِ هههه.

سوزان: الانَ أَصْبَحْتُ مِنْ عُشَاقِ الكُشَرِي المِصْرِي، كُشَرِي، كُشَرِي، سُوزان تُحِّبُ الكُشَرِي.

صفاء: أَلَمْ أَقُلْ لَكِ أَنَّهُ لَذِيذٌ جِداً ؟، كَمَا أَنَّهُ رَخِيصٌ فِعْلاً، ثَمَنُهُ الانَ لاَيَتَجَاوَزُ سَبْعَةَ اوْ ثَمَانِيَةَ جُنَيْهَاتٍ، وَبِالاضَافَاتِ وَالحُلوِ يُمْكِنُكِ أَنْ تَدْفَعِي مَا بَيْنَ خَمْسَةَ عَشَرَ الَى عِشرِينَ جُنَيْهاً مِصْرِياً.

الكلمات الجديدة

معناها	الكلمة
Koshery	الكُشَرِي
They are strolling / roaming	يَتَجَوَلُونَ
Downtown	وَسَطِ البَلَدِ
We shop	تَسَوَقنَا
The things / items	الأَشْيَاءَ
Pharaonic	الفِرْعَونِيَةَ
The statues	التَمَاثِيلَ
Papyrus	اوْرَاقَ البَرْدِيِّ
Ideal	مِثَالِيَةً
I can't wait to eat	لاَ أَصْبِرُ عَلَى الطَّعَامِ
Authentic	أَصِيلَةٌ
Finger licking' good: literally, you will eat your fingers afterwards	ستأكلين أَصَابِعَكِ وَرَاءَهُ
Black lentils	عَدْسٌ أَسْوَدٌ

191

Ingredients	مُكَوِّنَاتٌ
Additions	إِضَافَاتٌ
Hot pepper	الشَّطَّةِ الحَرَّاقَةِ
Very hot sauce	المُشَطْشَطَة
I think my stomach will blow up	اِنِّي أَعْتَقِدُ اَنَّ بَطْنِي سَيَنْفَجِرُ
Grated	المَبْشُورِ
Fried	المَقَلِّي
Crispy	المُقَرْمَش
Burns	يَحْتَرِقُ
Rice pudding	الرُزِ بِالحَلِيبِ
Will soothe the fire in your mouth	سَيُهَدِّئُ الحَرِيقَ فِي فَمِكِ
Dessert	الحُلْوُ
Cheap	رَخِيصٌ
Pounds	جُنَيْهَات

أَسْئِلَة:

1. For whom have Susan and Safaa gone shopping?

2. What do they buy?

3. Who do they intent to give gifts to?

4. In which country are the recipients of their gifts?

5. Which of the friends feel hungry first?

6. How do you say in Arabic, "my stomach is rumbling?"

7. Which type of food do they eat? What is the name of the restaurant?

8. Is this restaurant famous?

9. How do you say in Arabic that something is delicious?

10. Does this restaurant have table service?

11. Do they order the same food?

12. What are the ingredients of the dish they order?

13. After they finish eating, are they still hungry?

14. Is the food they eat spicy?

15. What do they eat for dessert?

16. How much should you expect to pay for koshery at this restaurant?

يَتَبَنَّى مَشْرُوعُ الدُّسْتُورِ التُّونُسِيِّ الْجَدِيدِ قِيَمَ الدَّوْلَةِ الْمَدَنِيَّةِ وَحُرِّيَّةَ الْمُعْتَقَدِ وَالضَّمِيرِ، وَاسْتَبْعَدَ فِي فُصُولِهِ النَّصَّ عَلَى أَنَّ الشَّرِيعَةَ الْإِسْلَامِيَّةَ مَصْدَرٌ أَسَاسِيٌّ لِلتَّشْرِيعِ، وَهِيَ مَضَامِينُ تَوَافَقَتْ عَلَيْهَا الْكُتَلُ دَاخِلَ الْمَجْلِسِ الْوَطَنِيِّ التَّأْسِيسِيِّ، غَيْرَ أَنَّهَا لَا تَزَالُ مَحَلَّ جَدَلٍ.

وَصَادَقَ نُوَّابُ الْبَرْلَمَانِ عَلَى الْبَابِ الْأَوَّلِ الْمُتَعَلِّقِ بِالْمَبَادِئِ الْعَامَّةِ الَّذِي يَنُصُّ عَلَى أَنَّ "تُونُسَ دَوْلَةٌ حُرَّةٌ مُسْتَقِلَّةٌ ذَاتُ سِيَادَةٍ، الْإِسْلَامُ دِينُهَا وَالْجُمْهُورِيَّةُ نِظَامُهَا".

وَرَغْمَ أَنَّ نَائِبَيْنِ مِنْ حِزْبِ حَرَكَةِ النَّهْضَةِ الَّذِي يَمْتَلِكُ أَغْلَبِيَّةَ الْمَقَاعِدِ اقْتَرَحَا أَنْ يَنُصَّ الْفَصْلُ الْأَوَّلُ عَلَى أَنَّ الْقُرْآنَ وَالسُّنَّةَ مَصْدَرٌ أَسَاسِيٌّ لِتَشْرِيعِ الْقَوَانِينِ، فَإِنَّ غَالِبِيَّةَ النُّوَّابِ رَفَضُوا النَّصَّ عَلَى أَنَّ الشَّرِيعَةَ الْإِسْلَامِيَّةَ جَوْهَرُ التَّشْرِيعِ.

The new Tunisian draft constitution adopts the values of the civil state and the freedom of religion and conscience. It has ruled out the stipulation that Islamic law is the essential source of legislation. This is agreed on by the members of the parties within the National Constituent Assembly, but it is still the subject of controversy.

The first section on general principles has been rectified by the MPs. These principles state "Tunisia is a free, independent, sovereign state. Islam is its religion and its system of government is republican".

Although two deputies from the Party of Renaissance Movement, which has a majority of seats in parliament, suggested that the first chapter states that the Quran and the Sunna is an essential source for legislation of laws, the majority of the House of Representatives refused this provision that the Islamic Sharia law is an integral part of the essence of legislation.

الإسكايب

We have a conversation here between a woman, her mother and her sister. They are talking over Skype and are comparing the different climates where they each are. New vocabulary will be weather-related.

الحوار

شيرين: أُمِّي، سَأُكَلِّمُ أُخْتِي نُور عَلَى الانْتَرنِتِ عَلَى بَرْنَامَجِ الاسْكَايبِي، الآنَ فَرْقُ التَّوْقِيتِ مُنَاسِبٌ بَيْنَنَا وَبَيْنَ كَنَدَا لِنَتَحَدَّثَ.

الأم: صَحِيحٌ، رَائِعٌ، لَقَد أوحَشْتِنِي كَثِيراً.

شيرين: تَعَالِي يَا أُمِّي، نُورٌ عَلَى الكَامِيرَا الآنَ، هَيَّا.

الأُمُّ: نُور، كَيفَ حَالُكِ يَا بِنتِي، وَكَيفَ حَالُ ابنِكِ؟

نور: الحَمْدُ للهِ يَا أُمِّي، كَيفَ حَالُكُم في مِصرَ؟

الأم: الحَمْدُ لله، لِمَاذّا تلبَسِينَ مِعطَفاً ثَقِيلاً، وَمَا هَذِهِ الثُّلُوجُ البَيضَاءُ التَّي وَرَاءَكِ؟ هَلْ الجَو بَارِدٌ؟

نور: أنَا أحَدِّثُكِ عَبرَ المُوبَايلِ مِنَ الجَامِعَةِ، وَنَحْنُ الآنَ في فصلِ الشِّتَاءِ، وَالبَرْدُ قَارِسٌ هُنَا.

الأم: سُبحَانَ الله، أخُوكِ في السُّعُودِيَةِ، وَالجَو هُنَاكَ حَارٌ جِداً، هُم في فصلِ الصَّيفِ، وَعِندَهُم عَوَاصِفُ رَمليَةٌ وَزَعَابِيبُ عَاصِفَةٌ، وَالرِّيحُ شَدِيدَةٌ، حَتَّى أنَّ شَرِكَاتِ الطَّيَرَانِ مَنَعَت الطَّائِرَاتِ لِوجُودِ رِياحٍ شَّدِيدَةٍ، أَتَمَنَى أن تَنزِلَ الأمطَارُ فَتُنَقِيَ الهَوَاءَ مِنَ الأترِبَةِ، عُمُوماً المُنَاخُ في السُّعُودِيَةِ لَيسَ مُمطِراً.

نور: يَبدُو أنَّ ذَلِكَ فَصْلُ الخَرِيفِ الذي يَلِي فَصْلَ الصَّيفِ يَاأُمِّي.

شيرين: مَعَكِ حَقٌّ يَاأختي، وَأعَانَكِ الله حتَّى فَصْلِ الرَّبيعِ الجَميلِ.

نور: الحَمدُ لله يَاشِيرِينَ، نَحنُ أفضَلُ مِن غَيرِنَا، هَلْ سَمِعتِي عَن اعصَارِ سَانِدِي بِأمريكَا عَلَى السَّواحِلِ الشَّرِقيَّةِ؟

شيرين: نَعَم، سَمعتُ وَشَاهَدتُ فِي نَشرَةِ الأخبَارِ وَ الأرصَادِ الجوّيَّةِ.

نور: أختُ زَوجي هُنَاكَ وقَلِقنَا عَلَيهَا، قَالَت لَنا أنَّهَا رِيَاحٌ شَديدَةٌ سُرعَتُهَا كَبيرَةٌ جِداً، صَاحَبَهَا بَرقٌ وَرَعدٌ وعَوَاصِفٌ وَفَيضَانَاتٌ، وَتَكثُرُ السُّحُبُ والغُيُومُ بِشَكلٍ مُفَاجِئٍ.

الأم: الحَمدُ لله عَلَى سَلامَتِهِم يَا بِنتِي.

نور: اوحَشَتِني مِصْرُ وأوحَشَنِي جَوهَا المُعتَدِلُ.

الكلمات الجديدة

الكلمة	معناها
الجَوُّ	Atmosphere, weather.
مَا أحلَى جَوِّك يَا بَلَدِي!	How wonderful the weather in my country!

197

Skype	الاسكَايِي
Time Difference	فَرْقُ التَّوقِيتِ
Via Mobile	عَبرَ المُوبَايِلِ
Storms	عَوَاصِفُ
Sand storm	زَعَابِيبُ
Purify	تُنَقِّي
Dust	الأَترِبَةِ
Climate	المُنَاخُ
Eastern coast	السَّواحِلِ الشَّرقِيَةِ
Meteorology	الأرصادِ الجوِيَةِ
Lightning	بَرق
Thunder	رَعدٌ
Flooding	فَيضَانَاتٌ
Cloud	السُّحُبُ
Clouds	الغُيُوم
Surprisingly	بِشَكلٍ مُفَاجِئٍ
Moderate	المُعتَدِلُ

أسئلة:

1. What are the names of the two sisters in this conversation?
2. Why does the mother choose this time to talk to her daughter?
3. How are they communicating in this conversation?
4. Does the mother miss her absent daughter?
5. In which country is her absent daughter?
6. Was the mother present at the beginning of the call?
7. Does the absent daughter have any children?
8. Where is the absent daughter originally from?
9. What was the absent daughter wearing when she appeared on the screen?
10. Was she indoors or outdoors?
11. Where exactly is the absent daughter calling from?
12. In which season is this conversation taking place?
13. How is the weather where the absent daughter is?
14. Where is the absent daughter's brother?
15. How is the weather where the brother is?
16. Why are the airlines grounding their planes where the brother is?
17. Why does the mother wish for rain where her son is?
18. Why does the mother get the season wrong where her son is?
19. Why do all three consider themselves lucky they are not on the east coast of the United States?
20. How did they hear about Hurricane Sandy?
21. Which one of them was in the United States? How does she describe the storm to the others?
22. What does the absent daughter miss most about her country of origin?

تَشْهَدُ مَنَاطِقُ شَمَالِ شَرْقِ الْوِلَايَاتِ الْمُتَّحِدَةِ تَسَاقُطًا كَثِيفًا لِلثُّلُوجِ أَدَّى إِلَى مَقْتَلِ عَدَدٍ مِن الْأَشْخَاصِ وَإِلْغَاءِ رِحْلَاتٍ جَوِّيَّةٍ وَإِغْلَاقِ الْمَدَارِسِ وَالْمَكَاتِبِ الْحُكُومِيَّةِ، خَاصَّةً فِي مَدِينَةِ بُوسْطُن الَّتِي تَبْدُو الْأَكْثَرَ تَأَثُّرًا بِأَوَّلِ عَاصِفَةٍ شَتْوِيَّةٍ كَبِيرَةٍ عَلَى الْمِنْطَقَةِ هَذَا الْعَامَ.

وَبَلَغَ سُمْكُ طَبَقَةِ الْجَلِيدِ فِي بُوسْطُن 45 سَنْتِيمِتْرًا تَقْرِيبًا، كَمَا تَرَاكَمَ فِي بَعْضِ الْبَلَدَاتِ إِلَى الشَّمَالِ مِنْهَا وَاقْتَرَبَ مِنْ مُسْتَوَى سِتِّينَ سَنْتِيمِتْرًا.

وَقَدْ غَطَّى الْجَلِيدُ أَيْضًا مُدُنًا كُبْرَى وَوَصَلَ ارْتِفَاعُهُ فِي نِيُويُورْكَ إِلَى 15 سَنْتِيمِتْرًا.

وَذَكَرَتْ هَيْئَةُ الْأَرْصَادِ الْجَوِّيَّةِ أَنَّ دَرَجَةَ الْحَرَارَةِ بِمِينِيسُوتَا انْخَفَضَتْ إِلَى 38 دَرَجَةً مِئَوِيَّةً تَحْتَ الصِّفْرِ، وَهِيَ أَقَلُّ دَرَجَةِ حَرَارَةٍ مُسَجَّلَةٍ فِي الْوِلَايَاتِ الْمُتَّحِدَةِ خَارِجَ وِلَايَةِ أَلَاسْكَا أَمْسِ الْجُمْعَةَ.

The northeastern regions of the United States have witnessed heavy snowfall that has led to the deaths of a number of people, cancelled flights and closing schools and government offices. The worst affected area is the city of Boston in this the first big winter storm in the region this year.

The total thickness of the snowfall in Boston is almost 45 centimeters, and accumulation in certain towns to the north has approached the level of sixty centimeters.

The snow has also covered the major cities and in New York has reached a height of 15 centimeters.

The Meteorological Agency said that the temperature dropped to 38 degrees Celsius below zero in Minnesota yesterday (Friday), the lowest temperature recorded in the United States outside of Alaska.

مَدْرَسَةُ هَامِلتُون هَايتس الابْتِدَائِيَة

There is a school in New York City that started to experiment with teaching Arabic to children. This article gives details about this experiment and describes how the parents of the children reacted to it .

تَبْدَأُ مَدْرَسَةٌ ابْتِدَائِيَةٌ حُكُومِيَةٌ مَحْدُودَةُ المَوَارِدِ، فِي حَيِّ "هَارلم" الشَّهِيرِ فِي مَدِينَةِ نِيويُورك، تَجرِبَةً لِتَعْلِيمِ الأَطْفَالِ اللُّغَةَ العَرَبِيَةَ أَثْنَاءَ اسْتِرَاحَةِ فَتْرَةِ الغَدَاءِ اليَومِيَةِ، ذَلِكَ إِذا رَغِبَ أَولِيَاءُ الأُمُورِ فِي اسْتِغْلالِ هَذِهِ الفُرْصَةِ السَّانِحَةِ لأَطْفَالِهِم.

فَمَدْرَسَةُ هَامِلتُون هَايتس الابْتِدَائِيَةِ لِلأَطْفَالِ الوَاقِعَةِ فِي حَيِّ "هَارلم" الشَّهِيرِ - وَهُوَ وَاحِدٌ مِنْ أَفْقَرِ أَحْيَاءِ مَدِينَةِ نِيويُورك - تَسْتَطِيعُ الآنَ أَنْ تَتَبَاهَى بِأَنَّهَا المَدْرَسَةُ الابْتِدَائِيَةُ الوَحِيدَةُ فِي المَدِينَةِ، التِّي تَعْرِضُ عَلَى تَلامِيذِهَا الصِّغَارِ خَيَارَ

تَعَلُّمِ اللُّغَةِ العَرَبِيَّةِ، ابْتِدَاءً مِنَ الخَرِيفِ القَادِمِ، كَفَعَالِيَاتٍ ثَقَافِيَّةٍ تُجْرَى أَثْنَاءَ اسْتِرَاحَةِ الغَدَاءِ.

وَمِنْ جَانِبِهِ، قَالَ مُحَمَّدٌ مَمْدُوح، وَهُوَ مُدَرِّسٌ لِلُّغَةِ العَرَبِيَّةِ "هَذِهِ المُبَادَرَةُ مِنْ قِبَلِ هَذِهِ المَدْرَسَةِ تَمَّتْ بِتَشْجِيعٍ وَتَمْوِيلٍ عَرَبِي، عَلَى أَمَلِ إِعْطَاءِ أَطْفَالِ الأُسَرِ المَحْدُودَةِ الدَّخْلَ فِي هَذَا الحَيِّ فُرْصَةً أَكْبَرَ لِلْتَنَافُسِ مُسْتَقْبَلاً فِي المَدَارِسِ الثَّانَوِيَّةِ وَالجَامِعَاتِ، فَـ77% مِنْ أُسَرِ هَؤُلَاءِ الأَطْفَالِ تَعْتَمِدُ فِي عَيْشِهَا عَلَى المَعُونَاتِ الحُكُومِيَّةِ.

أَمَّا بِلَامُون كَاسْتْرُو، وَهِيَ وَالِدَةُ أَحَدِ الأَطْفَالِ المُسَجَّلِينَ لِتَعَلُّمِ اللُّغَةِ العَرَبِيَّةِ فَعَلَّقَتْ قَائِلَةً: "أَعْرَاقُ التَّلَامِيذِ بَاتَتْ مُتَنَوِّعَةً الآنَ، وَمِنَ المُهِمِّ أَنْ يَتَعَلَّمَ تَلَامِيذُنَا، وَمِنْ بَيْنِهِمْ ابْنِي، لُغَاتُ الأَعْرَاقِ الأُخْرَى لِكَيْ نُصْبِحَ جُزْءًا مِنْهُمْ، وَيُصْبِحُونَ هُمْ جُزْءًا مِنْ مُجْتَمَعِنَا.

وَيُذْكَرُ أَنَّ 14% فَقَطْ مِنْ طُلَّابِ الوِلَايَاتِ المُتَّحِدَةِ يَتَحَدَّثُونَ لُغَتَيْنِ مُخْتَلِفَتَيْنِ، مُقَارَنَةً بِـ80% مِنَ الطُّلَّابِ فِي القَارَّةِ الأُورُوبِّيَّةِ، وَلِذَا رَحَّبَتِ الحُكُومَةُ المَحَلِّيَّةُ بِهَذِهِ المُبَادَرَةُ مِنْ خِلَالِ مُفَوَّضَةِ شُؤُونِ المُهَاجِرِينَ الَّتِي تَنْحَدِرُ نَفْسُهَا مِنْ جُذُورٍ عَرَبِيَّةٍ.

وَفِي هَذَا الصَّدَدِ قَالَتْ فَاطِمَةُ شَمَا، مُفَوَّضَةُ شُؤُونِ اللَّاجِئِينَ فِي الحُكُومَةِ المَحَلِّيَّةِ لِمَدِينَةِ نِيُويُورك: "مَا نَفْعَلُهُ كُلَّ يَوْمٍ فِي مَدِينَتِنَا هُوَ إِعْدَادُ أَطْفَالِنَا لَا لِدُخُولِ الجَامِعَاتِ وَالتَّخَرُّجِ وَحَسْبْ، بَلْ لِكَيْ يُصْبِحُوا جُزْءًا مِنَ المُجْتَمَعِ الدُّوَلِيِّ الَّذِي نَحْنُ جُزْءٌ مِنْهُ.

وَهَذِهِ المَدْرَسَةُ الابْتِدَائِيَّةُ لَنْ تَعْرِضَ عَلَى تَلَامِيذِهَا فِي الخَرِيفِ القَادِمِ تَعَلُّمَ اللُّغَةِ العَرَبِيَّةِ فَحَسْبُ بَلِ الصِّينِيَّةَ أَيْضًا، وَهُمَا لُغَتَانِ صَنَّفَتْهُمَا وَزَارَةُ الخَارِجِيَّةِ الأَمْرِيكِيَّةِ بِأَنَّهُمَا ضَرُورِيَّتَانِ لِضَمَانِ تَنَافُسِيَّةِ المُنْتَجَاتِ الأَمْرِيكِيَّةِ فِي الأَسْوَاقِ التِّجَارِيَّةِ العَالَمِيَّةِ المُهِمَّةِ، وَسَتَزِيدُ وَلَا شَكَّ مِنْ فُرَصِ نَجَاحِ هَؤُلَاءِ الأَطْفَالِ فِي

حَيَاتِهِمْ العَمَلِيَةِ مُسْتَقْبَلاً، وَقَدْ تُشَجِّعُ هَذِهِ التَّجْرُبَةُ المَدَارِسَ الأُخْرَى عَلَى تَقْلِيدِهَا.

الكَلِمَاتُ الجَدِيدَة

معناها	الكَلِمَة
Government primary school	مَدْرَسَةٌ ابْتِدَائِيَةٌ حُكُومِيَةٌ
Limited resources	مَحْدُودَةُ المَوَارِدِ
A break	اسْتِرَاحَةٍ
Period	فَتْرَةٍ
Opportunity	السَّانِحَةِ
Exploitation	اسْتِغْلَالِ
braggart	تَتَبَاهَى
Choice	خَيَارَ

Events	كَفَعَالِيَاتٍ
Finance	تَمْوِيلٍ
Encouragement	تَشْجِيعٍ
Government aid	المَعُونَاتِ الحُكُومِيَةِ
Races / ethnicities	أَعْرَاقٌ
Mixed	مُتَنَوعَةً
Became	بَاتَتْ
The continent	القَارَةِ
Commissioner for immigration	مُفَوَضَةِ شِؤُونِ المُهَاجِرِينَ
Both are classified	صَنَفَتْهُمَا
Comparative	تَنَافُسِيَةِ
Encourage	تُشَجِعُ
Guarantee	ضَمَانٍ

أَسْئِلَة:

1. What is the name of the school?

2. In which part of New York City is the school located?

3. Is it a private or public school?

4. What part of the day was Arabic taught to the students?

5. Is it a mandatory or optional choice to learn Arabic in this school?

6. Is this the only elementary school in New York City that taught Arabic in New York City at the time this article was published?

7. According to the article, when was the Arabic program to begin?

8. The article quoted an Arabic language teacher. What is his name?

9. How would you rate the income level of the families of Hamilton Heights?

10. What is the ultimate goal of offering Arabic education to the children of this school?

11. Between Europeans and Americans, which group speaks more than one language?

12. Who is financing this initiative?

13. The article quoted a parent of one of the children who approved of this experiment. What did she say that supported the Arabic program at Hamilton Heights?

لَمْ يَجِدْ لُؤَيُّ الْخَمِيسِيُّ -الْبَاحِثُ فِي الشُّؤُونِ الاجْتِمَاعِيَّةِ وَالتَّارِيخِيَّةِ- مَنَاصًا مِنَ السِّبَاحَةِ ضِدَّ التَّيَّارِ السَّائِدِ فِي بَلَدِهِ، فَقَدْ وَجَدَ الْمُجْتَمَعَ الشَّبَابِيَّ الْجَامِعِيَّ أَفْضَلَ نُقْطَةٍ لِإِطْلَاقِ حُلْمِهِ، فَأَنْشَأَ بَادِئَ الْأَمْرِ نَوَاةً لِمَا أَطْلَقَ عَلَيْهِ اسْمَ "مَدْرَسَةِ الْحُبِّ وَالسَّلَامِ"، وَكَانَتِ الْمُفَاجَأَةُ كَبِيرَةً بِالنِّسْبَةِ لَهُ حِينَ رَأَى اسْتِجَابَةً مِنْ شَبَابِ الْبَصْرَةِ.

Louay Khamisi - a researcher at the Social and Historical Affairs Office – had little choice but to swim against the current situation in his country. He found that the collegial youth community was the best launching pad for his dream. He established initially a nucleus of what he called "a school of love and peace" For him the surprise was great for he saw the response of the young people of Basra.

الأَلوَان

This dialogue follows a conversation that takes place in a clothing store in a mall in which customers are shopping for different clothes items of different colors. In this lesson, you will learn the colors, clothes items and accessories.

سوزان: أَرِيدُ أَجْمَلَ فُسْتَانٍ أَبْيَضَ لِزَفَافِي، يَاانِسَة.

توم: وَهَلْ هُنَاكَ بَذلَةٌ سَوْدَاءُ أَنِيقَةٌ، وَحِذَاءٌ أَسْوَدُ أَنِيقٌ يَاانِسَة.

البائعة: نَعَمْ، تَفَضَّل.

توم: يَاالَهِي، اِنَّهَا رَائِعَةٌ سَأَضَعُ وَرْدَةً بَيْضَاءَ هُنَا.

سَيِّدَةٌ عَجُوزٌ مقاطِعَةً: مِنْ فَضْلِك نَحْنُ هُنَا مُنْذُ وَقْتٍ طَوِيلٍ، اريدُ ان اجَرِّبَ القُبَّعَةَ الصَّفْرَاءَ ذَاتَ الشَّرِيطِ الأَصْفَرِ اللامِعِ والرِيشَتَيْنِ الصَّفْرَاوَيْنِ، اِنَّهَا أَجْمَلُ مِن كُلِّ القُبَّعَاتِ الصَّفْرَاوَاتِ الَّتِي لَدَيْكِ' فَصُفْرَتُهَا مُخْتَلِفَةٌ.

البائعة: لَدَيَّ مَاهُوَ أَفْضَلُ، قُبَّعَةٌ زَرْقَاءُ ذَاتُ شَرِيطٍ أَزْرَقٍ وَرِيشَتَانِ زَرْقَاوَانِ، اِنَّهَا اجْمَلُ القُبَّعَاتِ الزَّرْقَاوَاتِ، فَزُرْقَتُهَا مُمَيَّزَةٌ.

السيدة العجوز: رَائِعَةٌ، اِنَّهَا تُنَاسِبُ مَلابِسِي الزَّرْقَاءَ كُلَّهَا.

على وزنها أَحْمَرُ وأَخْضَرُ وأَصْفَرُ وأَبْيَضٌ وأَسْوَدٌ.

لانَقُولُ (زَرْقَاوَتَانِ، بَيْضَاوَتَانِ، خَضْرَاوَتَانِ) نَقُولُ (زَرْقَاوَانِ، بَيْضَاوَانِ، خَضْرَاوَانِ) اعرَابُهُمَا اعرَابُ المُثَنَّى يُرْفَعُ بِالالِف ويُنْصَبُ ويُجَرُ بِالْيَاءِ...(زَرْقَاوَيْنِ، بَيْضَاوَيْنِ، خَضْرَاوَيْنِ) ...الخ

جين: جَدَّتِي، مَارَأَيْكِ فِي هَذَا الحِذَاءِ البُنِّي.

البائعة: يَاطِفْلَتِي الجَميلَةَ انَّ ذَوْقَكِ رَائِعٌ وَلَدَيكِ عَينَانِ بُنِّيَتَانِ جَميلَتَانِ، انَّ هَذَا الحِذَاءُ مِنْ أجْمَلِ الأحْذِيَةِ البُنِّيَةِ اللَّونِ في المَكَانِ.

على وزنها بَنَفْسَجِيٌّ، بُرْتُقَالِيٌّ، رَمَادِيٌّ، وَرْدِيٌّ، سَمَاوِيٌّ، عَاجِيٌّ (اوف وايت)، قَمْحِيٌّ، نُحَاسِيٌّ، ذَهَبِيٌّ، فِضِّيٌّ.

سيدة شابة: مِنْ فَضْلِكِ اريدُ تَجْرِبَةً هَذَا الفُسْتَان.

البائعة: اخْتِيَارٌ مُوَفَّقٌ فَلَوْنُهُ يُنَاسِبُ السَّيِّدَاتِ البَيْضَاوَاتِ كَثيراً

أمَّا السَّيِّدَاتِ السوداوَاتِ يُنَاسِبُهُنَّ هَذَا اللَّونُ.

السيدة الشابة: سَاعِدِيني أيْضاً في اخْتِيَارِ قَميصٍ لِزَوْجِي.

البائعة: أزَوجُكِ أبْيَضٌ أمْ أسْوَدٌ أمْ قَمْحِيُّ اللَّونِ؟

السيدة الشابة: انَّهُ أبْيَضٌ.

البائعة: اذاً هَذَا القَميصُ رَائِعٌ، يُنَاسِبُ الرِّجَالَ البيضَ،

وَهَذَا يُنَاسِبُ الرِّجَالَ السُّودَ،

أمَّا ذَاكَ فَيُنَاسِبُ الرِّجَالَ قَمْحِيَّةَ اللَّونِ بِشَكلٍ خَاصٍّ.

السيدة الشابة: أشْكُرُكِ كَثيراً.

لاحِظ (قَمحِيَّةَ اللَّونِ)، هَذِهِ الصيغَةُ لِلجَمْعِ وَمثلُ ذلِكَ نُحَاسِي، بُنِّيٌّ، فِضِّيٌّ....الخ.

209

الكلمات الجديدة

معناها	الكلمة
The Mall	المُولِ
Colors	الألوان
Dress	فُسْتَانٍ
My wedding	زِفَافِي
suit	بَذَلَةٌ
Elegant	أَنِيقَةٌ
Interrupting	مقَاطَعَةٌ
Hat	القَبَعَة
Yellow	الصَفرَاءَ
Tape	الشَرِيطِ
Glossy	اللامِعِ
Two feathers	الرِيشَتَينِ
Blue	زَرْقَاءُ
Red	أحْمَرٌ
Green	أخْضَرٌ

Yellow	أَصْفَرٌ
White	أَبْيَضٌ
Black	أَسْوَدٌ
Brown	البُنِّي
Your taste is wonderful	ذَوْقَكِ رَائِعٌ
Violet	بَنَفسَجيٌّ
Orange	بُرْتُقَالِيٌّ،
Gray	رَمَادِيٌّ
Pink	وَرْدِيٌّ
Sky blue	سَمَاوِيٌّ
Ivory	عَاجِيٌّ
tan	قَمْحِيٌّ
Coppery	نُحَاسِيٌّ
Golden	ذَهَبِيٌّ
Silver	فِضِّيٌّ
Try out	تَجْرِبَةً
I want to try out this dress	اريدُ تَجْرِبَةً هَذَا الفُسْتَانِ
Good choice	اخْتِيَارٌ مُوَفَّقٌ

أسئلة:

1. What is the color of the dress that Susanne wants to buy for her wedding?

2. What is the color of the suit and shoes that Tom wants to buy?

3. What did the salesperson show to him?

4. What will Tom put in his suit?

5. Why was the old woman agitated?

6. What was the color of the hat she wanted to try on?

7. What distinguished this particular hat?

8. Why did the old woman think that this hat was prettier than other hats of the same color?

9. The salesperson offered the older woman a different color hat. What color was it?

10. Did the older woman like the hat? Why or why not?

11. What color are the shoes that Jeanne is looking at and what color are her eyes?

12. When the young woman asked to try on a dress, why did the saleswoman consider it an excellent choice?

13. A young woman asked the saleswoman to help in finding a shirt for her husband. Why was the color of his skin in a factor in the saleswoman's recommendation?

هَلْ تُحِبُّ القِرَاءَةَ؟

مُتعَتِي وَجَدتُهَا فِي القِرَاءةِ، إنَّهَا هِوَايَتِي

This is a conversation between friends about their reading hobby in which they are debating the benefits of reading.

سمير: حَسَناً، سَأذهَبُ اليَومَ الَى مَكتَبَةِ الاسْكَندَريةِ، هَلْ يُريدُ أَحَدٌ الذَّهَابَ مَعِي؟

أَحْمَد: رَائِع، أَنَا أُحِبُّ القِرَاءَةَ جِداً، وَمَكتَبَةُ الاسكَندَريةِ بِهَا كُتُبٌ وَمَرَاجِعٌ، وَمُؤَلَفَاتٌ وَأبحَاثٌ وَرِوَايَاتٌ وَقِصَصٌ وَمَجَلَّاتٌ وصُحُفٌ وَخَرَائِطٌ وَتَسجِيلاتٌ كَثِيرَةٌ وَمُفِيدَةٌ.

213

سمير: أمينُ المَكتَبَةِ في قِسمِ الأدبِّ العَرَبيُّ مُتعَاوِنٌ وَمُثَقَفٌ، وَيَطلُبُ التِزامَ الهُدوءِ مِن رُوّادِ المَكتَبَةِ، وَسَاعَدَني مَرَّةً في مَدِّ فَترَةِ الاستِعَارَةِ لِكُتُبٍ نَسِيتُ مَوعِدَ اعَادَتِهَا وتَسلِيمِهَا.

أحمد: سأذهَبُ مَعَكَ يَا سَمير، وَأنتَ يَا عُمَر، هَل تَذهَبُ مَعَنَا؟

عمر: لا، أنَا لأُحِبُّ القِرَاءَةَ، وَلِمَاذَا أقرَأ وَالانتَرِنتُ مِوجُودٌ؟ كُلُّ مَاابحَثُ عَنهُ أجدُهُ بِضغطَةِ زِرٍ.

أحمد: الانتَرِنتُ يُوفِّرُ المَعلُومَةَ السَّريعَةَ وَنَحنُ نَحتَاجُ المَعلُومَاتِ مِنْ مَصَادِرِهَا الأصلِيَةَ.

عمر: هَل تَعلَم أنَّهُ يُمكِنُكَ قِرَاءَةُ كِتَابٍ عَلَى جِهَازِ الكُمبيوتَر؟

أحمد: شكراً، أحِبُّ أنْ أمسِكَ بِالكِتَابِ بِيَدِي وَأقلِبَ الصَّفَحَاتِ بِنَفسِي.

سمير: اترُكهُ عَلَى رَاحَتِهِ يَا أحمَد، وَقُل لِي، أيُّ لَونٍ مِنَ الكُتُبِ تَقرَأُ؟ الأدَبِيَةُ أم العِلمِيَةُ أم الجُغرَافيَةُ أم التَّاريخِيَةُ أم العُلُومُ الانسانِيَةُ كَعِلمِ النَفسِ أم العُلُومُ الاجتِمَاعِيَةُ كَعِلمِ الاجتماعِ أم الطِّبُّ وَالصِّحّةُ أم الشِّعرُ وَالقصائِدُ أم الهِوايَاتُ أم الرِّيَاضَةُ أم اللُّغَاتُ أم الفُنُونُ المُختَلِفَةُ.

أحمد: أنا أحِبُّ الرِّوَايَاتِ البُوليسِيَةِ كَرَجُلِ المُستَحيلِ وَالخَيَالَ العَلمِي وَالأدَبَ المَسرَحِي، وَأُختِي مُنى تُحِبُّ كُتُبَ الطَّبخِ وَالزِراعَةِ وَالتجميلِ وَتَربِيَةِ الحَيَوَانَاتِ الأليفَةِ وَالطُّيورِ.

سمير: أنا أقرَأُ أدَبَ نَجيبٍ مَحفُوظٍ وَعَبَّاسِ العَقَّادِ وَالمَنفَلُوطِي وَالأدَبَ الغَربِي لِشِكسبيرٍ وَهِيمِنجوَاي.

214

أحمد: هَيَّا بِنَا الَى المَكتَبَةِ لِنقرأَ، سَأَساعِدُكَ فأَنَا اعرِفُ كُلَّ اقسَامِ المَكتَبَةِ وَرُفوفِهَا، وَنَترُكَ عُمَرَ العَنيدَ الجَاهِلَ بِأَهَمِيَةِ كُنُوزِ المَعرِفَةِ الحَقيقِيَةِ.

الكلماتُ الجديدة

معناها	الكلمة
My pleasure, do not use it as a response to thank you.	مُتعَتِي
And her grandmother	وجَدتُهَا
Check	مَرَاجِعٌ
Books	مُؤَلَفَاتٌ
Research	أبحَاثٌ
Novels	رِوَايَاتٌ
Stories	قِصَصٌ
Magazines	مَجَلَّاتٌ
Newspapers	صُحُفٌ

Maps	خَرائِطُ
Recordings	تَسجِيلاتٌ
Useful	مُفِيدَة
Librarian	أَمِينُ المَكتَبَةِ
Collaborator	مُتَعَاوِنٌ
Cultured	مُثَقَّفٌ
Commitment	الْتِزَامَ
Calm	الهُدُوءِ
Library patron	رُوَادِ المَكتَبَةِ
Extension	مَدِّ
Period metaphor	فَتْرَةِ الاستِعَارَةِ
Rapid information	المَعلُومَةَ السَرِيعَةَ
Original sources	مَصَادِرِهَا الأصلِيَةَ
And reading through pages	وَأَقلِبَ الصّفَحَاتِ
Leave it to comfort	اترُكهُ عَلَى رَاحَتِهِ
Literary	الأَدَبِيَةُ
Scientific	العِلمِيَةُ
Geographic	الجُغرافِيَةُ
Historical	التَّارِيخِيَةُ
Humanities	العُلُومُ الانسَانِيَةُ
Psychology	عِلمِ النَفسِ
Social Sciences	العُلُومُ الاجتِمَاعِيَةُ

As a science meeting	كَعِلْمِ الاجتِماعِ
Medicine	الطِّبُّ
Health	وَالصِّحَّةُ
Hair	الشِّعرُ
And poems	والقَصائدُ
Interests	الهِوايَاتُ
Sports	الرِّيَاضَةُ
Languages	اللُّغَاتُ
Various arts	الفُنُونُ المُختَلِفَةُ
Detective novels	الرِّوَايات البُوليسِيةِ
Sci-fi	الخَيَالَ العَلمِي
Dramatic Literature	الأدَبَ المَسرَحِي
Cooking	الطَّبخِ
And Agriculture	وَالزِراعَةِ
And cosmetics	والتَجميلِ
Breeding of pets	تَربِيةِ الحَيَوانَاتِ الأليفَةِ
Birds	الطُّيورِ
Western literature	الأدَبَ الغَربِي
Departments Library	اقسَامِ المَكتَبَةِ
Shelves	رُفوفِهَا
Stubborn	العَنِيدَ
Ignorant	الجَاهِلَ

أَسْئِلَة:

1. What is the name of the library that Samir is going to visit?
2. Who decided to go with him?
3. What distinguishes this library?
4. How would you describe the librarian at the Arabic literature section?
5. How often does he help people who forgot to return their books on their due dates?
6. How many people are going to the library all together?
7. What is the name of the person who does not like to read due to the availability of information on the internet?
8. Which one of the friends likes to read crime fiction?
9. Give examples of some of the books he likes to read.
10. Who likes to read science fiction?
11. What types of books does Mona like to read?
12. Who likes to read books by Hemmingway and Shakespeare?

تَعِجُّ بَنْغَازِي كُبْرَى مُدُنِ شَرْقِ لِيبْيَا بِالْحَرَكَةِ لَيْلًا ونَهَارًا، وَلَا يَكَادُ يُرَى فِيهَا أَثَرٌ لِفَوْضَى أَوِ انْفِلَاتٍ. لَكِنَّ الْحَيَاةَ الَّتِي تَنْبِضُ بِهَا الْمَدِينَةُ تُكَدِّرُ صَفْوَهَا أَعْمَالُ الْعُنْفِ الْمُتَوَاتِرَةُ الَّتِي تَسْتَهْدِفُ الْأَجْهِزَةَ الْأَمْنِيَّةَ وَبَعْضَ مُؤَسَّسَاتِ الدَّوْلَةِ وَالَّتِي تُثِيرُ قَلَقَ السُّكَّانِ.

إِلَّا أَنَّ ذَلِكَ لَا يَمْنَعُهُمْ مِنْ مُمَارَسَةِ حَيَاتِهِمْ بِصُورَةٍ طَبِيعِيَّةٍ. فَالْعَدِيدُ مِنَ الشَّوَارِعِ تَشْهَدُ حَرَكَةَ سَيْرٍ كَثِيفَةً فِي أَغْلَبِ سَاعَاتِ النَّهَارِ.

وَتَدِبُّ الْحَرَكَةُ فِي الْمَقَاهِي وَالْمَحَالِّ التِّجَارِيَّةِ فِي كُلِّ أَنْحَاءِ الْمَدِينَةِ مُنْذُ الصَّبَاحِ، وَيُقْبِلُ النَّاسُ عَلَى التَّبَضُّعِ حَتَّى سَاعَاتِ اللَّيْلِ الْأُولَى غَيْرَ آبِهِينَ بِقِصَصٍ تُرْوَى عَنِ اعْتِدَاءَاتٍ بِهَدَفِ السَّلْبِ تَحْدُثُ بَيْنَ الْفَيْنَةِ وَالْأُخْرَى.

Benghazi, the largest city in eastern Libya, is teeming with activity night and day. You hardly see the effect of the chaos and lawlessness, but the life that the city is pulsating with acts of violence targeting security forces and state institutions, which worry the population.

However, this does not prevent them from exercising their lives normally. Many of the streets experience heavy traffic at most hours of the day.

Signs of life start in the coffee shops and stores all over the city in the morning. People continue shopping until the early hours of the night without caring about the stories of looting which occur from time to time.

أَنَا بَطَلٌ رِيَاضِيٌّ

This conversation is about sport. The administrator in a sports club is registering new members. In this lesson, you will learn vocabulary relating to different sports activities and names of sports.

مَسؤُولُ النَّشَاطِ الرِّياضِي: اعلانٌ هَامٌّ لِأَعْضَاءِ النَّادِي الكِرَامِ الرَّاغِبِينَ فِي التَّسجِيلِ بِالأَنشِطَةِ الرِّياضِيةِ بِمُنَاسَبَةِ قُدُومِ الصَّيفِ، وَاستِغلالاً لِوقتِ الفَرَاغِ،

220

فَالعَقْلُ السَّلِيمُ في الجِسمِ السَّلِيم.

سَنَفتَحُ بَابَ التَّسجِيلِ في مَدرَسَةِ السِّبَاحَةِ وَجَمِيعِ الأنشِطَةِ الرِّيَاضِيَةِ المُختَلِفَةِ وَاليكُم عَدَدَ الحِصَصِ الأسبُوعِيَةِ لِكُل نَشَاطٍ:

السِّبَاحَةُ حَصَتان أسبُوعياً

الفُرُوسِية وَرُكُوبُ الخَيلِ ثَلاثُ حِصَصٍ

رِيَاضَاتُ القِتَالِ وَالدِّفَاعِ عَنِ النَّفسِ كَالجُودُو وَالكُونغ فُو وَالتَّايكُوندُو وَالكَارَاتيه وَالمُبَارَزَةِ بِسَيفِ الشِّيشِ كُلٌّ مِنهَا ثَلاثُ حِصَصٍ أُسْبُوعياً.

الألعَابُ الجَمَاعِيةُ كَكُرَةِ القَدَمِ، وَكُرَةِ السَّلَةِ، وَكُرَةُ الطَّائِرَةِ، وَكُرَةِ التِّنسِ وَتِنسِ الطَّاوِلَةِ وَالبِينِج بُونِج وَالاسكوَاشِ بِالاضَافَةِ الَى ألعَابِ الجُمبَازِ وَقَفزِ الحَوَاجِزِ بِمُعَدَّلِ أربَعِ حَصَصٍ في الأسبُوع.

وَلِيد: هَلْ هُنَاكَ تَدرِيبٌ لِكُرَةِ القَدَمِ الأمرِيكِيةِ يَاكَابتِن؟

المَسؤُولُ: لا يَابُنَي، لا يُوجَدُ لَدَينَا في مِصرَ لُعبَةُ كُرَةِ القَدَمِ الأمرِيكِيةِ، لَيسَ لَهَا شعبِيةُ هُنَا.

وَلِيد: اِذَن، سَأشتَرِكُ في تَدرِيبَاتِ كَمَالِ الأجْسَامِ أَوْ المُصَارَعَة.

المسؤُول: نَعَمْ كِلاهُمَا مَوجُودَانِ، لَكِنَكَ سَتَخضَعُ لاختِبَارَاتِ اللِّيَاقَةِ البَدَنِيَةِ، واذَا رَغِبتَ هُنَاكَ أيضاً المُلاكَمَة وَرَفعُ الاثقَال.

ندى: هَلْ يُوجَدُ مَدرَسَةٌ لِلبَالِيه أوْ السِّبَاحَةِ التَّوقِيعِيةِ أوْ تَعلِيمِ الرَّقصِ الشَّرقِي أوِ الغَربِي؟

المسؤُول: نَعَمْ، عَدَا الرَّقصَ الشَّرقِي، انَّهُ غَيرُ مَوجُودٍ.

221

أيمن: كُنتُ أرغَبُ في السُّؤَالِ عَنْ ألعَابِ القوى؟

المسؤُول: نَعَمْ جَمِيعُ ألعَابِ القوَى كالمَشْيِّ والجَرْيِّ والوَثْبِ والرَّمْيِّ، ورُكُوبِ الدَّرَاجَةِ مَوجُودَةٌ كَمَا نُشَارِكُ في البُطولاتِ الأوليمبيةِ التي تُقَامُ وَسِبَاقَاتِ المَارَثون.

نادية: أَنَا أُحِبُّ التَّزَلُّجَ عَلَى الجَلِيدِ.

المسؤُول: هُنَاكَ صَالَةٌ كَبِيرَةٌ لِلتَّزَلُّجِ والرَّقصِ عَلَى الجَلِيدِ.

نادر: أَنَا أُحِبُّ الجُولفَ والبُولينج والبِلْيَاردُو وَساشترِكُ بأَحَدِهِم.

المسؤُول: حَسَناً، سجِّل اسمَكَ في الادَارَةِ الرِّيَاضِيةِ، والانَ سَأُعَلِّقُ الاعلانَ عَلَى هَذَا الحَائِطِ وَيمكِنُكُم الاتصَالُ مُبَاشَرَةً بالمُدَرِبِ أو الكَابتِنِ المُختَصِّ بالنَشَاطِ.

الكلماتُ الجديدة

معناها	الكلمة
Club	نَادِي
Sixth of October City	مَدِينَةُ السَّادِس مِن أكتوبَر
I am the champion athlete	أَنَا بَطَلٌ رِيَاضِيٌّ

I won the trophy many times	فُزتُ بِالكَأْسِ مَرَّاتٍ عَدِيدَةٍ
Responsible	مَسؤُولٌ
Activity	النَّشَاطِ
Important Announcement	اعلانٌ هَامٌّ
Members	أعْضَاءِ
Distinguished	الكِرَامِ
Wishing	الرَّاغِبِينَ
Registration	التَّسجِيلِ
Sports activities	أنِشطَةِ الرِّياضِيَةِ
On the occasion of the advent of summer	بِمُنَاسَبَةِ قُدُومِ الصّيفِ
And exploitation	وَاستِغلالاً
A sound mind in a sound body	العَقلُ السَّليمُ في الجِسمِ السَّليمِ
Registration period	بَابَ التَّسجِيلِ
classes	الحِصَصِ
Equestrian	الفُرُوسِيَة

Riding	رُكُوبُ الخَيلِ
Combat Sports	رِياضَاتُ القِتَالِ
Self-defense	الدِّفَاع عَنِ النَّفسِ
Fencing	والمُبَارَزَةِ بِسَيفِ الشِّيشِ
Group games	الألعَابُ الجَمَاعِيَة
Gymnastics	الجُمبَازِ
At a rate of	بِمُعَدَّلٍ
Is not popular here	لَيسَ لَها شَعبِيةٌ هُنَا
Bodybuilding	كَمَالِ الأجسَامِ
Wrestling	المُصَارَعَةِ
Will be subject	سَتَخضَعُ
Tests	لاختِبَاراتٍ
Fitness	اللِّيَاقَةِ البَدَنِيَةِ
Boxing	المُلاكَمَة
Weightlifting	رَفعُ الاثقَالِ

Such as football	كَكُرَةِ القَدَم
Basketball	كُرَةِ السَّلَةِ
Volleyball	كُرَةِ الطَّائِرَةِ
Tennis	كُرَةِ التِّنِسِ
Table Tennis	تِنِسِ الطَّاوِلَةِ
Ping pong	البِيني بُونج
Squash	السكواش
Ballet	بَالِيه
Synchronized swimming	السِّبَاحَةِ التَّوقِيعِيَةِ
Belly Dancing	الرَّقصِ الشَّرِقِي
Athletics	ألعَابِ القوَى
Walking	كالمَشْيِّ
Running	الجَرْيِّ
Jumping	الوَثْبِ
And flinging	والرَّمْيِّ

The bike riding	وَرُكُوبِ الدَّرَاجَةِ
Olympic tournaments	البُطولاتِ الأُوليمبِيَةِ
Snowboarding	التَّزَلُّجُ عَلَى الجَليدِ
Dancing on ice	وَالرَّقصِ عَلَى الجَليدِ
Golf	الجُولفَ
And Bowling	وَالبُولِينج
And billiards	وَالبِليَاردُو
Sports management	الادَارَةِ الرِّيَاضِيَةِ
I will hang	سَأُعَلِّقُ
Announcement	الاعلانَ
Wall	الحَائِطِ

أسئِلة:

1. For which season are the new members signing up for?
2. How many sessions per week will the club offer swimming lessons?
3. How many sessions per week will the club offer horse riding instruction?
4. Name the self-defense classes that the club offer. How many classes per week will they offer?
5. Which team sports will the club offer? How many classes per week?
6. Will the club offer gymnastics and / or hurdles?

7. Why doesn't the club offer American football classes?

8. A member of the club, upon hearing that he could not do American football, decided to enroll in a different sport. Which sport is it? Does he require a medical test to enroll in this class?

9. Does the club offer boxing and / or weightlifting ?

10. Does the club offer synchronized swimming?

11. What type of dance classes does the club offer?

12. What type of track and field sports / athletics does the club offer?

13. Have members of the club ever participated in the Olympics?

14. Does the club offer instruction in marathon preparation?

15. What is the name of the new member who wants to ski?

16. One new member asks whether the club offers classes in golf, billiards and one other sport. What is it?

17. What should the members do in order to register for a class?

اكْتَشَفَ بَاحِثُونَ مِنْ جَامِعَةِ تَل أَبِيب آثَارًا عُمْرَانِيَّةً وَكُنُوزًا نَادِرَةً فِي مَنْطِقَةِ آرْسُوف التَّارِيخِيَّةِ دَاخِلَ الْخَطِّ الْأَخْضَرِ تَعُودُ لِفَتَرَاتِ الْحُكْمِ الْبِيزَنْطِيِّ وَالْإِسْلَامِيِّ. وَتُعْتَبَرُ آرْسُوفُ، الْمُجَاوِرَةُ لِقَرْيَةٍ فِلَسْطِينِيَّةٍ مَهْجُورَةٍ مُنْذُ نَكْبَةِ 48 تُدْعَى إِجْلِيلَ، مِنْ أَهَمِّ مُدُنِ فِلَسْطِينَ مُنْذُ أَنْ بُنِّيَتْ عَلَى أَيْدِي الْفِينِيقِيِّينَ فِي الْقَرْنِ الرَّابِعِ قَبْلَ الْمِيلَادِ.

Research from the Ministry of Tel Aviv discovered urban artefacts and rare treasures in the historical area of Asuf, inside the Green Line, dating back to the Islamic and Byzantine eras. Asuf, is adjacent to an abandoned Palestinian village from the catastrophe of '48 called Ijlil, which is one of the most important Palestinian cities since it was built by the Phoenicians in the fourth century BC.

In the Arabic world, the '48 war between Arabs and Israelis, which ended in the occupation of historical Palestine, is referred to as 'nakbah', which means catastrophe. There is a similar word naksaah, meaning 'setback' or 'relapse', and infers the Arab defeat at the hands of the Israeli's in 1967. By calling the first defeat a 'catastrophe', and the second a 'relapse', Arabs felt that the loss of Palestine is not irreversible, aiming in the future to reclaim their land.

وَعَثَرَ عُلَمَاءُ الْآثَارِ فِي آرْسُوفَ عَلَى مُنْشَآتٍ لِإِعْدَادِ الْمَحَاصِيلِ الزِّرَاعِيَّةِ وَمَعَاصِرَ وَأَدَوَاتٍ مَنْزِلِيَّةً مِنَ الْقَرْنِ الْخَامِسِ حَتَّى السَّابِعِ الْمِيلَادِي. كَمَا تَمَّ اكْتِشَافُ آبَارٍ اسْتُخْدِمَتْ لِلْقُمَامَةِ مِنَ الْفَتْرَةِ الْبِيزَنْطِيَّةِ يَبْلُغُ قُطْرُ أَكْبَرِهَا 30 مِتْرًا وَفِيهَا أَدَوَاتٌ فَخَارِيَّةٌ وَزُجَاجِيَّةٌ وَعِظَامٌ حَيَوَانِيَّةٌ.

In Asuf, archaeologists found facilities for the preparation of agricultural crops as well as household items from the 5th-17th century. Also, wells used for rubbish in the Byzantine period, the largest one with a diameter of 30 meters, were discovered containing pottery, glass tools and animal bones.

أَهْدَى الْمُلَاكِمُ الْجَزَائِرِيُّ مُحَمَّد فليسِي الْعَرَبَ مِيدَالِيَّتَهُمُ الْوَحِيدَةَ فِي بُطُولَةِ الْعَالَمِ لِمُلَاكَمَةِ الْهُوَاةِ الَّتِي اخْتُتِمَت الْيَوْمَ السَّبْتَ فِي مَدِينَةِ آلْمَاتِي الْكَزَاخِسْتَانِيَّةِ.

The Algerian boxer Mohamed Fleecy presented the Arabs with their only medal in the world championships for amateur boxing, which concluded on Saturday in the Kazakh city of Almaty.

وَخَسِرَ فليسِي النِّزَالَ النِّهَائِيَّ فِي وَزْنِ خَفِيفِ الذُّبَابَةِ أَمَامَ الْمُصَنَّفِ الْأَوَّلِ، الْكَازَخِسْتَانِي بِيرْزَهَان جَاكِيُبُوف، لِيَكْتَفِيَ بِالْمِيدَالِيَّةِ الْفِضِّيَّةِ فِي بُطُولَةٍ قَدَّمَ فِيهَا الْأَدَاءَ الْأَفْضَلَ فِي مَسِيرَتِه.

Fleecy lost his final bout in the lightweight fly section to the top contender Kazakh Beershan Jacquibov, taking only a silver model in the tournament in which he has given the best performance of his career.

وَكَانَتْ أَبْرَزُ إِنْجَازَاتِ الْمُلَاكِمِ الْجَزَائِرِيِّ، الْبَالِغِ مِنَ الْعُمْرِ 23 عَامًا، حُصُولُهُ عَلَى فِضِّيَّةِ الْبُطُولَةِ الْعَرَبِيَّةِ فِي الدَّوْحَةِ عَامَ 2011 وَأَيْضًا فِضِّيَّةِ دَوْرَةِ الْأَلْعَابِ الْأَفْرِيقِيَّةِ فِي الْعَامِ نَفْسِه.

The most significant achievement of the Algerian boxer, who is 23 years old, was receiving a silver medal in the Doha Arab Championship in 2011, as well as also winning silver in the African Games of the same year.

هَلْ تُمَارِسُ الرِّيَاضَةَ؟
بِالإِرادَةِ تُصْنَعُ المُعْجِزاتِ

This conversation is between two women discussing sport and losing weight. You will encounter vocabulary surrounding these issues.

الحِوَار

غادة: مَهَا، تَبْدِينَ رَشِيقةً جِداً!! كَيفَ خَسِرْتِ كُلَّ هَذا الوَزْنِ ؟

مها: اتَّبَعْتُ نِظَاماً غِذَائِياً صَارِماً وَذَهَبْتُ الَى الجِيم (صَالَةُ الألْعَابِ) وَأكثرُ شَئٍ نَفَعَني المَشَّايَةُ الكَهْرَبَائِيةُ وَتَمَارِينَ الأيْرُوبِيكس، فأنها تَحْرِقُ سُعْرَاتٍ حَرَارِيةً كَثِيرةً.

غادة: بِالارَادَةِ والصَّبْرِ تَتَحَقَّقُ المُعْجِزَاتُ.

مها: كُنْتُ سَمِينَةً جِداً، حَقاً الحُبُّ يَصْنَعُ المُعْجِزَاتِ.

غادة: هَيَّا اعترِفي أنَّ ذلكَ ما جعلكِ رَشِيقة، هههه.

مها: شَابٌ رِيَاضِيٌّ يَاغَادَةَ، وَسِيمٌ، مَفتُولُ العَضَلاتِ فَهُوَ يُمَارِسُ رِيَاضَةَ كَمَالِ الأجْسَامِ، وَحَازَ بُطُولَتَين في نَادِي الجَزيرَةِ الشهير وأخذَ الكَأسَ الذهَبِيّةَ في بُطُولَةِ الأولمبياد في دَورَةِ ألْعَابِ القُوَى الـ....

غادة: كفى كفى يَاعَاشِقَةً، دَعِينَا نَمْشِي في مَمْشَى النَّادِي، فالمَشْيُ أفضَلُ رِيَاضَةٍ عَلَى الاطْلاقِ لِلكَبيرِ والصَغِيرِ يَلِيهَا رُكُوبُ الدَّرَاجَةِ في نَظَرِي هههه.

مها: الان، كَمْ كُنْتُ أتَمَنَّى لَوْأنِّي لاعِبَةُ جُمْبَازٍ، أو سبَّاحَةٌ مَاهِرَةٌ، أوْ بَاليرِينَا (رَاقِصَةُ بَالِيه)، أوْ لاعِبَةُ كَارَاتِيه أوْ تَايْكُوندُو، أوْ كَابِتن مُدَرِّب لِفَرِيقِ كُرَةِ السَّلَةِ أوْ أيِّ شَئٍ أكُونُ فِيهِ قَرِيبَةً مِنْ عُمَرٍ.

مها: أوْ عَدَّاءَةٌ في فَريقِ النَّاشِئِين، أوْحَارِسَةُ مَرمَى فَريقِ كُرَةِ القَدَمِ، هههههه.

غادة: يَبْدُو أنَّني سَأرْمِي بِكِ في البِيسِينِ يامَهَا (حَمَّامُ السِّبَاحَةِ)، لَكِنِّي لَيْسَ لَدَيَّ وَقتٌ فَقَدْ حَانَ مَوعِدُ السَّاونَا والجَاكُوزِي، فَوَبَعْدَهَمَا جَلسَةُ مَسَاجٍ تَايلَندي مُرِيحٍ.

مها: رَائِع، يَبْدو ذلِكَ مُرَفَّهاً جِداً، تَمَنِياتِي لَكِ بِيْومٍ سَعِيدٍ يَاحَسْنَاءَ.

الكلماتُ الجديدة

معناها	الكلمة
With will power, miracles can be done	بِالارادةِ تُصْنَعُ المُعْجِزَاتِ
Agile	رَشيقةً
Strict	صَارماً
Treadmill	المَشَّايَةُ الكَهْرَبَائِيَةُ
Calories	سُعْرَاتِ
Fat	سَمِينَة

Bulging muscles	مَفتُولُ العَضَلاتِ
Body building	كَمَالِ الأَجْسَامِ
Athletics / track and field	أَلْعَابِ القُوَى
Lover	عَاشِقَةً
Walkway	مَمْشَى
In my opinion	فِي نَظَرِي
Gymnastics	جُمْبَازٍ
Nearby	قَرِيبَة
Runner / sprinter	عَدَّاءَة
Goalkeeper	حَارِسَة مُرمَى
Swimming pool	البِيسِينِ
Bumper life	مُرَفَهاً

أسئلة:

1. Why was Ghadah surprised when she saw Maha?
2. How did Maha lose weight?
3. Of all the exercises she did, which one benefited her the most? Why?
4. Why did Maha decide to lose weight?
5. Maha likes a man. What does he like to do?
6. Which sport is he into?
7. What sporting achievement has he accomplished?
8. From Ghadah's point of view, what is the best sport?
9. What is the name of the person Maha likes?
10. What does Maha practice in order to be close to the object of her affection?
11. Why does Ghadah threaten to throw Maha into a swimming pool?
12. What will Ghadah do after her conversation with Maha?

وَافَقَتِ السُّلُطَاتُ السُّعُودِيَّةُ عَلَى السَّمَاحِ لِلْبَنَاتِ بِمُمَارَسَةِ الرِّيَاضَةِ فِي الْمَدَارِسِ الْأَهْلِيَّةِ، وَفْقَ ضَوَابِطَ شَرْعِيَّةٍ.

The Saudi authorities have allowed girls to practice private sport in schools, according to Sharia guidelines.

وَذَكَرَتْ وِكَالَةُ الْأَنْبَاءِ السُّعُودِيَّةُ الرَّسْمِيَّةُ أَنَّ وَزِيرَ التَّرْبِيَةِ وَالتَّعْلِيمِ الْأَمِيرَ فَيْصَلَ بْنَ عَبْدِ اللَّهِ وَجَّهَ تَعْمِيمًا لِجَمِيعِ إِدَارَاتِ التَّرْبِيَةِ وَالتَّعْلِيمِ فِي الْمَمْلَكَةِ، يَقْضِي بِاعْتِمَادِ جُمْلَةٍ مِنَ الضَّوَابِطِ وَالِاشْتِرَاطَاتِ الَّتِي مِنْ شَأْنِهَا تَنْظِيمُ أَنْشِطَةِ اللِّيَاقَةِ الصِّحِّيَّةِ فِي مَدَارِسِ الْبَنَاتِ الْأَهْلِيَّةِ.

According to the Official Saudi news agency, the Minister of Education Prince Faisal bin Abdulla, issued directives to all departments of education in the Kingdom to establish guidelines and requirements that will regulate physical fitness activities in private girls' schools.

وَنَقَلَتِ الْوِكَالَةُ عَنِ الْمُتَحَدِّثِ الرَّسْمِيِّ بِاسْمِ وِزَارَةِ التَّرْبِيَةِ وَالتَّعْلِيمِ مُحَمَّدِ الدُّخَيْنِي قَوْلَهُ إِنَّ التَّعْمِيمَ نَصَّ عَلَى أَنَّ هَذَا الْإِجْرَاءَ يَنْطَلِقُ مِنْ تَعَالِيمِ دِينِنَا الْحَنِيفِ، الَّتِي أَبَاحَتْ لِلْمَرْأَةِ مُمَارَسَةَ هَذِهِ الْأَنْشِطَةِ وَفْقَ ضَوَابِطَ شَرْعِيَّةٍ.

The agency quoted the official spokesman of the Ministry of Education Mohammed Aldkhini, saying that the accessibility stemmed from the teachings of our true religion, which allows women to practice these activities according to the Sharia guidelines.

تَقْرَأُ أَوْ تَسْمَعُ كُلَّ يَوْمٍ عَنْ أَنْظِمَةٍ غِذَائِيَّةٍ جَدِيدَةٍ سَتُخَلِّصُكَ مِنَ الْوَزْنِ الزَّائِدِ وَتَجْعَلُكَ رَشِيقًا. وَلَكِنْ قَبْلَ اتِّبَاعِ أَيٍّ مِنْهَا يَجِبُ عَلَيْكَ التَّأَكُّدُ مِنَ الْأُمُورِ التَّالِيَةِ:

هَلْ تَحْتَوِي الْحِمْيَةُ عَلَى مَصَادِرَ مُنَوَّعَةٍ مِنَ الْغِذَاءِ؟
هَلْ تَسْمَحُ لَكَ بِتَنَاوُلِ أَطْعِمَتِكَ الْمُفَضَّلَةِ؟
هَلْ تُعْطِيكَ الْحِمْيَةُ الْحَدَّ الْمُنَاسِبَ مِنَ السُّعْرَاتِ الْحَرَارِيَّةِ، بِحَيْثُ لَا تَفْقِدُ أَكْثَرَ مِنْ كِيلُوغْرَامٍ وَاحِدٍ فِي الْأُسْبُوعِ؟
هَلْ تَتَضَمَّنُ بَرْنَامَجًا لِلنَّشَاطِ الْجَسَدِيِّ وَالرِّيَاضَةِ؟
إِذَا أَجَبْتَ عَنْ أَيٍّ مِنَ الْأَسْئِلَةِ السَّابِقَةِ بِـ"لا" فَهَذَا يَعْنِي أَنَّ الْحِمْيَةَ لَيْسَتْ صِحِّيَّةً.

Does your diet contain a variety of food sources?
Does that allows you to eat your favorite foods?
Is it the right diet to reduce calories, and so you do not lose more than one kilogram per week?
Does it include a program of physical activity and sport?
If you answered any of the previous questions "no" it means that the diet is not healthy.

مَحَطَّةُ سُورِ ٱلْأَزْبَكِيَةِ	مِتْرُوْ الْأَنْفَاقِ

There is a woman who wants to go to a part of Old Cairo called "Suur al-Azbakkya" which means "Azbakia Fence". Azbakkya Fence is a wall surrounding a park and from the outside, there are booksellers selling old and used books for very cheap prices by Egyptian standards. If you go to Cairo, make sure you visit this place. In this lesson, a young woman wants to go to "Suur al-Azbakkya" and is asking an older woman for directions. The vocabulary revolves around asking for and giving directions and touches on what you would expect to encounter in a subway car, which incidentally is similar to what you would expect to see in a New York subway car, i.e. sexual harassment, panhandlers, venders, and pickpockets. However, there is one major difference between the Cairo subway and the New York subway that we will read in the text.

234

الحوار

هبة: مِنْ فَضْلِكِ، أُرِيدُ الذَّهَابَ الَى سُورِ الأَزْبَكِيَةِ، مَكَانُ الكُتُبِ القَدِيمَةِ المُسْتَعْمَلَةِ بِأَسْعَارٍ بَسِيطَةٍ، أَيُّ مَحَطَّةِ مِتْرُو أَذْهَبُ؟

امرأة مسنة: بِمَا أَنَّكِ الانَ في الخَطِّ الثَّاني لِلمِترُو وَفي مَحَطَّةِ جَامِعَةِ القَاهِرَةِ، سَتَقْطَعِينَ تذكَرَةً الَى مَحَطَّةِ مِترُو السَّادَاتِ، لَكِنَّكِ سَتَنْزِلِينَ قَبْلَ مَحَطَّةِ السَّادَاتِ بِمَحَطَّةٍ وَاحِدَةٍ وَهِيَ مَحَطَّةُ العَتَبَةِ وَجَرَاجُ الأُوبِرَا،وَحَتَّى تَصِلِينَ الَيْهَا سَتَجْتَازِينَ مَحَطَّتَي مِترُو البُحُوثِ،وَالدُّقِي،وَسَتَخْرُجِينَ مِنْ سَلاَلِمِ المِترُو عَلَى يَمِينِكِ أَوْ شِمَالِكِ لِتَجِدِينَ نَفْسَكِ في سُورِ الأَزْبَكِيَةِ،لِتَشْتَرِي كُلَّ مَا تَحْتَاجِينَهُ مِنَ الكُتُبِ وَالمَجَلاَتِ القَيِّمَةِ.

هبة: أَيْنَ شُبَاكُ التذاكِرِ؟

المرأة: هَاهُوَ أَمَامُكِ، تَعَالِي مَعِي.

المرأة: الانَ وَبَعْدَ أَنْ قَطَعْنَا التَذَاكِرَ، لاتَرْمِيهَا، سَنَضَعُهَا في المَاكِينَةِ المُخَصَّصَةِ لِعبُورِالرُّكَابِ، حَتَّى تَسْمَحَ لَنَا بِالعُبُورِ.

هبة: رَائِعٌ.

المرأة: اذَا كُنْتِ سَتَرْكَبِينَ عَرَبِيَةَ السِّتَاتِ (عَرَبَةٌ مُخَصَّصَةٌ ْلِلنِسَاءِ)، يَجِبُ عَلَيْكِ أَنْ تَنْتَظِرِي في المُقَدِمَةِ حَتَّى يَأتِي المِترُو لأَنَّهَا أَوَّلُ عَرَبَةٍ في القِطَارِ خَلَفَ السَّائِقِ.

هبة: مُمْتَازٌ، لأَحَبُّ مُعَاكَسَاتِ وَمُضَايَقَاتِ الرِّجَالِ وَالشَّبَابِ في بَاقِي المِترُو، سَأَرْكَبُ عَرَبِيَةَ السِّتَاتِ.

المرأة ساخرةً: الرِّجَالُ فَقَطْ!!! انَّ اكْثَرَ مَا يُؤْذِيني البَاعَةُ الجَائِلِينَ الذينَ يَبيعُونَ أَيَّ شَيْءٍ وَيَقذِفُونَ بِمَا لَدَيهِم في حِجْرِكِ او في يَدِكِ لِتشتَري مِنهُم، الالْحَاحُ الذِّي قَدْ يَصِلُ الَى الشِحَاتَةِ (الشِّحَاذَةُ وَالتَسَّوُلُ)، احْذَريهِم يَا بِنتِي (ابنتي)، اِنَّهُم حَرَامِيَةٌ (لُصُوص)، يَسرِقُونَ الكُحْلَ مِنَ العَينِ (مُحْتَرِفي سَرِقَةٍ) خَاصَّةً في الزَحْمَةِ (الزِّحَام).

الكلماتُ الجديدة

معناها	الكلمة
Subway	مِترُو الأنْفَاقِ
Station	مَحَطَّةٌ
Wall	سُورِ
Used	المُسْتَعْمَلَةِ
Ticket	تذكَرَةٌ
Buy a ticket	سَتقطَعينَ تذكَرَةً
You are getting off	سَتَنْزِلينَ
You will cross	سَتَجْتَازينَ
Box office	شُبَّاكُ التذاكِرِ

Don't Throw It All Away	لاتَرْميهَا
Turnstile	المَاكِينَةِ المُخَصَّصَةِ لِعبُورِالرُّكَّابِ
Women only car	عَرَبَةٌ مُخَصَّصَةٌ لِلنِسَاءِ
The front	المُقَدِمَةِ
First car behind the motorman	أوَّلُ عَرَبَةٍ في القِطَارِ خَلَفَ السَّائِقِ
Flirting and harassment	مُعَاكَسَاتٍ وَمُضَايَقَاتٍ
Hawkers	البَاعَةُ الجَائِلِينَ
And threw what they have in your lap or in your hand to buy them	وَيَقذِفُونَ بِمَا لَدَيهِم في حِجْرِكِ او في يَدِكِ لِتشتَري مِنْهُم
Pressed	الالْحَاحُ
Begging and panhandling	الشِّحَاذَةُ وَالتَسَّولُ
Thieves	لُصُوص
Steel the eyeliner off you eye.	يَسرِقُونَ الكُحْلَ مِنَ العَينِ
Professionals theft	مُحْتَرِفي سَرِقَةٍ
cowed	الزِّحَامِ

أسئلة:

1. What is the name of the woman who is asking for directions?

2. Where does she want to go and why?

3. Which subway line is she traveling on?

4. What is the name of the subway station that is nearby to her destination?

5. What is the name of the subway station after that?

6. How far is the subway exit from her destination?

7. Where is the ticket booth?

8. Does she need the ticket to exit the subway system?

9. Does the subway have a car for women? If so, which one is it?

10. What is the reason for there being a car specifically for women?

11. What bothers the older woman most about the subway?

12. What does the older woman think of venders in the subway?

13. What does the idiom "stealing the Kohl from the eye" mean?

14. What is the most dangerous time to ride the subway?

بَعْد أَنْ ظَلَّ مَيْدَانُ اَلتَّحْرِيرِ لِنَحْوِ عَامِين مُنْطَلَقًا لِثَوْرَةِ الْمِصْرِيِّينَ عَلَى النِّظَامِ اَلسَّابِقِ وَذُيُولِهِ، شَهِدَ الْمَيْدَانُ اَلْوَاقِعُ فِي قَلْبِ اَلْقَاهِرَةِ حَشْدًا هُوَ اَلْأَكْبَرُ لِخُصُومِ الرَّئِيسِ مُحَمَّد مُرْسِي الَّذِينَ تَدَاعَوْا لِلتَّعْبِيرِ عَنْ رَفْضِهِمْ لِقَرَارَاتِهِ الصَّادِرَةِ الْأَخِيرَةِ، خُصُوصًا مَا تَعَلَّقَ مِنْهَا بِتَحْصِينِ قَرَارَاتِهِ مِنَ الْإِلْغَاءِ مِنْ طَرَفِ أَيِّ جِهَةٍ قَضَائِيَّةٍ حَتَّى إِقْرَارِ الدُّسْتُورِ وَانْتِخَابِ بَرْلَمَانٍ جَدِيدٍ.

Two years after Tahrir Square was the starting point of the Egyptian revolution against the former regime and its cohorts, the square, which is located in the heart of Cairo, witnessed another, bigger crowd, in opposition to President Mohamed Morsi. They were gathered to express their rejection of his latest resolutions, especially those that related to fortifying his own decisions from revocation by any judicial body until the adoption of the Constitution and the election of a new parliament.

الْمَيْدَانُ الَّذِي غَصَّ بِمِئَاتِ الْآلَافِ مِنَ الْمُرَحِّبِينَ بِفَوْزِ مُرْسِي بِانْتِخَابَاتِ الرِّئَاسَةِ فِي يُونْيُو الْمَاضِي، كَانَ فِي هَذِهِ اَلْمَرَّةِ سَاحَةً لِمُعَارِضِيهِ الَّذِينَ نَجَحُوا فِي تَحْقِيقِ أَكْبَرِ حَشْدٍ لَهُمْ ضَمَّ عَشَرَاتِ الْآلَافِ، فِي حِينِ تَحَوَّلَ مُؤَيِّدُو الرَّئِيسِ إِلَى شَرْقِ الْقَاهِرَةِ حَيْثُ نَظَّمُوا مُظَاهَرَاتِ تَأْيِيدٍ أَمَامَ الرِّئَاسَةِ.

The square, which was overcrowded with hundreds of thousands of people welcoming Morsi's victory in the presidential election last June, was this time the arena for his opponents, who have succeeded in gathering their biggest crowd, numbering in the tens of thousands. Meanwhile, those in support of the President moved to east of Cairo, where they organized demonstrations in his support in front of the Presidential palace.

فِي المَزْرَعَةِ فِي أُوكلاهُومَا

In this lesson, we will read a dialogue that is taking place between people on a farm in a certain state in the United States. The grammatical aspect of this lesson focuses on the feminine and the masculine and we will see how adjectives match the gender of the nouns they describe. You will also learn the difference between addressing males and females in Arabic.

ديانا: كَانَتْ فِكْرَةً مُمْتَازَةً يَافِيكِي أَنْ نَقْضِي عُطْلَةَ نِهَايَةِ الأَسْبُوعِ فِي مَزْرَعَةِ الجَدَّةِ فِي وِلايَةِ اوكلاهُومَا.

فيكي: نَعَمْ دِيَانا، أُحِبُّ هَذَا المَكَانَ الجَمِيلَ كَثِيراً.

الجدة: تَعَالَوا يَافتَيَات، لَقدعَادَ ادَمُ مِنَ الحَقلِ، هَاهُوَ يَضَعُ السَّيَارَةَ فِي الجَرَاجِ.

ادم: كَيْفَ حَالُكُنَّ يَا بَنَاتِ أَخِي الجَمِيلاتِ.

ديانا وفيكي: انظُرُوا الَى هَذَا العَمِّ الوَسِيمِ.

ديانا: تَبدُو شَاباً يَاعَمِّي، كَيفَ تَحْتَفِظُ بِهَذَا المَظْهَرِ الشَابِ هَكَذَا.

ادم: هَلْ انَا مِثلُ وَالِدِكُنَّ العَجُوزِ الكَسُولِ؟،هه، لَقَدْ أَنْسَتهُ حَيَاةُ المَدِينَةِ النَّشاطَ والعَمَلَ والحَرَكَةَ.

فيكي: لابُدَّ أَنَّ شَاباً مِثلَكَ تُغرَمُ بِهِ الفَتَيَاتُ هَيَا اعتَرِفْ.

ادم بخَجَلٍ: نَعَمْ، انَّها امرَأَةٌ رَائِعَةٌ وَجَمِيلَةٌ وَرَقِيقَةٌ تُنَاسِبُ رَجُلاً وَسِيماً وَقَوِّياً مِثلي.

الجدة: كُفُّوا عَنِ الكَلامِ والثرْثَرَةِ، الغَدَاءُ جَاهِزٌ.

ديانا وفيكي: مَاذَا اعدَدتِ يَاجَدَّتِي؟ رَائِحَةُ الشِّوَاءِ شَهِيَةٌ.

الجدة: اللَّحْمُ المَشوِّيُ وَسَلَطَةُ الكولِ سلو وَفَطِيرَةُ التفاح بِطَرِيقَةِ الجَدَّةِ.

ديانا: فِيكِّي، أَعْطِني الملعَقَةَ وَالشوكَةَ وَالطَّبَقَ والكوبَ والسِّكينَ مِنْ فَضْلِكِ.

ادم: المِلحُ والفُلفُلُ وَزُجَاجَةُ الكتشَبِ والخُبْزُ السَّاخِنُ يَا أمِّي مِنْ فضْلِكِ.

ادم: أَنَا جَائِعٌ جِداً يَاأمِّي، المَائِدَةُ جَاهِزَةٌ الانَ.

بَعْدَ الطَّعَامِ

240

فيكي: شُكراً جَدَّتِي عَلَى الوَجْبَةِ كُلِّهَا، لَقَدْ اكَلْتُ طَبَقِي كُلَّهُ.

ادم: سَاخُذُكُنَّ فِي جَوْلَةٍ بِالسَّيَّارَةِ لأريكُنَّ المَزْرَعَةَ وَاسطَبَلَ الخُيُول بَعْدَ التَوسِعَةِ، وَرُبَّمَا رَغِبْتُنَّ فِي النُزُولِ الَى البُحَيْرَةِ لِلسِبَاحَةِ وَالمَرَحِ.

ديانا: رَائِعٌ، عَمِّي، هَذا هُوَ الاسْتِجْمَامُ المِثالِي.

الكلماتُ الجديدة

معناها	الكلمة
Girls	فتَيَات
Field	الحَقلِ
Puts	يَضَعُ
My nieces	بَنَاتِ أخِي
The handsome Uncle	العَمِّ الوَسِيمِ
You looks young	تَبْدُو شَاباً
Keep this youthful appearance.	تَحْتَفِظُ بِهَذا المَظْهَرِ الشَابِ هَكَذَا.
Lazy	الكَسُولِ

You will enamored with	تُغْرَمُ بِهِ
Confess	إِعْتَرِفْ
The chatter	وَالثَّرْثَرَة
Roast	الشِّوَاءِ
Appetite	شَهِيَّة
Odor	رَائِحَة
Horses ' Stable	وَاسطَبلَ الخُيُول
Expansion	التَوسِعَةِ
Lake	البُحَيْرَةِ
Recreation	الاسْتِجْمَامُ

أسئلة:

1. What are the names of the two young women who are visiting the farm?

2. In which state is the farm located?

3. What is the relationship between the farm owners and the two young ladies?

4. What is their uncle's name?

5. Why do the girls think that he looks so young?

6. What type of activities does the girls' uncle do that their father does not do?

7. Who prepared the lunch?

8. What was for lunch?

9. After lunch, what will the girls do and with whom?

اِقْرَأْ

رَفَعَ خُبَرَاءُ اقْتِصَادِيُّونَ مَغَارِبَةٌ دَعْوَى قَضَائِيَّةً ضِدَّ الْبَنْكِ الدَّوْلِيِّ أَمَامَ إِحْدَى مَحَاكِمِ الرِّبَاطِ فِي أَوَّلِ سَابِقَةٍ فِي تَارِيخِ الْقَضَاءِ الْمَغْرِبِيِّ مُوَجِّهِينَ إِلَيْهِ تُهْمَةَ " تَزْوِيرِ نَتَائِجِ دِرَاسَةٍ" أَنْجَزُوهَا لِفَائِدَتِهِ فِي الْمَغْرِبِ.

وَأُثِيرَتْ هَذِهِ الْقَضِيَّةُ بَعْدَ تَكْلِيفِ الْبَنْكِ فَرِيقًا مِنَ الْخُبَرَاءِ الْبَاحِثِينَ الْمَغَارِبَةِ بِإِنْجَازِ دِرَاسَةٍ مَيْدَانِيَّةٍ حَوْلَ قِطَاعِ الزِّرَاعَةِ بِالْمَغْرِبِ، حَيْثُ قَالَ هَؤُلَاءِ الْخُبَرَاءُ إِنَّ الْمُؤَسَّسَةَ الدَّوْلِيَّةَ حَرَّفَتْ مَضْمُونَ الدِّرَاسَةِ ضِدَّ إِرَادَتِهِمْ وَرَغْمَ اعْتِرَاضَاتِهِمْ عَلَى نَشْرِهَا.

وَقَالَ مُحَامِي دِفَاعِ الْبَاحِثِينَ الْمَغَارِبَةِ إِنَّ الْهَدَفَ مِنْ هَذِهِ الدَّعْوَى هُوَ "تَنْبِيهُ السُّلْطَاتِ الْمَغْرِبِيَّةِ وَبَاقِي الدُّوَلِ إِلَى الْمُنَاوَرَاتِ الَّتِي يَعْتَمِدُهَا الْبَنْكُ الدَّوْلِيُّ فِي بَعْضِ الدِّرَاسَاتِ وَتَزْيِيفِهِ لِلنَّتَائِجِ بِهَدَفِ تَبْرِيرِ سِيَاسَتِهِ وَالضَّغْطِ عَلَى الدُّوَلِ لِقَبُولِ قُرُوضٍ مُعَيَّنَةٍ".

Moroccan economists started a lawsuit against the World Bank before a court in Rabat. This is the first precedent in the history of the Moroccan judiciary, charging the World Bank with "falsifying the results of the study" that they did for its own benefit in Morocco.

The issue was raised after the bank assigned a team of Moroccan experts to complete a field study on the agricultural sector in Morocco. Those experts said that the International Foundation misrepresented the content of the study against their will and in spite of their objections to the publication.

The defense attorney for the Moroccan researchers said, "The goal of this lawsuit is to alert the Moroccan authorities and the rest of the countries of the manipulation adopted by the World Bank of some studies, and its falsification of the results in order to justify their policies and to put pressure on states to accept certain loans".

مَنْ هُوَ مُطْرِبُكَ المُفَضَّلُ؟

This discussion is held before a concert at night by the Pyramids. The vocabulary will revolve around the theme of contemporary Arab music and Arab music in history. There will be a comparison of different types of music, and the interlocutors will give their reasons for their own musical preferences.

خالد: هُنَاكَ حَفْلٌ حَيٌّ اللَيْلَة عِندَ الاهرَامَاتِ، عِندَ الصَّوتِ والضَّوءِ، هَلْ أَحْجِزُ لَكَ مِقعَداً فِي الحَفلِ يازِيَاد؟

244

زِياد: يَبْدُو شَيْئاً سَاحِراً، الغِنَاءُ وَالرَّقصُ وَالأَضْوَاءُ وَالجَو الحَالِمُ وَالمَرَحُ، مَنْ سَيَقومُ بِالغِنَاءِ فِي الحَفلِ؟

خالد: انّهُ مُطرِبي المُفَضَّلُ، مُحَمَّدُ مُنير، أعِدُكَ أنّهُ سَيَكُونُ حَفلاً مِنْ أرْوَعِ مَاقَدَّمَهُ مُحَمَد مُنير.

زِياد: لِلْأَسَفِ لَسْتُ مِنْ مُحِبّي ألْحَانِ مُحَمَد مُنير وَلا أُحِبُّ طَريقَتَهُ فِي الغِنَاءِ.

خالد: نَعَمْ!!مَاذا تَقولُ؟. مُحَمَد مُنير مَلِكُ الغِنَاءِ وَلَهُ جُمْهُورٌ ضَخْمٌ.

زِياد: أنَا أفضِّلُ غِنَاءَ تَامِر حُسْني، غِنَاءٌ عَصرِيٌّ، وَغِنَاؤُهُ وَرَقصه رَائِعَان، لَو كَانَ هُنَاكَ لَكُنتُ ذَهَبْتُ الَى الحَفلِ طَبْعاً.

خالد: تَامِرُ حُسْني!!، أنتَ لاتحِبُّ طَريقَةَ مُحَمَد مُنير وَتُحِبُّ تَامِر حُسْني !!! لا أعْلَمُ عَنْ غِنائِهِ الّا أنْ يَفتحَ قَمِيصَهُ وَيَرقُّص كالمَجنون.

زِياد: لَا لَا، لَا تتكلَّمْ عَنْ نَجْمِي المُفَضَّلِ، انَّ لَهُ شَعْبِيَةً كَبِيرَةً فِي مِصرَ وَفِي قلْبِي، انَّهُ الأعْلَى أجراً عَلَى مَا أعْتَقِدُ، وَالمَطلوبُ بِشِدَّةٍ لإحْيَاءِ حَفَلَاتِ زِفَاف الأغْنِيَاءِ وَالطَّبَقَةِ الرَّاقِيَةِ.

خالد: وانتَ لاتعْلَمُ شَعْبِيَةَ مُحَمَد مُنيرٍ فِي مِصرَ، وَكَمْ يُقَدِّمُ مِنْ مِهْرَجَانَاتٍ غِنَائِيَةٍ، ولِمَاذَا تَتَكَلَّمُ عَنِ الطَّبَقَةِ الرَّاقِيَةِ، مُحَمَّدُ مُنير لايُقَدِّمُ غِنَاءً شَعْبِيًا هَابِطاً انّهُ يُقَدِّمُ الفَنَّ لِلْجَمِيعِ.

زِياد: عُمُوماً لَنْ نَختِلفَ يَاصَديقِي، فَاخْتِلَافُ الاذوَاقِ لايُفسِدُ لِلودِ قَضِيَةً وَكِلَاهُمَا فِعْلاً نَجْمَان عَرَبِيان.

245

خالد: فِعْلاً، أُمُّ كُلثُومٍ، وَصَبَاحُ، وَشَادِيَة، وَعَبْدُالحَلِيم حَافِظ، وَفَرِيد الأَطْرَش، وَمُحَمَّدُ فَوزِي كَانُوا نُجُوماً فِي زَمَنِهِم، نُجُومُ الزَّمَنِ الجَمِيل، الانَ الوَضْعُ مُخْتَلِفٌ، وَاخْتَلَفَ الغِنَاءُ وَأَصْبَحَ الابْهَار وَالتَّقنِيَّةُ الاليَّةُ مَطلَباً أَسَاسِياً فِي صِنَاعَةِ الأَغنِيَة وَالفِيدِيُو كِلِيبٍ.

الكلماتُ الجديدة

معناها	الكلمة
Who is your favorite singer?	مَنْ هُوَ مُطرِبُكَ المُفَضَّلُ
Live	حَيٌّ
Sound and light	الصَّوتِ والضَّوءِ
Magical	سَاحِراً
Dream-like atmosphere	والجَو الحَالِمُ
Who will sing at the concert?	مَنْ سَيَقومُ بِالغِنَاءِ فِي الحَفلِ
Unfortunately	لِلأَسَفِ
I am not a fan of the music	لَسْتُ مِنْ مُحِبِّي أَلْحَان
And I don't like the way he sings	وَلاأُحِبُّ طَرِيقَتَهُ فِي الغِنَاءِ
He unbuttons his shirt and dances like a	يَفتَحُ قَمِيصَهُ وَيَرْقُصَ كالمَجنونِ

madman	
He is the highest paid, as far as I know	الأَعْلَى أَجْراً عَلَى مَا أَعْتَقِدُ
Rich people's wedding	زِفَافِ الأَغْنِيَاءِ
The upper class	الطَّبَقَةِ الرَّاقِيَةِ
Music festivals	مِهْرَجَانَاتٍ غِنَائِيَةٍ
Agree to disagree (Literally, 'different opinions don't ruin our friendship')	فَاخْتِلاَفُ الاذوَاقِ لايُفسِدُ للِودِ قَضِيَةً
Dazzling	الابْهَارُ
Technology (of machines)	التَّقنِيَةُ الالِيَّةُ

أَسئِلة:

1. Where will the concert be held?

2. Is the concert live?

3. Who will reserve a seat for Khalid?

4. What does Ziad like the most about this concert?

5. Who will be the star singer of the concert? Is Ziad one of his fans? Why?

6. Is Ziad going to the concert or not?

7. Who is a fan of Tamer Hosny? Why?

8. What doesn't Khalid like about Tamer Hosny?

9. Is Tamer Hosny popular in Egypt?

10. Which singer charges the highest fee for a performance?

11. Which singer is in high demand?

12. Which singer's fans are usually found in the richest parts of society?

13. What is the difference between the singing of Mohammed Munir and Tamer Hosny?

14. Ziad and Khalid have different tastes in music. Do these differences affect their friendship?

15. Are Mohammed Munir and Tamer Hosny Arabs?

16. What are the names of the 'good old days' singers Khalid mentions when they are reminiscing about old styles of singing?

17. What is as important as having a good voice in today's show business?

الوِلادَةُ

This chapter presents a conversation in a hospital where a woman is giving birth. You will encounter vocabulary appropriate to this situation, including interactions with the medical staff.

السيدة ديانا: أَيْنَ أَنَا؟ اه ...أَشْعُرُ بِأَلَمٍ..أَيْنَ طِفْلِي؟

الممرضة: أَلْفُ مبرُوكٍ، لقد جَاءَكِ تَوْءَمَانِ جَمِيلانِ يُشْبِهَانِ أُخْتَهُمَا الَّتِي جَاءَتْ مَعَ وَالِدِهَا بِالأَمْسِ .

السيدة ديانا: حَقًّا! أُرِيدُ رُؤْيَتَهُمَا

الممرضة: لاتقُومِي مِنَ السَّرِيرِ، لَقَدْ أَمَرَنَا الطَّبِيبُ الَّذِي قَامَ بعمليةِ الولادةِ بأن تَرْتاحِي.

السيدة ديانا: أَيُّ طبيبٍ؟ طبيبُ التخديرِ ؟ أَمْ طبيبُ التوليدِ؟

الممرضة: لا تقلَقِي، الطبيبانِ اللَّذانِ قامَا بالولادَةِ مِنْ أَمْهَرِ أطباءِ المُسْتشفَى.

السيدة ديانا: لَسْتُ قلِقَةً، وأنا أَشْكُرُكِ وأَشْكُرُ المُمَرِّضَتانِ اللَّتانِ تناوَبتا على رِعَايَتِي قبلَ الوِلادَةِ.

الممرضة: لا شكرَ على واجبٍ، سَيدَتِي، فجَميعُ الأطبّاءِ والمُمَرِضينَ الَّذينَ يَعْمَلُونَ بالمُسْتَشْفَى، وجَميعُ الطبيباتِ والمُمَرِضاتِ اللاتي تعَمَلْنَ بالمُسْتَشْفَى على مُسْتَوَى مُرْتَفِعٍ مِنَ الكَفَاءَةِ.

السيدة ديانا: مَنْ يَعْمَلْ عَمَلَهُ بِاجتِهَادٍ يَسْتَحِقُّ الشُّكْرَ.

الممرضة: هَلْ كُنْتِ تَعلَمِينَ مَافِي بَطنِكِ؟

السيدة ديانا: لا لَمْ أَكُنْ أَعْلَمُ مَا في بَطني، طَلَبتُ مِنَ الطبيبِ الَّذي تَابَعَني ألَّا يُخْبِرَني بِنَوعِ الجَنينِ الَّذي في بَطني.

الممرضة: اللَّذان في بَطنِكِ، لَقَدْ كَانَا وَلَدَين توأَمَين.

السيدة ديانا: الحَمْدُ لله، خُذِي هَذه النقودِ واقتَسِميها مَعَ المُمَرِّضَاتِ اللَّاتي في خِدْمَتِي فأَنَا سَعيدَةٌ جداً بِالنَّبَأِ السَّعيدِ الَّذي قلتِيه، وأَتَمَنَى أَنْ أَرَى وَلَدَيَّ اللَّذين أَنْجَبتُهُما سَريعاً.

الكلماتُ الجديدة

معناها	الكلمة
I feel pain	أَشْعُرُ بألَمٍ
Congratulations	ألفُ مبروكٍ
Twins	تَوأَمَين
Resemble, looks like	يُشْبهَان
Don't get up	لا تقُومِي
Birth	الولادة
Anesthesiologist	طبيبُ التخدير

Obstetrician	طبيبُ التوليدِ
Take turns	تناوَبتا
My care	رِعَايَتِي
A high level of efficiency	عَلَى مُسْتَوَى مُرْتَفِعٍ مِنَ الكَفَاءَةِ
He who work hard deserve appreciation	مَنْ يَعْمَلْ عَمَلَهُ باجتِهَادٍ يَسْتَحِقُّ الشُّكْرَ
Did you know what your stomach were carrying / do you know the sex of the baby.	هَلْ كُنْتِ تَعْلَمِينَ مَا فِي بَطنِكِ
Type of embryo	بِنَوعِ الجَنِينِ
And split it	واقتَسِميهَا
The good news	النَّبَأَ السَّعِيدِ
I delivered them (the babies)	أنْجَبتُهُما

أسئلة:

1. What type of medical care does the woman need?

2. How did the woman feel on regaining her consciousness after being under anesthesia?

3. What did she ask about when she woke up?

4. Is this her first child?

5. How many children does she give birth to?

6. Who visited the woman on the day prior to this conversation?

7. Who do the newborn look like?

8. What were the doctor's orders after the birth?

9. How many doctors were involved in her care?

10. Are these doctors well qualified?

11. How many nurses helped care for the woman before she gave birth?

12. What is the general qualification of the people working at the hospital?

13. What is the sex of the newborn?

14. Did the woman know the sex beforehand?

15. Was it possible to know this?

16. Who tells the woman about the sex of the newborn?

17. How does the woman express her gratitude for the care she has received?

18. When does she want to see her newborn?

يَوْمٌ فِي حَيَاةِ طَالِبٍ جَامِعِي	مَنْ طَلَبَ العُلا سَهِرَ اللَيَالِي

الحوار

أحمد: هَلْ رَأَيْتَ خَالِداً يَامَحْمُود؟

محمود: لَا، لَمْ يَأْتِ اليَوْمَ عَلَى مَاأَظُنُّ.

أحمد: حَقّاً، لَقَدْ أَخَذْتُ مِنْهُ كَشْكُولَ المُحَاضَرَاتِ وَأُرِيدُ أَنْ أُعِيدَهُ اليهِ.

محمود: رُبَّمَا أَوْقَفَهُ الحَرَسُ الجَامِعِيُّ لِأَنَّهُ نَسِيَ كَارْنِيه الجَامِعَةِ (بِطَاقَةُ الهَوِيَةِ الجَامِعِيَةِ)، لاأَعْلَمُ.

أحمد: تَعَالَ نَذْهَبُ الَى مُدَرَّجُ(أ) فَهُنَاكَ مُحَاضَرَةٌ لِدُكْتُورِ مَادَّةِ تَارِيخِ الحَضَارَةِ، وَرُبَّمَا احْتَسَبْنَا غَائِبَيْنِ فِي السِيكْشَنِ.

محمود: مَعَكَ حَقٌّ، رُبَّمَا رَأَيْنَا خَالِداً هُنَاكَ، كَمَا انَّ الدُكْتُور سَيُشَغِّلُ جِهَازَ البِرُوجِيكْتُور وَسَيُرِينَا جُدَارِيَاتٍ فِرعَونِيَةً مُلَوَنَةً تُوَضِّحُ أَسَالِيبَ الزِرَاعَةِ عِنْدَ قُدَمَاءِ المِصْرِيينَ.

أحمد: لابُدَّ لَنَا أَنْ نَحْجِزَ مَكَاناً قَرِيباً فِي أَوَّلِ المُدَرَجِ لِنَرَى وَنَسْمَعَ جَيِّداً.

محمود: قَبْلَ ذَلِكَ قُلْ لِي هَلْ دَفَعْتَ لَنَا نُقُودَ الرِّحْلَةِ عِنْدَ اتِّحَادِ الطَلَبَةِ؟

أحمد: نَعَمْ، لَمْ أَنْسَ، لَكِنَّ خَالِداً حَصَلَ عَلَى هَذِهِ الرِحْلَةِ مَجَاناً.

محمود: نَعَمْ، مَاشَاءَ اللهُ، أَتَوَقَّعُ لِخَالِدٍ أَنْ يُصْبِحَ مُعِيداً وَيُعَيَّنَ بِالكُلِّيَةِ، انَّهُ مُجِدٌّ وَمُجْتَهِدٌ رُغْمَ ظُرُوفِهِ الصَّعْبَةِ، انَّهُ يَرْكَبُ الاوتُوبِيسَ(الباص) كُلَّ يَوْمٍ، وَنَحْنُ لَدينَا سَيَّارَاتُنَا الخَاصَّةِ وَلَسْنَا مُتَفَوِّقِينَ مِثلَهُ.

أحمد: صَحِيحٌ، مَاشَاءَ اللهُ، لَقَدْ طَلَبَ مِنْهُ عَمِيدُ الكُلِّيَةِ إلقَاءَ كَلِمَةً بِالنَّدوَةِ التِّي سَتقُامُ فِي مَسْرَحِ الطُّلابِ يَوْمَ الخَمِيسِ القَادِمِ.

محمود: مَاشَاءَ الله لاقُوَّةَ الا بِاللهِ.

أحمد: هَيَا نَذْهَبُ الَى المُحَاضَرَةِ وَبَعْدَهَا نَذْهَبُ الَى مَكتَبَةِ الكُلِّيَةِ، لَقَد وَعَدَنِي أَمِينُ المَكتَبَةِ أَنَّ الكُتُبَ التِّي أَرَدْتُهَا سَتَكُونُ مَوْجُودَةً اليَوْمَ.

محمود: وَبَعْدَهَا نَذْهَبُ لِتَنَاوِلِ الطَّعَامِ فِي كَافِيتِيرِيَا الكُلِّيَةِ (المَطْعَمِ)، ثُمَّ نُصَوِّرُ بَعْضَ الأوْرَاقِ فِي مَرْكَزِ التَّصْوِيرِ وَالأبْحَاثِ القَرِيبِ مِنْ مَحَطَّةِ الأتُوبِيسِ.

أحمد: هَيَاَ بِنَا إذنْ.

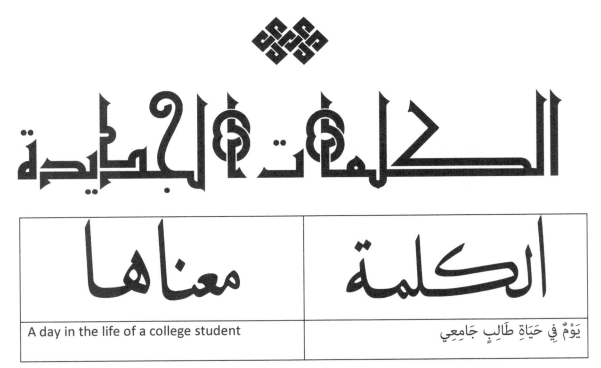

الكلمات الجديدة

الكلمة	معناها
يَوْمٌ فِي حَيَاةِ طَالِبٍ جَامِعِي	A day in the life of a college student

256

He who seek the top should stay up many nights (studying)	مَنْ طَلَبَ العُلا سَهِرَ اللَّيَالِي
As far as I know	عَلَى مَا أَظُنُّ
Lectures notebook	كَشْكُولَ المُحَاضَرَاتِ
Return it	أُعِيدَهُ
History of civilization	تَارِيخ الحَضَارَة
He was stopped	أَوْقَفَهُ
University guards	الحَرَسُ الجَامِعِيُّ
University ID	كَارْنِيه الجَامِعَة
University identity card	بِطَاقَةُ الهَوِيَةِ الجَامِعِيَةِ
I do not know	لا أَعْلَمُ
Lecture hall	مُدَرَجٌ
Lecture	مُحَاضَرَةٌ
Count the absentee	احْتَسَبْنَا غَائِبَيْنِ
You are right	مَعَكَ حَقٌّ
He will show us	سَيُرِينَا
Mural	جُدَارِيَاتٍ
pharaonic	فِرعَوْنِيَةً
Shows	تُوَضِّحُ
Methods	أَسَالِيبَ
Ancient Egyptians	قُدَمَاءِ المِصْرِيين

The price of the trip	نُقُودَ الرِّحْلَةِ
Student Union	اتِّحَادِ الطَلَبَةِ
Free	مَجَاناً
Will operate the projector	سَيُشَغِّلُ جِهَازَ البرُوجِيكتُور
What Allah's wish (has come to pass)	مَا شَاءَ اللهُ
Lecturer	مُعِيداً
And will be tenured in college	وَيُعَيَّنَ بالكُلِّيَةِ
Hard working	مُجِدٌّ
Diligent	مُجْتَهِدٌ
Hard worker	رُغْمَ
His situation is difficult	ظُرُوفِهِ الصَّعْبَةِ
High achievers	مُتَفَوِقِينَ
Dean of the College	عَمِيدُ الكُلِّيَةِ
Deliver a speech	إلقَاءَ كَلِمَةً
Symposium	النَّدوَةِ
Will be held	سَتُقَامُ
students Theater	مَسْرَحِ الطُّلابِ
Librarian	أمِينُ المكتَبَةِ
Photocopies some papers	نُصَوِّرُ بَعْضَ الأوْرَاقِ
Imaging Center and Research	مَركَزِ التَصْوِيرِ وَالأبْحَاثِ

258

أسئلة:

1. Where is Ahmed looking for Khalid?

2. Did Khalid come to university today?

3. What does Mahmoud think has happened to Khalid?

4. What is the role of university security guards?

5. What would university security guards do if someone forgot their ID?

6. What is the topic of the lecture in Lecture Hall A?

7. Is there a penalty for not attending lectures?

8. In the lecture, the professor uses a projector to show his students murals from ancient Egypt. What do these murals depict ?

9. Are these murals colorful?

10. Is the lecture hall big or small? How do you know?

11. The students re participating in a field trip. Where should they pay the fee for the trip?

12. Which student travels free? Why?

13. Why is Khalid expected to be hired by the college as part of their teaching staff?

14. Who is riding the bus to college and who drives his own vehicle?

15. What does the dean of the college ask Khalid to do? When and where should he do this?

16. After finishing the lectures, where do Ahmed and Mahmoud want to go?

17. What promise does the librarian give to Ahmed?

18. Where will Mahmoud and Ahmed have their meal?

19. Where is the photocopy center located? Why does Mahmoud want to go there

قَدْ يَكُونُ الْيَوْمُ الْأَوَّلُ للطِّفْلِ فِي الْمَدْرَسَةِ مِنْ أَجْمَلِ وَأَرْوَعِ الْأَيَّامِ، لَيْسَ فَقَطْ للطِّفْلِ، بَلْ لِوَالِدَيْهِ أَيْضًا. وَقَدْ يَكُونُ عَلَى النَّقِيضِ مِنْ ذَلِكَ تَمَامًا، حَيْثُ تَبْدَأُ مَعْرَكَةٌ يَوْمِيَّةٌ مِنَ الْبُكَاءِ وَالْهُرُوبِ وَالتَّمَارُضِ وَالرَّجَاءِ بِأَنْ لَا يَذْهَبَ إِلَى الْمَدْرَسَةِ، وَلَعَلَّ النِّسْبَةَ الْعُلْيَا -وَللْأَسَفِ- فِي مُجْتَمَعَاتِنَا الْعَرَبِيَّةِ هِيَ مِنَ النَّوْعِ الثَّانِي، فَمَعَ افْتِتَاحِ الْمَدَارِسِ تَبْدَأُ الشَّكَاوَى وَالْأَسْئِلَةُ تَرِدُ عَنْ أَفْضَلِ الْأَسَالِيبِ الَّتِي تُعَالِجُ هَذِهِ الظَّاهِرَةَ.

The first day in school for a child may be one of the most beautiful and wonderful of days, not only for the child, but also for his parents. But maybe, it will be the exact opposite, starting with a daily battle of crying, escape attempts, feigned illnesses, and begging not to go to school. Perhaps the highest percentage in our Arab society is of the second type, with the start of the school year bringing complaints and questions about what is the best method to address these issues.

وَلَعَلَّ الْإِجَابَةَ تَكْمُنُ فِي كَلِمَاتٍ بَسِيطَةٍ، وَهِيَ أَنْ "نَجْعَلَ الْمَدْرَسَةَ مَكَانًا جَاذِبًا للطِّفْلِ"، وَهَذَا لَيْسَ بِالشَّيْءِ الصَّعْبِ إِطْلَاقًا، لَكِنْ شَرِيطَةَ أَنْ تَقُومَ الْأُسْرَةُ بِدَوْرِهَا، وَكَذَلِكَ أَنْ تَقُومَ الْمَدْرَسَةُ بِدَوْرِهَا.

Perhaps the answer lies in the simple words, that we make the school an attractive place for the child. This is not a difficult thing at all, but the family must play its role, in addition to the school.

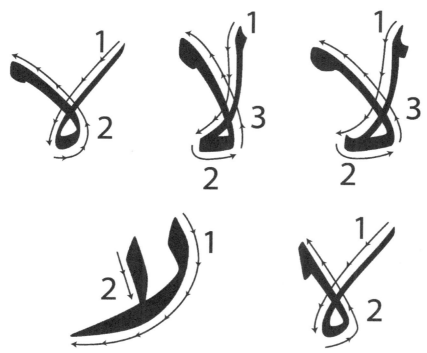

'La' means 'no'. When it is prefixed by the preposition 'baa', it will create 'bila', which means 'without'. 'La' by itself is a particle. When the 'ba' is attached, the 'la' changes into a noun. As 'la' is a noun attached to a preposition, 'bila' becomes a prepositional phrase جار ومجرور

He beat me without mercy.	ضَرَبَنِي بِلاَ رَحْمَةٍ
I helped Ahmed without hesitation.	سَاعَدْتُ أَحْمَدَ بِلاَ تَرَدُّدٍ
I kept working without getting tired.	أَخَذْتُ أَعْمَلُ بِلاَ تَعَبٍ
I faced him without fear.	وَاجَهْتُهُ بِلاَ خَوفٍ
I worked without fatigue.	عَمِلْتُ بِلاَ كَلَلٍ

'La' as a particle.

'La' can also come as an additional word with no grammatical effect; its function is to stress the negation of two nouns or verbs. For example, 'you will satisfy neither my father nor my mother'. 'Neither' does not translate as 'la', but the second negating word 'nor' will be 'la'.	'La' can also be an additional word in sentence with no grammatical effect on the word following it, and it will not precede a nominal clause. In some of the examples below, 'la' is preceded by hamza-tulwasl. In this case 'la' means 'not to'. This is one meaning among many in the examples that follow (although it always carries the connotation of negation).	When a present tense verb is preceded by 'la', this 'la' is a particle and is called a prohibiting 'la'. It is used as an imperative to not carry out the verb in question. When 'la' precedes a present tense verb, the verb will be in a state of jazem, which means you should place a sukuun on top of it, as you see in the examples below.
مَا كَانَ يُرْضِي ذَلِكَ أَبِي وَلاَ أُمِّي	مَامَنَعَكَ أَلاَّ تُذَاكِرَ	لاَتَشْرَبْ القَهْوَةَ الانَ
This satisfies neither my father nor my mother.	What prevents you from studying?	Do not drink the coffee now.
مَا كَانَ يُسَامِحُكَ مُحَمَدٌ وَلاَ أَنَا	مَا عَطَّلَكَ أَلاَّ تَحْضُرَ بِسُرْعَةٍ	لاَتَذْهَبْ الَى المَدْرَسَةِ اليَومَ
Neither Mohammed nor I will forgive you.	What delayed you in getting here sooner?	Do not go to the school today.
مَا أَنْكَرَ سَعِيدٌ وَلاَ اِعْتَرَفَ	مَا جَعَلَكَ أَلاَّ تُسَافِرَ	لاَتَاكُلْ هَذَا الطَّعَامَ
Sayyeed neither denied nor confessed.	What prevented you from travelling?	Do not eat the food.
مَا قَامَ مُحَمَدٌ وَلاَ تَحَرَّكَ مِنْ مَكَانِه	مَا مَنَعَكَ أَلاَّ تَعْمَلَ الوَاجِبَ	لاَ تَشْرَبْ الخَمْرَ
Mohammed did not get up, nor did he move from his place.	What prevented you from doing your homework?	Do not drink the wine.
مَا قَرَأْتُ الكِتَابَ وَلاَ لَخَصْتُهُ	مَا حَمَلَكَ أَلاَّ تَأْتِيَ	لاَ تَلْعَبْ مَعَ الكَلْبِ
I did not read the book, nor did I summarize it.	What prevented you from coming?	Do not play with the dog.
مَاكَانَ عَمِّي يَقْرَأُ وَلاَ يَكْتُبُ	مَا جَعَلَكَ أَلاَّ تَرْقُصَ مَعِي	لاَ تُقَامِرْ
My paternal uncle can neither read nor write.	What stopped you from dancing with me?	Don't gamble.

لَا إِلَهَ إِلَّا اللهُ

When 'la' precedes a noun

When 'la' precedes an indefinite noun		When 'la' precedes a definite noun, it should be repeated
'La' can also negate combining nouns, and here it will function as إن.	'La' could negate one noun, and in this case it functions like ليس. Its subject and predicate will be indefinite. The subject will always come before the predicate. You can precede the predicate with الا.	لَا خَالِدٌ مَحْبُوبٌ وَلَا أَحْمَدُ
		Neither Khalid nor Ahmed are loved.
لَا اِلَهَ اِلَّا اللهَ	لَا مَعْرُوفٌ ضَائِعًا	لَا رِيمٌ حَنُونَةٌ وَلَا وَفَاءُ
There is no God but Allah.	No good deed is lost.	Neither Reem nor Wafaa have compassion.
لَا طَالِبَ فِي الفَصْلِ اليَومَ	لَا كَاذِبٌ مَحْبُوبًا	لَا عَادِلٌ مُتَفَوِّقٌ وَلَا سَعِيدُ
There is no student in the class today.	No liar is loved.	Neither Adil nor Sayyeed excelled.
لَا حَيَاةَ عَلَى كَوكَبِ المَرِّيخ	لَاصَادِقٌ مَكْرُوهًا	لَا سَارَةٌ مَوهُوبَةٌ وَلَا نَادِيَةُ
There is no life on the planet Mars.	No truth-teller is hated.	Neither Sarah nor Nadia are talented.
لَا حَيَاءَ فِي الدِّينِ	لَا فَاشِلٌ مَوهُوبًا	لَا زِيَادٌ فَائِزٌ وَلَا طَارِقُ
There is no shame in the religion.	No failure is talented.	Neither Ziad nor Tarek are winners.

When 'la' precedes a verb

When 'la' precedes a past tense verb, it should be repeated.	When 'la' precedes a present tense verb, it should not be repeated.
لَا أَنْكَرَ وَلَا اِعْتَرَفَ	آنَا لَا أُحِبُّ الشَّايِ
He neither denied nor confessed.	I do not like tea.
فَلَا صَدَّقَ وَلَا صَلَّى	آنَا لَا أُحِبُّكَ
He neither prayed nor gave to charity.	I do not like you.
لَا تَكَلَّمَ وَلَا نَطَقَ	هُوَ لَا يُحِبُّ الْقِرَاءَةَ
He neither spoke nor uttered a word.	He does not like reading.
لَا بَاعَ وَلَا اِشْتَرَى	هِيَ لَا تُحِبُّ الْحَرَّ
He neither bought nor sold.	She does not like heat.
لَا ذَاكَرَ وَلَا اِجْتَهَدَ	نَحْنُ لَا نُحِبُّ السَّفَرَ
He neither studied nor worked hard.	She does not like heat.

الكلماتُ الجديدة

معناها	الكلمة
Mercilessly	بِلَا رَحْمَةٍ
Decidedly	بِلَا تَرَدُّدٍ

Tirelessly	بِلاَ تَعَبٍ
Fearless	بِلاَ خَوفٍ
Tirelessly	بِلاَ كَلَلٍ
Wine	الخَمْرَ
Do not gamble	لاَ تُقَامِرْ
What prevented you	مَا مَنَعَكَ
What delay you	مَا عَطَّلَكَ
To come	تَحْضُرَ
What made you	مَا جَعَلَكَ
What push you	مَا حَمَلَكَ
Dance	تَرْقُصَ
This will not satisfy you	مَا كَانَ يُرضِي
He will not forgive you	مَا كَانَ يُسَامِحُكَ
Denied	أَنْكَرَ
Confess	إِعْتَرَفَ
Move	تَحَرَّكَ
Summarized	لَخَّصْتُهُ

Affectionate	حَنُونَةٌ
Superior	مُتَفَوِّقٌ
Talented	مَوْهُوبَةٌ
Winner	فَائِزٌ
Known	مَعْرُوفٌ
Lost	ضَائِعًا
False	كَاذِبٌ
Beloved	مَحْبُوبًا
Honest	صَادِقٌ
Hatted	مَكْرُوهًا
Failure	فَاشِلُ
Gifted	مَوْهُوبًا
Mars	المَرِّيخِ
Shyness	حَيَاءَ

التَّحِيَّات

مَبْرُوكٌ، جَالَكَ وَلَدٌ.

This lesson will introduce you to many of the greetings, formalities and general well wishing in Arabic. These phrases permeate the Arabic language: often conversations will be heavily laden with greetings, farewells, and what may be called decorating language – often in Arabic you will hear whole conversations in which the interlocutors do not speak with a purpose per se, instead with humor and light-heartedness.

محمد: صَبَاحُ الخَيرِ يَا مَحْمُود.

محمود: صَبَاحُ النُّورِ يَا مُحَمَدٌ، كَيْفَ الحَالُ؟

محمد: بِخَيرٍ وَالحَمْدُ لله، كَيْفَ حَالُكَ؟

محمود: نَحْمِدُهُ، كَيْفَ حَالُ إبنتِكَ فَاطِمَةٌ؟

محمد: اِنَّهَا مَريضَةٌ، نَحْمِدُ اللهَ عَلَى كُلِّ حَالٍ.

محمود: الفُ لَابَأسَ عَلَيْهَا، شَفَاهَا اللهُ، وَكَيْفَ حَالُ ابنِكَ؟

محمد: اِنَّهُ بِخَيرٍ وَالحَمْدُ لله، لَقَدْ نَجَحَ في امْتِحَانِ الثانَوِيَةِ العَامَةِ.

محمود: بِسْمِ اللهِ مَا شَاءَ اللهُ، الفُ مَبْرُوكٍ، وَكَيْفَ حَالُ اخُوكَ احمَدٌ؟

محمد: اِنَّهُ يَسْتَعِدُّ لِلسَفَرِ الَى السُّعُودِيَةِ لِلعَمَلِ.

محمود: وَفَقَهُ اللهُ، يرُوحُ وَيَرْجِعُ بِالسَّلامَةِ انْ شَاءَ اللهُ.

محمد: ابُوكَ، اللهُ يَرْحَمُهُ وَيُحْسِنُ اليَهِ، عَمِلَ في السُّعُودِيَةِ لِفَتَرَةٍ طَوِيلَةٍ.

علي: السَّلامُ عَلَيْكُمْ وَرَحَمَةُ اللهِ.

268

محمود ومحمد: وَعَلَيْكُمُ السَّلَامُ وَرَحْمَةُ ۝ اللهِ وَبَرَكاتُهُ ، اتفَضَّلْ اجْلِسْ.

علي: شُكراً

محمد: الشُّكرُ للهِ، اتفَضَّلْ كُلْ مَعَنا، لُقمَة ۝ هَنِية ۝ تكفِي مِيه.

علي: شُكراً، بِالهَناءِ وَالشِّفاءِ وَمَطرَحُ ما يَسرِي يَمري، مَبرُوك عَلى نَجاحِ ابنِكَ حامِدٌ

محمد: اللهُ يُبارِكُ فِيكَ، عُقبَال ابنِكَ حَمدِي.

علي: مِنْ فَمِكَ الَى بَابِ السَّماءِ، انا خَائِفٌ عَلَيهِ.

محمد: لاتَخَفْ وَتَوَكَّل عَلَى اللهِ.

علي: وَنِعْمَ بِاللهِ، كَيفَ حَالُ صَدِيقِنَا حَمُودَه، سَمِعْتُ انَّهُ مَرِيضٌ.

محمد: للأسَفِ الشَّدِيدِ، انتَقَلَ الَى رَحمَةِ اللهِ.

علي: لاحَولَ وَلاقُوَّةَ إلا بِاللهِ. إنَّا للهِ وَإنَّا الَيهِ رَاجِعُونَ، اللهُ يَرْحَمُهُ وَيُحْسِنُ الَيهِ وَيَجعَلُ مَثْوَاهُ الجَنَّةَ.

محمد: هُوَ وَالسَّامِعِينَ يَاقَادِرُ يَاكَرِيْمُ، احْوَالُ عَائِلَتِه الانَ تُقطِّعُ القَلْبَ.

علي: رَبَّنَا يَسْتُرُهَا مَعَاهُم، وَيُوَقِّفُ لَهُم أولادُ الحَلالِ اللي يُسَاعِدُوهُم.

محمد: كُلُّنَا لَهَا، إنْ شَاءَ اللهُ سَنُحَاوِلُ مُسَاعَدَتَهُم عَلَى قَدرِ الامْكَانِ، هَذا وَاجِبٌ عَلَينا.

علي: بِدُونِ شَكٍ.

محمود: شُكراً عَلَى الاكْلِ وَالشُّربِ يَا اخُ مُحَمَدٍ.

محمد: العَفوُ يَا أخُ مَحْمُودٍ، إكْرَامُ الضَّيفِ وَاجَبٌ، بَلِّغ سَلامِي لِكُلَّ مَنْ يَسْأَلُ عَنِّي.

269

محمود: سَلامُكَ وَاصِلْ.

محمد: أَنَا هَامْشِي، فُوتَكَ بِعَافِيَةٍ يَامَحْمُود.

محمود: اللهُ يُعَافِيكَ، يَجْعَلُ لَكَ فِي كُلِّ خُطْوَةٍ سَلامَة ۝، فِي حِفْظِ اللهِ وَرِعَايَتِه، بَلِّغ السَّلامَ لِلحَاج عَامِرٍ.

محمد: أَمَّا انتَ ابنُ حَلالٍ صَحِيحٌ، دَه رَجَعَ مِنَ الحَجِّ، حَاضِرُ مِنْ عَيني.

محمود: تَكرُم ۝ عَينُكَ يَامُحَمَد، قُلْ لَه ۝ (حَجٌّ مَقبُولٌ وَذَنْبٌ مَغفُورٌ) ان شَاءَ اللهُ وَعُقْبَالُ السَّنَةِ القَادِمَة.

محمد: نَحْنُ وَانتُم ان شَاءَ اللهُ عَلَى جَبَلِ عَرَفَةٍ يَامَحْمُود.

محمود: اهٍ، نِفسِي وَمُنَى العَينِ يَامُحَمَد، سَمِعَ اللهُ مِنكَ، اللهُمَّ امِينْ.

سمية دخلت: السَّلامُ يَاعَم مَحَمَد عُقبَالُ عِندِكُم و عُقبَالُ الحَبَايِب ابنِي جَاله تَؤم، مُحَمَدٌ وَمَحْمُودٌ عَلَى اسمِكُم.

محمود: عَلَى اسمِي، الفُ مَبْرُوكِ يَاحَاجَة ۝ سُمَيَة ۝ وَيَترَبُونَ فِي عِزِّكِ وَعِزُّ ابُوهُم.

محمد: الفُ مَبْرُوكِ، الأخبَارُ الحُلوَة ۝، كَأَنَ ابنُكِ حَسْن مُتَزَوِجٌ امبَارِح وَكُنتُ اقُولُ لَه (مِنْكَ المَالُ وَمِنهَا العِيَالُ) وَ (بِالرَّفَاءِ وَالبَنُونِ)

سمية: يَا مِلحَ دَارِنَا كَثر عِيالُنَا يَاحَجُّ مُحَمَدٍ (الاولادُ زِينَة ۝ الحَيَاةِ الدُّنيَا).

محمد: وَأَعَزُّ الوِلْدِ وَلَدُ الوَلَدِ يَا حَاجَة ۝ سُمَيَة ۝.

سمية: عُقبَالُ نَادِيَة بِنتِكَ ان شَاءَ اللهُ.

محمد: اهٍ يَاحَاجَة مِنْ سَاعَةِ الطِّفلُ مَاتَ فِي بَطنِهَا وَهِيَ فِي نَارٍ.

270

سمية: رَبُّنَا قَادِرٌ يُبَرِّدُ قَلْبَهَا وَيُعَوِّضُهَا خَيْراً، عِوَضُ الصَّابِرِينَ يَارَبُّ.

محمد: يَسْمَعُ مِنكَ، رَبُّنَا يَكرِمُهَا بِشُوفَةِ ضَنَاهَا، ادْعِي لَهَا يَاحَاجَة ۞.

سمية: قَلْبِي مَعَاهَا وَمَعَ كُلِّ مَحْرُومٍ وَمُشْتَاقٍ يَارَبُّ.

محمود: وَهِبَة ۞تَصَالَحَتْ مَعَ زَوجِهَا.

سمية: لا، عَنِيدَة ۞وَرَأْسُهَا نَاشِفْ.

محمود: رَبُّنَا يَجْمَعُ شَمْلَهُمْ، وَيَهْدِي سِرَّهُمْ، وَيُحَنِنْ قُلُوبَهُمْ عَلَى بَعْضٍ.

سُمية: انَا كُنْتُ حَابَّة أزَوِّج سَعِيدَ اخُو حَسَنٍ مِنْ بِنتِكَ صَفَاءِ القَمَرِ يَاحَجُّ مَحْمُودٍ، وَابْنِي ابْنُكَ تَمَامٌ يَاحَاج.

محمود: يَزِيدُنَا شَرَفٌ، سُمْعَتُهُ سَابِقَاهُ، دَه احْنَا نُوصِلُهَا لِحَدِّ عِنْدِكُم وَصَفَاءُ بِنتِكِ يَاحَاجَة ۞وَانْتِ رَبَيْتِيهَا وَعَارْفَاهَا.

سمية: تَسْلَمُ يَاحَاج، صَفَاءُ بِنتِي وَنُثَقِّلُهَا بِالذَّهَبِ، مِنْ يَوم رَاهَا فِي فَرَحِ أخُوهِ، وَهُوَ لا عَلَى حَامِي وَلا عَلَى بَارِدٍ، وَيَقُولُ هِيَ هَذِهِ، حَلاوَةٌ وَنَقَاوَةٌ وَبِنتُ أُصُولٍ.

محمد: اللهَ اللهَ اللهَ، امتَى نُبلِّلُ الشربَاتَ؟ أَنَا أقولُ خَيْرُ البِرِ عَاجِلُهُ.

سمية: عَدَّاكَ العَيْبُ يَامُحَمَدَ، بَعْدَ جُمْعَتَينِ نَقرَأُ الفَاتِحَةَ

سَعِيدٌ سَيَصِلُ مِنَ الكُوَيتِ.

محمد: مِصْرُ هَتنَوَر بَعْدَ جُمْعَتَينِ.

سمية: مِصْرُ مُنَوَرَة ۞بِأهْلِهَا يَا حَاج مُحَمَد، أنَا كُنْتُ سَأخْطِبُ لَهُ بِنْتَكَ قَبْلَ مَا تُقْرَأُ فَاتِحَتُهَا، هههههه.

271

محمد:(مَالَهَاش فِي الطَّيْب نَصِيبٌ) يَاسْمَيَة ، (رُقَيَة بِنتُك وَصَفَاءُ بِنتُكِ)، (مَيَتَخَيَرُوش عَنْ بَعْضٍ).

شمس: صَبَاحُكُم أَبْيَض مِثلُ الحَلِيبِ.

سمية: صَبَاحِك فُلُّ الفُلَّ يَاشَمْس، (دَه اسْمُهُ كَلامٌ؟) (يَنفِعُ كِدَه؟) (انْتِ رُحْتِ وَقُلْتِ عِدُّوا لي؟) (ايه الغِيبَة الطَّوِيْلَة دِي؟) .

شمس: اصْلُ كَنْتُ بِعَافِيَةٍ شويةٍ.

سمية: خَيْرٌ؟ سَلامَتُك.

شمس: أَصْلُ بِنْتِي رَسَبَتْ فِي الامتِحَانِ، وَأَنَا زِعلْتْ زَعْل السِّنين.

سمية: لا حَوْلَ وَلا قُوَّةَ الا باللهِ، رَوَقِي نَفسِك، بُكرَه تَنجح.

شمس: دِي وَلا عَلَى بَالهَا، وَأَنَا ساجعَلهَا تُسَاعِدُني فِي السُّوقِ.

سمية: اصْبِري عَلَيهَا، عَشَان تِفلَحْ.

شمس: سِيبِك آنتي، الحَاجَة نَوال نَقَلتْ فِي بَيتِهَا الجَدِيدِ.

سمية: تَبَارَكَ الله، تَعَالِي نُبَارك لَهَا.

سمية: السَّلامُ عَلَيكُم يحاجه نَوَال، يَجْعَلهُ قَدَمَ السَّعدِ عَلَيكِ، وَيطرَحُ البَرَكَة فِيه.

نوال: عِشْتِ يَا سُمَيَة، خَطوَة عَزِيزَة يَاشَمس، يَادِي النُّور، يَادِي النُّور، اتفَضَلُوا الشَّاي.

سمية: يجعَلُه عَامِر وَفِي فَرْح عَلَى طُول يَارَب.

نوال: أَنَا نَوَيتُ والنِّيَّة للهِ أَنْ أذبَحَ عِجلاً وَأَفَرِقَهُ عَلَى الحَبَايب وَعَلَى الغلابَة.

272

سمية: خَمسةٌ وَخَميسةٌ في عِينِ اللّي مَايُصَلّي عَلَى النّبي.

نوال: شُكراً يَاعَزيزَة يَا غَالية.

سمية: اه، يَاحَاجة نَوَال يَارَب أفرَاحنَا تَزيد، وَيَجعَلُ الحُزْنَ بَعيْد، اعْمَلي مَعرُوف يَانَوَال تَذَكّري بَيْتَ الحَاجِ حَمُودَه، حَالهُمْ يَصْعَبُ عَلَى الكَافِرِ، وَأولادُهُ كَتَاكِيت، وَمرَاتُهُ في عزِّ شَبَابِهَا وَيُقَويهَا اللهُ عَلَى مَابَلاهَا.

نوال: مِن عَيِني، وَيَجعَلُهَا اخِرُالأحزَانِ، وَنَزُورُهم في الفَرح.

شمس: اللهُمَّ امِين، السَترُ مِنْ عِنْدَكَ يَارَبُّ.

الكَلمَاتُ الجَديدة

معناها	الكلمة
Congratulations, you have a boy! (The words translated as, 'you have a boy' is literally, 'a boy came to you')	مَبْرُوكٌ، جَالَكَ وَلَدٌ
Good morning (literally, 'morning of goodness')	صَبَاحُ الخَيرِ
Good morning (this is the answer to the first good morning; you answer 'morning of goodness' with this, 'morning of light')	صَبَاحُ النُّورِ

How are you? How is it going? (In Arabic, this is 'how is the situation?' 'How is your status?')	كَيْفَ الحَالُ
Okay, thank God (literally, 'with goodness, thanks to Allah')	بِخَيْرٍ وَالحَمْدُ للهِ
How are you?	كَيْفَ حَالُكَ
We thank Him (a typical answer to someone asking how you are – you thank Allah for both the good and the bad; you should be thankful regardless of your situation)	نَحْمِدُهُ
We praise Allah regardless of the situation (this could also be said when you are having a rough time. Muslims believe that no bad time will last forever, that good times will immediately follow bad situations)	نَحْمِدُ اللهَ عَلَى كُلِّ حَالٍ
One thousand no pain/suffering for her (said upon hearing that someone is sick; one thousand signifies the number of times you wish her to be well – you hear this in well-wishing, congratulations, sympathetic phrases, etc. People will mention the numbers sixty and one hundred beside one thousand to emphasize their statement. It is a common idiom in Arabic)	الفُ لابَأْسَ عَلَيْهَا
By the name of Allah, what Allah wished has come to pass (this is said upon hearing good news – success in exams, marriage, new job, etc. It is said to thwart any misconceptions that you envy the fortunate person)	بِسْمِ اللهِ مَا شَاءَ اللهُ
One thousand congratulations (a standard phrase to someone who has had success)	الفُ مَبْرُوكٍ
May Allah guide him to the right path (or, 'may Allah make him prosper': well-wishing upon hearing that someone is embarking	وَفَّقَهُ اللهُ

upon a new challenge)	
May he go and come back in safety, by the will of Allah (said when you hear that someone is travelling)	يرُوحُ وَيَرْجِعُ بِالسَّلامَةِ انْ شَاءَ اللهُ
May Allah have mercy on him and be charitable to him (said upon hearing that someone has passed away – also said after mentioning someone's name who has passed away. No one will mention the name of the recently deceased without saying anything)	اللهُ يَرْحَمُهُ وَيُحْسِنُ الَيْهِ
Peace be upon you, and Allah's mercy (a standard Islamic greeting – Christian Arabs don't use this greeting)	السَّلامُ عَلَيْكُمْ وَرَحمَةُ اللهِ
Peace be upon you, and Allah's mercy and his blessings (said in response to the above. Muslims believe that he who is greeted should respond with an equal or longer greeting)	وَعَلَيكُمُ السَّلامُ وَرَحْمَةُ اللهِ وَبَرَكاتُه
Please, go ahead (literally, 'condescension': said to someone "better" than you – they are doing you a favor by accepting your offering)	اتفَضَّلْ
Thank you (note 'thank you' is literally, 'thank you very much' – the grammatical construction emphasizes the thanks)	شُكرًا
Thanks to Allah (could also be said by someone who has been thanked, as any effort that he has been thanked for should be credited to Allah – this person believes that his act of kindness was facilitated by Allah. He is saying, 'don't thank me, but He who put me in the position to be of help')	الشُّكرُ للهِ
A wholesome morsel is enough for a hundred (said when you invite someone, but	لُقمَةٌ هَنِيَةٌ تَكفِي مِيَه

your guest declines as he sees there is not enough food for everyone – you say this to show that there is indeed enough)	
With happiness and healing – wherever it goes, it will exude health (when someone is invited to a meal, he will say this if he declines the offer to wish those who are eating happiness and good health)	بِالهَنَاءِ وَالشِّفَاءِ وَمَطرَحُ مَا يَسرِي يَمرِي
Congratulations (literally, blessed. There is an Arabic word for 'congratulations', but it is usually replaced by the word 'mabruk' meaning 'blessed')	مَبرُوك عَلَى
May Allah bless you (the answer to the above statement of congratulations)	اللهُ يُبَارِكُ فِيكَ
May the result happen also to your son (the breakdown of this exchange is: something good happens and a person congratulates you. Then the above is used to thank that person. You will then say this statement to wish the same good luck onto that person's son or daughter – as if the person has made that good thing happen and deserves to have the good fortune endowed upon his family)	عُقبَال ابْنِكَ
From your mouth to the door of the sky (this is the equivalent of, 'from your mouth to God's ear' – this would be blasphemous in Islam but the connotations are the same. Muslims believe there are doors in the sky; these are the doors which allow access to what is above the sky – there are seven skies)	مِنْ فَمِكَ الَى بَابِ السَّمَاءِ
Rely on Allah (said to someone who is about to embark on a task. It comes from the Koran, which states that he who relies on Allah will have the best ally in Allah)	وَتَوَكّلْ عَلَى اللهِ

And your life will be good and comfortable when you are following Allah (this phrase is said in response to the above statement as an affirmation of relying on Allah)	وَنِعْمَ بِالله
Unfortunately (literally, 'with deep sorrow' or 'with strong sorrow'; the situation where you say this is the same in English as in Arabic, but it carries a slightly stronger meaning in Arabic. If the situation is not severe, you will use 'with sorrow')	للأسف الشَّدِيد
He moved to within Allah's mercy (a Muslim declaration of a passing away: regardless of someone's deed, as long as he is a Muslim, and he believes in the oneness of Allah, his soul will be saved from the hellfire)	انتَقَلَ الَى رَحمَةِ اللهِ.
There is no power or strings, except those from Allah (said when you hear devastating news, such as the death of a person. Hearing the news of someone's death can trigger several statements that we are explaining now)	لاحَوْلَ وَلاقُوَّةَ إلا بِاللهِ
This is from the Koran: "Surely we belong to Allah and to Him we shall return." This phrase is said upon hearing bad news, in particular when a person has died. It can also be said when a risky venture is being embarked upon.	إِنَا لِلهِ وَإِنَا الَيهِ رَاجِعُونَ
On this person, may Allah have mercy, be charitable to him and make His eternal dwelling the paradise (another statement said upon hearing that someone has passed away)	اللهُ يَرْحَمُهُ وَيُحْسِنُ الَيهِ وَيَجْعَلُ مَثْوَاهُ الجَنَّةَ.
He and those who are listening – O! Omnipotent, O! Generous one! This phrase, written above, is a comment from someone wishing a good person mercy.	هُوَ وَالسَّامِعِينَ يَا قَادِرُ يَا كَرِيْمُ

He says 'him' to refer to he who has passed away. He asks mercy to all those who are listening – humans and genies: humans who are present and genies, another creation of Allah. The speaker invokes two special traits of Allah – omnipotence and generosity. He invokes omnipotence because of His capability to grant mercy and make paradise the man's ultimate destination. He invokes generosity because, despite being unworthy of Allah's mercy, He will still grant mercy.	
The condition of his family now tears up the heart. The expression 'tears up the heart' is the equivalent of 'breaks your heart' in English.	احْوَالُ عَائِلَتِهِ الانَ تُقطّعُ القَلْبَ
May Allah provide them with protection. This is often used when someone dies, leaving a family without great financial assets. It is used in the hope of preventing the family from asking others for help, especially money.	رَبِنَا يَسْتُرُهَا مَعَاهُم
May Allah send to them those good people who could help them. This phrase uses 'the children of halal' or 'awlad' to refer to good-hearted people who will provide the family with the help they need.	وَيُوَقِفُ لَهُم أولادُ الحَلالِ اللي يُسَاعِدُوهُم.
We are all going there. 'All' here is everyone who Allah created – everything with a soul – we will all meet our death one day. The destination is death.	كُلّنَا لَهَا
If Allah wills.	إنْ شَاءَ اللهُ
This is our duty.	هَذا وَاجِبٌ عَلَينَا
Without a doubt.	بِدُونِ شَكٍ

Honoring the guest is a duty.	إِكْرَامُ الضَّيْفِ وَاجَبٌ
Tell everyone who asks about me that I send my greeting.	بَلِّغْ سَلامِي لِكُلِّ مَنْ يَسْأَلُ عَنِّي.
Your greeting will be delivered.	سَلامُكَ وَاصِلٌ.
I leave you with good health.	قُوتَكَ بِعَافِيَةٍ يَا مَحْمُود
May Allah give you good health.	اللهُ يُعَافِيكَ
May Allah provide you with safety in every step.	يَجْعَلُ لَكَ فِي كُلِّ خُطْوَةٍ سَلامَة
In Allah's safeguard and care.	فِي حِفْظِ اللهِ وَرِعَايَتِهِ
Send my greeting to Haj Aamer.	بَلِّغْ السَّلامَ لِلْحَاجِ عَامِرٍ
You are truly a good man.	أَمَّا انتَ ابْنُ حَلالٍ صَحِيحٌ
I will do it gladly. ('Gladly' is literally, 'from my eye'. When something is said to be from the eye, it means it will be done with pleasure)	حَاضِرٌ مِنْ عَيِنِي
May your eyes be honored, Mohammed.	تَكرُمُ عَيِنُكَ يَا مُحَمَد
An acceptable Haj and a forgiven sin. (This is a greeting from someone who has just performed the Haj)	حَجٌّ مَقْبُولٌ وَذَنْبٌ مَغفُورٌ
If Allah wills. We hope to have the same outcome next year.	انْ شَاءَ اللهُ وَ عُقبَالُ السَّنَةِ القَادِمَةِ.
We , and you , God willing, on Mount Arafat Mahmoud	نَحْنُ وَانتُم انْ شَاءَ اللهُ عَلَى جَبَلِ عَرَفَةٍ يَا مَحْمُود
This is my wish and what I desired, Mohammed.	نِفسِي وَمُنَى العَينِ يَا مُحَمَد
May Allah hear you, amen.	سَمِعَ اللهُ مِنكَ، اللهُمَّ امِينْ

You may have the same outcome.	عُقبالُ عِندكُم
May the loved one have the same outcome.	عُقبالُ الحَبَايب
May they grow up in your glory and the glory of their father.	يَتَربُونَ فِي عِزِّكِ وَعِزُّ أبوهُم.
Good news.	الأخبَارُ الحُلوَة
From you the money and from her the offspring.	مِنْكَ المَالُ وَمِنْهَا العِيَالُ
Live in harmony and have many children. (Said to newlyweds)	بِالرَّفَاءِ وَالبَنِينِ
Oh the salt of house, make our offspring many.	مِلْحَ دَارِنَا كَثِّر عِيالَنَا
Children are the ornament of life on earth.	الاولادُ زِينَةُ الحَيَاةِ الدُّنيَا
The dearest child is the child of a child. (The child you love most is your grandchild)	وَأعَزُّ الوِلْدِ وَلَدُ الوَلَدِ
She is in a hellfire. (She is suffering)	وَهِيَ فِي نَارٍ
May Allah cool her heart and compensate her with goodness. (Usually said of someone who is deprived of a loved one – having a heart on fire is an Arabic metaphor for suffering)	رَبُّنَا قَادِرٌ يُبَرِّدُ قَلْبَهَا وَيُعَوِّضُهَا خَيْراً
May Allah compensate her the way He compensates those who have strong patience.	عِوَضُ الصَّابِرِينَ يَارَبُّ
	يَسْمَعُ مِنكَ
May Allah honor her by making her see her child.	رَبُّنَا يَكرِمُهَا بِشُوفَةِ ضَنَاهَا
Pray for her Haja.	ادعِي لَهَا يَاحَاجَة

My heart is with her and with everyone who is deprived and longing, oh God.	قَلْبِي مَعَاهَا وَمَعَ كُلِّ مَحْرُومٍ وَمُشْتَاقٍ يَارَبُّ
May God unify them. (Said when a family is scattered over many places in the hope of bringing them together)	رَبُّنَا يَجْمَعُ شَمْلَهُمْ
May God not divulge that they consider a secret that no outsider should be aware of.	وَيَهْدِي سِرَّهُمْ
May God make their hearts have compassion for each other.	وَيُحَنِّنْ قُلُوبَهُمْ عَلَى بَعضٍ.
It increases our honor.	يَزِيدُنَا شَرَفٌ
His reputation precedes him.	سُمْعَتُهُ سَابِقَاهُ
May you be safe, oh Haj.	تَسْلَمُ يَاحَاج
For us it is worth its weight in gold.	وَنُثَقِّلُهَا بِالذَّهَبِ
From the day he saw her at his brother's wedding.	مِنْ يَومِ رَاهَا فِي فَرَحِ أَخُوهِ
There are two types of contraction – hot and cold. When it is hot, you suffer and you deliver - and when it is cold, you suffer but you do not deliver. (When you describe someone as neither hot nor cold, he is bewildered and suffering. When a woman is about to birth, she can either have hot or cold contractions. If the contractions are hot you will deliver the baby; if it is cold, you won't deliver yet – but both times you have the pain of the contraction)	وَهُوَ لَا عَلَى حَامِي وَلَا عَلَى بَارِدٍ
The girl is sweet, select and from a deep-rooted family. (Describes a desirable girl – beautiful, unique among other girls and hailing from a noble family)	حَلَاوَةٌ وَنَقَاوَةٌ وَبِنتُ أُصُولٍ
When we will make the sweet drink wet. (Refers to adding water to make a sweet	امتَى نُبِلِّ الشربات

drink for those on a happy occasion)	
The best of good deeds is the fastest.	خَيْرُ البِرِ عَاجِلُهُ
This is good, Mohammed, shame has passed you by.	عَدَّاكَ العَيْبُ يَامُحَمَدَ
Egypt will be lit up.	مِصْرُ هَتِنَوَّر
Egypt is lit up by its inhabitants, Haj.	مِصْرُ مُنَوَّرَةٌ بِأَهْلِهَا يَا حَاج
She does not have a share in what is good.	مَالَهَاش فِي الطَّيْبِ نَصِيبٌ
Both are equally good.	مَيَتَخَيَّرُوش عَنْ بَعْضٍ
Your morning is good, like milk.	صَبَاحُكُم أَبْيَض مِثلُ الحَلِيبِ
Your morning is like the best of jasmine.	صَبَاحُكِ فُلُّ الفُلِّ
You left us and told us to count how many days I was away from you.	انْتِ رُحْتِ وَقُلْتِ عِدُّوا لِي؟
What is the reason behind his long absence?	ايه الغِيبَةُ الطَّوِيْلَة دِي؟
I did not feel very well.	اصْلُ كُنْتُ بِعَافِيَةٍ شويةٍ
Goodness? Your well-being.	خَيْرٌ؟ سَلامَتُكِ.
I was so upset, like someone who has been upset for years	زعِلْتُ زَعَلْ السِّنين
Cool down. (Literally, 'make yourself clear')	رَوَقِي نَفسِكْ
She did not pay attention / This was the last thing on her mind.	دِي وَلا عَلَى بَالِهَا
To help me in the market.	تُسَاعِدُنِي فِي السُّوقِ
Be patient with her.	اصْبِرِي عَلَيهَا
So she may be successful.	عَشَان تِفلَحْ

Glory to Allah	تَبَارَكَ الله
Let us go and congratulate her.	تَعَالَي نُبَارِك لَهَا
I hope this will bring her good luck. ('Good luck' here is literally, 'the feet of happiness')	يَجْعَلُه قَدَم السَّعدِ عَليكِ
May he cast a blessing in it.	وَيطرَحُ البَرَكَةَ فِيهِ
Long live Somayya. (Somayya is a name)	عِشْتِ يَا سُمَية
Thank you for visiting, Shams. ('A dear step, Shams' is the literal translation)	خَطوَة عَزِيزَة يَاشَمس
So glad to see you. (Literally, 'oh this light!')	يَادِي النُّور
May God make it full of people and happiness all the time, oh God!	يجعَلُه عَامِر وَفِي فَرْح عَلَى طُول يَارَب
I intended, and intention is for Allah.	أَنَا نَوَيتُ وَالنِّية لله
And I will distribute it to the loved ones.	وَأَفَرِقَهُ عَلَى الحَبَايب
And those in need.	وَعَلَى الغلابَةِ.
Five and five in the eye of he who does not praise the Prophet. (Five refers to the five fingers)	خَمسَةٌ وَخمِيسَةٌ فِي عِينِ اللِّي مَايُصَلِّي عَلَى النَّبِي
Please God, increase our happiness and make our sadness stay away.	يَارَب أفرَاحنَا تَزِيد، وَيَجعَلُ الحُزْنَ بَعِيد
An infidel would feel sorry for them. (Describes the bad condition of people – even an infidel who has not compassion for Muslims suffering, even he will feel sorry for them)	حَالهُمْ يَصعَبُ عَلَى الكَافِرِ
He children are chicks (i.e. very young) and his wife is in the prime of her youth.	وَأولادُهُ كَتَاكِيت
May God give him strength of what has	وَمرَاتُهُ فِي عِزّ شَبَابِهَا وَيُقَوِيهَا اللهُ عَلَى مَابَلاهَا.

befallen her.	
Gladly / from my eye.	مِن عَيني
May it be the last sadness we suffer.	وَيَجعَلُهَا اخِرُالأحزَانِ
Oh God, amen.	وَنَزُورُهم في الفَرح
Protection is from you, God.	اللهُمَّ امِين
Five and five in the eye of he who does not praise the Prophet. (Five refers to the five fingers)	السَترُ مِنْ عِنْدِكَ يَارَبُّ

أسئلة:

1. Whose daughter is Fatima?
2. What is her physical condition?
3. Who has passed his high-school exam, and what is his relationship to Mohammed?
4. Who is preparing to travel to Saudi Arabia? For what purpose? What is his relationship to Mohammed?
5. Is Mahmoud's father alive?
6. In which country did Mahmoud's father work for an extended period?
7. What were Mahmoud and Mohammed doing when Ali came to visit them?
8. For what does Mohammed wish Ali's son well?
9. Who is the mutual friend who recently died? How did he die?
10. How has his family's financial condition changed due to his death?
11. Which friend pledged to help this family?
12. Which friend has just returned from the Haaj?
13. A female acquaintance of the men told them the good news that her son has just had twins. What are their names? Why did they call them these names?
14. Mohammed's daughter has had a miscarriage. What is her name?
15. In this dialogue, there is a married couple who have been fighting. What is the name of the wife? Have they resolved their problem?
16. Sumaya wants one of her acquaintances to marry Mohammed's daughter. What are the names of the prospective couple? How does Mohammed react? Where is Sumaya's acquaintance now?
17. Shams has been absent recently – why?
18. A group of women went to visit Nawal to congratulate her. What are they congratulating her for?

19. Nawal will slaughter an animal to give the meat to her family and friends and also to the poor people in society. Which animal will she slaughter?

قَالَتْ صَحِيفَةُ نِيُويُورْكَ تَايِمز إِنَّ نَحْوَ 150 شَخْصًا يَعْتَنِقُونَ الإِسْلَامَ سَنَوِيًّا فِي مَسْجِدٍ بِضَاحِيَةِ كِريتاي بِالْقُرْبِ مِنَ الْعَاصِمَةِ الفَرَنْسَية حَيْثُ تُقَامُ لَهُمْ مَرَاسِمُ الدُّخُولِ فِي الدِّينِ الجَدِيدِ. هَذَا الْمَسْجِدُ أَصْبَحَ رمزًا لِلْوُجُودِ الإِسْلَامِيِّ الْمُتَعَاظِمِ فِي تِلْكَ الدَّوْلَةِ .

The New York Times reported that about 150 people convert to Islam yearly in a mosque in the suburb of Chritaa near the French capital, where they hold ceremonies to celebrate the conversion to the new religion. This mosque has become the symbol of growing Islamic presence in that state.

وَأَضَافَتِ الصَّحِيفَةُ فِي تَقْرِيرٍ مِنْ كريتاي أَنَّ مِنْ بَيْنِ الَّذِينَ يَأْتُونَ إِلَى المَسْجِدِ لِأَدَاءِ صَلَاةِ الجُمْعَةِ العَدِيدَ مِنَ الشُّبَّانِ مِنْ الكَاثُوليكِ الرُّومَانِ السَّابِقِينَ، "وَهُمْ يَرْتَدُونَ الجِلْبَابَ الطَّوِيلَ وَيَعْتَمِرُونَ قُبَّعَةَ الصَّلَاة ."

The newspaper said in a report from Chritaa, that among those who come to the Mosque for Friday prayers are many young men from Roman Catholic upbringings, 'wearing long robes and a prayer hat.'

وَجَاءَ فِي التَّقْرِيرِ أَنَّ أَعْدَادَ المُهْتَدِينَ إِلَى الإِسْلَامِ سَنَوِيًّا تَضَاعَفَ فِي السَّنَوَاتِ الـ25 المَاضِيَةِ، وَهُوَ مَا يَنْطَوِي فِي رَأْيِ خُبَرَاءَ - لَمْ تُشِرِ الصَّحِيفَةُ إِلَى هُوِيَّتِهِمْ-عَلَى تَحَدٍّ مُتَنَامٍ لِفَرَنْسَا الَّتِي تَتَّسِمُ نَظْرَةُ حُكُومَتِهَا وَالرَّأْيُ العَامُّ فِيهَا بِنَزْعَةٍ "خَرْقَاءَ وَأحيانًا عَدَائِيَّةٍ" تُجَاهَ الإِسْلَامِ.

The report, which involves the opinion of experts whose identity was not revealed by the newspaper, stated that the annual number of converts to Islam has doubled in the past 25 years. This is a growing challenge to France, whose government and public opinion is characterized by clumsy and sometimes hostile attitudes towards Islam.

الشُّعُورُ

There are two words in Arabic to denote 'feeling'. These are aHsas (which is used for sensory or physical feelings) and sha-or (used for emotional feelings).

How do you feel now? This sentence changes its meaning in Arabic depending on whether you use aHsas or sha-or. However, some people will use both words combined to ask how someone feels both physically and emotionally.	بِمَاذَا تَشعُرُ وتُحِسُّ الانَ؟
I feel, therefore I am. This is the Arabic equivalent of 'cogito ergo sum' - I think therefore I am. Arabs took the second part ('I am') but use 'feel' rather than 'think'. Arabs often use 'ergo sum' - 'therefore I am' - but use 'alive and provided with subsistence' instead of 'I am' to denote ongoing life.	أَنَا أَشعُرُ إِذَنْ أَنَا حَيٌّ أُرزَقُ.

الحِوَار

سَارَة: أُمِّي، أُمِّي، أَنَا أَشْعُرُ بِالسَّعَادَةِ وَالفَرَحِ وَالسُّرُورِ.

الأم: مَا سَبَبُ سَعَادَتِكِ وَفَرَحِكِ وسُرورِكِ؟ هَيَا أَسْعِدِيني مِثْلَكِ يَاسَارَة.

سَارَة: أَنْتِ تَعْلَمِينَ أَنَّني اعتدتُ أَنْ أَحْصُلَ عَلَى تَقْدِيرٍ مُمْتَازٍ فِي كُلِّ عَامٍ، وَأَكُونُ فِي حَالَةٍ مِنَ القَلَقِ والتَّوَتُّرِ وَالتَّرَقُّبِ طُوَالَ الوَقْتِ خَاصَةً عِندَ مَوْعِدِ الاعلانِ عَنِ النَتِيجَةِ.

الأم: نَعَمْ، فِعلاً، أَعرِفُ ذَلِكَ، لَكِن احْرِصِي عَلَى التَفَاؤُلِ يَابِنتِي، لأَنَّكِ تُذَاكِرِينَ بِجُهدٍ كَبِيرٍ، فَلِمَاذا القَلَقُ؟

سَارَة: أُمِّي، لَقَدْ حَصَلْتُ عَلَى تَقْدِيرٍ مُمْتَازٍ، وَالحَمْدُ لله.

الأم: حَقاً يَاسَارَة؟ حَقاً يَاحَبِيبَتِي؟ لَقَدْ أَدْخَلْتِ البَهجَةَ الَى قَلبي.

سَارَة: لقدْ كَادَ قَلبِي أَنْ يَقِفَ وَزَمِيلَتِي تَعلِنُ النَتِيجَةَ لَنا، وَلَمْ أَتَوَقَّفْ عَنِ الضَحِكِ عِندَمَا شَاهَدتُ النَتِيجَةَ بِنَفسِي، وَانتَابَتني حَالَةٌ مِنَ النَّشَاطِ والحَيَوِيَةِ والاثَارَةِ وَجِئتُ مُسرِعَةً لأخبركِ.

الأم: سَأشتَري لَكِ هَدِيةً ثَمِينَةً وَنُسَافِرُ فِي رِحْلَةٍ جَمِيلَةٍ، فَهَذا حَقُّكِ، الرَّاحَة بُعَدَ التَّعَبِ.

سَارَةُ: لَقَدْ هَنَّأتِني صَدِيقَتِي شِيرِين وَهَنَأتُها، فَقَد حَصَلْنا عَلَى تَقْدِيرٍ مُمَاثِلٍ، لَكِنَّها اكتَفت بِالابتِسَامِ، لأَنَّها تَشعُرُ بِالأَلَمِ وَالحُزنِ وَالغَمِّ والاكتِئَابِ والوَحْدَةِ حَتَّى أوشَكَتْ عَلى البُكَاءِ، وَعندَمَا تَعَجَبْتُ وأَصَابَني العَجَبُ والدَّهشَة مِنْ أمرِها، سَألتُها مِمَ أنتِ خَائِفَةٌ؟

أجَابَتني بِأَنَّ والِدَتَهَا في المُسْتَشفَى وحَالَتُهَا سَيِّئَةٌ، وتَشعُرُ بِالتشَاؤُم والارتِبَاك، كَمَا أنَّ الخَوفَ أن تَفقِدَهَا أصَابَهَا بِالأرَقِ، فَهِيَ لَم تَنَم جَيداً مُنذُ اسْبُوعٍ.

الأم: عَافَاهَا اللهُ، يَجِبُ أَن نَزُورَهَا، ان شَاءِ اللهِ.

نادية: السَّلامُ عَلَيْكُم، كَيْفَ حَالُكُم جَمِيعاً، هه، تَبدِينَ سَعِيدَةً يَاأختِي، مَاالسَبَبُ؟
الأم: بارِكِي لأختِكِ يَا نادِية لَقد نَجَحتْ بِتقدِيرٍ مُمتَازٍ.

نَادِية: مَعقُول!!!!مُمتاز دُفعَةً وَاحدةً!!!!أَنَا مُغتَاظَةٌ وأحسدُكِ وأغبطُكِ يَاسَارَة، وأشعُرُ بِالغَيظِ والحَسَدِ والغَيرَةِ، فَلَم أحصُلْ الا عَلَى تَقدِيرٍ مَقبُولٍ.
الأم: مَاهَذَا يَاسَارَة ؟!؟ أَنَا الانَ غَاضِبَةٌ مِنكِ، وأشعُرُ بِالغَضَبِ والضِّيقِ مِنكِ كَثِيراً، لَم تُهَنِّئي أختَكِ وتَحسِدِينَهَا
أَنَا مُندَهِشَةٌ!! تقدِيرُكِ جَاءَ نَتِيجَةَ الخُمُولِ واللَّعِب، كَمْ نَصَحتُكِ وَلَم تَسمَعِي يَا بِنتِي، أَنَا مُحتَارَةٌ في أمرِكِ، يَابنتِي لاتَفَوُّقَ بِدُونِ تَعَبٍ.
نادية: انا اسَفَةٌ يَا أمِّي، وَاسِفَةٌ يَا سَارَة، أشعُرُ بِالأسَفِ والخَجَلِ والنَدَم أَنْ قُلْتُ لَكِ ذَلِكَ، وأعتَذِرُ وَأَنَا خَجِلَة، وأشعُرُ بِالحَيرَةِ وَأَتَسَاءُل كَيف قُلتُ ذَلِكَ؟ فَأَنَا أُحِبُّ سَارَةَ وأتَمَنَّى لَهَا الخَيرَ، أَنَا لاأكرَهُ أختِي.
سارة: لا بَأس يا نادية، أنا أيضاً أحِبُّكِ وَأسَامَحُكِ ويُمكِننِي أَن أَسَاعدَكِ في دُرُوسِكِ لِتَحصُلِي عَلَى تَقدِيرٍ مُمتَازٍ.
نادية: مَا أجمَلَ التَّسَامُحَ وَالحُبَّ يَا أختِي.

الكلماتُ الجديدة

معناها	الكلمة
Feeling	الشُّعُورُ
Sensation	حِسٌّ
Then	إِذَنْ
Earning a livelihood/ Provided with a livelihood	أرزَقُ
Happiness	سَعَادَةِ
Joy	فَرَح
Pleasure	السُّرُورِ
Make me happy like you	أسعِدِيني مِثلَك
Excellent score (A+)	تَقدِيرٍ مُمتَازٍ
Anxiety	القَلَقِ
Tension	التَّوَتُّرِ
Anticipation	التَّرَقُّبِ
Optimism	التَفَاؤُلِ
Great Effort	جُهدٍ كَبِيرٍ
Cheerfulness	البَهجَة

My heart was about to stop	كَادَ قَلبِي أَنْ يَقَفَ
Laughter	الضَّحِكِ
Result	النَّتِيجَة
Activity	النَّشَاطِ
Vital	الحَيَوِيَةِ
Thrill	الاثَارَةِ
Speeding/ In a hurry	مُسرِعَة
Gift/ Present	هَدِيَة
Precious	ثَمِينَة
This is your right	هَذَا حَقُّكِ
Resting/ Relaxing after Fatigue	الرَّاحَة بُعدَ التَّعَبِ
She congratulated me	هَنَّأَتِني
Similar evaluation (the word "grades" in Arabic is often replaced by taqdeer which literally means "evaluation")	تَقدِيرٍ مُمَاثِلٍ
to estimate, assess, appraise, evaluate valuate, to appreciate	قَدَّر
She had enough	اكتَفت
Merely Smiled (aktafa literally means in this case "she was content with smiling"	اكتَفت بالابتِسَام
To feel pain (when saying "I feel pain", you need to use the baa as a connective prefix on the word for "pain")	تَشعُرُ بِالأَلَم
Sadness	الحُزنِ
Gloom	الغَمُّ
Depression	الاكتِئَاب

Loneliness	الوَحْدَةِ
She was about to cry	أوشَكَتْ عَلَى البُكَاء
I wondered	تَعَجَّبْتُ
I was astonished	أصَابَني العَجَبُ
Surprising	الدَّهشَة
By her behavior (as in "I was surprised by her behavior")	مِنْ أمرِهَا
Of/From what	مِمَ
She is scared	خَائِفَة
In a poor condition	حَالَتُهَا سَيِّئَة
Pessimistic	التشَاؤُم
Confusing	الارتِبَاكِ
Insomnia	الأرَقِ
She did not sleep well for a week	لَمْ تَنَم جَيداً مُنذُ اسْبُوعٍ
May Allah restore her health	عَافَاهَا اللهُ
We must visit her	يَجِبُ أنْ نَزُورَهَا
You look happy	تَبدِينَ سَعِيدَة
Congratulate	بارِكِي
Lump sum (an expression similar to "in one fell swoop")	دُفعَةً وَاحِدة
She is exasperated/ irritated	مُغتَاظَة
I envy you	أحسِدُكِ
I feel happy for you	أغبِطُكِ

I feel resentment	أَشْعُرُ بِالغَيْظِ
(The) Envy	الحَسَد
(The) Jealousy	الغَيرَة
She is angry	غَاضِبَة
I feel angry	أَشْعُرُ بِالغَضَبِ
Agitated	الضِّيقِ
Congratulate (this literally means "congratulate	تُهَنِّئِني
You envy her	تَحسِدينَهَا
She is surprised	مُندَهِشَة
Sluggishness	الخُمُولِ
Playing	اللَّعِبِ
How many times have I advised you?	كَمْ نَصحتُك
She is confused	مُحتَارَة
I'm confused by your behavior	مُحتَارَةٌ في أمرِكِ
You won't get ahead without hardships (literally means "no excelling without fatigue/being tired")	لاتَفَوُّقَ بِدُونِ تَعَبٍ
I feel sorry	أَشْعُرُ بِالأَسَفِ
And shame	وَالخَجَلِ
And remorse	وَالنَدَم
And I apologize	وَأَعتَذِرُ
Shy	خَجِلَة
Puzzled	الحَيرَة
I love you	أحِبُّك

And forgive you	وَأَسَامَحُكِ
I help you	أَسَاعِدَكِ
How wonderful tolerance and love is, my sister	مَا أجمَلَ التَّسَامُحَ وَالحُبَّ يَا أختِي

أَسئِلَة:

1. Write the names of the people involved in this conversation.

2. Why is Sara happy?

3. Why was she worried?

4. What will the mother reward her with?

5. Why was Shireen sad despite getting high grades?

6. Why grade did Nadia receive?

7. What type of help will Sara give her to get better grades?

8. What grade is she shooting for?

9. Please write in Arabic feelings that express well- being.

10. Please write the set of feelings in the text that express a more negative emotional state.

11. What advice did the mother give to Sara when she was feeling worried and tense?

12. Who announced the results of the exam?

أَصْدِقاءُ الطُّفُولَة

This conversation is between two **childhood friends** who have not seen each other for a long time and have just encountered one another.

الحِوَارُ

مَرْيَم: غَيْرُ مَعْقُولٍ!! سَارَةُ الشَرقَاوِي؟!!

سَارَة: لَا، مَرْيَمُ أَحْمَدُ المَنُوفِي؟!!

مريم: أَيْنَ اخْتَفَيْتِي يَاغَالِيَة؟ أَيْنَ أَخَذتْكِ الدُّنْيَا؟

سارة: اهٍ، يَا صَدِيقَةَ ۞ العُمْرِ، اعْتَرِفُ أَنِّي أَخْطَأتُ حِينَ تَرَكتُكِ دُون وَدَاعٍ وهَاجَرتُ الى أَمْرِيكَا مِن خَمْسِ سَنَوَاتٍ.

مريم: أَنتِ فِعْلاً صَدِيقَةٌ نَذلَةٌ (مُقَصِرَةٌ)، لَكِنِّي أُحِبُّكِ ويَكفِي أَنْ أَرَاكِ بِخَيْرٍ.

سارة: سَامِحِينِي يَا مَرْيَم يَا صَاحِبَتِي، أَنْتِ تَعْلَمِينَ ظُرُوفِي وَمَا حَدَثَ لِي بَعْدَ طَلاقِي، وَوَفَاةِ أُمِّي حُزْناً عَلَى حَالِي، فَهَاجَرتُ عِنْدَمَا تَمَّتِ المُوافَقَةُ عَلَى طَلَبِي لاكمَالِ دِرَاسَتِي هُنَاكَ لِلحُصُولِ على الدُّكتُورَاه، وَهَرَباً مِنَ الحُزْنِ.

مريم: وَكَيفَ حَالُكِ الانَ يا سُوسُو؟ (في العَادَةِ يُدَلِّلُ الأصدِقَاءُ بَعضَهُم).

سارة: تَزَوَجْتُ انسَاناً رائعاً بِمَعنَى الكَلِمةِ، وَالحَمْدُ لله، وَسَألتُ عَنْكِ فَورَ وُصُولِي، رُغمَ خَوفِي مِن رَدِّ فِعلِكِ.

مريم: رَائِعٌ، مَبرُوكٌ، هَل تَمْزَحِينَ؟ أَنْتِ تَؤُمِي، هَلْ تَذكُرِينَ أَيَامِنَا الجَمِيلَةِ وَأَيَامَ المَرَحِ وَالدِرَاسَةِ وَبَرَاءَةَ الطُّفُولَةِ؟ فَنَحنُ أَصدِقَاءٌ أَنتِيمٌ (أَصدِقَاءُ جِداً) مُنذُ الصِّغَرِ.

سارة: طَبْعاً، وَهَل هِيَ أَيَامٌ تُنْسَى؟ انَّهَا أَحلَى الذِّكرَيَاتِ.

مريم: نَعَم، كُورنيشُ الاسكَنْدَرِيَةِ شَهِدَ كَمْ تَمَشَّينَا وَحَكَينَا لَهُ أَسْرَارَنَا، وَأَكَلْنَا الذُّرَةَ المَشوِيَّةَ وَالفِشَارَ.

سارة: اه، ياحَبيبَتِي سَارِةِ، وياحَبيبَتِي يَا اسْكَنْدَرِيَةَ، أَحْلَى أَيَّامِ العُمْرِ.

الكلماتُ الجديدة

معناها	الكلمة
Unbelievable	غَيْرُ مَعْقُولٍ
You disappeared	اخْتَفَيْتِ
Wherever life takes you	أَيْنَ أَخَذَتْكِ الدُّنْيَا
Confess	اعْتَرِفُ
I made a mistake	أَخْطَأْتُ
I left you	تَرَكْتُكِ
Without goodbye	دُونَ وَدَاعٍ
Scoundrel	نَذْلَة
Indeed	فِعْلاً
Slacker / idler (someone who 'comes short')	مُقَصِّرَة
Enough	يَكْفِي

Forgive me	سَامِحِيني
You know my situation / circumstances	تَعْلَمِينَ ظُرُوفِي
My divorce	طَلاقِي
Grief	حُزْناً
Susu (nickname for someone, usually a female, whose names starts with an 's')	سُوسُو
With the whole meaning of the word	بِمَعنَى الكَلمةِ
Your reaction	رَدِّ فِعلِكِ
Are you kidding?	هَلْ تَمْزَحِينَ؟
My twin	تَوْءَمِي
Intimate friends	أَصدِقَاءٌ أنتِيمٌ
Since childhood	مُنذُ الصِّغَرِ
Sweetest	أحلَى
Memories	الذِّكرَيَاتِ
Corniche	كُورنِيشٌ
Witness	شَهِدَ
How many times did we stroll	كَمْ تَمَشَّينَا
Told it our secrets	وَحَكينَا لَه أسْرَارَنا
Grilled corn	الذُّرَة المَشوِّية
Popcorn	الفِشَارَ
Life's sweetest days	أحْلَى أيَّام العُمْرِ

أَسْئِلَة:

1. How many years has it been since they last saw each other?

2. What was the reason behind this separation?

3. Which university degree did one of the friends obtain and from which country?

4. The mother of one of the friends has passed away. Whose mother was it and what were the circumstances of her death?

5. What is Sara's nickname?

6. Is Sara currently married?

7. Why was she hesitant to contact her old friend?

8. What is the most lasting memory that they both share?

9. In which city did they grow up?

10. In their conversation, they talk about eating popcorn and grilled corn. Where did they used to eat it?

اِقْرَأ

رَغْمَ صِغَرِ سِنِّهِمْ أَصْبَحَتِ التِّقْنِيَّاتُ الْمُتَقَدِّمَةُ الْأَقْرَبَ إِلَيْهِمْ، حَيْثُ بَاتَتْ أَجْهِزَةُ الْإِنْتَرْنَتِ وَالْآيْبَادِ وَالْهَوَاتِفُ الْمَحْمُولَةُ بِكُلِّ تَطْبِيقَاتِهَا الْمُتَقَدِّمَةِ فِي مُتَنَاوَلِ الْأَطْفَالِ وَالْمُرَاهِقِينَ بَدَلًا مِنَ الْأَلْعَابِ التَّقْلِيدِيَّةِ، وَتَعَدَّتْ ذَلِكَ لِتَدْخُلَ إِلَى مَدَارِسِهِمْ وَصُفُوفِهِمِ الدِّرَاسِيَّةِ وَحَتَّى أُسَرِّتِهِمُ الدَّافِئَةِ.

هِيَ ظَاهِرَةٌ لَاقَتْ رَوَاجًا وَتَشْجِيعًا لَدَى الْكَثِيرِينَ فِي الْمُجْتَمَعَاتِ الْغَرْبِيَّةِ وَالْعَرَبِيَّةِ، عَلَى اعْتِبَارِهَا تُسَاعِدُ عَلَى تَوْسِيعِ مَدَارِكِ الْأَطْفَالِ وَتَجْعَلُ مِنْهُمْ أُنَاسًا مُثَقَّفِينَ مُسْتَقْبَلًا وَمُوَاكِبِينَ لِعَصْرِ تِكْنُولُوجْيَا

الْمَعْلُومَاتِ، دُونَ الِانْتِبَاهِ لِمَا قَدْ تُحْدِثُهُ مِنْ أَثَرٍ عَلَى صِحَّتِهِمْ وَتَفَاعُلِهِمْ مَعَ مُحِيطِهِمْ، فَضْلًا عَنْ تَعَرُّضِهِمْ لِلضُّغُوطِ النَّفْسِيَّةِ وَالِاجْتِمَاعِيّةِ وَالتَّحَرُّشِ وَالِاسْتِغْلَالِ حِينَ يَتَصَفَّحُونَ مَوَاقِعَ ضَارَّةً أَوْ شَبَكَاتٍ لِلتَّوَاصُلِ الِاجْتِمَاعِيِّ أَصْبَحَتْ هَدَفًا لِمُجْرِمِي الْإِنْتَرْنَت.

Despite their young age, have become advanced technologies closest to them , where are Internet devices , iPad and mobile phones with all applications developed in the reach of children and adolescents instead of traditional games , and exceeded that of the intervention to their schools and their classrooms and even their family warm .

Is a phenomenon met with popular and an encouragement to many in the Western and Arab societies , the mind helps to expand the perceptions of children and make them people educated in the future and abreast of the era of information technology , without paying attention to what might have an impact on their health and their interaction with their surroundings , as well as being subjected to psychological pressure and social harassment and exploitation while browsing malicious sites or networks of social networking has become a target for cyber criminals.

الفَرَحُ وَمَرَاسِمُ الزِّفَافِ

قَضَيْتُ شَهْرَ العَسَلِ فِي شَرْمِ الشَّيْخِ، وَأنتَ، أَيْنَ قَضَيْتَ شَهْرَ العَسَلِ؟

This lesson is about wedding ceremonies. You will learn vocabulary relating to happiness and festivity, and also formalities of Arab weddings. You will also see how Arabic culture has adopted the Western tradition of the Bachelor's Party, and how Arabic culture celebrates the day after the wedding.

الأم: لولي.

Arab weddings have a special form of celebrating. Women ululate in a high-pitched voice to show their joy. This is called the "zaghrouTah" (plural "zaghreeT"). Women perform this ululation, similar to a wail, by flicking their tongues against their upper lips rapidly: a flick from inside their mouths then from outside, and repeat continuously and very quickly, gradually releasing the air from their lungs. In order to make this sound you have to have lots of air in your lungs – the longer you can make this sound the more you will be appreciated. You will hear this sound at weddings and other celebrations, and if the women celebrate a newly elected president, for example. You might also hear this sound if somebody dies in battle, as this is considered just in Arab culture. The reason behind making this sound to share happiness with their neighbors. Usually the bride (or the person directly involved) will not make this sound, but rather her friends and family. The bride will often be somewhat embarrassed by it.

دينا: مَاهَذِهِ الزَّغرُودَةُ الجَمِيلَةُ يَاأُمِّي؟ أخجَلتِنِي.

الأم: دَعِينِي أُطلِقُ الزَّغَارِيدَ يَابِنتِي، نُرِيدُ أَنْ نفرَحَ.

الأب: اليَومَ قِرَاءَةُ الفَاتِحَةِ، قَدِّمِي الشَّربَاتَ لِعَرِيسِكِ، وَحَمَاتِكِ، وَحَمَاكِ يَادِينَا.

والد أحمد: نُرِيدُ أَنْ نَتَكَلَّمَ فِي التَّفَاصِيلِ، اطلُبُوا طَلَبَاتِكُم، ونَحنُ جَاهِزُون، دِينَا بِنتُ أُصُولٍ ونَزِنُهَا بالذَّهَبِ.

الأب: حَفِظَكَ اللهُ يَاسَيِد عَاطِف، أحمَدٌ وَلَدُنَا، وَنَحنُ نَشتَرِي رَجُلاً لِابنَتِنَا، يَصُونُهَا وَيَحمِيهَا، لَنْ نَختَلِفَ فِي التَّفَاصِيلِ ولَوَازِمِ الزَّوَاجِ.

والدة أحمد: وَنِعمَ الأَصلُ، دِينَا ابنَتِي أَنَا أيضاً والشَّئُ الذِي تُشِيرُ اليَهِ سَأشتَرِيهِ.

الأب: مَارَايُكُم أَنْ نَقسِمَ البَلَدَ نِصفَين، نِصفٌ عَلَينَا ونِصفٌ عَلَيكُم فِي كُلِّ شَئٍ، اليَومَ مَصَارِيفُ الزَّوَاجِ مُكَلَّفَةٌ جِداً، كَانَ اللهُ فِي عَونِ الشَّبَابِ، فِي زَمَانِي، كَانَ الزَّوَاجُ يَسِيراً وَمَطَالِبُهُ بَسِيطَة، وايجَارَاتُ الشُّقَقِ قَلِيلَةٌ، أمَّا الانَ، كُلُّ شَئٍ تَغَيَرَ.

والد أحمد: فِعلاً، إِذَنْ، اليَومَ نُقَدِّمُ الدِّبلَةَ وَالخَاتَمَ وَالمَحبَسَ أمَّا بِالنِسبَةِ الَى الشَّبكَةِ سَنَنزِلُ مَعاً الَى الصَّاغَةِ وَنَشتَرِي مَايعجِبُ عَروسَتَنَا.

والدة أحمد: مَارَأيُكُم أَنْ نَذهَبَ الَى مَدِينَةِ دُميَاطٍ وَقتَ شِرَاءِ العفشِ وَالأثَاثِ؟

الأب: مَدِينَةُ دِميَاطٍ مَشهُورَةٌ وَمَعروفَةٌ بِصِنَاعَةِ الأثَاثِ الرَّاقِي وَالمَتِينِ.

الأُم: فِكرَةٌ مُمتَازَةٌ ...حَسَناً. وَالقَائِمَةُ سَنَكتُبُ فِيهَا كُلَّ شَئٍ، مُوافِقُون؟

أحمد: مُوافِقُونَ طَبعاً، وسَأُوَقِّعُ القَائِمَةَ مُغمَضَ العَينَينِ، انَّهُ حَقُّ دِينَا، وَلَنْ يَحدُثَ طَلاقٌ انْ شَاءَ الله.

والدة أحمد: وَمَا رَأيُكُم أن تَكونَ الشَّبكَةُ وَكتبُ الكِتَابِ وَالدُّخلَةُ وَالزِّفَافُ فِي يَومٍ وَاحِدٍ؟

الأب: مُمتَاز، تَمَّ الاتِفَاقُ عَلَى كُلِّ شَئٍ، أَينَ تُحِبُونَ اقَامَةَ الفَرَحِ؟

والد أحمد: صَالاتُ الأفرَاحِ وَدُورُ المُنَاسَبَاتِ وَقَاعَاتُ الحَفَلاتِ كَثِيرَةٌ، وَيُمكِنُنَا الاختِيَارُ أو اقَامَتُهُ فِي احَدِ الفَنَادِقِ.

الأب: دَارُ الدِّفَاعِ الجَوِّي رَاقِيَةٌ وَمُنَاسَبةٌ أودَارُ المُشَاةِ أو فُنْدُقُ المُوفيمبيكِ أَوْ بَاخِرَةٌ نِيلِيَةٌ.

والد أحمد: اذَن، عَلَى بَرَكَةِ اللهِ نقرَأُ الفَاتِحَةَ جَمِيعاً.

الأب: بِسمِ اللهِ الرَّحمَنِ الرَّحِيمِ.........

يَومُ الحِنَّةِ

الأُم: هَيَا يَادِينَا، جَاءَتِ الحَنانَةُ لِتَنقُشَ الحِنَّاءَ عَلَى يَدَيكِ وَقَدَمَيكِ إذا رَغِبتِ.

302

دِينَا: أُرِيدُ نَقشاً عَلَى كَتِفِي أيضاً، هَيَا يَاصَاحِبَاتِي، لِنَرْقُص وَنُغَنِي وَنُصَفِق مَعَ المُوسِيقَى.....

أَلُو..... أَلُو..... أحمد...أحمد...لا أستَطِيعُ سَمَاعَكَ جَيداً...أَينَ أنتَ؟

أحمد: أَصَرَّ أصدِقَائِي أنْ يُقِيمُوا لِي حَفلَ وَدَاع العُزُوبِيَة وَخَرَجنَا قَلِيلاً.

يَومُ الفَرَحِ في الكُوَافِيرِ

مُصَفِفَةُ الشَّعرِ: مَبرُوك يَاانِسَة، الانَ وَقَد انتَهَينَا مِنْ السويتِ وَالحَمَّامِ المغربِي وَالبَادِيكِيرِ وَالمَانِيكِيرِ وَمِنْ تَصفِيفِ شَعرِكِ

وَالمكيَاجِ، سَتَأتِي خَبِيرَةُ لَفِ الطُّرَحِ لِتَلُفَ الحِجَابَ وَالطَّرحَةَ.

دِينَا: مِنْ فَضلِكِ، بِسُرعَةٍ، لَقَد حَانَ مَوعِدُ التَصوِيرِ، لَقَد حَجَزنَا مَوعداً مَعَ مَحَل تَصوِيرٍ مَعرُوفٍ لِيَأخُذَ لَنَا لَقَطاتٍ رَائِعَةٍ، وَهُوَ نَفسُهُ مَنْ سَيُصَوِرُ الحَفلَ بِالفِيدِيُو.

أحمد وَدِينَا يَنزلانِ مِن سَيَارَةِ الزِّفَافِ

الأم: تَبدِينَ فَاتِنَةَ يا ابنَتِي، مَبرُوك، هَيَا يَا أحمَد، الزَّفَةُ سَتَبدَأ، الفِرقَةُ تنتظِرُ وَالرَّاقِصَةُ سَتَزُفُكُم الَى بَابِ القَاعَةِ.

في القاعة

المُطرِب: الانَ، العَرِيسُ وَالعَرُوس يَرقُصَانِ، وَكُلُّ مَنْ يُرِيدُ مِنَ الأزوَاج وَالكَابلِز، الانَ، الدِّي جِيه وَالغِنَاءُ، هَيَا، أينَ أصدِقَاءُ وَصَدِيقَاتُ العَرُوسَينِ؟

بَعَد فَترَةٍ

والِدُ العَرِيسِ: لَقَد جَاءَ المَأذُونُ، لِيَعقِدَ القِرَانَ.

المأذون: أَيْنَ العَرِيسُ؟ وَأَيْنَ وَالِدُ العَرُوسِ؟ عَلَى بَرَكَةِ اللهِ.

بَعْدَ القُرَآنِ

المأذون: ادعُوا لَهُمَا بِالبَرَكَةِ وَالسَّعَادَةِ، بَارَكَ اللهُ لَهُمَا وَبَارَكَ عَلَيهِمَا وَجَمَّعَ بَينَهُمَا فِي خَيرٍ.

والد العروس: هَيَا يَا جَمَاعَةَ، لَقَد حَانَ مَوعِدُ البُوفِيهِ وَالعَشَاءِ.

صديق للعريس: مَا شَاءَ اللهُ، البُوفِيهُ مَلِئٌ بِأصنافٍ كَثِيرَةٍ، دُيُوكٌ رُومِيةٌ وَمَشوِيَاتٌ وَمَحَاشِي وَحَلوِيَاتٌ وَمَشرُوبَاتٌ،

هَيَا لِنَأكُلَ.

فِي الصَّبَاحِيَةِ

أم العروس: صَبَاحِيةٌ مُبَارَكَةٌ يَا أبنائِي، أحضَرنَا لَكُم افطَارَ الصَّبَاحِيَةِ، الفَطِيرُ المُشَلتَتُ وَالعَسَلُ وَالمُرَبَى وَالأجبَانُ وَالبَيضُ.

وَالِدُ العَرُوسِ: وَهَذا أَوَّلُ نُقُوطٍ لِلفَرَحِ.

العريس: هَذا كَثِيرٌ يَا عَمِّي، إذا أعطَانَا الأهْلُ وَالأَقَارِبُ نُقُوطاً مِثْلَ ذلِكَ، سَنَقضِي شَهْرَ العَسَلِ فِي تُركِيَا.

العروس: رَائِعٌ، أَنَا أحلُمُ بِذلِكَ.

304

الكلماتُ الجديدة

معناها	الكلمة
Wedding	الفَرَحُ
Weddings ceremonies	مَرَاسِمُ الزِّفَافِ
Honeymoon	شَهْرَ العَسَلِ
This is an onomatopoeic sound of the ululation	لولولوولولولولي
Ululation	الزَغْرُودَةُ
You embarrassed me	أخْجَلتِنِي
I will ululate	أُطلِقُ الزَغَارِيدَ
Reading the fatHa (the first surah of the Koran)	قِرَاءَةُ الفَاتِحَةِ
Give a sweet drink to your groom	قَدِّمِي الشَّربَاتَ لِعَرِيسِكِ
And your mother-in-law	وَحَمَاتِكِ
And your father-in-law	وَحَمَاكِ
The details	التَفَاصِيلِ
Request from us what you need	اطلُبُوا طَلَبَاتِكُم
And we are ready	ونَحنُ جَاهِزُون

305

Dina comes from a respected family (Dina in Arabic is Diana in English)	دِينَا بِنتُ أُصُولٍ
She is worth her weight in gold	وَنَزِنُهَا بِالذَّهَبِ
May Allah protect you	حَفِظَكَ اللهُ
We are buying a man for our daughter (this means that money is not an issue when you are finding a good husband for your daughter – you will do anything to secure the marriage)	نَشتَرِي رَجُلاً لِابنتِنَا
He will safeguard on her	يَصُونُهَا
And protect her	وَيَحمِيهَا
We disagree	نَختَلِفَ
The necessities for marriage	لَوَازِمِ الزَّواجِ
How wonderful this established origin (i.e., a person who comes from an established family, firmly rooted; a person of noble origin; high-born)	وَنِعمَ الأَصلُ
Referred to	تُشِيرُ اِلَيهِ
We split the country in two (this is an idiom that means to compromise between two parties)	نَقسِمَ البَلَدَ نِصفَينِ
Costly	مُكَلِّفَة
May Allah help young people	كَانَ اللهُ فِي عَونِ الشَّبَابِ
In my time	فِي زَمَانِي
Easily	يَسِيراً
Its demands	مَطَالِبُهُ
Simple	بَسِيطَة

Friends	ايجَارَاتُ
Apartments	الشُّقَقِ
Everything has changed	كُلُّ شَيْءٍ تَغَيَّرَ
We will present the wedding ring, the ring and the bracelet	نُقَدِّمُ الدَّبلَةَ وَالخَاتَمَ وَالمَحبَسَ
The wedding jewelry	الشَّبكَةِ
Goldsmiths	الصَّاغَةِ
Furniture and fittings	العفشِ وَالأَثَاثِ
The city of Damietta	مَدِينةِ دُميَاطِ
Upscale	الرَّاقِي
And solid	وَالمَتِينِ
The list	القَائِمَة
I will sign the list with my eyes closed	وَسَأُوَقِّعُ القَائِمَةَ مُغمَضَ العَينَينِ
Right	حَقُّ
Divorce	طَلاقٌ
The wedding night	الدُّخلَةُ
Wedding halls	صَالاتُ الأَفرَاحِ
House of occasions (something that hosts weddings and funerals, etc.; any other social occasion)	وَدُورُ المُنَاسَبَاتِ
Concert halls	وَقَاعَاتُ الحَفَلاتِ
The choice	الاختِيَارُ
House of air defense	دَارُ الدِّفَاعِ الجَوِّي
House of infantry	أوَدَارُ المُشَاةِ

Nile cruiser	بَاخِرَةٌ نِيلِيَة
With Allah's blessings	عَلَى بَرَكَةِ الله
Let's all read the fatHa	نَقرَأ الفَاتِحَةَ جَمِيعاً
Henna / tattoo artists	الحَنَانَة
To engrave the henna	لِتَنقُش الحِّنَاءَ
If you wish	إذا رَغِبتِ
I want an engraving on my shoulder	أُرِيدُ نَقشاً عَلَى كَتِفِي
And clap	وَنُصَفِّق
I can't hear you very well	لا أستَطِيعُ سَمَاعَكَ جَيداً
My friends insisted	أَصَرَّ أصدِقَائِي
Bachelor party	حَفلَ وَدَاعِ العُزُوبِيَةِ
Hairdresser	مُصَفِّفَةُ الشَّعرِ
Styling your hair	تَصفِيفِ شَعْرِكِ
A female expert in tying a scarf	خَبِيرَةُ لَفِ الطَّرَحِ
To wrap (something around your head)	لِتَلُفَّ
Wedding procession	الزَّفَّة
Singer	المُطرِب
DJ	الدِّي جِيه
In couples	وَالكَابِلز
Marriage official	المَأذُونُ
The buffet has many varieties of food	البُوفِيهُ مَلِئٌ بأصنافٍ كَثِيرَةٍ
Turkeys	دُيُوكٌ رُومِيةٌ

Barbeque	مَشوِيَاتٌ
Stuffed foods	مَحَاشِي
Desserts	حَلَوِيَاتٌ
The rings	مَشرُوبَاتٌ
The morning after the marriage consummation	الصَّبَاحِيَةِ
The blessed morning (after the marriage consummation)	صَبَاحِيَةٌ مُبَارَكَة
A type of unleavened bread	الفَطِيرُ المُشَلْتَتُ
Honey	العَسَلُ
Jam	المُرَبَّى
Cheeses	الأجبَانُ
Eggs	البَيضُ
Wedding donations	نُقُّوطِ
I dream of this	أَنَا أحلُمُ بِذلِكَ

أسئِلَة:

1. Who starts the first ululation?

2. Is the bride embarrassed by the sound?

3. On this day, which part of the wedding ceremony will take place?

4. Who comes to visit today?

5. What do they drink?

6. What are the names of the bride and groom?

7. The father of the groom wants to talk about 'details'. What does he refer to?

8. What does it mean in Arabic when you say somebody is worth his weight in gold?

9. What does it mean when you say 'we are buying a man' in Arabic?

10. Is there any disagreement at the outset of the wedding between the fathers of the bride and of the groom?

11. The family of the groom will buy something on this day for the bride. What is it?

12. What Arabic expression does the father of the bride use to mean, "Let's split it fifty-fifty"?

13. Are there any conditions to this agreement?

14. How does the father of the bride express his opinion about the cost of marriages these days?

15. Compare the costs of marriage between the two generations.

16. What type of jewelry will the family of the groom present to the bride on this day?

17. What is the name of the jewelry district where they will go to buy the present?

18. What is the name of the present?

19. In which Egyptian city do they go to buy the furniture? Why this city?

20. The mother of the bride talks about writing a list. What list is she referring to?

21. Who will sign the list?

22. The mother of the groom suggests one day to perform few wedding customs. What are these customs?

23. Do the two families have any disagreement on any aspects of this marriage?

24. Where does the father of the groom suggest they hold the wedding?

25. Where does the father of the bride suggest they hold the wedding?

26. Who suggests reading the opening of the Koran?

27. What is the name of the day that the henna artist will visit?

28. Will the henna decorate the bride or the groom?

29. Which body part does the bride ask to be decorated?

30. Does the bride or the groom have a bachelor's party?

31. What will the bride do at the hairdresser's salon?

32. Where will she go after this?

33. Is the photographer who takes the wedding portrait the same as the person filming the wedding?

34. Which artist will be involved with the wedding procession?

35. Will there be a DJ at the wedding party?

36. Who will officiate the wedding?

37. How will the food be served – a buffet or a la carte?

38. What type of food will be on offer?

39. What is the day after the consumption of the marriage called?

40. How is this day celebrated?

41. Why do the newlyweds have a big breakfast?

42. Who gives the newlyweds their first cash gift?

43. What is the reaction of the groom when he sees this gift?

44. Are the distant family expected to give cash gifts?

45. If the newlyweds receive as much money for their second gift as their first gift, what do they plan to do?

46. What is the bride's dream honeymoon destination?

غَزَل رَاقِي وَطَلَب زَوَاج

مِن غِير مَانتكلِّم بِتفهَمِني عِينيك

نَظرَاتَك بِتقيد فِيَا نَار

قُولِّي، ازاي دَه حَصَلْ وامتى؟

This dialogue illustrates classy or elegant flirtation, as it is described in Arabic. This type of flirtation is likely to take place between two educated people who know each other. In this dialogue are two work colleagues. This manner of conversation often comes as a prelude to talking about marriage.

الحِوَار

تامر: صَبَاح الخِير، يَا نِرمِين.

نرمين: صَبَاح الخِير يَا تَامِر

تامر: تِسمَحِيلِي أقعد شُوَيَة قَبْل مَاالزُملاء يجو.

نرمين: اتفضَّل يَا تامِر.

تامر: كُل سَنَة وأنتِ طَيِّبَةٌ.

نرمين: يَاه، انتَ عِرفت ازاي؟ مَحَدِّش يعرف عِيد مِيلادِي.

تامر: عِرِفْت يَا سِتِي مِن الأكونت بتَاعِك عَلَى الفِيس بُوك.
اللِّي بِيعِز حَدْ بِيعْرَف كُل حَاجَة عَنَّه.

ابتَسَمَتْ نِرمِينُ في خَجَلٍ

تامر: أنتِ أكِيد حَاسَّة بِيا مِن مُدَّةٍ كَبِيرَةٍ، أنَا مِش قَادِر أخبِّي شُعُورِي نَاحِيتِك أكتَر من كِدَه، أنَا اتأكِّدت ان حُبِّي لِيكِي حَقِيقِي، وبامُوت فِيكِي، وَباتمنَّى يُكُون شُعُور مُتَبَادَل مِن نَاحِيتِك.

نرمين: مِش عَارفَة أقول لِك ايه يَا تَامِر، انتَ فَاجِئتِنِي، انتَ انسَان أي بِنت تِتمَنَّاه، مِش عَارفَة ....

313

تامر: مَتقُوليش حَاجَة خَالِص، يَا رِيمُو، أَنَا مِن سَاعِةِ مَاشُوفتِك وَأَنَا مُعجَب بِيكِي، وَلَمَاعرفتِك أكتر، حَبِيت نِرمِين مِن جُوه اكتر، وقُلت دِي الانسانة اللي باتمَنَّى تِشَاركِني حَيَاتِي، وَأَدِيلهَا قَلبِي وَحَيَاتِي، قُولِي اه بَس وَأَنَا أَجِيب الوَالِد وَالوَالِدَة وأرُوح أطلُب ايدِك مِن الوَالِد.

أومأت نِرمِين رَأسَهَا مُوَافِقةً وَمُبتَسِمَةً في خَجَلٍ

تامر: أَنَا أَسعَد انسَان دِلوَقتِي، أَنَا حَبِيت أَصَارحَك في نَفس يُوم عِيد مِيلادِك يَا أَحلَى حَاجَة في حَيَاتِي.

الكلماتُ الجديدة

معناها	الكلمة
Flirtation	غَزَل
Upscale	رَاقِي
Your eyes understand me	بِتفهَمِني عِينيك
The way you look at me	نَظرَاتَك
Set me on fire	بِتقِيد فِيَا نَار
Tell me	قُولِّي

Do you allow me ... ?	تِسمَحِيلي
A little	شُوَيَة
They will come / arrive	يجو
Please, go ahead	اتفضَّل
Happy birthday	كُل سَنَة وأنتِ طَيِّبَة
How did you know?	انتَ عرفت ازاي
No one knows my birthday	محَدِّش يعرف عِيد مِيلادِي
My lady	سِتي
Your Facebook account	الأكونت بتَاعِك عَلَى الفِيس بُوك
He who loves someone knows everything about them	اللِّي بِيعِز حَد بِيعرَف كُل حَاجَة عَنه
She smiled	ابتَسَمْت
Shyness	خَجَلٍ
I am sure / certain you've had feelings for me for a long time	أنتِ أكيد حَاسَّة بِيَا مِن مُدَّةٍ كَبِيرَةٍ
More than that	أكتَر مِن كِدَه
My love for you is real	حُبِّي لِيكِي حَقِيقِي
I can't hide my feelings towards you	مِش قَادِر أخبِّي شُعُورِي نَاحِيتِك
I love you to death	بَامُوت فِيكِي
The feelings are mutual	شُعُور مُتبَادَل
From your side	نَاحِيتِك
Remo (a female nickname)	رِيمُو
Any girl would be lucky to have you	انتَ انسَان أي بِنت تِتمَنَّاه

Don't say anything at all	مَتقُوليش حَاجَة خَالِص
I love Nermin's inside more (said when you admire someone's personality more than their beauty – in the West, this could be considered less than flattering, but in the Arab world, it means that you have more than purely carnal intentions)	حَبِّيت نِرمين مِن جُوه اكتر
The person who I wish to share my life with	الانسانة اللي باتمَنَّى تِشارِكني حَيَاتي
And I will give her my heart and life	وَأديلهَا قَلبي وَحَيَاتي
Just say yes	قُولي اه بَس
And I will ask your father for your hand	وأرُوح أطلُب ايدِك مِن الوَالِد
She nodded	أومأت
She agreed	مُوَافقَة
And smiling	وَمُبتَسِمَة
With shyness	في خَجَلٍ
I want to be honest with you	أنَا حَبِّيت أصَارحَك
On your birthday, Oh! You are the sweetest thing in my life	في نَفس يُوم عيد مِيلاِدك يَا أحلَى حَاجَة في حَيَاتي

أسئلة:

1. What are the names of the two people in this conversation? Which is the male and which is the female?
2. Where is this conversation taking place?
3. Are there people around them?
4. How does the male know the female's birthday?
5. Does anyone else know her birthday?
6. Do they both have Facebook accounts?
7. Does the man have feelings for the woman?
8. If so, how does he express his feelings?

9. Does the man think that the woman is aware of his feeling towards her?
10. Is the woman surprised by the man telling her he likes her?
11. Are his feelings reciprocated?
12. Does the woman think other women are attracted to the man?
13. What is the nickname the man gives to the woman?
14. When did his feelings for the woman start?
15. What does the man mean when he says, 'I like you better on the inside than on the outside'?
16. Whom will he bring with him when he asks for her hand in marriage?
17. Whom does he need to ask to marry her (as well as herself)?
18. Does the woman consent to his proposal?
19. What is her reaction to his proposal?
20. On which particular and personal day does he propose?

قد أثر هذا الانقسام بين الشعب على الاقتصاد المصرى، تأثيرًا عظيمًا، وباتت الخسائر تتوالى وراء بعضها البعض. المصريون يعيشون فى حالة من الارتباك النفسى، والانقسام فى الرأى بطريقة مقلقة للغاية.

(1) المُعَاكَسَاتُ فِي الشَّارِعِ

الثُّقل صَنعَة يَا جَمِيل

مُعَاكَسَة مُستَوى بِيئَة (مُستَوى لُوكَال)

This is a conversation between a man flirting with a woman in the street. The language of this lesson is Egyptian colloquial Arabic and is laden with idioms and uses words and expressions that are less sophisticated, but are well known in the language. The English word "local" is used in Egyptian Arabic to mean "low class".

رجل: طَيِّب عَبرنَا يَاجَميل

فتاة: ايه أصلُه دَه؟

رجل: هيفَاء وَهبي يَانَاس، دَه انتِ مُزَّة جَامدَة تَمَام

زَي مَابيقُول الكِتَاب.

الفتاة تضحك من منظر الرجل وتحاول أن تُخفِي ضحكتها

الرجل: قِشطَة بِالصَلاةُ النَّبِي، يَاوَعدِي، أمُوت أنَا.

الفتاة: أنتَ وَاد هَايِف، مِش نَاوِي تِجِيبهَا لِبر؟ امشِي أحسَن لَك.

الرجل: اخُد نِمرِة المُوبَايل يَاعَسَل.

الفتاة: اتاخِدِت رُوحَك يَابعِيد، وِامشِي أحسَن ألِم عَليك أُمة لا إله الا الله.

الرجل: ايه بس؟ لِيه كده؟ اللُّون الوِحش ده؟ هَاودِيني يَاقَمر، مَحسُوبِك قَصدُه خِير، وأنا جَدَع وأعجِبِك أوي.

الفتاة: مُش هَيحصَل خِير أبَداً، يَابن النَّاس امشِي، يالا يَارُوح أُمَّك.

الرجل: انتِ شَربَات صَحِيح، وحِتَة مِشَفِيَة مِن غِير عَضم، بَس لِسَانك زَالِف وطويل، بس لُوز والنَّبِي.

319

الفتاة: قَطْع لِسَانَك انتَ يَاض، يَاللا يَاخَفِيف، زُق عَجَلَك، ايه البَلاوي اللي بِتتحدِّف عَلَى الصُبح دِي؟

الرجل: مَاشِي يَاوَحش، الصَّبر حِلو يَاجَمِيل، ده أنَا بَاستَنَّى تَعدِي مِن هِنَا كُل يُوم، عَشَان أكحَل عِيِني بشُوفتَك يَا قَاسِي، ادلَّع واتقل بِرَاحتَك يَا بَا.

الفتاة تضحك مِن كَلامِه وتقول: بَلاوي!!

الكلماتُ الجَديدة

معناها	الكلمة
Flirtations	المُعَاكَسَاتُ
Composure- describes someone that does not get easily excited, and in this context, the man describes the woman as having composure good enough to be a profession	الثُّقل
Workmanship/ Profession	صَنعَة
Composure- describes someone that does not get easily excited, and in this context, the man describes the woman as having composure good enough to be a profession	الثُّقل صَنعَة يَا جَمِيل

320

Haifa Wehbe is a Lebanese singer and actress who is considered by Arabs to be of the utmost beauty. Comparing a woman to her means that the woman is very beautiful.	هيفَاء وَهبِي
Oh beautiful (this is considered a flirtatious word – notice that the word is masculine, even though you might be talking to a woman)	يَا جَميل
Environment (as in their upbringing, family, friends, etc.)	بِيئَة
A level environment (this is used about someone from a low class – also used is the English word 'local')	مُستَوى بِيئَة (مُستَوى لُوكَال)
Pay attention to us	عَبرنَا
What is the story? / What is going on? (In Arabic, Where's this from / its origin?)	ايه أصلُه دَه
Haifa Wehbe, oh people (used when you are asking for help – she is so beautiful, you need help handling her beauty)	هيفَاء وَهبِي يَانَاس
Hot woman	مُزَّة
Rigid / strong (this is another word to describe a hot woman)	جَامدَة
Rigid / strong, exactly as the book said (this latter phrase means, in the English, 'textbook hot' – the ideal definition)	جَامدَة تَمَام زَي مَا بيقُول الكِتَاب
She hid	تُخفِي
And tried to hide her laughter	وتحاول أن تُخفِي ضحكتها
Cream with praising the Prophet ('cream' is used as a metaphor for the sweetness or the	قِشطَة بِالصَلاة ۝ النَّبِي

beauty of a woman or situation, and it is combined with praising the Prophet because you want to thank the divine act in making this beauty)	
Oh, my promise (this is an exclamation that you say when you are really astounded at your good luck, as in when somebody's promise to you is fulfilled)	يَاوَعدِي
I die (this is a play on the phrase 'it's to die for!' – something that you love)	أمُوت أنَا
You're a lightweight, boy	أنتَ وَاد هَايِف
You do not have any intention to bring it to shore (said when someone does not seem like they want to end an intimidating or aggressive situation – as in a boat in a stormy sea where you do not have the intention to bring it back to the calm shore. This is used in English when 'there's a storm brewing' is used metaphorically, or in literature where the sea symbolizes danger)	مِش نَاوِي تِجِيبها لِبر
It is better for you to walk away (said to someone who harasses another and who has no intention of going away)	امشِي أحسَن لَك
I want to take your mobile number, oh honey ('honey', like in English, is used flirtatiously)	اخُد نِمرِة المُوبَايل يَاعَسَل
May your soul be taken from you, oh you who is far away (when a person says the above to the girl, she plays on the verb 'to take' to wish that his soul is taken, i.e. he will die. By saying 'you who is far away', she makes it clear that she doesn't want to be close to that person)	اتاخِدت رُوحَك يَابِعِيد

And go away / keep walking, or I will gather all around you the nation of no God but Allah (the woman tells the man that she will scream so that other people will take her side and do something bad to him; the whole nation of Islam is clearly a very large number)	وِامِشي أحسَن ألِم عَليك أُمِة لا إله الا الله
Bad color (refers to the bad attitude or reaction from someone they don't expect this from – this literally means a bad personality / attitude / reaction)	اللُون الوِحِش
Be lenient towards me, oh moon (moon is another flirtatious word describing a beautiful woman)	هَاوِديني يَاقَمر
Your friend / ally has good intentions (the man is telling the woman that he just wants to talk to her, and this intention could be good, like marriage, or something that is not haram)	مَحسُوبِك قَصدُه خِير
I am a good man and you will like me very much (the word translated as 'good man' refers to somebody who is trustworthy, who comes to the aid of those who need his help, and who is generous)	وأنا جَدَع وأعِجِبِك أوي
Nothing will come from this (this is a threatening phrase promising that bad things will happen)	مُش هَيحصَل خِير أَبداً
Oh, son of people, keep walking ('son of people' refers to someone who comes from a good family; the woman tells him that he comes from a good family; that this is his last chance to retain some dignity in the situation – he must stop bothering her and just keep walking)	يَابن النَّاس امِشي

OK let's go, oh! the soul of your mother (said as an insult to an adult man, because his mother is still very much attached to him)	يَاللا يَارُوح أُمَّك
You are a real sweet drink (similar to, 'you are really sweet' – even if a man is not being talked to kindly by a woman, it might still sound pleasant purely because it is coming from her mouth)	انتِ شَربَات صَحِيح
You are a piece of boneless meat (considered a flirtatious statement for low-class people. Needless to say it is an insult in Western society – but in certain circles in Arab cultures, meat is very expensive: the enjoyment someone will get from eating boneless meat is the equivalent to talking to this woman)	وحِتَة مِشَفِيَة مِن غِير عَضم
But your tongue is long, and it is closing in (meaning someone is impolite – they are talking about someone who they shouldn't be)	بَس لِسَانِك زَالِف وِطويل
But you are almonds, by the Prophet (almonds are considered a delicacy, like honey; 'by the Prophet' means you are swearing to the Prophet that what you say is true)	بس لُوز والنَّبي
May your tongue get cut, oh boy (his words are always bad / insulting / mischievous, so he deserves his tongue to be cut off)	قَطْع لِسَانَك انتَ يَاض
Let's go, oh you lightweight! (said to someone who is not respected; 'lightweight' describes a weak or unstable mind)	يَاللا يَاخَفِيف
Push your wheels ('go away')	زُق عَجَلَك
What are these disasters being thrown at me so early in the morning? (describing the	ايه البَلاوي اللي بِتتحِدّف عَلَى الصُبح دِي

woman's experience when she meets the undesirable man)	
OK, oh bad (woman) (the man is referring to the woman's unfair reaction to his attempted flirtation)	مَاشِي يَاوَحش
Patience is sweet ('good things happen to those who wait')	الصَّبر حِلو
I want to eyeline with kohl my eyes with your image (this metaphor means that he wants to imprint her image onto his eyes, like a woman would do with eyeliner – 'kohl' is the material used in eyeliner)	أكحَل عِيني بشُوفتَك
Be spoilt and composed as much as you like (the man is saying that the woman's indifference to his advances is an attempt to hide her true, positive feelings towards him)	ادلَّع واتقل بِرَاحتَك يَا بَا
Disasters / afflictions (when you describe someone as a disaster, they obviously haven't made an impression on you)	بَلاوي

أسئلة:

1. Which actress does the man say resembles the woman he is flirting with?

2. Was the woman receptive to the man?

3. Was this a spur of the moment encounter between the two or did the man plan on meeting her?

4. He describes the woman as "cream". What does this mean?

5. Did the woman give the man her cell phone number?

6. As he is flirting with the woman, he calls her "a piece of meat". What does this mean in this context?

7. In general, did the woman consider the man funny or obnoxious?

رُخْصَةُ ٱلْقِيَادَةِ

DRIVER LICENSE رخصة القيادة

No. 1062345336

Exp. 15/03/2014

Date of Birth
15/03/2014

١٦٢٣٤٥٣٣٦

تاريخ الانتهاء

تاريخ الميلاد

12398912V 189433 53898R9TRY-QW

مَا نَوعُ رُخْصَةِ القِيَادَةِ الَّتِي تَحْمِلُهَا؟ رُخْصَةٌ خَاصَّةٌ؟
أم مِنَ الدَّرَجَةِ الأُولَى أم الثَّانِيَةِ أم الثَّالِثَةِ؟ أم رُخْصَةٌ مُؤَقَّتَةٌ؟

This is a conversation between a driving instructor and his student. This lesson contains
vocabulary that pertains to driving and traffic.

مُدَرِّبُ السِّوَاقَةِ: لِمَاذَا تَأَخَّرْتَ يَا عُمَرُ؟ هَذا وقْتٌ إِضَافِيٌّ، سَأُحَاسِبُكَ عَلَيهِ.

عُمَرُ: كَمَا تَعْلَمُ يَاأُسْتَاذ، أَنَّهُ لَيْسَ لَدَيَّ سَيَّارَةٌ خَاصَّةٌ بَعْدُ، لِأَنِّي لازِلْتُ أَتَعَلَّمُ السِّوَاقَةَ (القِيَادَةَ)، فَاضْطُرِرْتُ الَى التَشَعْبُطِ (التَعَلُّقِ) بِأوتُوبِيس النَّقْلِ العَام (حَافِلَةُ النَّقلِ العَام)، وَلَكِنْ لِلأَسَفِ لَقَدْ سُرِقْتُ فِي الزِّحَام وَأَنَا أَدْفَعُ ثَمَنَ التَذْكَرَةِ لِلكُمْسَرِيِّ (المُحَصِّل).

مُدَرِّبُ السِّوَاقَةِ: يَا رَبِّي، حَسَنٌ، اذَنْ لَنْ أَحْتَسِبَ هَذَا الوَقْتَ يَاعُمَرُ، هَيَّا، الانَ اشَارَةُ المُرُورِ خَضْرَاءُ، وَالعَسْكَرِيُّ (شُرْطِيُّ المُرُورِ) يُلَوِّحُ بِصَفَّارَتِه أَنْ تَحَرَّكُوا، اتَّجِه يَمِيناً (انْعَطِف يَمِيناً)، وَأَدِرْ عَجَلَةَ القِيَادَةِ بِثَبَاتٍ، سِرْ لِلأَمَام، خُذْ هَذَا المَلَفَّ (الدَوَرَان أو المُنْعَطَف)، ثُمَّ اتَّجِه شَمَالاً (انْعَطِف لِلشَّمَال)، قِفْ حَالاً، سَائِقُ المِيكْرُوبَاص قَادِمٌ بِسُرْعَةٍ هَائِلَةٍ.... أَنْتَ يَاسَائِقَ المِيكْرُوبَاص، لِمَاذَا لاتَلْتَزِمُ بِقَوَاعِدِ وَقَوَانِينِ المُرُورِ، أَغْلَبُكُم كَذَلِكَ، سَأُبْلِغُ عَسْكَرِيَّ المُرُورِ عَنْكَ.

سَائِقُ المِيكْرُوبَاص: أَنْتَ المُخْطِئُ، أَنْتَ مَنْ يَسِيرُ بِبُطْءٍ زَائِدٍ، والتَّاكْسِيُّ (سَيَّارَةُ الأُجْرَةِ) الذي وَرَائِي يَسْتَعْجِلُنِي.

مُدَرِّبُ السِّوَاقَةِ: هَلْ أَصَابَكَ العَمَى؟ ألا تَرَى أَنَّ هَذِه السَّيَّارَةَ تَابِعَةٌ لِمَدْرَسَةِ تَعْلِيْمِ القِيَادَةِ، وَأَنَّ السَّائِقَ طَالِبٌ يَتَعَلَّمُ القِيَادَةَ، كَمَا أَنَّ الازْدِحَامَ شَدِيْدٌ.

سَائِقُ المِيكْرُوبَاص: نَعَمْ، أَنَا اسِفٌ حَقّاً، سَامِحْنِي.

مُدَرِّبُ السِّوَاقَةِ: حَسَناً، لَقَدْ اعْتَذَرْتَ، لَقَدْ كِدْتَ تَصْدِمُنَا وَتَتَسَبَبُ بِحَادِثٍ، الحمد لله أَنَّ خَطَّ عُبُورِ المُشَاةِ (مَكَانَ عُبُورِ المُشَاةِ) كَانَ خَالِياً مِنَ المَارَّةِ، لَوْ كَانَ شَئٌ حَدَثَ لِسَيَّارَةِ المَدْرَسَةِ، كُنْتُ أَخَذْتُكَ الَى المِيكَانِيكِي فِي وَرْشَةِ اصْلاح السَّيَّارَاتِ وَدَفَّعْتُكَ ثَمَنَ الاصْلاحَاتِ.

سَائِقُ المِيكْرُوبَاص: لَمْ أَتَمَكَّنْ مِنْ سَحْبِ الفَرَامِلِ (المَكَابِحِ)، الحَمْدُ لِلَّه، قَدَّرَ وَلَطَفَ، سَامِحْنِي يَابُنَيَّ.

عُمَرُ: اَلحَمْدُ لِلَّه أَنْ لَطَفَ بِنَا، الانَ، لَقَدْ تَأَخَّرْتُ كَثِيراً، وعِنْدِي مَوْعِدٌ مَعَ وَالِدِي القَادِم مِنَ الصَّعِيدِ بِالقِطَارِ، وَيَجِبُ أَنْ أَذْهَبَ الَى مَحَطَّةِ القِطَارِ بِرَمْسِيس.

مُدَرِّبُ السِّوَاقَةِ: عُموماً يَا عُمَرَ، لَقَدْ تَقَدَّمْتَ كَثيراً فِي القِيَادَةِ، وَيُمْكِنُكَ الانَ أَنْ تَجْتَازَ اخْتِبَارَ القِيَادَةِ بِنَجَاحٍ، وَتَحْصُلَ عَلَى رُخْصَةِ قِيَادَةٍ خَاصَّةٍ سَرِيعاً، فَقَطْ تَدَرَّبْ عَلَى الرَّكْنِ كَثيراً.

عُمَرُ: رَائِعٌ، طُموحِيَ القَادِمُ أَنْ أَحْصُلَ عَلَى رُخْصَةِ قِيَادَةٍ مِنَ الدَّرَجَةِ الأُولَى، لأَسَافِرَ وَأَعْمَلَ بِالخَليجِ سَائِقاً لِلشَّاحِنَاتِ وَنَقْلِ البَضَائِعِ فِي خِلالِ سَنَتَينِ.

مُدَرِّبُ السِّوَاقَةِ: انْ شَاءَ اللهُ وَوَفَّقَكَ لِمَاتُرِيدُ، فَقَطْ تَذَكَّرْ، أَنَّ فِي العَجَلَةِ النَّدَامَةَ، وَفِي التَّأَنِّي السَلامَةُ، وَدَائِماً دُعَاءُ الرُّكوبِ (سُبْحَانَ الَّذِي سَخَّرَ لَنَا هَذا وَمَا كُنَّا لَهُ مُقْرِنِينَ، وإنَّا الَى رَبِّنَا لَمُنْقَلِبُونَ، وَانَّا لله وَانَّا اليَهِ رَاجِعُونَ).

الكلِماتُ الجَديدة

الكَلِمة	معناها
المُرُورُ وَالمُوَاصَلَاتُ	Traffic and transportation
رُخْصَةِ القِيَادَةِ	Driving license (in Arabic this is a general license)
الَّتِي تَحمِلُهَا	That you carry
رُخْصَة ُخَاصَّة	Driving license (a special license used only

328

for your private means)	
First class	الدَّرَجَةِ الأُولَى
Temporary license	رُخْصَةٌ مُؤَقَّتة
Driving instructor	مُدَرِّبُ السِّوَاقَة
Extra time	وقْتٌ إِضَافِيٌّ
I will charge you for it	سَأُحَاسِبُكَ عَلَيه
After	بَعْدُ
People who hang from the doors of crowded buses / trains	التَّشَعْبُطِ
Hanging	التَّعَلُّق
General public transportation	أوتُوبِيس النَّقلِ العَامِ
Bus	حَافِلَة
It was stalling	سُرِقْتُ
Conductor (ticket collector)	المُحَصِّل
Oh my God!	يَا رَبِّي
Traffic warden (traffic police or agent in Arabic)	شُرْطِيُّ المُرُور
Wave with his whistle	يُلَوِّحُ بِصَّفَارَتِه
Turn right	انْعَطِف يَمِيناً
Steering wheel	عَجَلَةَ القِيَادَة
Go straight ahead	سِرْ لِلأَمَام
Go around the roundabout / traffic circle	خُذْ هَذَا المَلَفَّ

Roundabout / traffic circle	الدَوَرَانُ
Traffic lights	اشارَةُ المُرُورِ
Turn north	اتَّجِه شَمَالاً
Stop immediately	قِفْ حَالاً
With very high speed	بِسُرْعَةٍ هَائِلَةٍ
I will report	سَأُبْلِغُ
You are wrong	أنْتَ المُخطِئُ
Extremely slow	بِبُطءٍ زَائِدٍ
He is rushing me	يَسْتَعْجِلُني
Are you blind?	هَلْ أَصَابَكَ العَمَى
The traffic is heavy	الازْدِحَامَ شَدِيدٌ
I am really sorry	أنَا اسِفٌ حَقاً
Forgive me	سَامِحني
You were about to hit us	لَقَدْ كِدْتَ تَصْدِمُنَا
And cause an accident	وَتَتَسَبَبُ بِحَادِثٍ
Pedestrian crossing	خَطَّ عُبُورِ المُشَاةِ
Pedestrian-free	خَالِياً مِنَ المَارَّةِ
Auto repair shop	وَرْشَةِ اصلاحِ السَيَّاراتِ
I'll make you pay for the repairs	وَدَفَّعْتُكَ ثَمَنَ الاصلاحَاتِ
I couldn't hit the break	لَمْ أَتَمَكَّنْ مِنْ سَحْبِ الفَرَامِلِ

The break	المَكَابِح
It is by the grace of God that nothing bad happened	قَدَّرَ وَلَطَفَ
Forgive me, son	سَامِحْني يَابُنَيَّ
Upper Egypt	الصَّعيدِ
Driving test	اخْتِبَارَ القِيَادةِ
Practice parking a lot	تَدَرَّبْ عَلَى الرَّكْنِ كَثيراً
My next ambition	طُمُوحِيَ القَادِمُ
Truck driver	سَائِقاً للشَّاحِنات
According to your wishes	وَوَفَّقَكَ لِمَا تُريدُ
Rushing causes regret	في العَجَلَةِ النَّدَامَة
Slowing down results in safety (an Arab proverb advising people not to rush)	وَفِي التَّأَنِّي السَلامَةُ
Riding prayer (a prayer a Muslim will recite upon riding any mode of transportation)	دُعَاءُ الرُّكوبِ

أسئلة:

1. Why was the driving instructor upset with Umar and does he penalize him?
2. Does Umar have a private car, and why or why not?
3. What happened to Umar on the way to his lesson and when?
4. Upon starting his first driving lesson, which direction did he go?
5. How did the instructor teach him how to turn the wheels?
6. Why did the driving instructor tell him to start the car immediately?
7. There was an exchange between the driving instructor and a driver of a minivan. What did the driving instructor accuse the minivan driver of and what did he do about it?
8. Whom did the minivan driving accuse in turn?
9. What type of vehicle was driving behind the mini van?

331

10. In the exchange between the minivan driver and the driving instructor, which one accused the other of being blind and why?

11. What are the two reasons that the instructor gave to the minivan driver to take account of the way he was driving?

12. Was the minivan driver remorseful for his actions?

13. How was a traffic accident avoided during this dialogue?

14. If the accident happened, who would have paid for repairs?

15. Who is older, the instructor or the minivan driver?

16. Where will Umar go after finishing his lesson?

17. What does Umar need to practice more?

18. Does the instructor believe that Umar can pass the road test at his current level?

19. What type of license does Umar want to get and why?

20. What proverb did the instructor give to Umar that says he should always be cautious and slow down?

21. What type of prayer did he advise him to say while driving?

ستار بَكس كَافِيه

عِندَك وَاحِد شَاي فِي الخَمسِينَة، وَصَلَحُه...

This is a conversation between a young man and his grandfather who are visiting a Western coffee shop. The grandfather is surprised by the style of this coffee shop and the items they offer and is explaining the difference between the traditional coffee shop and the modern version.

وَليد: نَاو جِرَاند بَا، لِيتس جو، ذَاتس ذَا گَافيه.

الجد: يَاابني كَلَمِني بِالعَرَبِيَةِ، مُنذُ أَن عُدتَ مِن أمريكَا وَأَنَالا أفهَمُ مُعظَمَ كَلامِكَ.

وليد: انزِل يَاجَدِّي، وَصَلنَا الَى الكَافِيه، ستَاربَكس گَافِيه، هَا هِيَ، في مُولِ سِيتي ستَارز بِمدِينَةِ نَصٍ.

الجد: مَا هَذَا؟ هَلْ أتَيتَ بِنَا الَى مَطعَم أو گَافِيتِيرِيَا؟ أيْنَ القهوَةُ يَاحَفِيدِي؟ دِيكُورَاتُ المَكَانِ عَصرِيَةٌ جِداً، وَالطَّاوِلاتُ وَالكَرَاسِي نَاعِمَةٌ ولامِعَةٌ.

وليد: هاهاها، جَدِّي، هَلْ كُنتَ تعتَقِدُ انَّها قَهوَةٌ شَعبِيَةٌ وَصَبِيُّ القَهوَجِي، وَالاحسَاس الشَّرقِي (الأورِينتَال)؟

تَعَالَ، هَيَّا.

الجد: طَيِب، سَنَرَى يَاوَليد.

فِي الگَافِيه

الجد: ما هذا يَا وَليد؟، طَاقَمُ العَمَلِ يَرتَدُونَ زِيَاً واحِداً، وَالمَكَانُ يُشبِهُ المَطعَم.

وَلِيد: نَعَم، انَّهُم يُقَدِّمُون سَاندوتشَاتٍ (شَطَائِرَ)، وَحَلَوِيَاتٍ خَفِيفَةً أَيْضاً.

الجَد: اطْلُب أنتَ لَنَا شَيئا، فَأَنَا لا أَعْرِفُ شَيئاً مِنْ قَائِمَةِ المَشرُوبَاتِ الَّتي أَمَامِي.

وَلِيد: مِن فَضلِك، وَن كَافِيه لِيتِيه، وَن شوكلِيت مُوكَا، اند تُو مَاربِلْ بَاوند كِيكس.

النَادِل: أوكِ، هَافَ أنَايس دَاي سِير.

الجَد: نَعَم، مَاذَا قُلْتْ؟ مَاهَذَا البَارِبِل بُوند الَّذِي طَلَبتَه؟

وَلِيد: هَاهَاهَا، جَدِّي، لَقَدْ طَلَبتُ لَكَ قَهوَةً بِالحَلِيبِ، ولي قَهوَةٌ بِالشُوكُولاته، وقِطعَتَينِ مِن الكَعكِ، سَتَتَذُوقُ أفضَلَ قَهوَةٍ بَالحَلِيب.

الجَد: أفضَلُ قهوَةٍ!! يَا بُنَي، رَحِمَ اللهُ أيَّامَ قَهوَةِ عَمِّكَ صَالح بالحُسَينِ، والرَّادِيُو وَالسَّيدَةُ أمُّ كلثُوم وَيَالِيل يَاعِين، و(عَظَمَة يَاست) وَأحلَى مَشرُوب سَحلَبٍ سَّاخِنٍ أو فِنجَانِ قهوَةِ سَادَةٍ أو زِيَادَةٍ أو مَضبُوط.

وَلِيد: يَاجَدِي، أنَا أرِيكَ التَّطورَ لِكُلِ شَئٍ، انَّهَا سِلسِلَةُ كَافِيهَاتٍ مَشهُورَةٌ وَفُرُوعُهَا فِي جَمِيع أنحَاءِ العَالَمِ، وانتَشَرَتْ فُرُوعُهَا فِي مِصرَ أَيْضاً.

الجَد: أنَا أرَى أنَّ مُعظَمَ الزَّبَائِنِ مِنَ الشَّبَابِ الرَّاقِي، أو الكِبَارِ الذِّينَ رُبَّمَا عَاشُو فِي بِلادِ أجنَبِيَةٍ.

النَادِل: هَذَا مَا طَلَبتَهُ سَيدِي.

الجَد: مَاهَذِهِ الرَّغوَةُ الَّتِي تُشبِهُ رَغوَةَ الصَّابُون فَوقَ وَجهِ القهوَةِ؟

وَلِيد: صَابُون؟ يَاجَدِّي انَّها رَغوَةٌ مِن كِرِيمَةِ الحَلِيبِ فَوقَ قَهوَتَكَ.

الجَد: رَحَمَ الله أيَّامَ القَهوَةِ التِّي بِوَجه أو دُونَ وَجهٍ.

335

تُقال فِي مِصرْ، بِوشّ أومِن غَيرِ وِشّ

وليد: الانَ، مَارَأيُكَ جَدِّي؟

الجد: انَّهَا لَذِيذَةٌ.

وليد: رَائِعٌ.

الجد: لكِنْ، أتعلَمُ شَيئاً؟

وليد: مَاذَا؟

الجد: لَيسَ هُنَاكَ أفضَلُ مِن فِنجَان البُنِّ المُحَوَّجِ فِي القَهوَةِ البَلَدِي يَا وَلِيد، تَضبَطُ المِزَاجَ فَعلاً، أو كُوبِ شَاي كُشَرِي، وَصَوتُ صَبِيُّ القَهوَجِي وَهُوَ يَقُولُ وَعِندَك وَاحِد شَاي كُشَرِي وصَلَحُه.

وليد: مَاهُوَ شَّايُ الكُشَرِي؟ وَمَا مَعنَى وَصَلَحُهُ؟

الجد: كشَرِي تَعنِي أن يَضَعُ الشَّاي النَّاعِمَ وَلَيسَ شَايَ الأكِيَاسِ كَمَا الانَ، والسُّكر فِي كوبٍ، وَيَصُبُّ عَلَيهِم المَاءَ المَغلِي، وصلحه تعني احسِن صُنعَهُ واضبِطهُ،

وَهُنَاك (شَاي فِي الخَمسِينَة) وَتَعنِي فِي كُوبٍ صَغِيرٍ
وَأيضاً (سُكَرْ بَرَّه) مَعنَاهَا أنْ يُقَدَّمَ السُّكَرُ لِمَنْ يُرِيدُونَ اضَافَتَهُ بِأنفُسِهِمْ، و(شَايٌ فِي المِيزُو) تَعنِي شَايٌ بِالحَلِيبِ فِي القاهِرَةِ، لَكِنَّهَا فِي الاسكَندَرِيةِ تَعنِي شَايٌ فِي كوبٍ صَغِيرٍ، وَ (الشَّايُ المَقطُوعُ نَفَسُهُ) تَعنِي شَايٌ تَمَّ غَليَانُهُ كَثِيراً، الانَ شَئٌ بِالفَانِيلِيَا وَشَئٌ بِالفَرَاوِلَةِ وَاخَرُ بِالرَّغوةِ!!!

وَعَولَمَةُ الأمَاكِنِ والمطَاعِم والمَحَلاتِ والمَقَاهِي!!!

336

وليد: حَاضِر يَا جَدِّي، المَرَّةُ القَادِمَةُ سَتَكُونُ فِي قَهوَةِ الفِيشَاوِي فِي الحُسَينِ، فَهِي تُعجِبُنِي كَثِيرا،ً

فَلِكُلِّ مَكَانٍ طَابِعُهُ يَا جَدِّي، وَمَهمَا تَغَيَّرَتِ الأُمُورُ نَشتَاقُ الَى الأَصَالَةِ.

الكلماتُ الجديدة

معناها	الكلمة
Speak Arabic to me	كَلَمنِي بِالعَرَبِيَةِ
I don't understand most of what you said	وَأَنَالا أفهَمُ مُعظَمَ كَلامِك
Modern	عَصرِيَة
Soft	نَاعِمَة
Shiny	لامِعَة
Popular coffee shop	قَهوَةٌ شَعبِيَة
Barista apprentice (this is a boy who helps the man make and serve coffee to learn the trade secrets)	صَبِيُّ القَهوَجِي
Oriental atmosphere	الاحسَاس الشَّرقِي
Staff	طَاقَمُ العَمَل

Uniform	زِيّاً
Drinks menu	قَائِمَةِ المَشْرُوبَاتِ
Cakes	الكَعكِ
Your Uncle SaleH's coffee shop in el-Hussain (a district in Old Cairo)	قَهوَةِ عَمِّكَ صَالِحٍ بِالحُسَينِ
The lady Ummkulthum (the most famous singer in the history of the Middle East – read about her online)	السَّيدَةُ أُمُّ كلثُوم
Oh night, oh I (this refers to oriental music and singing)	يا لِيل يَاعِين
Greatness, oh lady (a greeting that listeners will express when they hear Ummkulthum sing)	عَظَمَة يَاسِت
Saloob (a drink made from salep)	سَحلَبْ
Black coffee	قهوَةً سَادَةٍ
Increase (this means you need more sugar)	زِيَادَةٍ
Exact / equal (this means the amount of coffee powder is the same as the sugar)	مَضبُوط
Evolution	التَّطوَّرَ
Form	الرَّغوَةُ
The face of the coffee (the top, which often has cream or foam)	وَجهِ القهوَةِ
Coffee with or without a face	القَهوَةِ التَّي بِوَجه أو دُونَ وَجهٍ
Coffee mixed with spices	البُنِّ المُحَوَّج
Popular	البَلَدِي

338

Set / get you into the mood	تَضبَطُ المِزَاجَ
Koshery cup of tea	كُوبِ شَاي كُشَرِي
Soft tea	الشَّاي النَّاعِمَ
Pour liquid	يَصُبُّ
Boiled	المَغلِي
Make it perfect	وصلحه
Sugar on the side	سُكَّرْ بَرَّه
Demitasse (small cup usually for Turkish coffee)	المِيزُو
Out of breath tea (refers to tea leaves which have been used many times)	الشَّايُ المَقطُوعُ نَفَسُهُ
Vanilla	بالفَانِيلِيَا
Strawberry	بالفَرَاولةِ
Globalization	وَعَولَمَة
We long for	نَشتَاقُ
Originality	الأَصَالَة

أسئلة:

1. What is the name of the coffee shop that they are visiting?

2. In which language did the young man start talking to his grandfather?

3. Did the grandfather understand him?

4. In which foreign country does the young man live?

5. How did they get to the coffee shop?

6. The coffee shop is located in a mall. What is the name of the mall?

7. What features of the coffee shop surprised the grandfather?

8. What features of the traditional coffee shop were missing from this modern coffee shop?

9. Do the people who work in traditional coffee shops wear uniforms?

10. Why did the grandfather think that the modern coffee shop looked more like a restaurant?

11. Why did the grandfather ask his grandson to order his drink?

12. What drinks did the grandson order?

13. Which one of them will have the marble pound cake?

14. What will the grandfather have to drink?

15. What will the grandson have to drink?

16. What does the grandfather miss the most about the traditional coffee shops?

17. Does this company have more coffee shops in Egypt, or is this the only one?

18. What types of customers, in the grandfather's opinion, would frequent this place?

19. What did the grandfather compare the foam to?

20. A traditional coffee can be called a coffee with or without a face. What does this mean?

21. Did the grandfather enjoy his coffee?

22. How do you prepare a cup of "shay koshari?"

23. In traditional coffee shop language, what does 50s mean?

24. How do you order a drink with sugar on the side?

25. How do you order tea with milk?

26. What is "out-of-breath" tea?

27. What is the name of the coffee shop these two intend to go to next time? Is it a traditional or modern coffee shop?

بِمُشَارَكَةِ 62 فِيلْمًا مِنْ 19 دَوْلَةً أُورُوبِّيَّةً وَالْبَلَدِ الْمُضِيفِ مِصْرَ انْطَلَقَتْ فَعَّالِيَّاتُ الدَّوْرَةِ الثَّانِيَةِ مِنْ مِهْرَجَانِ الْأُقْصُرِ لِلسِّينَمَا الْمِصْرِيَّةِ وَالْأُورُوبِّيَّةِ، وَتَحْضُرُ السِّينَمَا الْأَلْمَانِيَّةُ ضَيْفَ شَرَفٍ عَلَى الْمِهْرَجَانِ الَّذِي يُفْتَتَحُ بِالْفِيلْمِ الْمِصْرِيِّ الْجَدِيدِ "لَا مُؤَاخَذَةَ" لِلْمُخْرِجِ عَمْرِو سَلَامَة.

وَتَدُورُ أَحْدَاثُ الْفِيلْمِ حَوْلَ يَوْمِيَّاتِ طِفْلٍ مَسِيحِيٍّ وَعَلَاقَتِهِ بِزُمَلَائِهِ الْمُسْلِمِينَ فِي الْمَدْرَسَةِ، مُلْقِيًا الضَّوْءَ عَلَى قَضِيَّةِ الْفِتْنَةِ الطَّائِفِيَّةِ فِي الْمُجْتَمَعِ الْمِصْرِيِّ بِأُسْلُوبٍ بَسِيطٍ مِنْ خِلَالِ عَلَاقَاتِ الْأَطْفَالِ فِي الْمَدْرَسَةِ بِزَمِيلِهِمُ الْمَسِيحِيِّ، وَدَوْرِ الْكِبَارِ فِي هَذِهِ الْعَلَاقَةِ.

وَيَضُمُّ الْمِهْرَجَانُ -الَّذِي تَمَّ تَأْجِيلُهُ مِنْ شَهْرِ سَبْتَمْبَرَ/أَيْلُولَ الْمَاضِي بِسَبَبِ الظُّرُوفِ السِّيَاسِيَّةِ وَالْأَمْنِيَّةِ فِي مِصْرَ-هَذَا الْعَامَ مُسَابَقَتَيْنِ، الْأُولَى لِلْأَفْلَامِ الطَّوِيلَةِ وَالْأُخْرَى لِلْأَفْلَامِ الْقَصِيرَةِ وَأَفْلَامِ التَّحْرِيكِ.

With the participation of 62 films from 19 European countries and the host country Egypt, the second session of the Luxor Festival of Egyptian and European Cinema kicked off. German Cinema attended as a guest of honor at the festival, where the new Egyptian film "Excuse Me" opens, directed by Amr Salama.

The film revolves around the daily life of a Christian child and the relationship with his Muslim classmates at school. It highlights the issue of sectarian strife in Egyptian society through a simple relationship between children in school with their Christian classmate, and the role adults play in this relationship.

The festival – which was postponed from September due to political and security conditions in Egypt – includes for the first time two competitions: the first for long movies and the other for short and animated films.

الطَّبْخُ وَالاكْلُ وَالمَطَاعِمُ
يُرِيدُني أَحْمَدُ شِيف، أَستَاذةٌ فِي فَنِّ الطَّبخِ!!!

In this text, a husband is bickering with his wife because of her poor culinary skills.

أحمد: أَنَا تَعِبْتُ مِنْ هَذَا الأَكْلِ، يَا هَانِم!!مَتَى تَتَعَلَّمِينَ أَصُولَ المَطْبَخِ وَالطَّبِيخِ؟؟ أنتِ
فَقَط مَاهِرةٌ فِي رَصِّ الأَطبَاقِ، وَالأَكوَابِ، وَالمَلَاعِقِ، وَالشُّوَكَاتِ، وَالسَّكَاكِينِ،

343

دَوْرَقُ المَاءِ(الشَّفشَق)هُنَا، المَلَّاحَةُ هُنَاكَ، وَاتِيكِيتُ (آداب) الطَّعَام كَذَا وَكَذَا ..الخ...الخ...الخ

لَكِنِ الرَّائِحَةُ وَالطَّعْمُ مَعْدُومَان، كَمْ أَتَمَنَّى أَنْ أَشَمَّ رَائِحَةً طَيبَةً لِلقِدْرِ أوِ الحَلَّةِ الَّتي عَلَى البُوتَاجَازِ(المَوقِد)، كَمْ أَتَمَنَّى أَنْ أَشَمَّ اللَّحْمَ الذي في الفُرْنِ وَرَائِحَةَ الشِّوَاءِ، مَلَلتُ افطَارَ وَغَدَاءَ وَعَشَاءَ دَائماً مِنَ الأكلِ المَحْفُوظ وَالمُعَلَّبِ.

مَنى: النَّاسُ تَقُولُ (بِسم اللهِ) قَبْلَ الأكلِ، وَانتَ كَلَامُكَ يَسُدُّ الشَّهِيَةَ (النَّفس)!!!
أحمد: يَسُدُّ الشَّهِيَةَ (النَّفس)!!أَيْنَ هِيَ تِلكَ الشَّهِيَةُ؟ حَتَّى في رَمَضَانَ شَهْرُ الصِّيَام، مِنْ أَوَّلِ يَومٍ لِاخِرِ يَومٍ، لَمْ أَكُلْ وَجْبَةً جَيدَةً وَاحِدَةً، لا في افطَارٍ أوسُحُورٍ، لَوْلَا أَنْ تَعْزِمَنَا أمِّي مِنْ وَقتٍ لِاخَرٍ بِأكلٍ بَيتِي شَهِي، مِنْ عَمَلِ يَدِهَا، لَقدْ أوْشَكتُ عَلَى الافطَار في مَوَائِدِ الرَّحْمَنِ عِدَّة مَرَّاتٍ هَرَباً مِنْ طَبِيخِكِ السَّيِّءِ.

مَنى: وَالِدَتُكَ! اِهٍ، نَعَمْ، تَعْزِمُنَا حَمَاتِي عُزومَةً رَائِعَة (تدعُونَا)، وَأتَوَرَّطُ أنَا في غَسِيلِ كَوْمَةٍ مِنَ المَوَاعِينِ وَالأطْبَاقِ وَدَعْكِ وَجَلِي الحُلَلِ والقُدُورِ، وَتنظيفِ الأرْضِيَةِ والبُوتُوجَازِ(المَوْقِد)، وَوَضْعِ بَرَّادِ الشَّاي الكَبِيرِ عَلَى النَّارِ، وَتَجْلِسُ أخَوَاتُكَ كَالضُّيوف.

أحمد: مُنَى، احْفَظِي أَدَبَكِ وَأنتِ تتحَدَّثِينَ عَنْ وَالِدَتي.

مَنى: انَا أقصِدُ أنَّهَا لاتَمْلِكُ غَسَّالَةَ أطبَاقٍ يَارُوحي.

أحمد: نِسَاءٌ لا يَعْرِفنَ الطَّبْخَ وَلاَ النَّفْخَ وَلاَ أعْمَالَ المَنْزِل.
مَنى: اجْلِسْ فَقَطْ يَا حَبيبِي عَلَى الكُرْسِي، وَانْظُرْ مَاذَا اعْدَدْتُ لَكَ عَلَى المَائِدَةِ (التَّرَابِيزَة)، جَرِّبْ هَذِه الشُّورَبَة (الحَسَاء)، سَأَضَعُ لَكَ قَلِيلاً بِالمِغْرَفَةِ في طَبَقِكَ.
أحمد: شُورَبَةُ!! أنَا رَجُلٌ اتعَبُ وَأشْقَى خَارِجَ البَيْتِ كُلَّ يوم لأَحْلُمَ بِوَجْبَةٍ شَهِيَةٍ مُشبِعَةٍ لأَجِدُ الا الشُّورَبَة اوِالطَّعَامَ البَائِتَ (غَيْرُ طَازَج)، أَيْنَ الطَّعَامُ الطَّازِجُ؟ أَيْنَ

اللَّحْمُ وَالدَّجَاجُ وَالسَّمَكُ؟ أَيْنَ الفَوَاكِهُ وَالخُضَرَوَاتُ؟ أَيْنَ السَّلَطَاتُ وَالمُخَلَّلَاتُ وَفَوَاتِحُ الشَّهِيةِ(المُقِبلَات)؟ الجَّوُ حَارٌ أَيْنَ العَصيرُ وَالمُثلَجَاتُ؟ أَيْنَ الحَلَوِيَاتُ؟

منى: أَحْمَدُ يَاقلْبِي، الانَ اِحْجِزْ لَنَا فِي مَطعَم، غَدَاءً لِشخْصَيْنِ أَنَا وَانتَ فَقَط.

أحمد: هَاهَاهَا، يَامُنَى يَا حَبِيبتِي أَتَمَنَّى أَنْ تَتَعَلَمِي فُنُونِ اعْدَادِ الطَّعَامِ وَأُصُولِ المَطبخِ، المَشوِّي وَالمَقلِّي، المَسْلُوقُ وَالمَحْشِّي، المَطهِي وغَيْرَ المَطهِي، المُتَّبَّلَ وَالمُفَلْفَلَ، أُرِيدُكِ أُسْتاذَةً فِي فَنِّ الطَّهْي.

لَقَدْ اعْتَادَ الجَرْسُونُ (النَّادِلَ) وُجُودَنَا زَبائِنَ دَائِمِينَ، وَتَجِيئُنِي فَاتُورَةُ الحِسَابِ (الشِّيكِ) بِمَبْلَغٍ وَقَدْرِهِ

اهِ يَا جَيِبِي مِنكِ يَاَ حَيَاتِي، لَكِنْ سَتَتَعَلَمِين، أَلَيسَ كَذَلِكَ؟

الكلماتُ الجديدة

معناها	الكلمة
Good	طَيّبة
etc.	الخ...الخ...الخ..
Cooking	الطَّبْخُ
Eating	الاكْلُ
Restaurants	المَطَاعِمُ
Professor	أستَاذةٌ
Cookery / Art of Cooking	فَنِّ الطَّبْخِ
Tired	تَعِبْتُ
Principals	أصُولَ
And cooking	وَالطَّبيخِ
Organize	رَصِّ
Skilled	مَاهِرة

Forks	الشَّوَكاتِ
Knives	السَّكاكِينِ
Spoons	المَلَاعِقِ
Water Jug	دَوَرَقُ المَاءِ
Slate shaker	المَلَّاحَة
Smell	الرَّائِحَة
Taste	الطَّعْمُ
Don't exist	مَعْدُومانِ
Good	طَيَّبَة
Pot	قِدْرِ
Burner	المَوقِد
Roast	الشِّوَاءِ
Tired	مَلَلْتُ
Frozen and Canned food	الأَكْلِ المَحْفُوظِ وَالمُعَلَّبِ
Lost the appetite	يَسُدُّ الشَّهِيَة
Invite us	تَعْزِمَنَا
From time to time	وَقتٍ لاخَرِ
Home cooking	أَكْلِ بَيْتِي
delicious	شَهِي
Made by her hands.	عَمَلِ يَدِهَا

Near/about	أَوْشَكْتُ
Tables of the merciful one	مَوَائِدِ الرَّحْمَنِ
And get bogged down	أَتَوَرَّطُ
Pile	كَوْمَةٍ
Rubbing	دَعْكِ
cleaning	جَلِي
Tea pot	بَرَّادِ الشَّاي
Like guests	كَالضُّيُوفِ
Watch what you saying, behave	احْفَظِي أَدَبَكِ
Dishwasher	غَسَّالَةَ أَطْبَاقٍ
To blow	النَّفْخَ
Stew	الحَسَاء
Ladle	مَغْرَفَةٍ
Work hard,	أَشْقَى
stalled	البَائِتَ
Table	المَائِدَةِ
Try	جَرِّبْ
Boiled	المَسْلُوقُ
Stuffed	المَحْشِّي
Stew	المَطِهِي

Uncooked	غَيْرَ المَطْهِي
Spicy	المُتَبَّلَ
Fried	المُفَلْفَلَ
The waiter	النَّادِلَ
Patrons, regular customers	زَبَائِنَ دَائِمِينَ
The bill	فَاتُورَةُ الحِسَابِ
The amount of	بِمَبْلَغٍ وَقَدْرِهِ
Is it so?	أَلَيْسَ كَذَلِكَ

أَسْئِلَة:

1. What is the name of the husband and what is his wife's name?

2. What culinary skills does the wife possess?

3. Does the woman know about proper table manners?

4. What is lacking in her food?

5. What scents does the husband want to smell?

6. What type of food does he always have for breakfast, lunch, and dinner?

7. Did the couple's bickering take place before or after their meal?

8. In the context of the dialogue, when will people say "In the name of God"?

9. Mona, the wife, described something as unappetizing. What was it?

10. What is the biggest grievance the husband has in regards to his wife's cooking?

11. What type of solace does his mother give him?

12. What does "the tables of the merciful one" mean and did the husband eat there?

13. What did Mona dislike about being invited by her mother-in-law for a meal?

14. Why does her mother-in-law own a dishwasher?

15. Ahmed described his wife as one of the women who does not know how to cook nor blow nor take care of house chores. What does it mean to say that she does not know how to blow?

16. What did Mona offer him for food at this point in the conversation and was Ahmed graceful in accepting what she had offered?

17. What type of food does he not like?

18. What type of food did he miss?

19. When the weather is hot, which kind of drink does he like to have?

20. Does he miss eating dessert?

21. Mona asked Ahmed to make a reservation in a restaurant. How many seats did she reserve?

22. What types of culinary skills did Ahmed request that his wife learn?

23. What did Ahmed hate the most about going to the restaurant?

24. Ahmed's pocket is in pain. Who caused this and why?

25. What is the word that expresses feeling pain?

تَأَخَّرتُ قَليلاً

خَرَجْتُ في الصَّباحِ السَّاعةَ السَّابِعةَ إلى عَمَلي، رَكِبْتُ سَيَّارتي الفِضِّيَّةَ اللَّونِ، وبَدَأْتُ أَسيرُ في شَوارعِ المدينةِ، الطَّريقُ كانَ مُزْدَحِمًا جِدًّا ومَليءٌ بالنَّاسِ والسَّيَّاراتِ، حاوَلْتُ الوُصولَ إلى مَكْتَبي مُبَكِّرًا لَكِنْ لِلأَسفِ وَصَلْتُ مُتَأَخِّرًا خَمْسَ دَقائقَ، لَمْ أَعْتَدْ أَبَدًا التَّأَخُّرَ عَنْ عَمَلي أَوْ أَيِّ مَوْعِدٍ لي.

فِي دَارِ أَزْيَاءِ مَارِي لُوي

هَلْ تُفَضِّلُ المَلابِسَ الكَاجوَال، أمْ الكلاَسِيكِيَة؟

This is an interview with a fashion designer named Mary Loui. In this interview, you will learn a number of words related to clothing.

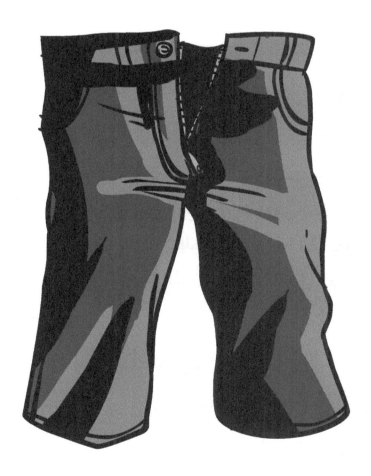

الجواهر

المذيعة: سَيِّدَاتي وَسادَتي، المَظهَرُ مهمٌّ جداً، نَحْنُ عَلَى لِقاءٍ مَعَ مُصَمِّمَةِ الأزْيَاءِ الشهيرَةِ، وَالفَنَانَةِ المُبدِعَةِ، السَّيِّدَةُ مَاري لُوي، أهلاً بِكِ مَعَنا في بَرنَامَج (نَظرَةٌ عَلَى المُوضَةُ).

ماري: أهلاً وَسهلاً، وَأشكُرُكِ.

المذيعة: مَا الجَدِيدُ يَامَاري، في هَذِهِ السَنَةِ؟

ماري : اقتَرَبَ مَوعِدُ العَرْضِ، وَمَجْمُوعَةُ الصَّيفِ جاهِزَة، خَطُّ أزْيَاءِ مَاري لُوي للأزْيَاءِ الرَّاقِيَةِ له سُمْعَتُهُ في مصرَ، وَمَحَلاتُنا مَشهُورَةٌ، مَلابِسُنَا لَيسَت رَخِيصَةً، انّها غَالِيَةٌ وَثَمِينَةٌ، أنَا لا أبِيعُ قِطَعِي وَتصَامِيمِي عَلَى الرَّصِيفِ، أنَا أقُومُ بِتَفصِيلِ القِطَعِ في مَصنَعِي لِلمَلابِسِ الجَاهِزَة، فَأنَا أهتَمُ بِكُلِّ شَيئٍ مِنَ اليَاقَةِ الى أسْوَرَةِ القَمِيصِ، الأزرَار وَالعَرَاوي، السَّحَابُ (السُوْستة)، الكُمُّ، وَالبَابِيُونُ هَذِهِ التَّفَاصِيلُ الصَّغِيرَةُ تجَعلُ التَشطِيبَ عَلَى أعْلَى مُستَوَى.

المذيعة: مَارَأيْكِ في ذَوقٍ وَمقَاس المَرأةِ المِصرِيَةِ؟

ماري: المَرأةُ المِصرِيةُ مِثْلُ أيِّ امرَأةٍ، تَعْشَقُ المرأةَ والأنَاقَةَ، دُولابُهَا مَلِئٌ بالمَلابِس وَالشَّمَاعَاتِ وَالمَلابِسِ القُطنِيةِ المُريحَةِ في الصَّيفِ، والصُّوفِيَة في الشَّتَاءِ، كَالبَالطُو وَالمِعطَفِ، والقُفَازِ (الجوَانتي).

لكِنَّ المقَاسَاتِ تَختَلِفُ عَنْ المَرأةِ الصِّينِيَةِ والمَرأةِ الأُورُوبِيَةِ، المَرأةُ المُمتَلِئَةُ تُنَاسِبُهَا المَلابِسُ الفَضفَاضَةُ الوَاسِعَةُ وَالعَبَاءاتُ وَالجِلبَابُ المَغرِبيُ، وَالمَرأةُ النّحِيفَةُ يُنَاسِبُهَا

352

البَنْطَلُونُ الضَّيِّقُ وَالجَاكِيتُ وَالصَّدِيري أو الصَّدِيري القَصِيرُ وَالشورتُ القَصِيرُ وَالأَحْزِمَةُ التَّي تُبْرِزُ الخَصْرَ، هَلْ تَعْلَمِينَ أَنَّ حَمَّالاتِ الصَّدرِ تُؤَثِّرُ في تَغَيُّرِ المَقَاسَاتِ؟ ، لِذَلِكَ لَدَيْنا خَطُّ انتاج مَلابِسٍ دَاخِلِيَةٍ، وَفانِلاتٍ دَاخِلِيَةٍ.

المذيعة: مَا الذي يُكمِلُ أَنَاقَةَ المَلابِسِ في رَأيكِ؟

ماري: الاكسِسْوَارَاتُ طَبعاً في المُنَاسَبَاتِ كَالسَّاعَةِ وَالخَاتَمِ وَالعِقدِ وَالحَلَقِ وَالحَقِيبَةِ (الشَّنطَةِ) وَالحِذاءِ (الجَزمَةِ) وَالصَّنَدَلِ وَالشَّبْشِبِ المُرِيحِ.

المذيعة: وَمَاذَا تُقَدِمِينَ لِلرِّجَالِ هَذا العَامَ؟

ماري: بِالطَبعِ، نَهتَمُّ بِالرِّجَالِ، انَّهُم نِصفُ المُجتَمَعِ، الرَّجُلُ يَهتَمُّ بِكُلِّ التَفَاصِيلِ الصَّغِيرَةِ كِرِبَاطِ العُنُقِ(الكَرَافَتة)،

وَرِبَاطِ الحِذاءِ، لَونُ الحِذاءِ (الجَزمَةِ)، المِندِيلُ الذي يَضَعُهُ في جَيبِ البَدَلَةِ.

المذيعة: من زَبَائِنُكُم مِنَ الرِّجَالِ؟

زَبَائِنُنَا مِنَ العَالَمِ العَرَبِي والغَرَبِي، وَالخَلِيجِ أَيْضاً، الذين يَلبَسُونَ الغترَةَ وَالعِقَالِ، لَكِنَهُم يُحِبُّونَ مُوضَةَ العَصرِ.

الكلمات الجديدة

معناها	الكلمة
Fashion house	دَارِ أَزْيَاءِ
Casual (notice this is phonetically written in Arabic, and has the same meaning)	الكَاجوَال
Classical (regarding clothes; this is also written phonetically. The word differs from the English according to the Arabic grammar rules. In this case, the definite article is added, and the word is changed into a relational adjective by suffixing a 'nisba')	الكلاَسِيكِيَّة
Ladies and gentlemen	سَيِّدَاتِي وَسَادَتِي
Appearance	المَظْهَرُ
Female fashion designer	مُصَمِّمَةِ الأزْيَاءِ
Famous	الشهيرَةِ
Creative female artist	الفَنَانَةِ المُبدِعَةِ
Look	نَظْرَة
Fashion	المُوضَةُ
Summer collection	مَجْمُوعَةُ الصَّيفِ

Ready-to-wear clothes	جاهِزَة
His reputation	سُمْعَتُهُ
My pieces	قِطَعِي
On the sidewalk (in Arabic, when someone says 'I don't sell it on the sidewalk' they mean what they are selling is expensive. This is similar to English where street vendors sell products cheaply)	عَلَى الرَّصِيفِ
Collar	اليَاقَةِ
Cuff (of a shirt sleeve)	أَسوَرَةِ القَمِيصِ
And buttonholes	وَالعَرَاوِي
Zipper	السَحَابُ
Sleeve	الكُمُّ
Bow-tie	البَابِيُونُ
Small details	التَّفَاصِيلُ الصَغِيرَةُ
Finishing touches	التَشطِيبَ
Taste	ذَوقِ
Size	مقَاس
Hangers	الشَّمَاعَاتِ
Comfortable	المُريحَةِ
Light coat	البَالطُو
Coat	المِعطَفِ

Glove	القُفَّازِ
Full figure	المُمتَلِئَة
Baggy	الفَضفَاضَة
Gowns	العَبَاءاتُ
Moroccan robes	الجِلبَابُ المَغرِبيُّ
Vest	الصِّدِيري
Waist	الخَصرَ
Bras	حَمَّالاتِ الصَّدرِ
Affect	تُؤَثِّرُ
Production line	خَطُّ انتَاج
Underwear	مَلابِسٍ دَاخِلِيَةٍ
Undershirt	وَفانِلاتٍ دَاخِلِيَةٍ
For an hour	لسَّاعَةِ
Ring	الخَاتَمِ
Contract	العِقدِ
Throat	الحَلَقِ
Satchel	الحَقِيبَةِ
Shoes	الحِذاءِ
Sandal	الصَّنَدَلِ
Slippers	الشِّبشِبِ

Half of the society	نِصفُ المُجتَمَعِ
Necktie	رِبَاطِ العُنُقِ
Shoelace	رِبَاطِ الحِذَاءِ
Handkerchief	المِنديِلُ
Pocket	جَيبِ
Headdress (worn by men in the Gulf area)	الغترَةَ
Band (used to keep the headdress in place)	العِقَالِ
Contemporary fashion	مُوضَةَ العَصِرِ

أسئلة:

1. What is the name of the program on which this interview took place?

2. Which seasonal clothing line does this interview discuss?

3. Is this clothing line high end, or is it directed at the average consumer?

4. Where were these clothes manufactured?

5. How did the fashion designer describe Egyptian women's taste in clothing and how did she describe their size?

6. What type of clothes should you expect to see in an Egyptian woman's closet in the summer and in the winter?

7. According to the fashion designer, what suits a full-figured woman well and what suits a slim body type?

8. Which body type is the Moroccan robe suitable for?

9. Does the bra effect the size of the clothing?

10. Does Mary Loui have an underwear line?

11. What types of accessories does Mary Loui recommend be worn with clothes?

12. What will Mary Loui offer for men this season?

13. Are all of Mary Loui's male customers Arab?

357

الخَاطِبَةُ الذَّكِيَّةُ لِمُوَاجَهَةِ العُنُوسَةِ وَالتَّوفِيقِ فِي الحَلالِ فِي المُجْتَمَعِ السُّعُودِي.

This lesson is about a university professor who became a matchmaker as a way to combat spinsterhood.

الرِّيَاض ــ أَمَلاً فِي كَسْبِ الأَجْرِ، وَلِلتَّوفِيقِ بَيْنَ رَأْسَيْنِ فِي الحَلالِ، عَمَدَتْ أُسْتَاذَةٌ جَامِعِيَّةٌ فِي إِحْدَى الجَامِعَاتِ بِالرِّيَاضِ إِلَى التَّحَوُّلِ إِلَى مِهْنَةٍ (خَاطِبَةٍ) لِلحَدِّ مِنْ نِسْبَةِ العُنُوسَةِ وَتَزْوِيجِ الطَّالِبَاتِ لِلرَاغِبِينَ فِي الزَّوَاجِ مِنَ الشَّبَابِ الجَادِّينَ فَقَطْ.

وَأَكَّدَتِ الأُسْتَاذَةُ الجَامِعِيَّةُ أَنَّهَا تَسْتَهْدِفُ حَفَلاتِ التَّخَرُّجِ لِمُعَايَنَةِ الطَّالِبَاتِ وَجْهًا لِوَجْهٍ، وَمِنْ ثَمَّ تَسْعَى إِلَى تَحْقِيقِ مُتَطَلَّبَاتِ الشَّبَابِ فِي القَوَائِمِ الَّتِي تَصِلُهَا مِنْ أَجْلِ اخْتِيَارِ الأَنْسَبِ لِلطَرَفَيْنِ.

وَذَكَرَتِ الأُسْتَاذَةُ الجَامِعِيَّةُ (الخَاطِبَةُ) الَّتِي رَفَضَتِ الإِفْصَاحَ عَنْ هَوِيَتِهَا لِـ"الجَزِيرَةِ أونْلاين" أَنَّهَا لا تَتَقَاضَى أَجْرًا مَادِيًّا إِزَاءَ التَّوفِيقِ بَيْنَ خَرِيجَاتِ الجَامِعَةِ وَالرَّاغِبِينَ فِي الزَّوَاجِ، مُرْجِعَةً ذَلِكَ لأَنَّ الفَتَاةَ فِي المُجْتَمَعِ لا يَسْتَطِيعُ الشَّابُ رُؤْيَتَهَا، لافِتَةً إِلَى أَنَّ

358

المُوَاصَفَاتِ الَّتِي يَطْلُبُهَا الزَّوجُ بِشَرِيكَةِ حَيَاتِه دَقِيقَةٌ لا تَحْتَاجُ إِلَى إِغْفَالِهَا، حَيْثُ يُسَبِّبُ عَدَمُ دِقَّتِهَا رَفْضَ الرَّجُلِ لِلفَتَاةِ بَعْدَ الرُّؤْيَةِ الشَّرْعِيَّةِ، مِمَّا يُسْهِمُ فِي دُخُولِ الفَتَاةِ حَالَةً مِنَ الكَآبَةِ.

وَحَمَّلَتْ بِدَوْرِهَا فَوضَى الخَاطِبَاتِ فِي المَمْلَكَةِ إِلَى جَهْلِ الخَاطِبَاتِ بِمُوَاصَفَاتِ الفَتَاةِ، وَذَلِكَ لِأَنَّهَا لَمْ تَرَهَا، مُشَدِّدَةً عَلَى أَنَّ الكَسْبَ المَادِّيَ لَدَى بَعْضِ الخَاطِبَاتِ يُفْقِدُ ثِقَةَ الرَّجُلِ وَالفَتَاةِ بِهِنَّ.

الكلماتُ الجديدة

معناها	الكلمة
Matchmaker	الخَاطِبَةُ
Smart	الذَّكِيَّةُ
Confrontation	مُوَاجَهَةِ
Spinsterhood	العُنُوسَةِ
Go between two people in (permitted in Islam) manner, it means to act as match maker that could lead to (lawful in Islam) marriage	التَّوفِيقِ فِي الحَلالِ
Hoping to earn a reward (from God)	أَمَلاً فِي كَسْبِ الأَجْرِ

And to reconcile between two heads within the lawful. (Reconciling between two heads refers to mediating between two people getting married. Within the lawful means according to Islamic law – 'halal'.)	وَلِلتَّوفِيقِ بَيْنَ رَأَسَينِ فِي الحَلَالِ
For people with serious intentions only.	الجَادِينَ فَقَطْ
Targeting / aiming	تَسْتَهدِفُ
The graduation	التَّخَرُّجِ
Viewing	مُعَايَنَةِ
Face-to-face	وَجْهًا لِوَجْهٍ
Requirements	مُتَطَلَبَاتِ
Realization	تَحْقِيقِ
Lists	القَوائِمِ
Suited to both parties	الأَنْسَبَ لِلطَرَفَينِ
She refused to disclose her identity	رَفَضَتْ الإفْصَاحَ عَنْ هَوِيَتِهَا
She charged	تَتَقَاضَى
Cash fee	أَجْرًا مَادِيًا
Towards / about	إزَاءَ
Because	مُرْجِعَةً
Exact / specific	دَقِيقَةٌ
Description / specification	المُوَاصَفَاتِ
Overlooked	إغْفَالِهَا

Legitimate viewing (this refers to the opportunity for the groom to see his future bride, since it is not legal in Islam to sit with a woman who is not his wife – in the case of someone who is serious about marrying a woman, he may sit with her at her house so they can get to know each other).	الرُّؤْيَةِ الشَّرْعِيَةِ
Depression	الكَآبَةِ

أَسْئِلَة:

1. What are the two goals that prompted the professor to become a matchmaker?

2. In which setting would she like to meet the female students who are looking to get married ?

3. How do the males and females communicate the qualities they are looking for in a mate to the matchmaker?

4. Was the professor anonymous or not?

5. Which news channel covered this story?

6. Does the matchmaker charge a fee for her service?

7. Why is it difficult for a young man to meet a young woman face to face?

8. What does "legal viewing" mean?

9. Why it is that matchmakers' efforts are so often futile?

10. Why have young women and men lost confidence in traditional matchmakers?

11. In which society did this story take place?

12. In which city did the university professor work?

الْحَق حَرَامِي!!!

وقعتْ فِي شَرِّ أعمَالَك يَاابن الكَلب..

He got his comeuppance; he got his just deserts; he got what was coming to him.
("He fell (he was caught) doing the most evil of all his bad deeds.")

This lesson shows a heated exchange between two men who have been involved in a car accident. You will see how the incident was in fact staged in order to cheat one of the drivers. This lesson will therefore expose you to the vocabulary of an argument about a road incident.

الحوار

أحمَد: انزل لي يَاحُمار، انتَ أعمَى؟ انت غَبِي؟ انتَ خَبَطت الاكصَدام والعَرَبِيَة مِن وَرَى.

سَائِق المِيكرُوبَاص: أستَغفِرُ اللهَ العَظِيم، أنَا اصطَبَحت بِوش مِين عَالصُّبح؟

النَهَار دَه يُوم مَاطِلعتلُوش شمس.... مَاتِحترم نَفسَك عَالصُّبح بَدَل مَا أهزَقَك...وزَرَابِينِي تطلَع عَلِيك..

أحمَد: وَاللهِ مَاأنا سَايبَك غِير فِي القِسم...

النَّاس: صَلُوا عَلى النَّبِي يَاجَمَاعَة...واقصِرُوا الشَّر

اسْتَهدُوا بِالله، انتَ اللي غَلطان يَاسَوَّاق المِيكرُوبَاص

ولازِم تدفع لَه ثَمَن تَصلِيح الاكصَدام.

سَائِق المِيكرُوبَاص: وَأنا ماقُلتِش حَاجَة يَاعَم، بَس مِن غِير شِتِيمَة، احنَا اسفِين.

أحمد: طيب يَعنِي يرضِيك كِدَه؟ العَرَبِيَة لِسَه عَلِيهَا أقسَاط.

سَائِق المِيكرُوبَاص: مَاقُلت لَك هَنرُوح مِيكَانِيكِي وَأصلَحهَالك، خَلاص فُضَّهَا سِيرَة.

أحمد: ايه ده يَاحَرَامِي يَابن الكَلب، يَانَاس حَرااامِي!!

الحرامي: ايه يابيه أنَا مَخدتش مِنك حَاجة ...

363

أحمد: فَاكِرِنِي سَهل يَاض بِتثَبتني بِمطوَاة في جَمبي، ادي المطوَاة رَميتَهَالك، بِتنشِلني في الزَّحمَة، ده انتَ هَتاخُد مني عَلقِة مُوت يَاعِين أُمَّك.

الحرَامِي: اعمِل مَعرُوف يَاباشا، أنَاغَلبَان وبجري عَلَى أُمِّي العَيَانَة، واخواتِي اليَتَامَى، مَعلِش حَقَك عَلَيَا.

أحمد: انتَ هَتقُوللِّي ابصَر ايه ومَاادرِك ايه، وَهتحكِيلي قَصة حَيَاتَك!!!

سَائِق المِيكرُوبَاص: خلاص يَاعَم اديلُه جُوزين اقلام، وسِيبَك مِنُه، ابن الحَرَامِيَه دَه، عَشَان نِنجِز فِي مَوضوعنَا.

أحمد: شَكلُكُم طَابخِينهَا سَوا، والله مَا هَسِيبكُم غِير في القِسم، يَا ولاد النَّشَالَة ..

النَّاس: صَحِيح، ولاد الحَرَام مَا خَلُّوش لِولاد الحَلال حَاجَة.

الكلمات الجديدة

معناها	الكلمة
Catch. Someone in distress who needs helps usually says this word. It has the connotations of catching up with someone in trouble - 'catch up with me to help me!'	الْحَق
Thief	حَرَامِي

You fell down	وقعتْ
Your worst deed (i.e. the worst thing you have ever done)	شَرِّ أعمَالَك
Come down and talk to me	انزل لي
Blind	أعمَى
Stupid	غَبي
Hit / collided	خَبَطت
Bumper	الاكصدَام
From behind	مِن وَرَى
Minivan	المِيكرُوبَاص
I beg Allah for forgiveness	أستَغفِرُ اللهَ العَظِيم
The first thing I see in the morning	أنَا اصطَبَحت
Face	وِش
This expression blames the first face you saw in the morning for a bad thing that happens. In Arab culture, seeing somebody's face could constitute a good or a bad omen. If something bad happens during the day, you would avoid that person in the future. This has nothing to do with the person you see (his reputation or relationship to you) but it is a superstition common in the culture: Arabs associate people with good or bad luck.	أنَا اصطَبَحت بِوش مِين عَالصُّبح
today	النهَار دَه
This expression describes a very bad day – the literal translation is, "this is day on which the sun has not shined". Similar phrases in English are, "it's one of those days", "what a bloody day!" or sometimes, "it's been a dark day today". The Arabic phrase is usually meant severely, for particularly bad days.	مَاطِلِعتلُّوش شَمس

Why don't you respect (yourself)	مَاتِحترِم
Yourself	نَفسَك
Instead	بَدَل
Humiliate	أهزَقَك
Anger	وزَرَابِيني
Reflected or exits	تطلَع
Leave you.	سَايَبَك
Police station	القِسم
Calm down for the sake of Allah	اسْتَهدُوا بِالله
Wrong	غَلطان
Must	لازِم
Pay him	تدفع لَه
Price	ثَّمن
Fixing	تَصلِيح
I did not say anything, oh uncle ('uncle' is used to address certain people even if they are not in your family)	وَأنا ماقُلتِش حَاجَة يَاعَم
But without cursing	بَس مِن غِير شِتِيمَة
We are sorry	احنَا اسفِين
Okay	طيب
Does that satisfy you?	يَعنِي يرضِيك كِدَه؟
I have not completed paying for the car	العَرَبِية لِسَه عَليهَا أقسَاط.
I already told you that we will see a mechanic, and he will fix it for you	مَا قُلت لَك هَنرُوح مِيكَانِيكِي وَأصلَحهَا لك

Enough talk about the biography (this is said to someone who is talking excessively about something already settled)	خَلاص فُضَّهَا سِيرَة
I did not want your life story. This phrase is the same in English: when somebody is talking a lot and you do not have the time or the desire to listen.	وَهتحكيلي قَصِة حَياتَك
Biography	سِيرَة
Disengage it (said to someone to stop them talking)	فُضَّهَا
Oh people – a thief!	يَانَاس حَراامي
Oh Bayh (this is a Turkish title)	يابِيه
I have not taken anything from you	أنَا مَخدتش مِنك حَاجة
Do you think I am ...?	فَاكِرِني
Do you think I am vulnerable?	فَاكِرِني سَهل
Oh boy! (a disrespectful way to talk to someone beneath you – in age or class)	يَاض
Is this a hold-up?	بِتثَبتِني
Pen-knife	المطوَاة
I threw it away for you	رَميتَهَالك
You pickpocketed me	بِتنشِلِني
The crowd	الزَّحمَة
You will take	هَتاخُد
A beating	عَلقة
A deadly beating	عَلقة مُوت
Oh your mother's eye (a disparaging phrase meaning someone's mother loves him as much as her own eye)	يَاعِين أُمَّك
Do me a favor	اعمِل مَعرُوف

Bashar	بَاشَا
Poor man	غَلبَان
Look after / support	وبجري
I am supporting my sick mother	وبجري عَلَى أُمِّي العَيَانَة
And my orphaned siblings	واخواتي اليَتَامَى
Never mind	مَعَلِش
I'll make it up to you	حَقَك عَلَيَا
Are you going to tell me …?	هَتقُولِّي
Rubbish / nonsense story	ابصَر ايه ومَاادرك ايه
Are you going to tell me a story?	وَهتحكيلي
Your life story	قَصة حَيَاتَك
OK / it's over	خلاص
Next to me	جَمبِي
Give him	يَاعَم
Oh uncle	اديلُه
Slap his face	أقلام
Leave him alone / he's not worth it	سِيبَك مِنُه
This is the son of a female thief	ابن الحَرَامِيَه دَه
Because	عَشَان
Accomplish something	نِنجز
Our problem / subject	مَوضوعنَا
You look like you all look	شَكلُكُم

You cook it	طَابِخِينهَا
I'm not going to leave you	مَا هَسِيبكُم
Anywhere but the police station	غِير فِي القِسم
Oh, you sons of a female pickpocket	يَا ولاد النَّشَالَة
It is true	صَحِيح
The bastards have ruined it for the legitimate children (idiom meaning people who commit many crimes and offences make all good people suffer - it is usually said as a form of apology to good people who are smeared with the wrongdoings of criminals, despite their innocence)	ولاد الحَرَام مَا خَلُّوش لِولاد الحَلال حَاجَة

أسئلة:

1. How many people are involved in the car accident?
2. What types of car are involved in the accident?
3. Does the accident attract the attention of people on the street?
4. Is the exchange between the people involved in the accident polite?
5. Can you tell who is to blame for the accident?
6. Which part of the car needs repairing because of the accident?
7. What kind of compensation does one driver demand from the other?
8. Is the driver who is blamed willing to take responsibility for the accident?
9. Whose car has not been fully paid for?
10. Which driver becomes the victim of a pickpocket during the argument?
11. With what weapon does the thief threaten this man?
12. Why does the victim think the thief is working with the other driver?
13. Do you think this accident was staged and why?
14. Where does the victim say he will take the other driver and the thief?

التَّحَرُّشَات الجِنْسِيَّة

This lesson is about an incident of sexual harassment on a public bus. This lesson uses colloquial Egyptian Arabic. You will exposed to vocabulary and expressions relating to a quarrel or a fight among people. How does the fight start? How does it escalate? How does it dissolve? How do people react? What is the tone of the language used in this lesson?

فِين شَهَامِة وِلاد البَلَد؟ بِيتحَرَش بِيَا فِي الأوتوبيس يَاناس!!!

سمية: انت يا أستاذ وسَّع شُوَية، مِش مَعقول كِدَه، الدُّنيَا زَحمَة ومُش طَالبَة قِلِة الأدَب دِي.

الرجل: حَد جَه جَمبِك يَاسِت؟

سمية: وكَمان بتتبَجَّح !! يَابن الكَلب.

الرجل: يَافَتَّاح يَاعَلِيم، يَا رزَّاق يَاكَرِيم.

سمية: شُوف ازاااي!!! عَمَّالة أقولْ لَك وَسَع، عِيب كِدَه، مَايصحش مِن الصُّبح، البِعِيد.... مَفِيش فَايدة.

الرجل: دَه انتِ وِليَة بِنت سِتِين كَلْب، صَحِيح، انتِ فَاكرَة نَفْسِك سِت؟ دَه انتِ سِتْ أُشهُر.

سمية: يَالَهوي!!! الله يِخرِب بِيتَك، انتَ مَال أهلَك بيَا؟

شاب اخر: مَاتِلِم نَفسَك يَالا، انتَ مَعَنْدَكش اِخوَات بَنَات؟

الرجل: خَلِيك في حَالَك يَابَا، مَاشِي، بَدَل مَااطلعهُم عَلِيك، يَاعَم الأمُور، فتَح عِينَك كِدَه وشُوف بِتكَلِم مِين...

الشاب: بَكَلِّم وَاحِد ابْن جَزْمَة، عَاوز يِتربَّي، وَيَاخُد بالجَزْمَة القَدِيمَة.

الرجل: طيب وَرِيني هَتعمِل ايه يَارُوح أُمَك.

الشاب: تَعَالَ وَأنَا أوَرِيك رَاجِل لِرَاجِل يَا خَوَل.

أحَد رُكَّاب الأُوتوبِيس:

مَا تصَلُّوا عَالنَبِي يَاجَمَاعَة، واقصِرُوا الشَّرْ، يَاللا يَاابني انتَ وهُوَ، اتِكلُوا عَلَى الله، وانتِ يَاسِت تَعَالِ اقعُدِي مَكَاني وأَنَا هَقُف مَكَانك.

سمية: انْ شَاء الله يِسعِدَك يَا خُويَا، ويِهِد اللي مَايتسَمَّى، حَسْبِيَ الله وَنعمَ الوَكِيل، قَادِر يجِيب لِي حَقِي، رَبِّنَا يِهِد المُفتَري، رَبِّنَا ينتِقِم مِنُّه.

الكَلِمَاتُ الجَدِيدَة

معناها	الكَلِمَة
Fights	الخِنَاقَات
Harassments	المُضَايقَات
Magnanimity	شَهَامِة
Sons of the Country (an expression used to describe a group of people who are most likely of the working class, who are generous and trustworthy-in Britain these people would be called working class heroes.)	وِلاد البَلَد
He is harassing	بِيتحَرَش

Me (when you are using the word "harassing", you have to attach the letter baa to either the pronoun or to the name of the person that is the subject of harassment)		بِيَا
Oh people (this is a call for help or attention)		يَانَاس
Make room (in the imperative)		وسَّع
That is impossible, Incomprehensible (used to ridicule someone's actions or to express a disapproval of someone's behavior)		مِش مَعقول كِدَه
The world/the earth/life in this world/the present life (used to describe the current situation, i.e. "it is cold" would be translated as "the world is cold")		الدُنيَا
Crowded		زَحمَة
Impolite (literally, this means a lack of manners)		قِلةِ الأَدَب
(female) student		طَالبة
Boasting/ Bragging/ Bravado		بتَبَجَّح
Son of a dog (the most used curse in the Arab world because the dog is for the most part a despised animal)		يَابن الكَلب
Oh God (this literally invokes an attribute of God, fattaH which connotes the one who provides a way out of a problem and also means conqueror. This utterance is usually said by Muslims and non- Muslims when starting the day. More often than not, people will say it when they encounter an unexpected problem in the morning as they		يَافتَّاح

are starting their day and call upon God to provide them with a way out)	
Oh Omniscient One (usually "oh fattaH" and "oh omniscient" are said together so that one would say "ya fattaH ya 3aliim")	يَاعَلِيم
Razzaq (this literally means "provider" and is one the attributes of God)	يَارَزَّاق
Oh Generous One (These four attributes will most likely be invoked together upon encountering an unexpected problem early in the workday. This is not to say that a Muslim will only say these four attributes upon encountering a problem. Sometimes, they like to invoke these attributes to ask for help. So, these four utterance when put together call upon God to help them get out of problems which are encountered, and because he is all knowing and generous, he will be able to provide in abundance.)	يَاكَرِيم
See how (notice the elongation of the alif, so it reads "shuf izaaaaay", used to ridicule an implausible explanation, as when you know someone is wrong about something and might say sarcastically in English "oh really?")	شُوف ازَااي
Keep/ Keeping	عَمَّالة
I keep telling you	عَمَّالة أقولْ لَك
This is not right/ This should not be done/ This act is impolite (literally means "this is shameful"	عِيب كِدَه

This is not right	مَايصحش
He who is far away (usually this is said when you do not wish to mention the name of somebody who is giving you grief or acting in a manner that is abhorrent to you. By not mentioning him by name and replacing it with "he who is far away", it is as if you are wishing that he would stay as far away as possible from you due to his actions or behavior, troubles and problems. The mere mentioning of the name would bring back bad memories, so this term is invoked to replace the name)	البِعِيد
There is no use/ no point (literally means "there is no benefit")	مَفِيش فَايدة
A woman, usually of low class, literally means a friend (in classical Arabic)	وِلِيَة
She is a daughter of sixty dogs. This is one of the most common curses in the Arabic language. It will usually be said as 'son of a dog' or 'daughter of a dog'; when 'sixty dogs' is used, the insult becomes more severe (like if you were say 'get the hell out' rather than just 'get out').	بِنت سِتين كَلْب
Do you consider yourself a woman? This means that a woman is not acting in a well-mannered manner.	انْتِ فَاكَرَة نَفْسِك سِت؟ ،
You are like six months. The Arabic word for a woman and the Arabic word for number six are the same. When somebody replaces the word 'lady' with 'six months', he compares enduring six months in prison with spending time with the woman.	دَه انْتِ سِتْ أُشهُر

Oh my God! This is mostly a woman's invocation and should not be used by men.	يَالَهوي
May Allah harm your house! This is a frequent insult and can also be used humorously.	الله يِخَرِب بِيتَك
Leave me alone. Literally, this means 'what has your family got to do with me?' The word 'family' is in this phrase to emphasize that nobody (not even the family) should bother the speaker.	انتَ مَال أهلَك بِيَا
Mind your own business. This phrase literally means 'collect yourself'. This likens a person who interferes with another's business to something that has spilled, spread itself and needs to be reined in from where it should not be.	مَاتِلِم نَفسَك
Let us go / Come here / Go away! This word is said when somebody wants to urge another into action. The word in truncated: it was originally 'yo Allah'. The reason Allah is used is to ask His help to enact proceedings.	يَالا
Don't you have any sisters? This phrase is said to somebody who is disrespecting women. It reminds the person that he should behave towards women in the manner he would towards his own sisters. In Arabic you literally say, 'Do you have girl / female siblings?' The word 'akhwat' means 'siblings', so you must clarify the gender of the siblings by saying 'benat'.	مَعَنْدَكش إخوَات بَنَات
Mind your own business. This literally means 'remain in your situation', i.e. do not venture into other people's affairs.	خَلِيك في حَالَك

Oh father! One of the words for 'father' is 'baba'. When you say 'ba', then combine it with the evocative particle 'ya', the meaning comes across as low-class and very casual.	يَابَا
OK. Literally 'walking' or 'going'.	مَاشِي
Otherwise, I will release them and you. This is a literal translation that evokes an irritated feeling of the speaker, who will release on the interlocutor his evil spirits (every Muslim believes people suppress bad spirits). The speaker is saying that he is so angry he is out of control.	بَدَل مَااطلعهُم عَليك
Oh cute uncle! This phrase, when it is said to somebody who is acting aggressively, belittles the recipient by comparing him to a 'cute' child. It has an undertone of a warning not to fight with adults.	يَاعَم الأُمُور
Open your eyes and see whom you are talking to. It is equivalent to the English phrase, 'do you know who I am?'	فَتَح عِينَك كِدَه وشُوف بِتكِّلم مِين
I am talking to a son of a shoe. The shoe is the dirtiest item a man can handle. When you describe somebody as a son of a shoe, it means he is worthless. This is an answer to the above phrase: the English conversation would be, 'Do you know who I am?' 'You're nobody.'	بَكِّلم وَاحِد ابْن جَزْمَة
He needs more upbringing. This refers to a coarse person who needs more adult instruction – he needs to modify his behavior.	عَاوز يِتربَّى
And will be beaten with an old shoe.	وَيَاخُد بِالجزْمَة القَدِيمَة.

OK.	طيب
Show me. In English, we would say 'let's wait and see' or simply 'we will see'.	وَرِيني
What are you going to do? Literally 'what you will do?'	هَتعمِل ايه
Oh you are a mommy's boy! In Arabic, this means that the person is as dear to his mother as to be her soul.	يَارُوح أُمَك
Man to man. This is very close to the English phrase.	رَاجِل لِرَاجِل
Homosexual. Derogatory word for homosexual. 'Khoual' refers to a group of men who dressed as woman and danced at parties. They did this because the Sultan of Egypt banned female dancers.	خَوَل
Why don't you praise the Prophet, oh group [of people]! You will hear this when you see an aggressive situation escalating – people say this to prevent violence by reminding people of the Prophet. Violence will probably cease.	مَا تصَلُّوا عَالنَبِي يَاجَمَاعَة
And cut short the evil. In other words, 'do not let evil take hold of you'. This is said when somebody is embarking on a violent or aggressive path.	واقصِرُوا الشَّرُ
Let us keep going my son, you and him. Used for telling people to disburse in order to avoid a violent clash, both combatants and spectators.	يَاللا يَاابني انتَ وهُوَ
Rely on Allah. This could be said in many different situations. In this context, the speaker is telling people to go separate ways and rely on Allah to provide sustenance and	اِتِكلُوا عَلَى الله

guidance.	
And you, lady, come and sit in my place, and I will stand in your place.	وانتِ يَاسِت تَعَالِ اقعُدِي مَكَانِي وأَنَا هَقُف مَكَانِك.
Allah's will shall make you rejoice, my brother.	انْ شَاء الله يِسعِدَك يَا خُويَا
May Allah demolish he who has no name. When people wish harm on somebody who is powerful, they use the verb 'demolish', 'hadd'. When they abhor the person, they say he has no name.	ويِهِد اللي مَايتسَمَّى
Allah is enough for me, and he is the best guardian. This phrase means that Allah is sufficient in my life so I do not need anybody else. He is the best all those who can act on my behalf: he will defend me and avenge me.	حَسْبِيَ الله وَنِعمَ الوَكِيل
He is capable of bringing me what rightfully I should have.	قَادِر يجِيب لِي حَقِي
May Allah demolish the slanderer.	رَبِنَا يِهِد المُفتَري
And may Allah take revenge on him.	رَبِّنَا ينتِقِم مِنُه

أَسئِلة:

1. The language used in this lesson is modern standard Arabic (MSA) and Egyptian colloquial Arabic.

2. What is the name of woman who has been harassed?

3. Whom does she ask for help?

4. What is the reaction of the accused man?

5. Who is the first person to cast an insult? What is this insult?

6. What time of day does this incident occur?

7. Does the victim ask the accused man not to get so close to her?

8. What does the man say about her appearance?

9. Do other people get involved in the incident?

10. How many people get involved in the fight? What are their approximate ages?

11. How is the situation resolved? By whom?

قَالَتِ الشُّرْطَةُ فِي مَدِينَةِ نيوتاون بِوِلَايَةِ كونِّكْتِيكَتْ بِشَمَالَ شَرْقِ الْوِلَايَاتِ الْمُتَّحِدَةِ إِنَّ 26 شَخْصًا بَيْنَهُمْ 20 طِفْلًا قُتِلُوا الْجُمُعَةَ بِرَصَاصٍ أَطْلَقَهُ مُسَلَّحٌ دَاخِلَ مَدْرَسَةٍ ابْتِدائِيةٍ بِالْمَدِينَة.

Police in the Northeastern U.S. city of Newtown, in the state of Connecticut, say that 26 people, including 20 children, were killed on Friday by bullets fired by a gunman inside an elementary school in the city.

وَأَعْلَنَتِ الشُّرْطَةُ أَنَّهَا تَمَكَّنَتْ مِنْ قَتْلِ مُطْلِقِ النَّارِ، الَّذِي ذَكَرَتْ قَنَوَاتٌ تَلْفَزَةٍ أميرْكِيَةٍ أَنَّهُ فِي الرَّابِعَةِ وَالْعِشْرِينَ مِنَ الْعُمُرِ، وَأَنَّهُ قَتَلَ وَالِدَهُ دَاخِلَ مَنْزِلِهِ قَبْلَ أَنْ يَتَوَجَّهَ إِلَى الْمَدْرَسَةِ وَيُطْلِقَ النَّارَ عَلَى التَّلَامِيذِ وَالْمُعَلِّمِينَ وَمِنْ ضِمْنِهِمْ وَالِدَتُهُ الَّتِي تَعْمَلُ مُدَرِّسَةً هُنَاكَ.

The police announced that they were able to kill the gunman, who American TV channels have reported was 24 years old. He also killed his father inside his home before heading to the school and shooting students and teachers, including his mother, who was working as a teacher there.

وَقَدْ عَبَّرَ الرَّئِيسُ الأميرِكي بَارَاك أُوباما عَنْ حُزْنِهِ الْبَالِغِ لِهَذَا الْحَادِثِ، دَاعِيًا فِي خِطَابٍ مُوَجَّهٍ إِلَى الأميركيين إِلَى تَنْحِيَةِ السِّياسَةِ جَانِبًا وَاتِّخَاذِ إِجْرَاءٍ فَعَّالٍ لِمَنْعِ تَكْرَارِ هَذِهِ المَأْساةِ فِي الْمُسْتَقْبَل.

The U.S. President Barack Obama expressed his deep sadness in relation to the incident, calling in a speech to the American people to put aside politics and take effective measures to prevent the recurrence of such tragedy in the future.

فِي البَيتِ

وَأَنْتَ، مَا ذَوقُكَ؟ كِلاسِيكِيٌّ (قَدِيمٌ)، أَمْ مُودِرنُ (حَدِيثٌ) أَمْ نِيوكِلاسِيكِيٌّ (مَزِيجٌ بَيْنَ هَذَا وَذَاكَ)؟

This conversation is between two friends. One of them has just bought a new house and is telling his friend. The vocabulary will include words about buying a house, household appliances, utilities and décor.

طارق: خَالِدُ، بَارِكْ لِيَّ الانَ.

خالد: مَبْرُوكٌ، لَكِنْ، لِمَاذَا يَاطَارِق؟ هَيَّا أَخْبِرْني.

طارق: هَذِهِ الفِيلاَ الَّتي أَنْتَ عَلَى وَشَكِ أَنْ تَدْخُلَهَا لَيْسَتْ لِعَميلٍ جَديدٍ كَمَا أَخْبَرْتُكَ، انَّهَا مُلْكِي، اشْتَرَيْتُهَا مُنْذُ يَوْمَيْنِ فَقَطْ بِعَقْدِ تَمْلِيكٍ خَالِصٍ، لَقَدْ مَلَلْتُ ايجَارَ الشَّقَّةِ المُبَالَغ فِيهِ، فانَا أَدْفَعُ الكَثِيرَ بِالاضَافَةِ الَى فَاتُورَةِ النُّورِ وَالكَهْرَبَاءِ وَالغَازِ وَالمَاءِ، وَمَشَاكِلِ العِمَارَةِ، وَالمِصْعَد(الأَسَانِسِير) الَّذِي يَعْطُلُ عَنِ العَمَلِ، التَّمْلِيكُ أَفْضَلُ شَيْءٍ.

خالد: صَحِيحٌ؟ أَلْفُ مَبْرُوكٍ يَاطَارِق، أَلَدَيكَ فِيلاَ بِالتَّجَمُّعِ الخَامِسِ؟ اللَّهُمَ اجْعَلْهَا فَأَلَ خَيرٍ وَبَرَكَةٍ عَلَى طَارِقٍ، كَانَتْ هَذِهِ مُفَاجَأَةً إِذَنْ.

طارق: جِيرَاني هُنَا مِنَ المُجْتَمَعِ الرَّاقِي، وَجَارِي القَرِيبِ رَجُلٌ مُحْتَرَمٌ، انظُرْ انَّ الفِيلاَ مِنْ طَابِقَيْنِ، دَورٌ عُلْوِيٌّ وَدَورٌ أَرْضِيٌّ وَالسَّطْحُ، انَّ السَّطْحَ مُبَلَّطٌ وَمُحَاطٌ بِسُورٍ عَالٍ، وَعَلَى اليَمِينِ جَرَاجٌ (مِرَابٌ) وَاسِعٌ لِسَيَّارَتَيْنِ أَوْثَلاَثٍ.

خالد: مَاشَاءَ اللهُ لاقوَّة اَلاَّ بِالله .

طارق: هَيَّا نَفتَحُ بَوَّابَةَ الحَدِيقَةِ، لَدَيَّ حَدِيقَةٌ أَمَامِيَّةٌ وَاسِعَةٌ، وَحَدِيقَةٌ خَلْفِيَةٌ لَكِنَّهَا أَقَلُّ مِسَاحَةً .

أَيَنَ المِفتَاحُ؟ رُبَّمَا في جَيبِي!!

لَقَدْ أَغْلَقتُ البَوَّابَةَ بِقِفلٍ كَبِيرٍعِنْدَمَا اشْتَرَيْتُهَا، حَتَّى أُرَكِّبَ كَالُوناً جَدِيداً.

خالد: يُمْكِنُكَ عَمَلَ نَافُورَةِ مَاءٍ هُنَا أَوْحَمَّامَ سِبَاحَةٍ (بِيسِين) مُتَوَسِّطِ الحَجْمِ أَوْ شَلَّالٍ صِنَاعِي فِي الحَدِيْقَةِ يَاطَارِقَ.

طارق: رَائِعٌ!!، أَنْتَ أَفْضَلُ مُهَنْدِس دِيكُورٍ وَتَصْمِيمٍ دَاخِلِي في مَجَالِكَ يَاخَالِدَ.

خالد: شُكْراً لَكَ، انظُرْ، اقْتَرِحُ أَنْ يَكُونَ بَابُ الفِيلا مُزْدَوَجاً، وَاحِدٌ مِنَ الحَدِيد المَشْغُولِ(الفِيرفُورْجِيه) لِلأَمَانِ، وَاخَرُ مِنَ الزُّجَاجِ المُعَشَّقِ المُلَوَّنِ لِلجَمَالِ، وَيُمْكِنُكَ جَعْلُ النَّوَافِذَ وَالشَّبَابِيكَ وَالشُّرَفَاتِ (البَلَكُونَات) كَذَلِكَ أَيْضاً.

طارق: الانَ، أَمَامَكَ الطَّابِقُ السُّفْلِي وَيَضُمُّ الاسْتِقبَالَ وَالضِّيَافَةَ (الصَّالُون) وحَمَامَينِ وَمَطْبَخاً كَبِيراً وَغُرْفَةَ السُّفرَةِ (الطَّعَام)، أُرِيدُكَ أَنْ تُحَدِّدَ لِي أَمَاكِنَ مَفَاتِيحَ الكَهْرَبَاءِ وَأَزْرَارَ النُّورِ، وَأَمَاكِنَ مَرَاوِحِ السَّقفِ أَوْأَجْهِزَةِ التَكيِيفِ(المُكِيفَات)، وَلاَ تَنْسَ مَكَانَ الثلاَّجَةِ وَالغَسَّالَةِ،

وَأَمَاكِنَ الحَنَفِيَاتِ(الصَّنَابِيرِ) وَالبَانِيُو (حَوْضِ الاسْتِحْمَامِ) وَكَابِينَةِ الصَّرْفِ للِحَمَّامِ وَمَا اِلَى ذَلِكَ.

خالد: سَنَقُومُ بِعَمَلِ اضَاءَةٍ غَيرَ مُبَاشِرَةٍ (سبُوت لايت) وَأَبَالِيكَ هُنَا، سَتُظْهِرُ وَتُبْرِزُ جَمَالَ مَا سَتَقُومُ بِشِرَاءِهِ مِنْ أَبَاجُورَاتٍ وَتُحَفٍ وَأَنتِيكَاتٍ.

طارق: رَائِعٌ، هَذَا مَا أُسَمِيه عَمَلَ المُحْتَرَفِينَ، يَاصَدِيقِي، هَنَاكَ سُلَّمٌ يُؤَدِّي الَى الدَّورِ العُلوِّي، المُكَوَّنِ مِنْ حَمَامَينِ وَخَمْسَةِ غُرَفِ نَوْمٍ، مِنْهُم غُرْفَةٌ أُرِيدُهَا مَكتَباً لِي أُؤَدِّي فِيهِ أَعْمَالِي وَأَحْتَفِظُ فِيهِ بِأَوْرَاقِي، وَغُرْفَةُ جُلُوسٍ (لِيفِينج).

خالد: سَيَكُونُ دَرَابْزِينُ السُّلَمِ (سُورُ السُّلَمِ) مِنَ الاسْتَنلِ ستِيلِ النَّاعِمِ اللَّامِعِ (مَعْدَنٍ مُقاوِمٍ للِصَدَأِ)، وَاقتَرِحُ لِغُرَفِ النَّومِ انْ تَبْعُدَ عَنِ التَّكَلُّفِ وَالمُبَالَغَةِ، مَثَلاً، دَهَانَاتٌ (طِلاَءٌ) هَادِئَةُ الأَلْوَانِ، وَسَتَائِرٌ بَسِيطَةٌ جِداً، لأَحَبِّذُ سَتَائِرَ البَرَاقِعِ (الدَّرَابِيه)، وَهُنَا دَوَالِيبُ (خَزَائِنُ مَلَابِسٍ) مُدَمَجَةٌ (بِيلْت اِنْ)، وَالسَّرِيرُ وَالمَرَاتِبُ وَالمُخَدَّاتُ (الوِسَادَة) وَثِيرَةٌ، وَ هُنَا أَدْرَاجٌ طَائِرَةٌ (مُثَبتةعَلَى الحَائِطِ دُونَ قَوَائِمَ)، وَبِكُلِّ غُرْفَةِ نَومٍ مِقعَدَانِ وَثِيرَانِ مُرِيحَانِ، امَّا غُرْفَةُ الجُلُوسِ فَسَتَكُونُ مَكتَبَةُ التِلِيفِزيُون بَسِيطَةً، وَسَنَضَعُ كُرْسِياً هُنَا وَكَنَبَةً (أَرِيكَةً) هُنَاكَ، وَسَنَضَعُ الكَثِيرَمِنَ الخُدَدِيَاتِ المُلَوَّنَةِ تَتَنَاسَبُ مَعَ لَونِ السَّجَادَةِ، ممم، وَسَنَتَبِعُ الطِّرَازَ الذي تُفَضِّلُهُ.

الكلماتُ الجديدة

الكلمة	معناها
ذَوقُكَ	Your taste

Old	قَدِيمٌ
Modern	حَدِيثٌ
Mixed	مَزِيجٌ
Between this and that	بَيْنَ هَذَا وَذَاكَ
Congratulate	بَارِكْ
Congratulate me	بَارِكْ لِيَ
About to	عَلَى وَشَكِ
Client	عَمِيلٍ
Contract of full ownership	بِعَقْدِ تَمْلِيكٍ خَالِصٍ
I am tired	مَلَلْتُ
The rent for the apartment is overpriced	ايْجَارَ الشَّقَّةِ
	المُبَالَغَ فِيهِ
The lighting bill	فَاتُورَةِ النُّورِ
Lighting and electricity bill	فَاتُورَةِ النُّورِ وَالكَهْرُبَاءِ
The building problems	مَشَاكِلِ العِمَارَةِ
The elevator	المِصْعَدِ
Fifth compound (name of a residential area)	بِالتَّجَمُّعِ الخَامِسِ
May Allah make it an omen of blessing and goodness for Tarek	اللَّهُمَّ اجْعَلْهَا فَأَلَ خَيرٍ وَبَرَكَةٍ عَلَى طَارِقٍ
Surprise	مُفَاجَأَةً
High society	المُجْتَمَعِ الرَّاقِي

Two levels	طَابِقَيْنِ
The villa	الفِيلاَ
Upper level	دَورٌ عُلوِّيٌّ
The ground floor	وَدَورٌ أَرْضِيٌّ
And the roof	وَالسَّطْحُ
Paved	مُبَلَّطٌ
And surrounded	وَمُحَاطٌ
With a high fence	بِسُورٍ عَالٍ
Garage	مِرْآبٌ
What Allah wills will pass, There is no power except by or from Allah	مَاشَاءَ اللهُ لاقُوَّةَ اِلاَّ بِالله
Front garden	حَدِيقَةٌ أَمَامِيَّةٌ
Back garden	حَدِيقَةٌ خَلفِيَة
Less space	أَقَلُّ مِسَاحَة
Gate	البَوَّابَة
With a lock	بِقِفلٍ
A door lock	كَالُوناً
Fountain	نَافُورَة
Swimming pool	حَمَّام سِبَاحَةٍ
Average size	مُتَوَسِطِ الحَجْم
Artificial waterfall	شَلاَّلٍ صِنَاعِي

Interior designer	مُهَنْدِس دِيْكُورٍ
Interior design	تَصْمِيمٍ دَاخِلِي
Your domain	مَجَالَك
The double door of the villa	بَابُ الفِيلاَ مُزْدَوَجاً
Wrought iron	الحَدِيدِ المَشْغُولِ
For safety	لِلأَمَانِ
Stain glass	الزُّجَاجِ المُعَشَّقِ المُلَوَّنِ
Reception	الاسْتِقْبَالَ
Hospitality	الضِّيَافَةَ
Dining room	غُرْفَةَ السُّفَرَةِ
Electrical switches	مَفَاتِيحِ الكَهْرُبَاءِ
Light switches	وَأَزْرَارَ النُّورِ
Ceiling fans	مَرَاوِحِ السَّقْفِ
Air conditioner	أَجْهِزَةِ التَكِيِيفِ
Refrigerator	الثلاَّجَةِ
Washing machine	الغَسَّالَةِ
Faucets	الصَّنَابِير
Bath tub	حَوْض الاسْتِحْمَام
Toilet cistern	كَابِينَةِ الصَّرْفِ لِلحَمَّام
Indirect lighting	اضَاءَةٍ غَيرَ مُبَاشِرَةٍ

Wall lamp	أَبَالِيكَ
Bedside lamp	أَبَاجُورَاتٍ
Antiques	تُحَفٍ
Antiques	أَنتِيكَاتٍ
Professionals	المُحْتَرِفِينَ
Ladder	سُلَّمٌ
Lead	يُؤَدِّي
Living room	غُرْفَةُ جُلُوسٍ
Handrail	سُورُ السُّلَّمِ
Metal	مَعْدَنٍ
Anticorrosive	مُقَاوِمٍ لِلصَدَأ
In good taste	تَبْعُدَ عَنِ التَّكَلُّفِ
Excessive	المُبَالَغَةِ
Paint	طِلاَءٌ
Quiet colors	هَادِئَةُ الأَلْوَانِ
Simple curtains	وَسَتَائِرٌ بَسِيطَة
I don't recommend	لاَ أَحَبِّذُ
Heavy curtains	سَتَائِرَ البَرَاقِعِ
Closets	خَزَائِنُ مَلاَبِسٍ
Built-in	مُدْمَجَة

Mattresses	المَرَاتبُ
Pillows	الوِسَادَة
Soft	وَثِيرَة
Flying drawers	أدْرَاجٌ طَائِرَة
Supported on	مُثَبَتة عَلَى
Legs	قَوَائِمَ
Very comfortable	وَثِير
Sofa	أريكة
Small pillows	الخُدَدِيَات
Carpet	السَّجَادَة
Trim	الطِّرَاز

أسئلة:

1. What is the name of the person who bought the house?
2. What type of house is it?
3. Why is the friend surprised when he hears that the house he visits belongs to his friend?
4. Who does the friend think is the owner of the house?
5. When did the man buy the house?
6. What type of contract has he signed?
7. What was the reason behind him buying the house?
8. What type of house did he live in before?
9. What type of bills did he pay in his old house?
10. Does his old house have problems? What are they?
11. What type of neighbors does the man have around his new house ?
12. What does his next-door neighbor do for a living?
13. How many floors does his new house have?
14. What distinguishes his roof from others?

15. Does the new house have a garage?

16. If so, how many cars can fit in the garage?

17. How many gardens does the new house have?

18. Which garden is bigger?

19. Does the house have a fountain or a swimming pool?

20. What does the new homeowner's friend do for a living?

21. The new owner plans to build an artificial waterfall. Where does he plan to build it?

22. The friend suggests the homeowner builds a new two-door front door. With what materials does he suggest he build it?

23. What type of security feature does the friend suggest he installs ?

24. What types of room are on the lower floor?

25. Is the house ready for occupancy?

26. How will the friend help the owner with the electricity and plumbing?

27. What types of room are on the upper floor?

28. How many bathrooms does the house have?

29. How many bedrooms does the house have?

30. On which floor will his private office be?

31. On which floor will the living room be?

32. Which material will the handrails be made out of?

33. How exactly will he decorate the living room?

34. What type of closets will be in the bedroom?

35. What type of chest of drawers will he have?

36. How many chairs will each bedroom have?

37. What will the color of the pillows match?

هَيْمَنَتِ التَّحَوُّلَاتُ السِّيَاسِيَّةُ وَالْأَحْدَاثُ الرَّاهِنَةُ الَّتِي تَعْصِفُ بِالْمَنْطِقَةِ الْعَرَبِيَّةِ عَلَى اجْتِمَاعِ الْمَكْتَبِ الدَّائِمِ لِلِاتِّحَادِ الْعَامِّ لِلْأُدَبَاءِ وَالْكُتَّابِ الْعَرَبِ الَّذِي اخْتَتَمَ أَعْمَالَهُ الْأَرْبِعَاءَ بِالْعَاصِمَةِ الْعُمَانِيَّةِ مَسْقَط، وَذَلِكَ عَلَى الرَّغْمِ مِنْ سَيْطَرَةِ الصِّبْغَةِ الثَّقَافِيَّةِ الْكَامِلَةِ عَلَى الْفَعَالِيَّاتِ الْمُصَاحِبَةِ لِلِاجْتِمَاعِ طَوَالَ فَتْرَةِ انْعِقَادِهِ مِنْ 24 إِلَى 27 نُوفَمْبِر/تَشْرِينَ الثَّانِي الْجَارِي.

389

وَقَدِ انْعَكَسَ هَاجِسُ التَّحَوُّلَاتِ السِّيَاسِيَّةِ بِالْمَنْطِقَةِ بِوُضُوحٍ عَلَى الْبَيَانَاتِ الثَّلَاثَةِ الَّتِي أَصْدَرَهَا الِاجْتِمَاعُ الَّذِي كَانَ مُغْلَقًا، وَهِيَ الْبَيَانُ الْخِتَامِيُّ، وَالثَّقَافِيُّ، وَبَيَانُ الْحُرِّيَّاتِ فِي الْوَطَنِ الْعَرَبِيِّ، الَّتِي كَشَفَ مَضْمُونُهَا عَنْ تَخَوُّفِ الْمُبْدِعِينَ وَالْكُتَّابِ الْعَرَبِ مِنَ التَّأْثِيرِ السَّلْبِيِّ لِتِلْكَ التَّحَوُّلَاتِ عَلَى مَسِيرَةِ الْإِبْدَاعِ الْأَدَبِيِّ وَالْفِكْرِيِّ بِالْمَنْطِقَةِ.

Political transformations and current events that beset the Arab region dominated discussions at a meeting of the Permanent Bureau of the General Union of Arab Writers. The meeting concluded on Wednesday in Muscat, Oman. This political angle took place in spite of the dominance of the cultural character of the events associated with the meeting, which was held throughout the convention's session from 24 to 27th November.

The obsession with political transitions in the region was reflected clearly in the three statements issued by the convention, which was conducted behind closed doors. These are the final statement, the cultural statement and the freedom statement of the Arab world. The contents of the freedom statement revealed the fear those with talent and Arab writers have of the negative impact of these political changes on the march of literary and intellectual creativity in the region.

فِي الفُنْدُقِ

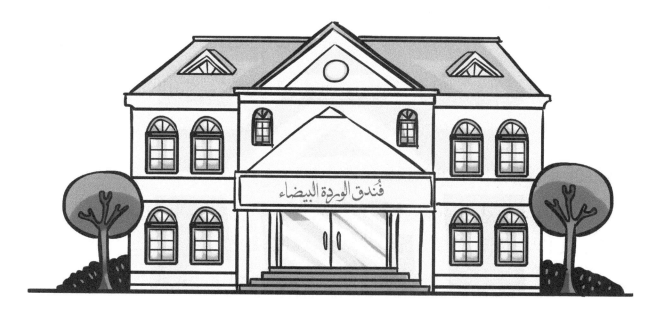

In this lesson, we will introduce you to vocabulary that is useful in a hotel setting. In what follows, there is a conversation between a guest and a front-desk agent while he is checking in. The agent is describing the amenities that the hotel has to offer.

موظف الاستقبال: اهْلاً وَسَهْلاً بِسِيَادَتِكَ فِي فُنْدُقِ الوَرْدَةِ البَيْضَاءِ.

النزيل: أَهْلاً بِكَ، اِسْمِي مُحَمَدُ مُنِير، عِنْدِي حَجْزُ غُرْفَةٍ لِشَخْصَينِ.

موظف الاستقبال: نَعَمْ، نَحْنُ نَتَوَقَّعُ وُصُولَكَ يَا أُسْتَاذ مُحَمَّد، كُلُّ المَعْلُومَاتِ اللَّازِمَةِ لَدَيْنَا، وَالِدُكَ اللهُ يَرْحَمُهُ كَانَ مِنْ أَفْضَل ضُيُوفِنَا، لِذَا أَوْجَدْنَا لَكَ غُرْفَةً رَائِعَةً رَغْمَ صُعُوبَةِ الحَجْزِ هَذِهِ الأَيَّام فَالفُنْدُقُ كَامِلُ العَدَدِ حَتَّى آخِرِ الشَّهْرِ القَادِم لِاسْتِضَافَتِنَا مُؤْتَمَرًا خَاصًّا بِرِجَالِ الأَعْمَال ، وَهَذَا مِفْتَاحُ الغُرْفَةِ رَقَم مِئَةٍ وَعِشْرِينَ فِي الطَّابِقِ العَاشِرِ، سَيَصْحَبُكَ صَابِرُ حَمَّالُ الحَقَائِبِ إِلَى غُرْفَتِكَ.

النزيل: نَعَمْ وَالِدِي الله يَرْحَمُهُ كَانَ يُحِبُّ النُّزُولَ فِي فُنْدُقِ الوَرْدَةِ البَيْضَاءِ، كُنْتُ أُرِيدُ أَنْ أَعْرِفَ إِذَا كَانَ سِعْرُ الغُرْفَةِ يَتَضَمَّنُ أَيَّ وَجَبَاتٍ.

موظف الاستقبال: نَعَمْ، يَتَضَمَّنُ وَجْبَةَ الافْطَارِ فِي مَطْعَم لَيَالِي الشَّرْقِ وَهُوَ فِي الطَّابِقِ الثَّالِثِ، المَطْعَمُ يُوَفِّرُ ثَلَاثَ وَجَبَاتٍ، الافْطَارُ مِنَ السَّاعَةِ السَّادِسَةِ إِلَى الحَادِيَةِ عَشَرِ، وَالغَدَاءُ مِنَ الثَّانِيَةِ عَشَرِ إِلَى الثَّالِثَةِ، وَالعَشَاءُ مِنَ السَّادِسَةِ حَتَّى مُنْتَصَفِ اللَّيْلِ، وَأَيْضًا هُنَاكَ بَار إِذَا أَرَدْتَ أَيَّ مَشْرُوبَاتٍ كُحُولِيَةٍ.

النزيل: أَنَا لَا أَشْرَبُ الكُحُولِيَاتِ، هَلْ عِنْدَكُم خِدْمَةُ الغُرَفِ؟

موظف الاستقبال: نَعَمْ، وَهِيَ مُتَاحَةٌ عَلَى مَدَارِ السَّاعَةِ.

النزيل: مُمْتَازٌ، أُرِيدُ قَائِمَةَ الطَّعَام لِخِدمةِ الغُرَفِ.

موظف الاستقبال: سَتَجِدُهَا فِي غُرْفَتِكَ بِجِوَارِ الهَاتِفِ.

النزيل: سُؤَالٌ آخَرٌ، كَيْفَ أَتَصِلُ هَاتِفِيًّا مِنْ غُرْفَتِي؟

موظف الاستقبال: لِخِدْمَةِ الغُرَفِ اضْغَطْ رَقَم وَاحِد وَانْتَظِر رَدًّا، وَلِلِاسْتِعْلامَاتِ اضْغَطْ رَقَم اِثْنَان، وَلا جْرَاءِ اِتِّصَالاتٍ مَحَلِّيَّةٍ، اِضْغَطْ رَقَم تِسْعَةٍ وَانْتَظِر حَتَّى تَسْمَعَ الحَرَارَةَ وَبَعْدَ ذَلِكَ اِضْغَطْ الرَّقَمَ الَّذِي تُرِيدُ، وَلِلْمُكَالَمَاتِ الدَّوْلِيَةِ، اِضْغَطْ رَقَم ثَلَاثَة وَعِنْدَمَا تَسْمَعُ الحَرَارَةَ، أَكْمِل اتِّصَالَكَ بِالرَّقْمِ الدَّوْلِي الَّذِي تَرْغَبُ.

النزيل: مُمتازٌ، وَمَاذَا عَنْ النَّادِي الصِّحِي؟

موظف الاستقبال: عَلَى مُسْتَوَى عَالٍ مِنَ التَّجْهِيزِ وَالكَفَاءَةِ،
وَبِهِ كُلُّ مَا تَحْلُمُ بِهِ، التَّدْلِيكُ والاسْتِرْخَاءُ وحَمَّامُ البُخَارِ، وَسَيُعْجِبُ السَّيِّدَةَ حَرَمَ
سِيَادَتِكَ كَثِيرًا، الحَمَّامُ المَغْرِبِي وَأَقْنِعَةُ الوَجْهِ وَالجِسْمِ.

النزيل: رَائِعٌ، سَتَجِدُ زَوْجَتِي مَاتَقُومُ بِهِ أَثْنَاء انْشِغَالِي فِي حُضُور جَلَسَاتِ مُؤْتَمَرِ رِجَالِ
الأَعْمَالِ العَرَبِ فِي قَاعَةِ المُؤْتَمَرَاتِ هُنَا.

موظف الاستقبال: أُحِبُّ أَنْ أُخبِرَكَ أَنَّهُ يُوجَدُ لَدَيْنَا بِالفُنْدُقِ مَكْتَبٌ لِخِدْمَةِ رِجَالِ
الأَعْمَالِ، بِهِ جَمِيعُ الخَدَمَاتِ كَالفَاكِس والكُومبيُوتَر والانْتَرْنِت وَالطِّبَاعَةِ وَغَيْرِهَا، وَإِنْ
أَرَدْتَ يُمْكِنُكَ أَنْ تَسْتَخْدِمَ الكُمبيُوتَر المَحْمُولَ الخَاصَ بِكَ وَاسْتِخْدَامِ خِدْمَةِ الانْتَرْنِت
اللاسِلْكِيَةِ.

النزيل: بِالتَّأْكِيدِ سَأْحْتَاجُ كُلَّ ذَلِكَ.

موظف الاستقبال: إِقَامَةٌ سَعِيدَةٌ يَاسَيِّدِي.

النزيل: شُكْرًا لَكَ، وَسَأَكُونُ أَسْعَدَ لَوكَانَتِ الغُرْفَةُ بَعِيدَةً عَنْ الضَّوضَاءِ والازعَاج.

موظف الاستقبالُ: لا تَقْلَق يَاسَيِّد مُحَمَد، فَالغُرْفَةُ بَعِيدَةٌ عَنْ حَمَّامِ السِّبَاحَةِ
وَالضوضَاءِ، ومُطِلَّةٌ عَلَى مَنْظَرِ البَحْرِ الجَمِيلِ.

النزيل: رَائِعٌ!

موظف الاستقبال: هَلْ تَرْغَبُ يَا أُسْتَاذُ مُحَمَد فِي تَأْكِيدِ طَلَبٍ لِسَيَّارَةِ تَاكْسِي تُوصِلُكَ إِلَى
المَطَارِ عِنْدَ المُغَادَرَةِ؟

النزيل: لَا، شُكْرًا، مَعِي سَيَّارَتِي الخَاصَة فِي جَرَاجِ الفُنْدُقِ وَلَنْ أَذْهَبَ إِلَى المَطَارِ.

موظف الاستقبال: أَنَا في خِدْمَتِكَ دَائِمًا.

النزيل: الحَقِيقَةُ أَنَا بِحَاجَةٍ اِلَى كَيَّ بَعْضِ المَلَابِسِ.

موظف الاستقبال: لَقْد أَصْبَحَتْ غُرْفَةُ سِيَادَتِكَ جَاهِزَةٌ، اِنْتَهَى مَسْؤُلُوا نَظَافَةِ الغُرَفِ مِنْ عَمَلِهِم، وَوَصَلَتْ حَقَائِبُ سِيَادَتِكَ اِلَى هُنَاكَ أَثْنَاءَ حَدِيثِنَا، سَأُرْسِلُ لَكَ عَامِلاً مِنْ المَغْسَلَةِ لِتَطلُبَ مَاتُرِيدُ مِنْهُ مِن غَسِيلٍ وَكَيٍّ.

النزيل: حَقًّا! شُكْرًا لَكَ.

موظف الاستقبال: أُسْتَاذ مُحَمَد، شَيْءٌ وَاحِدٌ أُحِبُّ أَنْ أُخْبِرَكَ بِهِ، التَّدْخِينُ مَمْنُوعٌ في الغُرَفِ.

النزيل: لامُشْكِلَة، أَنَا لا أُدَخِنُ.

موظف الاستقبال: مُمْتَازٌ، أَتَمَنَّى لَكَ اِقَامَةً مُرِيحَةً.

النزيل: أَشْكُرُكَ كَثِيرًا.

الكلمات الجديدة

معناها	الكلمة
Receptionist	موظف الاستقبال
I have a reservation	عِنْدِي حَجْزٌ
We expect	نَتَوَقَّعُ
We have	لَدَيْنَا
God bless his soul	اللهُ يَرْحَمُهُ
No vacancy	الفُنْدُقُ كَامِلُ العَدَد
For hosting us	لِاسْتِضَافَتِنَا
Conference	مُؤْتَمَرًا
Valet, porter.	حَمَّالُ الحَقَائِب
Price	سِعْرٌ
Meals	وَجَبَاتٍ
Alcoholic beverages	مَشْرُوبَاتٍ كُحُولِيَةٍ
Available	مُتَاحَةٌ
Room service	خِدْمَةِ الغُرَف
Press number one and wait for a response	اِضْغَطْ رَقَم وَاحِد وَانْتَظِر رَدًّا

For queries/information	وَلِلاسْتِعْلَامَاتٍ
And to make local calls	وَلَا جْرَاءِ اِتِّصَالَاتٍ مَحَلِّيَّةٍ
Tone (as in wait for the tone)	الحَرَارَة
The health club	النَّادِي الصِّحِي
Wife.	حَرَم
And face masks	وَأَقْنِعَةُ الوَجْه
Laptop	الكُمبِيُوتَر المَحْمُولَ
Noise	الضَوضَاءِ
disturbance	الازعَاج
Confirmation Order	تَأْكِيد طَلَب
I am always at your service	أَنَا فِي خِدْمَتِكَ دَائِمًا
So that	كَيِّ
Housekeeping	مَسْؤُلُوا نَظَافَةِ الغُرَف
Laundry	المَغْسَلَة
Smoking is prohibited in rooms	التَّدْخِينُ مَمْنُوعٌ فِي الغُرَف
A comfortable stay	إِقَامَةٌ مُرِيحَةً

أسئلة:

1. What is the name of the hotel?

2. What is the name of the guest?

3. What type of room did he reserve?

4. Why does the front desk agent consider him a special guest?

5. Why is the hotel full until the end of next month?

6. What is the number of his room and on which floor?

7. What is the name of the porter?

8. Does the room rate include any meals? If so, which one?

9. What is the restaurant's name and where is it located?

10. How many meals does the restaurant serve and during which hours?

11. Does the restaurant have a bar?

12. Does the guest drink alcohol?

13. Does the hotel have room- service? If so, at what time?

14. Where can the guests find a menu?

15. How can a guest make an outside call?

16. What is the number for information?

17. What number should a guest press to make a local call, and what number should a guest press to make an international call?

18. What services does the health club offer?

19. Does the guest's wife accompany him?

20. What is the purpose of the guest's visit?

21. What type of service does the business center offer?

22. Describe the location of the guest's room.

23. Does the guest need a taxi after having checked in?

24. Does he need some clothes to be ironed?

25. Is his room for smokers or non-smokers?

إكْرام المَيت دَفْنُهُ

مَلائِكَةُ الرَّحْمَةِ وَالانْسَانِيةِ

This is a dialogue taking place in a hospital. A woman has brought her grandfather who has been hit by a car. He is bleeding. In this lesson, you will learn vocabulary concerning hospital environments, emergency care and tragic endings.

نُهَى: أَرْجُوكُم بِسُرْعَةٍ، جَدِّي يَمُوتُ، صَدَمَتْهُ سَيَّارَة، انَّهُ يَنْزِفُ.

مُوَظَّفُ الاسْتِقبالُ: هُناكَ رُسُومٌ يَجِبُ عَلَيكِ دَفْعُها قَبْلَ أَيِّ شَئٍ، لَنْ نَسْتَقبِلَهُ حَتَى يَدْفَعَ.

نُهَى: أَليسَ لَديكُم رَحْمَة؟ خُذوهُ حَتَّى أحْضِرَ الفُلوس(المَالَ)

مُوظَّفُ الاسْتِقْبَالُ: اذهَبِي وَأحضِرِي المَالَ، هَذَا مُسْتَشْفَى اسْتِثمَارِي خَاص، وَتِلكَ اللَّوائِحُ، واذَا ذهبْتِ بِهِ الى مُسْتَشْفَى حُكُومِي كَالقَصْرِ العَينِي أومُسْتَشْفَى المُنيرَةِ لَنْ تَجِدِي أمَاكِنَ، وَسَتَسُوءُ حَالَتُهُ.

نُهَى: يَالَكُم مِن طمَّاعِين (جَشِعِينَ)!! خُذ كَارتَ الفِيزَا الخَاص بِيُ.

الطبيب: النَزْفُ شَدِيدٌ، المُصَابُ يَحْتَاجُ الَى نَقلِ دَمٍ فَوراً، فَصِيلَةُ دَمِهِ نَادِرَةٌ، وَبَنْكُ الدَم لَا يُوجَدُ بِهِ مَايَكفِي.

نُهَى: مَاذَا؟ تَصَرَّف يَادُكْتُور، فَصِيلَةُ دَمِي مُخْتَلِفَةٌ.

الطبيب: ابْحَثِي عَنْ مُتَبَرِّعٍ بِالدَم.

تَدَخَلَتْ المُمَرِضَةُ هَامِسَةً: أعْرِفُ مُتَبَرِعينَ بِالدَم، لَكِن بِضِعفِ سِعْرِ بَنْكِ الدَم.

نُهَى يَائِسَةً: مُوافِقَةٌ.

دَخَلَ تَمَرْجِيٌّ مُسْرِعاً: يَا دُكْتُور، يَادُكْتُور، مَريضُ الطَّوارِئ الذِي فِي جِهَازِ التَّنَفُّسِ الصَّنَاعِي قَدْ مَاتَ.

الطبيب: هل أعطَيتَهُ حُقنَةَ البِينجِ المَوضِعِي (مُسَكِنُ الألَم)؟

التَمَرْجِي: نَعَمْ.

الطبيب: كَيفَ؟ انَّهُ رَجُلٌ عَجُوزٌ وَينزِفُ، مَنْ أمَرَكُمْ بِذَلِكَ؟ كَانَ يَجِبُ ادخَالُهُ غُرْفَةَ الانْعَاشِ (العِنَايَةَ المُرَكَّزَةِ).

صَرَخَتْ نُهَى: لَايُمْكِن!! سَأقَاضِيكُم بِتُهمَةِ الاهمَالِ، لَنْ أترُكَكُم.

الطبيب: انَّا لله وانَّا اليهِ رَاجِعُونَ ياانِسَةَ، أنَا مُجَرَّدُ دُكتُورٍ هُنَا، النِّظَامُ أنَّكِ لِتَأخُذي جَدَّكِ، يَجِبُ أنْ تَدفَعي بَاقِي الحِسَابِ والاَّ وُضِعَ في ثَلاجةِ المَشْرَحَةِ حَتَّى تَدفَعي كَامِلَ حِسَابِ المُسْتَشفَى.

سَيِّدَةٌ مُسِّنَةٌ: يَابِنتي اكرَامُ المَيِّتِ دَفنُهُ، أسرِعي وادفِني جَدَّكِ، ثُمَّ تَعَالي، حَاسِبيهِم وَقاضِيهِم، وأنَا شَاهِدَةٌ مَعَكِ.

الكلماتُ الجديدة

معناها	الكلمة
Hospital	المُسْتَشفَى
Angels of mercy and humanity	مَلائِكَةُ الرَّحْمَةِ والانْسَانِيةِ
My grandfather is dyeing	جَدِّي يَمُوتُ
He was hit by a car	صَدَمَتهُ سَيَارَة
He is bleeding	انَّهُ يَنزِفُ
Fees	رُسُومٌ

400

We will not admit him until he pay	لَنْ نَسْتَقْبِلَهُ حَتَى يَدْفَعَ
Don't you have mercy	أَليسَ لَديكُم رَحْمَة
A private investment hospital	مُسْتَشْفى اسْتِثمَاري خَاص
Regulations	اللَّوائِحُ
Government hospital	مُسْتَشفَى حُكُومي
You will not find places	لَنْ تَجِدِي أمَاكِنَ
His condition will worsen	سَتَسُوءُ حَالَتُهُ
How greedy you are	يَالَكُم مِن طمَّاعين
Severe bleeding	النَزْفُ شَديدٌ
Patient needs a blood transfusion immediately	المُصَاب يَحْتاجُ الَى نَقلِ دَمٍ فَوراً
Rare blood group	فَصِيلَة دُمِه نَادِرَة
The blood bank does not have enough	وَبَنْكُ الدَم لاَ يُوجَدُ بِه مَا يَكْفِي
Blood Donor	مُتَبَرِّع بِالدَم
Double	بِضِعف
Emergency patient	مَريضُ الطوَارئِ
Ventilator	جِهَاز التَّنَفُّس الصِّنَاعي
Local anesthetic injection	حُقنَة البينج المَوضِعِي
Painkiller	مُسَكِّنُ الألَم
Intensive Care	العِنايَةَ المُرَكَّزَة
I will charges you of negligence	سَأقَاضيكُم بِتُهَمَة الاهمَال

We are form Allah, and him we shall return	اِنَّا لله وَاِنَّا اِليهِ رَاجِعُونَ
I'm just Dr. working her	أنَا مُجَرَّدُ دُكتُورٍ هُنَا
System	النِّظَامُ
You have to take your grandfather	أنَّكِ لِتَأخُذِي جَدَّكِ
You should pay the balance	يَجِبُ أَنْ تَدفَعِي بَاقِي الحِسَابِ
Morgue Refrigerator	ثَلاجةِ المَشْرَحَةِ
hospital Full balance due	كَامِلَ حِسَابِ المُسْتَشفَى
To honor the dead is to bury him.	اكرَامُ المَيِّتِ دَفنُهُ
I will hold them accountable and sue them	حَاسِبِيهِم وَقاضِيهِم
You can consider me as your witness	وَأنَا شَاهِدَةٌ مَعَكِ

1. What is the condition of the injured man?

2. What is his relationship to the woman who brought him to the hospital?

3. Was he bleeding?

4. The receptionist asked the woman to do something before the hospital admits the patient. What is it?

5. Does the woman have what is asked of her?

6. What is the difference between a government-run hospital and a privately owned hospital?

7. The receptionist mentioned two types of government-run hospital. What are they?

8. If the woman were to take her grandfather to a government-run hospital, what would to his physical condition? Why?

9. Why does the woman describe the people running the privately run hospital as greedy?

10. What type of credit card does she propose to use?

11. Does the grandfather have a rare blood type?

12. Does he need an immediate blood transfusion?

13. Does the hospital have enough blood?

14. Does the woman's blood type match that of her grandfather?

15. If a patient has a rare blood type which is unavailable in the hospital, who can provide him with blood? How much does this usually cost?

16. To which department of the hospital is, the patient sent? Is this right place for him? Where should he have gone?

17. Is he given any painkiller?

18. What does the male nurse inform the doctor about?

19. Why does the woman threaten the hospital with a lawsuit? What is the charge she brings against them?

20. After her grandfather dies, what must the woman do to retrieve his body?

21. Where will his body be kept?

22. Was there a witness to this incident?

اِقْرَأ

يَقْتَادُ مُلَّاكُ الْإِبِلِ مِنْ مَنَاطِقَ مُتَفَرِّقَةٍ فِي الْمَمْلَكَةِ الْعَرَبِيَّةِ السُّعُودِيَّةِ أَجْمَلَ مَا عِنْدَهُمْ مِنْها لِلْمُشَارَكَةِ فِي مُسَابَقَةِ أَجْمَلِ الْإِبِلِ فِي "مِهْرَجَانِ أُمِّ رقيبة لِمَزايِن الْإِبِلِ" الْمُقَامِ حالِيًّا فِي مَنْطِقَةِ أُمِّ رقيبة بِشَرْقِ السُّعُودِيَّةِ.

وَيَبْلُغُ عَدَدُ النُّوقِ الْمُشَارَكَةِ فِي مِهْرَجَانِ هَذَا الْعَامِ 10350 نَاقَةً يَمْلِكُهَا 289 مُشَارِكًا.

يَقُولُ جَزَا الْعُصَيْمِي وَهُوَ وَكِيلُ أَعْمَالِ أَحَدِ الْمُشَارِكِينَ بَعْدَ أَنْ أَبْرَمَ صَفْقَةً بِقِيمَةِ 120 مِلْيُونَ رِيالٍ إِنَّ الْمِهْرَجَانَ مَشْرُوعٌ اقْتِصَادِيٌّ يَعُودُ بِالنَّفْعِ عَلَى الْوَطَنِ وَتَنْشَطُ عَلَى هَامِشِهِ حَرَكَاتُ بَيْعٍ أُخْرَى كَبَيْعِ الْخِيَّامِ وَلَوَازِمِهَا وَالسَّيَّارَات.

Camel owners from different areas in Saudi Arabia escorted the most beautiful of their animals from different parts of the country to participate in the competition of the most beautiful camel. This festival is called 'Mahrajan Um raqiba le mazayen al ibel', and it is in Um Raqibah in eastern Saudi Arabia. The number of camels to participate in this year's festival is 10,350. These camels belong to 289 owners. Jaza Usaimi (an agent for one of the participants) said, after one of the participants concluded that a deal worth 120 million riyals, that the festival is an economic project for the benefit of the whole nation. At the sidelines of this festival, other sales transactions are taking place, such ash as the sale of cars, tents and their supplies.

هَذِهِ عَائِلَتِي

هَذِهِ شَجَرَةُ الْعَائِلَةِ، حَدِّثْنِي عَنْ عَائِلَتِكَ...

This lesson is about a family tree in which you will be introduced to vocabulary pertaining to relationships and occupations, ancestries and backgrounds.

الحِوَارُ

أَهْلاً وَسَهْلاً بِطُلَّابِ اللُّغَةِ العَرَبِيَةِ

أُرِيدُ انْ أُعَرِّفَكُمْ بِعَائِلَتِي.

وَلَكِنْ اوَلاً يَجِبُ انْ آَعَرِّفَكُمْ بِنَفْسِي.....

اسْمِي شَمْسٌ، وَعُمْرِي عِشْرُونَ سَنَةً، وَانَا طَالِبَةٌ فِي كُلِّيَةِ الطِّبِّ.

هَذِهِ اخْتِي الصَّغِيرَةُ قَمَرٌ، وَعُمْرُهَا عَشْرُ سَنَوَاتٍ، وَهِيَ طَالِبَةٌ فِي مَدْرَسَةٍ ابْتِدَائِيَةٍ.

وَهَذَا اخِي التَّوْأَمُ، نَجْمٌ، وَهُوَ ايْضاً طَالِبٌ فِي كُلِّيَةِ الطِّبِّ.

هَذَا ابِي، اسْمُهُ أَصِيل، وَهُوَ صَيدَلِي.

هَذِهِ أُمِّي، اسْمُهَا جَمِيلَةٌ، وَهِيَ لاتَعْمَلُ، انَّهَا رَبَّةُ بَيتٍ.

هَذَا خَالِي، اسْمُهُ خَمِيسٌ، وَهُوَ رَجُلُ اعْمَالٍ.

وَهَذِهِ خَالَتِي، اسْمُهَا زَهْرَةٌ، وَهِيَ ايْضاً صَيْدَلِيَةٌ مِثْلُ ابِي.

هَذَا خَطِيبِي، وَهَذِهِ خَطِيبَةُ اخِي، كِلاهُمَا يَدْرُسَانِ فِي كُلِّيَةِ الحُقُوقِ.

هَذَا ابْنُ خَالِي، اسْمُهُ أَحْمَدُ، وَهُوَضَابِطٌ بِالجَيشِ، وَهَذِهِ نُهَى أُخْتُ أَحْمَدِ، وَابْنَةُ خَالِي.

وَهَذِهِ لَطِيفَةُ ابْنَةُ خَالَتِي وَهِيَ ضَابِطَةُ شُرْطَةٍ، وَذَاكَ عَادِلٌ أَخُوهَا، وَابْنُ خَالَتِي.

هَذَا عَمِّي عُمَرٌ، انَّهُ بَقَّالٌ.

وَهَذَا ابْنُ عَمِّي مُصْطَفَى، وَيَعْمَلُ مُحَاسِباً.

وَهَذِهِ ابْنَةُ عَمِّي نيفِيْنُ، وَهِيَ مُذِيْعَةٌ بِالتِلِفِزْيُونِ.

وَهَذَا ابْنُ ابْنِ عَمِّي، وَاسْمُهُ بَاسِمٌ، وَهَذِهِ ابْنَةُ ابْنِ عَمِّي وَاسْمُهَا بَسْمَةُ.

تَعَالِي يَاعَمَّتِي....، اسْمُهَا نُورَان، وَمَعَهَا ابْنُ عَمَّتِي أَيْمَنُ، وَابْنَةُ عَمَّتِي سُهَيْلَةُ، وَهَذَانِ أَبْنَاؤُهُمَا حَاتِمُ ابْنُ ابْنِ عَمَّتِي، وَايْلِين ابْنَةُ ابْنَةِ عَمَّتِي.

وَأَخِيْراً، هَذَا جَدِّي عَلِيُّ، وَهُوَ طَبِيبٌ مُتَقَاعِدٌ، وَهَذِهِ جَدَّتِي مَلَكُ، وَهِيَ خَيَّاطَةٌ.

نَحْنُ نَنْحَدِرُ مِنْ أُصُولٍ تُرْكِيَةٍ ،فَجُدُودِي أَتْرَاكُ،مِنْ عَائِلَةٍ عَرِيْقَةٍ وَغَنِيَةٍ، كَانَ وَالِدُ جَدِّي تُرْكِياً، وَاسْمُهُ حِكْمَتْ كَارْجِي، وَكَانَ تَاجِراً غَنِياً، يُسَافِرُ عَبْرَ البِحَارِ لتِجَارَةِ الأقمِشَةِ، وَفِي ايْطَالِيَا تَعَرَّفَ الَى فَتَاةٍ أمْرِيكِيَةٍ جَمِيْلَةٍ،أَحَبَّهَا وَأَحَبَّتْهُ، وَتَزَوَّجَا رُغْمَ مُعَارَضَةِ وَالِدَتِه، السَّيِّدَةُ نَازْلِي هَانُمْ، وَوَالِدِهِ كَارْجِي بِيك، كَانَا يُرِيدَانِه أَنْ يَتَزَوَجَ مِنَ ابْنَةِ عَمِّه نَازِك لَكِنَّ الحُبَّ انْتَصَرَ،وَهَاجَرَ جَدِّي الكَبِيْرُ حِكْمَتْ الَى أُمْرِيكَا مَعَ زَوْجَتِه كَارِين وَتَرَكَ اسْطَنْبُولَ اسِفاً، وَبَدَأَ حَيَاتَهُ هُنَاكَ مِنَ الصَّفِر،وَحَصَلَ عَلَى الجِنْسِيَةِ الأُمْرِيكِيَةِ، وَحَصَلَ جَمِيْعُ أَحْفَادِهِ عَلَيْهَا، وَأَنْشَأَ مَصْنَعاً لِصِنَاعَةِ المَفَارِشِ التُّرْكِيَةِ الفَاخِرَةِ وَالمُطَرَزَةِ.

وَتَوَارَثَتْ عَائِلَتِي هَذِهِ الصِّنَاعَةَ، لابُدَّ مِنْ أَحَدٍ يُدِيرُ المَصْنَع وَحَالِياً هَوَعَمُّ والِدِي وَاسْمُهُ سُلَيْمَان بِيك،

وَهَذَا سَبَبُ لَقَبِ عَائِلَتِي المُمَيَزِ، عَائِلَة كَارْجِي، وَأَنَا حَفِيدَةُ عَائِلَةِ كَارْجِي.

فَاسِمِي هُوَ شَمْس أَصِيْل عَلِي كَارْجِي، وَأَحمِلُ الجِنْسِيَةَ الأُمْرِيكِيَةَ.

وَالانَ، عَرِّفْنَا بِأُسْرَتِكَ الكَرِيْمَةِ.....

الكلماتُ الجديدة

معناها	الكلمة
Family tree	شَجَرَةُ العَائِلَة
Tell me	حَدِّثْني
I want to introduce you to	أريدُ انْ أُعَرِّفَكُمْ
Elementary school	مَدْرَسَةٍ ابْتِدَائِيَةٍ
Twins	التَوَّمُ
Pharmacist	صَيْدَلِي
Housewife	رَبَّةُ بَيتٍ
Businessman	رَجُلُ اعْمَالٍ
Law school	كُلِّيَةِ الحُقُوقِ
An officer in the army	ضَابِطٌ بالجَيش
My female maternal cousin	ابْنَةُ خَالِي

A female police officer	ضَابِطَةُ شُرْطَةٍ
Grocer	بَقَّالٌ
Accountant	مُحَاسِباً
TV presenter	مُذِيعَةٌ بِالتِلِفِزْيُونِ
Retired doctor	طَبِيبٌ مُتَقَاعِدٌ
Female tailor	خَيَّاطَة
Descended	نَنْحَدِرُ
Turkish origin	أصولٍ تُرْكِيَةٍ
Deep-rooted family	عَائِلَةٍ عَرِيْقَةٍ
Merchant	تَاجِراً
Overseas	عَبْرَ البِحَارِ
Textiles Trading	لِتِجَارَةِ الأقمِشَةِ
He met an American Girl	تعَرَّفَ الَى فَتَاةٍ أمْرِيكِيَةٍ
He loved her and she loved him	أحَبَّهَا وَأحَبَّتْهُ
Despite the opposition of his mother	رُغْمَ مُعَارَضَةِ وَالِدَتِه
Unfortunately	اسِفاً
And began his career there from scratch	وَبَدَأ حَيَاتَهُ هُنَاكَ مِنَ الصِّفر
Factory	مَصْنَعاً
Turkish made luxury industry placemats and	صِنَاعَةِ المَفَارِشِ التُرْكِيَةِ الفَاخِرَةِ وَالمُطَرَزَةِ

embroidered	
Inherited	تَوَارَثَتْ
He run the factory	يُدِيرُ المَصْنَعِ
Title	لَقَبِ
Distinguished	المُمَيَّزِ

أسئلة:

1. Who is a student in the college of medicine?

2. How old is Qamar and in which grade is she?

3. What is Najm's relationship to Qamar?

4. How many people studied to be doctors?

5. What does Najm's father do for a living?

6. What are the names of Qamar's mother and father?

7. What does Jamila do for a living and what is her relationship to Qamar?

8. How old is Shams and how old is Qamar?

9. How many people in Shams' family work as pharmacists, what are their names, and what are their relationships to her?

10. Is she engaged?

11. Which people in her circle of friends and family studied to be lawyers?

12. What is Noha's relationship to Shams and does she have a brother? If so, what does he do for a living?

13. Which one of her relatives works in law enforcement?

14. How many children does her maternal aunt have?

15. What does her maternal cousin do for a living and what is his name?

16. What does her uncle do for a living?

17. What does her paternal cousin do for a living?

18. There are two people among her relatives with names related to smiling. What are their names and what are their relationships to Shams?

19. Who is Nuran?

20. Is this family a Muslim family?

21. Who came with Nuran to visit them?

22. How many children does her female cousin Suhaila have?

23. Which member of her family is a retired doctor and who works as a tailor?

24. What is her grandmother's name?

25. What are this family's ancestries?

26. What did her great grandfather do for a living? Was he a rich man?

27. A beautiful American girl was introduced to the family. What is her name and what are the circumstances of her being introduced to the family?

28. The mother of her grandfather did not approve of her great grandfather doing something. What was it and why did she object?

29. What was the reason behind her great grandfather's immigration to America?

30. Did his wealth help him in his new life there?

31. Where did the great grandfather live in Turkey prior to his immigration?

32. How did the great grandfather of Shams make a living in America?

33. Who is currently running her great grandfather's business in America? What is his name and what his relationship to Shams' father?

34. What is Shams' nationality?

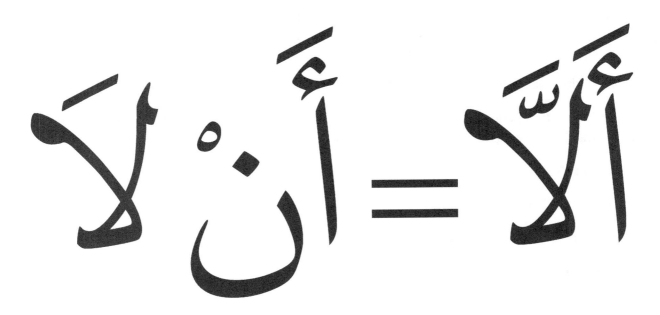

The above word 'alla' means, 'no', 'not', 'in order not to' or 'that ... not to.' It is a truncation of two particles: 'an' which means 'that' and 'la' which means 'not'. Please read the following examples to see how 'nn' is used in the positive sentences and 'alla' is used in the negative sentences.

In the positive sentences below, the English sometimes does not contain 'that' but the Arabic still does: the literal translation of the first example would therefore be: 'I wish that you would answer my cell phone.' 'An' always comes before a positive verb. It is necessary to place it before a positive verb to indicate a verbal noun. This constitutes a verb conjugated into the appropriate tense and with the appropriate noun, and is preceded by 'an'. This is the equivalent to the infinitive form in English (placing 'to' before a verb). Although 'an' in Arabic indicates a verbal noun, this does not always translate into English, as the examples demonstrate.

I asked you **that to answer** my cell phone.	أَطْلُبُ مِنْكَ أَنْ تَرُدَ عَلَى هَاتِفِي المَحمُولِ.
I asked you not **to answer** my cell phone.	أَطْلُبُ مِنْكَ أَلاَّ تَرُدَ عَلَى هَاتِفِي المَحمُولِ.
Please go **to meet** my paternal uncle at the airport.	أَرْجُو أَنْ تَذْهَبَ لِمُقَابَلَةِ عَمِّي فِي المَطَارِ.
Please do not go **to meet** my paternal uncle at the airport.	أَرْجُو أَلاَّ تَذْهَبَ لِمُقَابَلَةِ عَمِّي فِي المَطَارِ.
I wish **that** you would meet my grandfather.	أَتَمَنَّى أَنْ تُقَابِلَ جَدِّي.

I wish you would not **meet** my grandfather.	أَتَمَنَّى أَلَّا تُقَابِلَ جَدِّي.
What do you think about **telling** your father of this matter?	مَا رَأْيُكَ أَنْ تُخْبِرَ وَالِدَكَ عَنِ الْمَوْضُوعِ؟
What do you think about not telling your father of this matter?	مَا رَأْيُكَ أَلَّا تُخْبِرَ وَالِدَكَ عَنِ الْمَوْضُوعِ؟
I prefer **to listen** to popular songs.	أَفَضِّلُ أَنْ أَسْمَعَ الْأَغَانِي الشَّعْبِيَةَ.
I prefer not **to listen** to popular songs.	أَفَضِّلُ أَلَّا أَسْمَعَ الْأَغَانِي الشَّعْبِيَةَ.

In Arabic, there are two ways to express similarity. With some grammatical condition (we will not discuss this right now) you can use the letter 'kaaf' as a preposition, or you can use the particle 'methlu.'

This girl is like the moon (or as beautiful as the moon, an object used to compare beauty to)	هذه الفَتَاةُ مِثْلُ القَمَرِ.
	هذه الفَتَاةُ كَالقَمَرِ.
This girl is exactly like her mother.	هذه البِنْتُ مِثْلُ أُمِّهَا تَمَامًا.
	هذه البِنْتُ كَأُمِّهَا تَمَامًا.
Eiman is as strong as a lion.	أَيْمَن قَوِيٌّ مِثْلُ الأَسَدِ.
	أَيْمَن قَوِيٌّ كَالأَسَدِ.
My hair is soft like your hair.	شَعْرِي نَاعِمٌ مِثْلُ شَعْرِكِ.
	شَعْرِي نَاعِمٌ كَشَعْرِكِ.
My shoes are like your shoes.	حِذَائِي مِثْلُ حِذَائِكَ.

	حِذائي كَحِذائِكَ.

لَيْلَةُ الزِّفاف

اِسْتَيْقَظْتُ صباحَ يومِ عُرْسي أُفَكِّرُ ماذا أَفْعَلُ اليومَ؟ وكيفَ أُرَتِّبُ أَشْيائي؟ وكيفَ سيكونُ يومي؟ ...

ذَهَبْتُ إلى الحلّاقِ، حَلَقْتُ شَعري وذَقْني.
ذَهَبْتُ لِأَشْتَري بدلةً جديدةً، واشْتَرَيْتُ قَميصًا جديدًا.

اِشْتَرَيْتُ عِطْرًا جميلًا، واشْتَرَيْتُ كلَّ مُسْتَلْزَماتِ الحياةِ اليوميةِ التي سوفَ أَحْتاجُها بعدَ زَواجي ..

414

In this section of the book you will learn the basics of singular and plural words, personal pronouns (he, she and they in masculine and feminine), adjectives (which should match its noun's definiteness, gender and number)), tanween (the writing of two vowels marks on the top of each other to denote indefiniteness, making a 'nuun' sound) and case endings in the nominative.

Singular Words

Singular words denote just one of something. They can be masculine or feminine.

Dual

Dual nouns are two of something. These words are written as single nouns, and then suffixed with alif and 'nuun' or 'yaa' and 'nuun', depending on the grammatical function of the word.

Plural:

Sound masculine plural nouns are limited to proper nouns and adjectives under certain condition. It is best to memorize plural nouns as you encounter them since some of them take different forms. Sound masculine plural nouns end in a 'waaw nuun' or 'yaa nuun', depending on its Iɛrab. Sound feminine plural nouns end in 'alif-taa'.

The word sound in 'sound masculine plural' means 'salim', or 'intact'. When singular words are made into SMP, all the letters in its singular form remain intact, whilst broken plural words change some letters in the singular form.

Gender:

Every Arabic noun has a gender, either masculine or feminine: there are no neutral nouns. This is also true of pronouns, so there is no word in Arabic for 'it', for instance.

Case ending: 'Iɛrab'

Iɛrab is the placement of any of the vowel marks (fatHa, dumma, kasra) on the last letter of a word according to its grammatical function in a sentence. If the word is definite, there will be just one mark; if it is indefinite there will be two, and in this case, it will be called tanween. Both are illustrated in the examples given in the lesson. بٌ بَ

Iɛrab also can be applied in different ways: as above, by changing vowel marks, and also by changing the letters of a word. An example of this is, in the case of sound masculine plural, the waaw of the 'waaw nuun' changing to 'yaa'.

Adjectives

Adjectives usually follow the noun it describes. It will match the noun in number, gender and definiteness. If the noun is non-human (books, cars, etc.), it is possible for the gender and number of the adjective not to match the noun. Adjectives also follow their noun in I3rab.

The definite article al; the

The definite article is the most frequently used word in Arabic. It is prefixed to the noun regardless of gender or number.

The indefinite article:

There is no indefinite article in Arabic. For a word to be described as indefinite, tanween must be placed above the last letter of the word. This is a double vowel mark, with one vowel mark above another.

The absence of the verb 'to be' in nominal sentences

The verb 'to be' is not used in a simple sentence such as 'He is a doctor' or 'I am a professor'. In Arabic, these sentences would literally be, 'He doctor' and 'I professor'.

The pronouns he, she, they; masculine and feminine

In this lesson you will also be introduced to the pronouns 'he', 'she' and 'they'. In Arabic, there are two words denoting 'they', one masculine and one feminine.

Next, you will see example of the topics we have discussed. We will learn how words come in different 'I3rab', how they can be definite and indefinite, how they become plural.

Here you will see how words are organized in these grammatical functions.

أَبَاءٌ طَيِّبُون	أبٌ طَيِّبٌ	أب.ج. اباء
هُوَ أبٌ طَيِّبٌ	الأبُ الطَّيِّبُ	الأبُ طَيِّبٌ
		هُم اباءٌ طَيِّبُون

This table has examples of the different grammatical features we have been discussing:

The first word (on the right) is 'father' in the singular. The 'jiim' is then written to denote plurality: 'jiim' is the first letter of the word	أب.ج. اباء

Description	Arabic
'jam3' ('plural'). Then 'fathers' is written.	
Here is a singular noun with an adjective. Notice that both words are indefinite as they have the tanween. Both words are singular.\n\nThis means, 'a good-hearted father'. Remember, adjectives follow nouns in Arabic.	أَبٌ طَيِّبٌ
The same words are here, but written in the plural. The noun is broken plural, whilst the adjective is sound masculine plural. Also note that when a word in is the sound masculine form, it does not take tanween. Tanween is only used for singular and broken plural words.	أَبَاءٌ طَيِّبُون
This noun has been prefixed with the definite article 'al'. Do not translate this as 'the good-hearted father' but rather, 'the father is good-hearted'. The alif must appear before both the noun and adjective for the meaning to become 'the good-hearted father'. Also, notice the absence of the verb 'to be'. The word 'father' loses the tanween, whilst 'good-hearted' has kept it.	الأَبُ طَيِّبٌ
Here the definite article prefixes both the noun and the adjective. Thus, 'the good-hearted father'.\n\nNotice the disappearance of tanween, as both words have become definite.	الأَبُ الطَّيِّبُ
In this sentence the meaning is, 'he is a good-hearted father'.You are introduced to the personal pronoun 'he'. There is no verb 'to be' again here.	هُوَ أَبٌ طَيِّبٌ
'They are good-hearted fathers.' Look at which word has tanween and which has not. Notice there is no verb 'to be'.	هُم اباءٌ طَيِّبُون

Vocabulary section:

Study the following vocabulary. These words will come in examples below.

Actor	مُمَثِّلٌ		Airport	مَطَارٌ		Alarm o'clock	مُنَبِّه

Annoying	مُزْعِجٌ	Director	مُدِيرٌ	Large	كَبِيرٌ
Assiduous	مُجْتَهِدٌ	Donkey	حِمَارٌ	Lion	أَسَدٌ
Award	جَائِزَة	Door	بَابٌ	Local	مَحَلِيَة
Bathroom	حَمَّام	Factory	مَصْنَعٌ	Long	طَوِيلٌ
Beautiful	جَمِيلَة	Family	عَائِلَة	Love	حَبٌّ
Beds	سَرِيرٌ	Fat	سَمِينَة	Magazine	مَجَلَّة
Beefy	سَمِينٌ	Fellow	زَمِيلٌ	Man	رَجُلٌ
Book	كِتَابٌ	Fruit	فَاكِهَة	Many	كَثِيرٌ
Boy	وَلَدٌ	Glossy	لامِعٌ	Mosque	مَسْجِدٌ
Bright	مُشْرِقَة	Have	دِيكٌ	Mount	جَبَلٌ
Broadcast	إذاعَة	Head	رَئِيسٌ	Napkin	مِنْدِيلٌ
Brother	أَخ	Hen	دَجَاجَة	Never	قَطُّ
camel	جَمَلٌ	Horse	حِصَانٌ	New	جَدِيدٌ
Capital	عَاصِمَة	House	بَيْتٌ	New	جَدِيدٌ
Capital	مَالٌ	In	وَفِيٌّ	Newspaper	صَحِيفَة
Car	سَيَّارَة	Key	مِفْتَاحٌ	Office	مَكْتَبٌ
Chair	كُرْسِيٌّ	Known	مَعرُوفٌ	Old	عَجُوزٌ
City	مَدِينَة	known	مَعرُوفَة	Old	قَدِيمٌ
Classroom	فَصْلٌ	Ladder	سُلَّمٌ	Pair	زَوْجٌ
Deft	مَاهِرٌ				

Pen	قَلَمٌ	Tree	شَجَرَة
Perfumed	مُعَطَّرٌ	Tutor	مُدَرِّسٌ
Pharmacy	صَيْدَلِيَّة	University	جَامِعَة
Photographer	مُصَوِّرٌ	Village	قَرْيَة
Physician	طَبِيبٌ	WC	مِرْحَاضٌ
Playground	مَلْعَبٌ	Wide	وَاسِعٌ
Prince	أمِير	Window	نَافِذَة
Ravenous	مُفْتَرِسٌ	Woman	امْرَأَةٌ
Refrigerator	ثَلاجَة	Women	نِسَاءٌ
Room	غُرْفَة		
Sea	بَحْرٌ		
Shirt	قَمِيْصٌ		
Sick	مَرِيْضٌ		
Small	صَغِيْرٌ		
Star	نَجْمٌ		
Street	شَارِعٌ		
Student	طَالِبٌ		
Sun	شَّمْسٌ		
Train	قِطَارٌ		

هُم اباَءٌ طَيِّبون	هُوَ أبٌ طَيِّبٌ	الأبُ الطَّيِّبُ	الأبُ طَيِّبٌ	أباَءٌ طَيِّبون	أبٌ طَيِّبٌ	أب.ج. اباَء

Using your understanding of the above words and the vocabulary provided, translate these sentences (first highlighted in grey) into Arabic.

أُمَّهَاتٌ طَيِّبَاتٌ	أُمٌّ طَيِّبَةٌ	أم.ج. أُمَهَات
هِيَ أُمٌّ طَيِّبَةٌ	الأُمُّ الطَّيِّبَةُ	الأُمُّ طَيِّبَةٌ
The good-hearted mother likes shopping because it helps her family grow healthily		هُنَّ أُمَّهَاتٌ طَيِّبَاتٌ

إذاعَاتٌ مَحَلِيَةٌ	إذاعَةٌ مَحَلِيَةٌ	إذاعَة.ج. إذاعَاتٌ
هِيَ إذاعَةٌ مَحَلِيَةٌ	الإذاعَةُ المَحَلِيَةُ	الإذاعَةُ مَحَلِيَةٌ
The local radio station, which only had ten members of staff, was popular across the whole of southern Egypt.		هِيَ إذاعَاتٌ مَحَلِيَةٌ

نِسَاءٌ جَمِيلاتٌ	امْرَأَةٌ جَمِيلَةٌ	امْرَأَةٌ.ج. نِسَاءٌ
هِيَ امْرَأَةٌ جَمِيلَةٌ	المَرْأَةُ الجَمِيلَةُ	المَرْأَةُ جَمِيلَةٌ
The beautiful women are famous because of their good looks, and because they are all sisters.		هُنَّ نِسَاءٌ جَمِيلاتٌ

والِدُون طَيِّبُون	والِدٌ طَيِّبٌ	والِد.ج. والِدُون
هُوَ والِدٌ طَيِّبٌ	الوالِدُ الطَّيِّبُ	الوالِدُ طَيِّبٌ

A good father would help his son with his homework, but only if he was struggling.		هُمْ وَالِدُون طَيِّبُون

إخْوَةٌ طَيِّبُون	أخٌ طَيِّبٌ	أخ. ج. إخْوَةٌ
هُوَ أخٌ طَيِّبٌ	الأخُ الطَّيِّبُ	الأخُ طَيِّبٌ
Good brothers look after each other, even when times are tough.		هُمْ إخْوَةٌ طَيِّبُون

أُسُودٌ مُفتَرِسَةٌ	أَسَدٌ مُفتَرِسٌ	أَسَدٌ. ج. أُسُودٌ
هُوَ أَسَدٌ مُفتَرِسٌ	الأَسَدُ المُفتَرِسُ	الأَسَدُ مُفتَرِسٌ
The ferocious lion, having not eaten for a week, attacked the zebra mercilessly.		هِيَ أُسُودٌ مُفتَرِسَةٌ

أُمَرَاءٌ مَعرُوفُون	أمِيرٌ مَعرُوفٌ	أمير. أُمَرَاءٌ
هُوَ أمِيرٌ مَعرُوفٌ	الأمِيرُ المَعرُوفُ	الأمِيرُ مَعرُوفٌ
A renowned prince travelled to Saudi Arabia in order to purchase their traditional dress.		هُمْ أُمَرَاءٌ مَعرُوفُون

أبْوَابٌ كَبِيرَةٌ	بَابٌ كَبِيرٌ	بَابٌ. ج. أبْوَابٌ
هُوَ بَابٌ كَبِيرٌ	البَابُ الكَبِيرُ	البَابُ كَبِيرٌ

Do not let the door hit you on the way out. (In Arabic, we say, 'a camel can pass through the door' - the door is big enough for a camel to leave, so you certainly can! Both are expressions telling someone to get out.)	هِيَ أَبْوَابٌ كَبِيرَةٌ

بِحَارٌ كَبِيرَةٌ	بَحْرٌ كَبِيرٌ	بَحْرٌ. ج. بِحَارٌ
هُوَ بَحْرٌ كَبِيرٌ	البَحْرُ الكَبِيرُ	البَحْرُ كَبِيرٌ
Abdullah sailed his boat across the big, deep sea when he was searching for his long-lost brother.		هِيَ بِحَارٌ كَبِيرَةٌ

بِيُوتٌ كَبِيرَةٌ	بَيْتٌ كَبِيرٌ	بَيْتٌ. ج. بِيُوتٌ
هُوَ بَيْتٌ كَبِيرٌ	البَيْتُ الكَبِيرُ	البَيْتُ كَبِيرٌ
Historically, the largest houses in the region were built in Damascus during the nineteenth century.		هِيَ بِيُوتٌ كَبِيرَةٌ

ثَلاجَاتٌ جَدِيدَةٌ	ثَلاجَةٌ جَدِيدَةٌ	ثَلاجَةٌ. ج. ثَلاجَاتٌ
هِيَ ثَلاجَةٌ جَدِيدَةٌ	الثَّلاجَةُ الجَدِيدَةُ	الثَّلاجَةُ جَدِيدَةٌ
My grandfather's house in Alexandria has a new refrigerator, which he bought from Morocco.		هِيَ ثَلاجَاتٌ جَدِيدَةٌ

جَوَائِزُ كَبِيرَةٌ	جَائِزَةٌ كَبِيرَةٌ	جَائِزَةٌ. ج. جَوَائِزُ

الجَائِزَةُ كَبِيرَةٌ	الجَائِزَةُ الكَبِيرَةُ	هِيَ جَائِزَةٌ كَبِيرَةٌ
هِيَ جَوَائِزٌ كَبِيرَةٌ	There is a big prize, as you would expect, for those who esteem themselves in Saudi diplomacy.	

جَمَلٌ. ج. جِمَالٌ	جَمَلٌ كَبِيرٌ	جِمَالٌ كَبِيرَةٌ
الجَمَلُ كَبِيرٌ	الجَمَلُ الكَبِيرُ	هُوَ جَمَلٌ كَبِيرٌ
هِيَ جِمَالٌ كَبِيرَةٌ	The mother camel was very upset when her baby was slaughtered to make a meal for the owner's guests.	

جَامِعَةٌ. ج. جَامِعَاتٌ	جَامِعَةٌ مَعرُوفَةٌ	جَامِعَاتٌ مَعرُوفَةٌ
الجَامِعَةُ مَعرُوفَةٌ	الجَامِعَةُ المَعرُوفَةُ	هِيَ جَامِعَةٌ مَعرُوفَةٌ
هِيَ جَامِعَاتٌ مَعرُوفَةٌ	SOAS, a university based in London, is the most renowned place of study for the Arabic language and culture.	

جبل. ج. جِبَالٌ	جَبَلٌ كَبِيرٌ	جِبَالٌ كَبِيرَةٌ
الجَبَلُ كَبِيرٌ	الجَبَلُ الكَبِيرُ	هُوَ جَبَلٌ كَبِيرٌ
هِيَ جِبَالٌ كَبِيرَةٌ	Omar travelled to the big mountain, which towered above the capital city.	

حِصَانٌ. ج. أَحْصِنَةٌ	حِصَانٌ قَوِيٌّ	أَحْصِنَةٌ قَوِيَّةٌ

هُوَ حِصَانٌ قَوِيٌّ	الْحِصَانُ الْقَوِيُّ	الْحِصَانُ قَوِيٌّ
One can find many strong horses in the land surrounding the ancient city of Beirut.		هِيَ أَحْصِنَةٌ قَوِيَةٌ

حَمِيرٌ صَغِيرَةٌ	حِمَارٌ صَغِيرٌ	حِمَارٌ. ج. حَمِيرٌ
هُوَ حِمَارٌ صَغِيرٌ	الْحِمَارُ الصَّغِيرُ	الْحِمَارُ صَغِيرٌ
When he was a child, Mohammed would ride a small donkey around his village.		هِيَ حَمِيرٌ صَغِيرَةٌ

حُبُوبٌ كَثِيرَةٌ	حَبٌّ كَثِيرٌ	الْحَبُّ. ج. الْحُبُوبُ
هُوَ حَبٌّ كَثِيرٌ	الْحَبُّ الْكَثِيرُ	الْحَبُّ كَثِيرٌ
The Sudanese farmer scattered many seeds in the fertile valley of the River Nile.		هِيَ حُبُوبٌ كَثِيرَةٌ

حَمَّامَاتٌ كَبِيرَةٌ	حَمَّامٌ كَبِيرٌ	حَمَّامٌ. ج. حَمَّامَاتٌ
هُوَ حَمَّامٌ كَبِيرٌ	الْحَمَّامُ الْكَبِيرُ	الْحَمَّامُ كَبِيرٌ
My friend in Tehran has one of the most expensive houses in the city, including a very big shower.		هِيَ حَمَّامَاتٌ كَبِيرَةٌ

]

دَجَاجَاتٌ سَمِينَةٌ	دَجَاجَةٌ سَمِينَةٌ	دَجَاجَةٌ. ج. دَجَاجَاتٌ

هِيَ دَجَاجَةٌ سَمِينَةٌ	الدَجَاجَةُ السَمِينَةُ	الدَجَاجَةُ سَمِينَةٌ
I have to slaughter five plump chickens to feed all my guests at the wedding.		هِيَ دَجَاجَاتٌ سَمِينَةٌ

دِيُوكٌ كَبِيرَةٌ	دِيكٌ كَبِيرٌ	دِيكٌ.ج. دِيُوكٌ
هُوَ دِيكٌ كَبِيرٌ	الدِيكُ الكَبِيرُ	الدِيكُ كَبِيرٌ
The big rooster, who lives in a nearby house in the village, wakes me up every morning at six o'clock.		هِيَ دِيُوكٌ كَبِيرَةٌ

رِجَالٌ أَقْوِيَاءٌ	رَجُلٌ قَوِيٌّ	رَجُلٌ.ج. رِجَالٌ
هُوَ رَجُلٌ قَوِيٌّ	الرَّجُلُ القَوِيُّ	الرَّجُلُ قَوِيٌّ
Saddam Hussein was the strongman of Iraq until the Western forces brought him down.		هُمْ رِجَالٌ أَقْوِيَاءٌ

رُؤَسَاءٌ جُدُدٌ	رَئِيسٌ جَدِيدٌ	رَئِيسٌ.ج. رُؤَسَاءٌ
هُوَ رَئِيسٌ جَدِيدٌ	الرَّئِيسُ الجَدِيدُ	الرَّئِيسُ جَدِيدٌ
Many Arab countries will elect new presidents in the coming years because of the Arab Spring.		هُمْ رُؤَسَاءٌ جُدُدٌ

زُمَلاءٌ أَوفِيَاءٌ	زَمِيلٌ وَفِيٌّ	زَمِيلٌ.ج. زُمَلاءٌ
هُوَ زَمِيلٌ وَفِيٌّ	الزَّمِيلُ الوَفِيُّ	الزَّمِيلُ وَفِيٌّ

Although Mahmoud is married to my sister, he has also proven to be a very loyal colleague.		هُمْ زُمَلاءٌ أوفِيَاءٌ

أزوَاجٌ أوفِيَاءٌ	زَوْجٌ وَفِيٌّ	زَوْجٌ. ج. أزوَاجٌ
هُوَ زَوْجٌ وَفِيٌّ	الزَّوْجُ الوَفِيُّ	الزَّوْجُ وَفِيٌّ
My sister does not think that Abdul-Rahman is a very loyal husband.		هُمْ أزوَاجٌ أوفِيَاءٌ

أسِرَّةٌ جَدِيدَةٌ	سَرِيرٌ جَدِيدٌ	سَرِيرٌ. ج. أسِرَّةٌ
هُوَ سَرِيرٌ جَدِيدٌ	السَرِيرُ الجَدِيدُ	السَرِيرُ جَدِيدٌ
My brother, who lives in a large house in Cairo, has just purchased a new bed.		هِيَ أسِرَّةٌ جَدِيدَةٌ

سَلالِمٌ طَوِيلَةٌ	سُلَّمٌ طَوِيلٌ	سُلَّمٌ. ج. سَلالِم
هُوَ سُلَّمٌ طَوِيلٌ	السُلَّمُ الطَوِيلُ	السُلَّمُ طَوِيلٌ
When I was younger, I grew up in a house that had a lobby and a long staircase.		هِيَ سَلالِمٌ طَوِيلَةٌ

سَيَّارَاتٌ جَدِيدَةٌ	سَيَّارَةٌ جَدِيدَةٌ	سَيَّارَةٌ. ج. سَيَّارَاتٌ
هِيَ سَيَّارَةٌ جَدِيدَةٌ	السَيَّارَةُ الجَدِيدَةُ	السَيَّارَةُ جَدِيدَةٌ
There are so many new cars in Dubai; it is like being on a TV commercial when you visit.		هِيَ سَيَّارَاتٌ جَدِيدَةٌ

أَشْجَارٌ عَالِيَةٌ	شَجَرَةٌ عَالِيَةٌ	شَجَرَةٌ . ج. أَشْجَارٌ
هِيَ شَجَرَةٌ عَالِيَةٌ	الشَّجَرَةُ العَالِيَةُ	الشَّجَرَةُ عَالِيَةٌ
When the sun is high, you can still cool down in the shade of high trees.		هِيَ أَشْجَارٌ عَالِيَةٌ

شُمُوسٌ مُشْرِقَةٌ	شَمْسٌ مُشْرِقَةٌ	شَمْسٌ . ج. شُمُوسٌ
هِيَ شَمْسٌ مُشْرِقَةٌ	الشَّمْسُ المُشْرِقَةُ	الشَّمْسُ مُشْرِقَةٌ
In many Arab countries, you can have the pleasure of a shining sun all year long.		هِيَ شُمُوسٌ مُشْرِقَةٌ

شَوَارِعُ طَوِيلَةٌ	شَارِعٌ طَوِيلٌ	شَارِعٌ . ج. شَوَارِعُ
هُوَ شَارِعٌ طَوِيلٌ	الشَّارِعُ الطَّوِيلُ	الشَّارِعُ طَوِيلٌ
My cousin, originally from Baghdad, now lives in Tunis on a long street in the city.		هِيَ شَوَارِعُ طَوِيلَةٌ

شُبَّانٌ أَقْوِيَاءٌ	شَابٌّ قَوِيٌّ	شَابٌّ . ج. شُبَّانٌ
هُوَ شَابٌّ قَوِيٌّ	الشَّابُّ القَوِيُّ	الشَّابُّ قَوِيٌّ
Oman are recruiting for their new-look army, aiming to attract strong young men from all parts of society.		هُمْ شُبَّانٌ أَقْوِيَاءٌ

427

صُحُفٌ مَعرُوفَةٌ	صَحِيفَةٌ مَعرُوفَةٌ	صَحِيفَةٌ . ج. صُحُفٌ
هِيَ صَحِيْفَةٌ مَعرُوفَةٌ	الصَّحِيفَةُ المَعرُوفَةُ	الصَّحِيفَةُ مَعرُوفَةٌ
A renowned newspaper broke the news of the resignation of the president.		هِيَ صُحُفٌ مَعرُوفَةٌ

أَصدِقَاءٌ أَوفِيَاءُ	صَدِيقٌ وَفِيٌّ	صَدِيقٌ . ج. أَصدِقَاءُ
هُوَ صَدِيقٌ وَفِيٌّ	الصَّدِيقُ الوَفِيُّ	الصَّدِيقُ وَفِيٌّ
As the Arab proverb says, there are three impossibilities: an ogre, a phoenix and a loyal friend.		هُمْ أَصدِقَاءٌ أَوفِيَاءُ

صَيْدَلِيَّاتٌ صَغِيرَةٌ	صَيْدَلِيَّةٌ صَغِيرَةٌ	صَيْدَلِيَّةٌ . ج. صَيْدَلِيَّاتٌ
هِيَ صَيْدَلِيَّةٌ صَغِيرَةٌ	الصَّيْدَلِيَّةُ الصَّغِيرَةُ	الصَّيْدَلِيَّةُ صَغِيرَةٌ
The small pharmacy, like most places of business, closes when it time to pray.		هِيَ صَيْدَلِيَّاتٌ صَغِيرَةٌ

طُلَّابٌ مُجْتَهِدُونَ	طَالِبٌ مُجْتَهِدٌ	طَالِبٌ . ج. طُلَّابٌ
هُوَ طَالِبٌ مُجْتَهِدٌ	الطَّالِبُ المُجْتَهِدُ	الطَّالِبُ مُجْتَهِدٌ
The hardworking student passed all his exams, whereas the lazy student failed his.		هُمْ طُلَّابٌ مُجْتَهِدُونَ

أَطِبَّاءٌ مَعرُوفُون	طَبِيبٌ مَعرُوفٌ	طَبِيبٌ. ج. أَطِبَّاءٌ
هُوَ طَبِيبٌ مَعرُوفٌ	الطَّبِيبُ المَعرُوفُ	الطَّبِيبُ مَعرُوفٌ
A renowned Pakistani doctor helped capture Osama bin Laden in his hideaway.		هُمْ أَطِبَّاءٌ مَعرُوفُون

عَوَاصِمٌ كَبِيرَةٌ	عَاصِمَةٌ كَبِيرَةٌ	عَاصِمَةٌ. ج. عَوَاصِمٌ
هِيَ عَاصِمَةٌ كَبِيرَةٌ	العَاصِمَةُ الكَبِيرَةُ	العَاصِمَةُ كَبِيرَةٌ
Cairo is the largest capital city in Egypt, and indeed in the whole Arab world.		هِيَ عَوَاصِمٌ كَبِيرَةٌ

عَائِلَاتٌ مَعرُوفَةٌ	عَائِلَةٌ مَعرُوفَةٌ	عَائِلَةٌ. ج. عَائِلَاتٌ
هِيَ عَائِلَةٌ مَعرُوفَةٌ	العَائِلَةُ المَعرُوفَةُ	العَائِلَةُ مَعرُوفَةٌ
Despite being infamous, bin Laden is from what is considered one of the most renowned families in Saudi Arabia.		هِيَ عَائِلَاتٌ مَعرُوفَةٌ

عَجَائِزٌ مُسِّنُون	عَجُوزٌ مُسِّنٌ	عَجُوزٌ. ج. عَجَائِزٌ
هُوَ عَجُوزٌ مُسِّنٌ	العَجَائِزُ المُسِّنُون	العَجُوزُ مُسِّنٌ
An old man, very advanced in years, travelled all the way from Libya to Jordan on a camel.		هُمْ عَجَائِزٌ مُسِّنُون

غُرَفٌ صَغِيرَةٌ	غُرْفَةٌ صَغِيرَةٌ	غُرْفَةٌ . ج. غُرَفٌ
هِيَ غُرْفَةٌ صَغِيرَةٌ	الغُرْفَةُ الصَّغِيرَةُ	الغُرْفَةُ صَغِيرَةٌ
When I was studying Arabic in Yemen, I lived in a small room next to a mosque.		هِيَ غُرَفٌ صَغِيرَةٌ

فَوَاكِهٌ كَثِيرَةٌ	فَاكِهَةٌ كَثِيرَةٌ	فَاكِهَةٌ . ج. فَوَاكِهٌ
هِيَ فَاكِهَةٌ كَثِيرَةٌ	الفَاكِهَةُ الكَثِيرَةُ	الفَاكِهَةُ كَثِيرَةٌ
There is hardly any fruit growing in the Empty Quarter in Saudi Arabia.		هِيَ فَوَاكِهٌ كَثِيرَةٌ

فُصُولٌ كَبِيرَةٌ	فَصْلٌ كَبِيرٌ	فَصْلٌ.ج. فُصُولٌ
هُوَ فَصْلٌ كَبِيرٌ	الفَصْلُ الكَبِيرُ	الفَصْلُ كَبِيرٌ
Ehab studied Arabic literature at school in a large classroom.		هِيَ فُصُولٌ كَبِيرَةٌ

قُرَى صَغِيرَةٌ	قَرْيَةٌ صَغِيرَةٌ	قَرْيَةٌ . ج. قُرَى
هِيَ قَرْيَةٌ صَغِيرَةٌ	القَرْيَةُ الصَّغِيرَةُ	القَرْيَةُ صَغِيرَةٌ
Although I was born in a small village, now I live in Riyadh, a large city.		هِيَ قُرَى صَغِيرَةٌ

أقلامٌ جَدِيدَةٌ	قَلَمٌ جَدِيدٌ	قَلَمٌ. ج. أقلامٌ
هُوَ قَلَمٌ جَدِيدٌ	القَلَمُ الجَدِيدُ	القَلَمُ جَدِيدٌ
Musa wrote a novel, about spies in Arab countries, using his new pen.		هِيَ أقلامٌ جَدِيدَةٌ

قُمْصَانٌ جَدِيدَةٌ	قَمِيصٌ جَدِيدٌ	قَمِيصٌ. ج. قُمْصَانٌ
هُوَ قَمِيصٌ جَدِيدٌ	القَمِيصُ الجَدِيدُ	القَمِيصُ جَدِيدٌ
We went to the mosque to pray wearing new shirts bought from the large mall.		هِيَ قُمْصَانٌ جَدِيدَةٌ

قِطَطٌ صَغِيرَةٌ	قِطٌّ صَغِيرٌ	قِطٌّ. ج. قِطَطٌ
هُوَ قِطٌّ صَغِيرٌ	القِطُّ الصَّغِيرُ	القِطُّ صَغِيرٌ
A small kitten, found in the rubble of a destroyed building, survived the fighting in Iraq.		هِيَ قِطَطٌ صَغِيرَةٌ

قِطَارَاتٌ سَرِيعَةٌ	قِطَارٌ سَرِيعٌ	قِطَارٌ. ج. قِطَارَاتٌ
هُوَ قِطَارٌ سَرِيعٌ	القِطَارُ السَّرِيعُ	القِطَارُ سَرِيعٌ
Saudi Arabia is building a new express train that will connect Mecca to Medinah.		هِيَ قِطَارَاتٌ سَرِيعَةٌ

كِلابٌ وَفِيَةٌ	كَلْبٌ وَفِيٌّ	كَلْبٌ .ج. كِلابٌ
هُوَ كَلْبٌ وَفِيٌّ	الكَلْبُ الوَفِيُّ	الكَلْبُ وَفِيٌّ
Although he was let down by his friends, Ahmed knew he could trust his loyal dog.		هِيَ كِلابٌ وَفِيَةٌ

كَرَاسِي قَدِيمَةٌ	كُرْسِيٌّ قَدِيمٌ	كُرْسِيٌّ .ج. كَرَاسِي
هُوَ كُرْسِيٌّ قَدِيمٌ	الكُرْسِيُّ القَدِيمُ	الكُرْسِيُّ قَدِيمٌ
The famous coffee shops of Damascus house old men smoking shisha, sitting in old chairs.		هِيَ كَرَاسِي قَدِيمَةٌ

كُتُبٌ كَبِيرَةٌ	كِتَابٌ كَبِيرٌ	كِتَابٌ .ج. كُتُبٌ
هُوَ كِتَابٌ كَبِيرٌ	الكِتَابُ الكَبِيرُ	الكِتَابُ كَبِيرٌ
The library of Alexandria is home to many large books about Egyptian history.		هِيَ كُتُبٌ كَبِيرَةٌ

لُغَاتٌ صَعْبَةٌ	لُغَةٌ صَعْبَةٌ	لُغَةٌ .ج. لُغَاتٌ
هِيَ لُغَةٌ صَعْبَةٌ	اللُّغَةُ الصَّعْبَةُ	اللُّغَةُ صَعْبَةٌ
		هِيَ لُغَاتٌ صَعْبَةٌ

أَمْوَالٌ كَثِيرَةٌ	مَالٌ كَثِيرٌ	مَالٌ. أَمْوَالٌ
هُوَ مَالٌ كَثِيرٌ	المَالُ الكَثِيرُ	المَالُ كَثِيرٌ
Complicated grammar rules make Arabic such a difficult language for non-Arab people.		هِيَ أَمْوَالٌ كَثِيرَةٌ

مَسَاجِدٌ صَغِيرَةٌ	مَسْجِدٌ صَغِيرٌ	مَسْجِدٌ. ج. مَسَاجِدٌ
هُوَ مَسْجِدٌ صَغِيرٌ	المَسْجِدُ الصَّغِيرُ	المَسْجِدُ صَغِيرٌ
The FBI raided a small mosque in Brooklyn looking for terrorists.		هِيَ مَسَاجِدٌ صَغِيرَةٌ

مَكَاتِبٌ كَبِيرَةٌ	مَكْتَبٌ كَبِيرٌ	مَكْتَبٌ. ج. مَكَاتِبٌ
هُوَ مَكْتَبٌ كَبِيرٌ	المَكْتَبُ الكَبِيرُ	المَكْتَبُ كَبِيرٌ
Sometimes I work from home, but I get more done in my big office.		هِيَ مَكَاتِبٌ كَبِيرَةٌ

مَلاعِبٌ وَاسِعَةٌ	مَلْعَبٌ وَاسِعٌ	مَلْعَبٌ. ج. مَلاعِبٌ
هُوَ مَلْعَبٌ وَاسِعٌ	المَلْعَبُ الوَاسِعُ	المَلْعَبُ وَاسِعٌ
Qatar are building many vast stadiums for the football world cup in 2018.		هِيَ مَلاعِبٌ وَاسِعَةٌ

مُدَرِّسُونَ مَاهِرُونَ	مُدَرِّسٌ مَاهِرٌ	مُدَرِّسٌ. ج. مُدَرِّسُونَ
هُوَ مُدَرِّسٌ مَاهِرٌ	المُدَرِّسُ المَاهِرُ	المُدَرِّسُ مَاهِرٌ
There are not many skilled Arabic teachers in the Western world.		هُمْ مُدَرِّسُونَ مَاهِرُونَ

مُدِيرُونَ جُدُدٌ	مُدِيرٌ جَدِيدٌ	مُدِيرٌ. ج. مُدِيرُونَ
هُوَ مُدِيرٌ جَدِيدٌ	المُدِيرُ الجَدِيدُ	المُدِيرُ جَدِيدٌ
We expanded our company into Abu Dhabi and hired a new manager.		هُمْ مُدِيرُونَ جُدُدٌ

مُصَوِّرُونَ مُحْتَرِفُونَ	مُصَوِّرٌ مُحْتَرِفٌ	مُصَوِّرٌ. ج. مُصَوِّرُونَ
هُوَ مُصَوِّرٌ مُحْتَرِفٌ	المُصَوِّرُ المُحْتَرِفُ	المُصَوِّرُ مُحْتَرِفٌ
We hired a professional photographer for our wedding in Algiers last spring.		هُمْ مُصَوِّرُونَ مُحْتَرِفُونَ

مُمَثِّلُونَ مَعْرُوفُونَ	مُمَثِّلٌ مَعْرُوفٌ	مُمَثِّلٌ. ج. مُمَثِّلُونَ
هُوَ مُمَثِّلٌ مَعْرُوفٌ	المُمَثِّلُ المَعْرُوفُ	المُمَثِّلُ مَعْرُوفٌ
Omar Sherif is a renowned actor from Egypt; he has starred in many movies and TV shows.		هُمْ مُمَثِّلُونَ مَعْرُوفُونَ

مَرَاحِيضٌ جَدِيدَةٌ	مِرْحَاضٌ جَدِيدٌ	مِرْحَاضٌ. ج. مَرَاحِيضٌ
هُوَ مِرْحَاضٌ جَدِيدٌ	المِرْحَاضُ الجَدِيدُ	المِرْحَاضُ جَدِيدٌ
Our house in Khartoum has been refurbished with a new toilet.		هِيَ مَرَاحِيضٌ جَدِيدَةٌ

مَفَاتِيْحُ قَدِيمَةٌ	مِفْتَاحٌ قَدِيمٌ	مِفْتَاحٌ. ج. مَفَاتِيْحُ
هُوَ مِفْتَاحٌ قَدِيمٌ	المِفْتَاحُ القَدِيمُ	المِفْتَاحُ قَدِيمٌ
Many Palestinian refugees still carry the old keys to their houses from Palestine.		هِيَ مَفَاتِيْحُ قَدِيمَةٌ

مَنَادِيْلُ مُعَطَّرَةٌ	مِنْدِيْلٌ مُعَطَّرٌ	مِنْدِيْلٌ. ج. مَنَادِيْلُ
هُوَ مِنْدِيْلٌ مُعَطَّرٌ	المِنْدِيْلُ المُعَطَّرُ	المِنْدِيْلُ مُعَطَّرٌ
For his birthday, I bought my father a fragrant handkerchief - a specialty from the Arab world.		هِيَ مَنَادِيْلُ مُعَطَّرَةٌ

مَجَلَّاتٌ مَعْرُوفَةٌ	مَجَلَّةٌ مَعْرُوفَةٌ	مَجَلَّةٌ. ج. مَجَلَّاتٌ
هِيَ مَجَلَّةٌ مَعْرُوفَةٌ	المَجَلَّةُ المَعْرُوفَةُ	المَجَلَّةُ مَعْرُوفَةٌ
A renowned magazine published an interview with the deposed Tunisian president.		هِيَ مَجَلَّاتٌ مَعْرُوفَةٌ

مُدُنٌ صَغِيرَةٌ	مَدِينَةٌ صَغِيرَةٌ	مَدِينَةٌ . ج. مُدُنٌ
هِيَ مَدِينَةٌ صَغِيرَةٌ	الْمَدِينَةُ الصَّغِيرَةُ	الْمَدِينَةُ صَغِيرَةٌ
Most Egyptian intellectuals were born in villages or small cities, rather than big metropolis.		هِيَ مُدُنٌ صَغِيرَةٌ

مَرْضَى مُسِنُّونَ	مَرِيضٌ مُسِنٌّ	مَرِيضٌ . ج. مَرْضَى
هُوَ مَرِيضٌ مُسِنٌّ	الْمَرِيضُ الْمُسِنُّ	الْمَرِيضُ مُسِنٌّ
The old patient in the hospital was always praying - he was preparing to meet his maker.		هُمْ مَرْضَى مُسِنُّونَ

مَصَانِعُ جَدِيدَةٌ	مَصْنَعٌ جَدِيدٌ	مَصْنَعٌ . ج. مَصَانِعُ
هُوَ مَصْنَعٌ جَدِيدٌ	الْمَصْنَعُ الْجَدِيدُ	الْمَصْنَعُ جَدِيدٌ
Many new factories were built in Bahrain during the last fifty years		هِيَ مَصَانِعُ جَدِيدَةٌ

مَطَارَاتٌ وَاسِعَةٌ	مَطَارٌ وَاسِعٌ	مَطَارٌ . ج. مَطَارَاتٌ
هُوَ مَطَارٌ وَاسِعٌ	الْمَطَارُ الْوَاسِعُ	الْمَطَارُ وَاسِعٌ
Dubai International Airport is the largest in the region.		هِيَ مَطَارَاتٌ وَاسِعَةٌ

مُنَبِّهَاتٌ مُزْعِجَةٌ	مُنَبِّهٌ مُزْعِجٌ	مُنَبِّهٌ . ج. مُنَبِّهَاتٌ
هُوَ مُنَبِّهٌ مُزْعِجٌ	المُنَبِّهُ المُزْعِجُ	المُنَبِّهُ مُزْعِجٌ
My baby brother is always crying at night like a disturbing alarm clock.		هِيَ مُنَبِّهَاتٌ مُزْعِجَةٌ

نُجُومٌ لامِعَةٌ	نَجْمٌ لامِعٌ	نَجْمٌ . ج. نُجُومٌ
هُوَ نَجْمٌ لامِعٌ	النَّجْمُ اللامِعُ	النَّجْمُ لامِعٌ
When you walk through the desert, you see the brightest stars in the universe.		هِيَ نُجُومٌ لامِعَةٌ

نَوَافِذُ صَغِيرَةٌ	نَافِذَةٌ صَغِيرَةٌ	نَافِذَةٌ . ج. نَوَافِذُ
هِيَ نَافِذَةٌ صَغِيرَةٌ	النَّافِذَةُ الصَّغِيرَةُ	النَّافِذَةُ صَغِيرَةٌ
The small windows of the mosque were decorated with Islamic ornamentation.		هِيَ نَوَافِذُ صَغِيرَةٌ

أولادٌ سِمَانٌ	وَلَدٌ سَمِينٌ	وَلَدٌ. ج. أولادٌ
هُوَ وَلَدٌ سَمِينٌ	الوَلَدُ السَّمِينُ	الوَلَدُ سَمِينٌ
The fat boy ate so much schwerma he was sick all the next week.		هُمْ أولادٌ سِمَانٌ

الشواذ

This lesson discusses the precarious lives of gay people in Iraq and those who criticize and often attack them. Iraq is traditionally a very conservative country and new liberties are struggling to take hold.

As this is a relatively long text, the questions will be asked chronologically.

يَتَجَمَّعُونَ فِي مَقَاهٍ وَأَمَاكِنَ عَامَةٍ مُنْتَشِرَةٍ فِي أَنْحَاءِ بَغْدَادٍ وَالْبَصْرَةِ وَالنَّجَفِ وَمُدُنٍ أُخْرَى، يُفَرِّقُ كُلُّ وَاحِدٍ مِنْهُمْ شَعْرَهُ الطَّوِيلَ مِنَ النَّصْفِ، وَيَثْقُبُ بَعْضُهُمْ أُذُنَهُ، كَمَا يَضَعُ الْمَسَاحِيقَ عَلَى وَجْهِهِ، وَيَتَحَدَّثُ بِطَرِيقَةٍ نِسَائِيَةٍ أَثْنَاءَ إِرْتِشَافِهِ الشَّايِ، وَلَا يَخْجَلُ مِنْ أَنْ يَظْهَرَ بِمَظْهَرِ الشَّاذِّ عَلَى الْمَلَأِ.

هَؤُلَاءِ مَجْمُوعَةٌ مِنَ الشَّوَاذِ جِنْسِيّاً الَّذِينَ بَدَءُوا فِي الِانْتِشَارِ فِي الْفَتْرَةِ الْأَخِيرَةِ بِالْعِرَاقِ؛ بِسَبَبِ مَا أَرْجَعَتْهُ صَحِيفَةُ نِيُويُورك تَايمز الْأَمْرِيكِيَةِ إِلَى "الْأَمْنِ وَالِانْفِتَاحِ وَالْحُرِّيَةِ الَّتِي جَلَبَهَا الْغَزْوُ الْأَمْرِيكِيُّ لِهَذَا الْبَلَدِ" فِي 9 أَبْرِيل 2003. وَقَالَتْ الصَّحِيفَةُ الْأَمْرِيكِيَةُ فِي تَقْرِيرٍ نَشَرَتْهُ الثُّلَاثَاءَ تَزَامُنًا مَعَ الذِّكْرَى السَّادِسَةِ لِاحْتِلَالِ بَغْدَادَ: إِنَّ "الْأَمْنَ وَالْهُدُوءَ سَمَحَ لِلْعِرَاقِيينَ أَنْ يَتَمَتَعُوا بِالْحُرِّيَاتِ (الْأَمْرِيكِيَّةِ)، وَمِنْ بَيْنِهَا حُرِّيَةُ الشُّذُوذِ، وَالَّتِي لَمْ يَكُنْ مِنَ الْمُتَصَوَّرِ أَنْ تَحْدُثَ قَبْلَ بِضْعَةِ أَعْوَامٍ".

بَاسِم (23 عَامًا) أَحَدُ مُمَارِسِي الشُّذُوذِ، وَيُفَضِّلُ أَنْ يُنَادَى عَلَيْهِ بِـ "بَسِيمَة"، قَالَ: إِنَّ " ثَلَاثَةً مِنْ أَقْرَبِ أَصْدِقَائِي قُتِلُوا خِلَالَ الْأُسْبُوعَيْنِ الْمَاضِيَيْنِ فِي مَدِينَةِ الصَّدْرِ (الَّتِي يُقِيمُ فِيهَا مِلْيُونَا نَسَمَةٍ، وَكَانَتْ تَحْتَ سَيْطَرَةِ الزَّعِيمِ الشِّيعِي مُقْتَدَى الصَّدْرِ، وَمِيلِشِيَاتِ جَيْشِ الْمَهْدِّي التَّابِعَةِ لَهُ)". وَأَضَافَ الشَّابُ الَّذِي يَعْمَلُ مُصَفِّفَ شَعْرٍ: أَنَّهُ وَزُمَلَاءَهُ "كَانُوا يُخَطِّطُونَ لِلذَّهَابِ إِلَى مَقْهًى بَعِيدٍ عَنْ مَدِينَةِ الصَّدْرِ؛ لِأَنَّهُمْ لَا يَشْعُرُونَ بِالْأَمَانِ فِي الْمَدِينَةِ، وَبِالْفِعْلِ ذَهَبَ عَدَدٌ مِنْهُمْ، لَكِنَّهُمْ قُتِلُوا فِي الطَّرِيقِ أَثْنَاءَ ذَهَابِهِمْ.. وَلَكِنَّهُ لِحُسْنِ حَظِّهِ لَمْ يَكُنْ مَعَهُمْ".

وَقَالَ بَاسِمٌ الَّذِي يَضَعُ عَلَى وَجْهِهِ الْمَسَاحِيقَ، وَيُسْدِلُ شَعْرَهُ حَتَّى أَسْفَلِ أُذُنِهِ، بِطَرِيقَةٍ غَيْرِ مَعْهُودَةٍ لِلشَّبَابِ الْعِرَاقِيينَ: إِنَّهُ "يَعْرِفُ مَا لَا يَقِلُّ عَنْ 20 شَابًا يُمَارِسُونَ الشُّذُوذَ اخْتَفُوا مِنْ مَدِينَةِ الصَّدْرِ مُؤَخَرًا"، مُضِيفًا أَنَّهُ "عَلِمَ لَاحِقًا بِأَنَّهُمْ قُتِلُوا".

وَشَهِدَتِ الأَشْهُرُ الأَخِيرَةُ مَقْتَلَ نَحْوَ 25 شَابًا وَرَجُلاً يُشْتَبَهُ فِي مُمَارَسَتِهِمُ الشُّذُوذَ فِي مَدِينَةِ الصَّدْرِ بِالعِرَاقِ، عَلَى أَيْدِي مُسَلَّحِينَ، وَذَلِكَ بَعْدَ أَنْ تَبَرَّأَتْ مِنْهُمْ قَبَائِلُهُمْ، فَقَرَّرَتِ التَّخَلُّصَ مِنْهُمْ وَإِحْرَاقَ المَقَاهِي الَّتِي يَتَجَمَّعُونَ فِيهَا.

وَقَالَتِ الشُّرْطَةُ : إِنَّ جُثَثَ هَؤُلَاءِ تُوجَدُ فِي الطُّرُقَاتِ وَعَلَيْهَا آثَارُ إِطْلَاقِ نَارٍ، وَيُرْفَقُ بِالعَدِيدِ مِنْهَا وَرَقَةٌ مَكْتُوبٌ عَلَيْهَا كَلِمَةُ "مُنْحَرِف"، بِحَسَبِ نِيُويُورْك تَايِمْز. وَتَقُولُ الشُّرْطَةُ العِرَاقِيَّةُ: "لَيْسَتْ فِرَقُ المَوْتِ الشِّيعِيَّةُ فَقَطْ هِيَ الَّتِي تَسْتَهْدِفُ الشَّوَاذَ، لَكِنْ أَيْضًا أَفْرَادُ العَائِلَاتِ وَالقَبَائِلِ، تَفْعَلُ ذَلِكَ "، مُشِيرَةً إِلَى أَنَّ المُسَلَّحِينَ يَسْتَهْدِفُونَ بِشَكْلٍ كَبِيرٍ الشَّوَاذَ مِنَ الرِّجَالِ. شَعْبٌ مُتَدَيِّنٌ وَفِي إِطَارِ التَّصَدِّي لِهَذِهِ الظَّاهِرَةِ تَقُومُ الشُّرْطَةُ بِحَمْلَةٍ وَاسِعَةٍ لِتَعَقُّبِ الشَّوَاذَ، وَذَلِكَ بِالتَّزَامُنِ مَعَ جُهُودٍ تَوْجِيهِيَّةٍ مِنْ عُلَمَاءٍ فِي مَدِينَةِ الصَّدْرِ تَهْدِفُ لِاسْتِئْصَالِ شَأْفَةِ الشُّذُوذِ مِنَ المُجْتَمَعِ .

وَفِي هَذَا الصَّدَدِ قَالَ المُثَنَّى سَعْد، ضَابِطَ شُرْطَةٍ فِي حَيِّ الكَرَادَةِ وَسَطَ بَغْدَاد، وَالَّذِي أَصْبَحَ مَعْرُوفًا بِانْتِشَارِ الشُّذُوذِ فِيهِ: إِنَّ "اللُّوَاطَ مُخَالِفٌ لِلْقَانُونِ، وَهُوَ أَمْرٌ يُثِيرُ الاشْمِئْزَازَ". وَأَضَافَ المُثَنَّى سَعْد: أَنَّ "الأَشْهُرَ الأَرْبَعَةَ المَاضِيَةَ شَهِدَتْ حَمْلَةً، شَارَكَ فِيهَا الضُّبَّاطُ لِتَطْهِيرِ الحَيِّ مِنْ هَؤُلَاءِ الشَّوَاذِ"، مُشِيرًا إِلَى أَنَّ قُوَّاتِ الأَمْنِ "لَا تَمْلِكُ القَبْضَ عَلَى أَيِّ شَخْصٍ إِلَّا إِذَا كَانَ مُتَلَبِّسًا بِمُمَارَسَةِ هَذَا الفِعْلِ".

وَبِرُغْمِ تَزَايُدِ أَعْدَادِ الشَّوَاذِ فِي العِرَاقِ بِحَسَبِ الصَّحِيفَةِ فَإِنَّهَا تُؤَكِّدُ أَنَّ الشَّعْبَ العِرَاقِيَّ فِي الجُمْلَةِ "مُتَدَيِّنٌ"، وَمُحَارَبَةُ الشُّذُوذِ مِنْ بَيْنِ أَهْدَافِ العُلَمَاءِ الشِّيعَةِ وَالسُّنَّةِ ، لَكِنَّ أَعْمَالَ العُنْفِ وَعَمَلِيَّاتِ القَتْلِ قَدْ غَطَّتْ عَلَى الجُهُودِ الَّتِي يَبْذُلُونَهَا فِي مُوَاجَهَةِ هَذَا الأَمْرِ. فَفِي عَامِ 2005، أَصْدَرَ المَرْجِعُ الشِّيعِيُّ، عَلِي السِّيسْتَانِي، فَتْوَى بِمُعَاقَبَةِ الشَّوَاذِ جِنْسِيًّا عَنْ طَرِيقِ القَتْلِ، قَائِلاً: "إِنَّهُمْ لَابُدَّ أَنْ يُقْتَلُوا شَرَّ قَتْلَةٍ"، بِحَسَبِ الصَّحِيفَةِ الأَمْرِيكِيَّةِ. مِنْ جِهَتِهِ قَالَ الشَّيْخُ إِبْرَاهِيمُ الغَرَاوِيُّ، عُضْوٌ فِي مَكْتَبِ التَّيَّارِ الصَّدْرِيِّ: إِنَّ "الشُّذُوذَ الجِنْسِيَّ أَصْبَحَ أَكْثَرَ انْتِشَارًا مُنْذُ أَنْ فَقَدَ جَيْشُ المَهْدِيِّ السَّيْطَرَةَ عَلَى مَدِينَةِ الصَّدْرِ، وَكَذَلِكَ بِسَبَبِ انْتِشَارِ

440

آلأَفْلَامِ الجِنْسِيَةِ، وَالقَنَوَاتِ الفَضَائِيَةِ، وَغِيَابِ الرَّقَابَةِ الحُكُومِيَةِ". وَيُشِيرُ تَقْرِيرٌ لِلأُمَمِ المُتَّحِدَةِ، صَدَرَ نِهَايَةَ عَام 2006، إِلَى أَنَّ عَنَاصِرَ بَعْضِ التَّنْظِيمَاتِ المُسَلَّحَةِ تَبْعَثُ بِرَسَائِلَ لِعَائِلَاتِ الشَّوَاذِ تُهَدِّدُهُم فِيهَا بِاسْتِهْدَافِ أَفْرَادٍ مِنَ العَائِلَةِ، إِذَا لَمْ يَتِمَّ تَسْلِيمُ الشَّاذِ إِلَيْهَا أَو تَصْفِيَتِه.

معناها	الكلمة
Gays	الشَّوَاذ
Parting hair	يُفَرِّقُ
Pierces	يَثْقُبُ
Powders, makeup	المَسَاحِيقَ
Sipping	إِرْتِشَاف
In public	عَلَى المَلَأ
Hairstylist	مُصَفِّف شَعْرٍ
Unusual	غَيرِ مَعْهُودَةٍ
Pervert	مُنْحَرِف
In the context of addressing	فِي إِطَارِ التَّصَدِي
Guided efforts	جُهُودٍ تَوْجِيهِيَةٍ
To eradicate	لِاسْتِئصَالِ شَأَفَة

Disgust	الاشْمِئْزَازَ
Liquidate him	تَصْفِيَتِهِ

أسئلة:

1. What is the literal meaning of 'a gay person' in Arabic?
2. Where do gay people usually congregate in Iraq?
3. What are the specific features of a typical Iraqi gay person?
4. Do they use make-up?
5. Do they talk in an effeminate manner?
6. Are they ashamed of who they are?
7. In which American newspaper was this article originally published ?
8. What is the date of this article's publication?
9. The article was published on which anniversary of the invasion of Iraq?
10. What is the name of the gay person interviewed for this article?
11. Why does he choose to be called by this version of his name?
12. How many of his closest friends were killed? When and where were they killed?
13. What does this young man do for a living?
14. Is it common in Iraq for young men to have long hair?
15. How many gay people who he knows have been killed?
16. Who are the usual suspects when gay people are murdered?
17. Were the tribes of gay people supportive of them?
18. What is the outcome of this?
19. How do the police distinguish gay people's corpses from others?
20. What other groups of people besides Shi'a death squads target gay people?
21. Do the police serve any role in cracking down on gay people?
22. Is homosexuality illegal?
23. What is the role of religious scholars or imams in forming public perceptions of gay people?
24. Under what conditions can gay people be arrested ?
25. Is the population of gay people in Iraq increasing or decreasing?
26. Why is the killing of gay people not given more prominence in the media?
27. What type of punishment should gay people receive according to Grand Ayatollah Sistani's fatwa?

28. Does the spread of porn, satellite TV and the absence of tight government control increase the homosexuality?

29. How do armed groups threaten the families of gay people?

العَلَف دَاخِلَ الرُولزرُويس

A luxury car manufacturer is suing an Arab citizen because he is doing something with the luxury car that does not fit in with the company's image.

قَامَتْ صَانِعَةُ السَّيَّارَاتِ البِرِيطَانِيَةِ "رُولز رُويس" بِتَقْدِيمِ طَلَبِ مُحَاكَمَةِ مُوَاطِنٍ إِمَارَاتِي فِي مَحْكَمَةِ أَبُوظَبِي وَذَلِكَ لِقِيَامِهِ بِتَحْمِيلِ العَلَفِ وَالبَرْسِيمِ فَوقَ وَدَاخِلَ السَّيَّارَةِ، وَقَدْ أَرْسَلَتْ وَكَالَةُ أَبُوظَبِي مُوتُورز وَكِيلَ شَرِكَةِ رُولْز رُويس فِي مَدِينَةِ أَبُوظَبِي أَحَدَ مَسْؤُولِيهَا إِلَى المُوَاطِنِ لِإِجْبَارِهِ عَلَى التَّوَقُّفِ عَنْ هَذَا الفِعْلِ وَالَّذِي يُعْتَبَرُ اِنْقَاصًا لِسَيَّارَةِ رُولْز رُويس الجَدِيدَةِ مِنْ نَوعِ رِيث، الشَّرِكَةُ قَدَّمَتْ لَهُ العَدِيدَ مِنَ الخَيَارَاتِ مِنْ ضِمْنِهَا شِرَاءُ السَّيَّارَةِ غَيرَ أَنَّهُ رَفَض.

وَيَقُولُ المُوَاطِنُ أَنَّ السَّيَّارَةَ حَصَلَ عَلَيهَا هَدَيَّةً مِنْ اِبْنِهِ حَيثُ يَعْمَلُ المُوَاطِنُ فِي تِجَارَةِ الإِبِلِ وَلَهُ سُمْعَةٌ كَبِيرَةٌ بَينَ أَبْنَاءِ مَدِينَةِ أَبُوظَبِي فِي الإِبِلِ وَالمُتَاجَرَةِ فِيهَا وَالمُشَارَكَةِ فِي المُسَابَقَاتِ بِهَا، وَلَازَالَتْ الشَّرِكَةُ فِي صَدَدِ العَمَلِ عَلَى القَضِيَةِ فِي مَحَاكِمِ مَدِينَةِ أَبُوظَبِي حَتَّى الآنَ.

معناها	الكلمة
Feed	العَلَف
Trial	مُحَاكَمَة
For having	لِقِيَامِه
To load	بِتَحْمِيلِ
Trefoil	البَرْسِيم
Officials	مَسْؤُولِيهَا
Citizen	المُوَاطِنِ

445

To force him	لِإجْبارِهِ
A reduction	إنْقَاصًا
Options	الخَيَارَاتِ
Good luck	حَظًّا سَعيداً
Including	مِنْ ضِمْنِهَا

أسئلة:

1. What is the name and the nationality of the car manufacturer?
2. What is the nationality of the Arab man being sued?
3. In which city is the case happening?
4. What was he accused of?
5. What is the option that the manufacturer's representative offered the man to stop the company's image being harmed?
6. Why do the company consider the way the man was using his car is harmful to their image?
7. What is the model of the car in question?
8. Did the car owner consent to the request of the car manufacturer?
9. How did the car owner acquire the car?
10. What does the car owner's son do for a living?
11. Has the issue been settled?
12. How do you think the man justifies using the car in this manner?

اَلشُّذُوذ

While gay people in Iraq have a hard time due to their lifestyle, the opposition to gay people in Egypt is not so severe: it is rare for anyone to be killed for being gay in Egypt. This conversation will expose you to the vocabulary that gay people typically use among themselves, and the kind of language that opponents to homosexuality often use; you will see both hostile and religious vocabularies regarding homosexuality. There is a mix of MSA and Egyptian colloquial vocabulary.

المَشْهَد: شَابٌ وَسِيمٌ يَتَبَخْتَرُ في مَشْيَتِهِ في شَارِعِ جَامِعَةِ الدُّوَلِ العَرَبِيَّةِ بِحَيِّ المُهَنْدِسِينْ الرَّاقِي في القَاهِرَةِ.

وَائِل: اِلْحَق يَاض يَاكَرِيمْ! شُوف المُزَّة اللِّي جَايَة هِنَاك دِي!

كَرِيم: فِين؟ أَنَا مِش شَايف يَعني وَحْدَة مَاشْيَة!!!

وَائِل: دَه أَجْمَد مِنْ أَي وَاحْدَة...بُص..العِينين والحَوَاجِب اللِّي تِسحر واللَّا رِقْتُهُ أَمُوتْ أَنَا.....

كَرِيم: اِيه دَه يَاعَم وَائِلْ ؟ اِنْتَ مِنْهُم واللَّا اِيه؟ لَا يَاعَم مَالِيش في الجَّو دَه، أَنَا مَاأَعْرَفْش إِنْ اِنْتَ كِدَه!!

وَائِل: قِشْطَة ...سِيبْلي القُطَّة دِي أَظَبَّطْهَا...

اِلْتَفَتَ أَحَدُ أَصْحَابِ المَحَالِ الذِي سَمِعَ الحِوَارَ مِنْ بِدَايَتِه...غَاضِباً

صَاحِبُ المَحَّلِ: أَسْتَغْفِر الله العَظِّيم يَارَب...أَعُوذُ بالله مِنْ غَضَب الله!

جَرَى اِيه في الدُّنْيَا!؟..يَاللَّا يَاض يَاخَوَّلْ مِنَّك لِيه ...يَاللَّا يَا وِلاَد الكَلْب مِنْ هِنَا...مِش عَاوِز خَلَقْكُم الغَبْرَة هِنَا...

وَائِل : جَرَى اِيه يَا عَم ! هُوَ حَد كَلِّمَك؟!

صَاحِبُ المَحَّلِ: نَعَمْ يَاخَوَّلْ !! غُور مِنْ هِنَا يَاض...أَنَا مِش فَاتِح مَعْرَسَة يَا مِعَرَّس اِنْتَ وهُوَ ...دِي مَنَاظِر رِجَالَة؟!...وانْتَ يَالاَ...يَاللِّي هِنَاك ..حَاطِطْ رُوج وعَامِل حَوَاجْبَك ومَسقَّط البَنْطَلُون وتِتْهَز يمِين وشِمَال..اِسْمَك اِيه يَالاَ؟ أَنَا بَشُوفَك هِنَا عَلَى طُولْ كُلْ يُوم بَعْد العِشَاء!

الشَّاذ بِدَلَال: يَاسم!...اِنْتَ مَالَك بِيَا يَا اِنْتَ؟

صَاحِبُ المَحَّلِ: طَبْ اِرْمِي اللَّبَانَة مِنْ بُقَّك يَامَدِيحَة واللَّاّ يَاسَمِيحَة اِنْتِ! دَه اِنْتَ مِتْزَّوق وَلاَ بَنَات الجَّامْعَة...غُور يَا حَيَوَانْ يَاخَوَّل مِنْ هِنَا لَا جِيبْكُم مِنْ شَعْرُكُم الطَّويل دَه أَمْسَح بِيه رَصِيف الشَّارع...اِحْنَا نَاقْصِين نَجَاسَة يَاولاَد الكَلْب؟!

مَشَى الجَمِيعُ بَعِيدًا عَنْ صَاحِبِ المَحَّلِ ...

كَرِيم: عَاجَبَك كِدَه التَّهْزِيق دَه؟! وعَشَان اِيه؟

وَائِل: المُزَّة اِسمَهَا اِيه؟

أَزَالَ الشَّاذُ شَعرَهُ مِنْ عَلَى وَجهِهِ بِدَلَالٍ كَمَا تَفْعَلُ الفَتَيَاتُ قَائِلاً

الشَّاذ: اِسمِي دِينَا...يَاهِيرُو اِنتَ...يَاي تِجَنِّن..عِندَك مَطرَح يَا....؟

كَرِيم: لَا لَا ...أَنَا مَاشِي...أَنَا غَلْطَان اِنِّي آمْشِي مَعَاك بَعْد كِدَه.

وَائِل: كَرِيم...اِستَنَّى ...أَنَا بَاعمِل كِدَه غَضب عَنِّي..مِش عَارِف لِيه؟

وعَارِف اِنَّك مِش كِدَه وَمَاطَلَبْتِش مِنَّك تِكُون كِدَه..بَس مَاتِزْعَلْش.

فِي أَثْنَاءَ ذَلِكَ فُوجِئَ الجَمِيعُ بِرَجُلٍ مُسِّنٍ يَتَدَخَّلُ فِي الحِوَار...

الشَّيخ: السَّلَام عَلِيكُم يَاوِلَاد.. أَنَا سَامِع كَلَامْكُم مِنْ بَدْرِي ...مِنْ لَمَّا خَرَجْت مِنْ الجَامِع...أَنَا خَايف عَلِيكُم مِنْ خُسَارة الدُّنْيَا والآخَرَة..اللِّي اِنتُو بِتعْمِلُوه دَه فِعْل قَوم سَيِّدنَا لُوط اللِّي أَهْلَكَهُم رَبَّنَا بِعَذَابِه...يَاوِلَاد رَبَّنَا خَلَق مِنْ كُل مَخْلُوق ذَكَر وَأُنْثَى حَتَّى النَّبَات...وخَلَقْكُم رِجَالَة فِيكُو طَاقَة وصِحَّة عَشَان تُسْتَخْدَم فِي مَكَانْهَا الصَّحِيح...مَكَان الحَرْث والنَّسْل...دَه حَتَّى البَهَايم مَابِتعْمِلَش كِدَه أَبَدًا...صَحِيح الاِنْسَان ظَالِم لِنَفْسُه.

كَرِيم: لَا يَاسَيِّدنَا الشَّيخ ..أَنَا مِش كِدَه...أَنَا مَاكُنْتِش أَعْرَف حَاجَة...

الشَّيخ: يَاإِبْنِي ..أَنَا مِش بَحَاسِبْكُم ...الحِسَاب عَنْد رَب الحِسَاب..أَنَا مِسْتَخْسَرْكُم فِي الضَّيَاع والنَّجَاسَة...اِنْتُو الأَمَل بِتَاع النَّهَارْدَة وبُكْرَة...

اِنْتُو عَارْفِين الأَمْرَاض وضَعْف الصِّحَة مِن القَرَف دَه غِير غَضَب الله وسُخْطُه عَلِيكُم..والنَّفَس مَعْدُود وَمَاحَدِّش عَارِف الأَجَل اِمْتَى؟

تِمُوتُ عَالمَعْصِية؟!!!!

وَائِل وَهُوَ يَبْكِي بُكَاءً حَادًا: أَنَا خَلَاص ضَايع ضَايع يَاسِيدِنَا الشِّيخ ...أَنَّ عَمَلْتْ بَلَاوِي كِتِير وفَاتْ الأَوَان...

الشِّيخ: اِسْتَهْدَى بَالله يَابْنِي...رَبِّنَا قَال فِي كِتَابِه الكَرِيم:" وَالَّذِينَ إِذَا فَعَلُوا فَاحِشَةً أَوْ ظَلَمُو أَنْفُسَهُم ذَكَرُوا اللَّهَ فَاسْتَغْفَرُوا لِذُنُوبِهِمْ وَمَنْ يَغْفِرُ الذُّنُوبَ إِلَّا اللَّهُ وَلَمْ يُصِرُّوا عَلَى مَا فَعَلُوا وَهُمْ يَعْلَمُونَ"...تُوبْ اِنْتَ وَرَبِّنَا بِينَادِيك تِرْجَع لِطَرِيق الحَقّ...وَلَمَّا تِلَاقِي نَفْسَك فِي طَاعْتُه وتِحِسْ اِن رَبِّنَا رِضِي عَنَك ...اِتْوَكِّل عَلَى الله واتْجَوِّز...وكَمِّل نُص دِينَك فِي حَلَال رَبِّنَا وِبالحَلَال....

وَائِل: بِيسْلَم بُقَّك يَاحَاج...رَبِّنَا يَسَرَك فِي طَرِيقِي عَشَانْ أَحِس اِن لِسَّه فِي أَمَل فِيَا...يَالَّا بِينَا عَالجَامِع نِتْوَضَّا ونْصَلِّي رَكْعِتِين تُوبَة ونَدَم وصِدْق العَهْد مَعَ الله....ويَارِيت يَاأَخ دِينَا تِفَكَر اِنْتَ كَمَان وتْبَطَّل تِغْوِي الشَّبَاب وتوَقَّعْهُم وتُقَع فِي نَار مَالْهَاش قَرَار..شَبَابَك مَحْسُوب عَلَيك...ومُمْكِنْ تِمُوت مُوتة الكِلَاب..وَالا تُقَعْ فِي اِيد بَلْطَجِي مَابِيرْحَمْش..ويبْقَى لَادُنْيَا ولَاآخَرَة..أَسْتَغْفِرُ الله وَأَتُوب اِليه ....

الكلمات الجديدة

معناها	الكلمة
Scene	المَشْهَد
Handsome young man	شَابٌّ وَسِيمٌ
Strutting / parading	يَتَبَخْتَر
The way he walks	مَشْيَتِه
Hurry up!	اِلْحَق

450

Oh, boy	يَاض
Hot / beautiful woman	المُزَّة
Literally, 'solid': this means someone is very attractive, and is used in the comparative ('hotter')	أَجْمَد
Cast a spell (metaphorically, as her eyebrows have cast a spell on him)	اللِّي تِسْحِر
Or	وَاللَّا
His tenderness	رِقتُهُ
To die for	أَمُوتْ أَنَا
Are you one of them?	اِنتَ مِنهُم
Or what?	وَاللَّا ايه
I am not into that. Literally, 'I am not into this weather / atmosphere'	مَاليشْ في الجَّو دَه
I didn't know you were like that	أَنَا مَاأَعْرَفْش اِنْ اِنتَ كِدَه
Cream	قِشْطَة
Let me fix this cat (usually referring to a beautiful person; 'fix' could also be 'calibrated'. It means that he will get *her* to do what he wants, usually sexually)	سِيبْلِي القُطَّة دِي أَظَبَّطْهَا
The store owner	صَاحِبُ المَحَّل
I beg the forgiveness of Allah the greatest, oh Lord	أَسْتَغْفَر الله العَظِّيم يَارَب
I don't know what the world is coming to!	جرَى ايه في الدُّنْيَا
Keep moving, all you faggot boys	يَاللَّا يَاض يَاخَوَل مِنَّك لِيه

Keep moving away from here, you sons of dogs	يَاللَّا يَا ولَاد الكَلْب مِنْ هِنَا
I don't need your dusty features here ('dusty' could also be 'ashen', an insult in the Arab world)	مِش عَاوِز خِلَقْكُم الغَبْرَة هِنَا
Does anyone talk to you?	هُوَ حَد كَلِّمَك
I am not running a whore house, you two!	أَنَا مِش فَاتِح مَعْرَسَة يَا معَرَّس اِنْتَ وهُوَ
Is this what men look like? (ridiculing the way the gay people look)	دِي مَنَاظِر رِجَالَة
Lipstick	رُوج
Did you do your eyebrows?	وعَامِلْ حَواجْبَك
And your pants are sagging (when your trousers are around your thighs)	مسَقَّط البَنْطَلُون
And shaking right and left (referring to the gay people shaking their buttocks in a feminine manner)	وتِتْهَز يِمين وشِمَال
Oh poison (usually said by women as an expression of mild displeasure of someone who is flirting with her; hence it is used by gay men when they imitate the way women talk)	يَاسِم
Stop bothering me (literally, 'why are you so into my business, oh you?')	اِنْتَ مَالَك بِيَا يَا اِنْتَ
Oh you (when this pronoun comes at the end of a phrase, it is indicative of a female addressing someone – this is why the gay people use it)	يَا اِنْتَ
OK, spit the chewing gum from your mouth, MadiHa (the man insults the gay person by calling him by a female name; chewing gum	طَبْ اِرْمِي اللِّبَانَة مِنْ بُقَّك يَامَدِيحَة

is usually a female habit in Arab culture because it can seem sexually appealing)	
Or you, SamiHa (another female name)	اللأ يَاسَمِيحَة اِنْتِ
You're dolled up better than university girls (another insult, as university girls supposedly wear lots of make-up)	دَه اِنْتَ مِتْزَوَّق وَلاَ بَنَات الجَامْعَة
Get the hell outta here, you faggot animal	غُور يَا حَيَوَانْ يَاخَوَل
Or I will pull you by your long hair	لاَ جِيبْكُم مِنْ شَعْرُكُم الطَّوِيل دَه
I will mop the sidewalk / pavement with it	أَمْسَح بِيه رَصِيف الشَّارِع...
Filth is the last thing we need, you sons of dogs	اِحْنَا نَاقْصِين نَجَاسَة يَاولاَد الكَلْبْ.
Do you like the way they are humiliated?	عَاجْبَك كِدَه التَّهْزِيق دَه
What is the hot woman's name? (She is spoken to in the third person, a sign of respect in Arabic)	المُزَّة اِسْمَهَا اِيه
Dina	دِينَا
Oh hero, you!	يَاهِيرُو اِنْتَ
You are driving me crazy	يَاي تِجَنِّن
Do you have a place?	عنْدَك مَطْرَح يَا
I would be at fault if I were to go out with you again	أَنَا غَلْطَان اِنِّي آَمْشِي مَعَاك بَعْد كِدَه
Wait	اِسْتَنَّى
I'm doing that in spite of myself	أَنَا بَاعمِل كِدَه غَضْب عَنِّي
I know you are not like that	وعَارِف اِنَّك مِشْ كِدَه
And I didn't ask you to be like that	وَمَاطَلَبْتِش مِنَّك تِكُون كِدَه

Everyone was surprised	فُوجِئَ الجَمِيعُ
With an old man	بِرَجُلٍ مُسِّنٍ
He joined in the conversation	يَتَدَخَّلُ فِي الحِوَار
I was listening to you for a while	أَنَا سَامِع كَلَامْكُم مِنْ بَدْرِي
I'm worried that you'll lose life on earth and in the hereafter	أَنَا خَايف عَلِيكُم مِنْ خُسَارة الدُّنْيَا والآخِرَة
What you are doing is the deed of the people of our Lord Lot, who were destroyed by God's punishment	اللِّي إِنْتُو بِتعْمِلُوه دَه فِعْل قَوم سَيِّدْنَا لُوط اللِّي أَهْلَكَهُم رَبِّنَا بِعَذَابُه
God created every creature as a male and female, even plants	رَبِّنَا خَلَق مِنْ كُل مَخْلُوق ذَكَر وَأَنْثَى حَتَّى النَّبَات
And he created you as men	وخَلَقْكُم رِجَالَة
You have energy and health so you can use it in its right place	فِيكُو طَاقَة وصِحَة عَشَانْ تُسْتَخْدَم فِي مَكَانْهَا الصَّحِيح
To cultivate the land and reproduce (i.e. getting married and having children)	مَكَانْ الحَرْث والنَّسْل
Even cattle would not condescend to do that! (Cows are a lowly animal in Arab culture; in English we might use pigs instead)	دَه حَتَّى البَهَايم مَابِتعْملَش كِدَه أَبَدًا
It is true that a human being is always doing unjust acts to himself	صَحِيح الإِنْسَان ظَالِم لِنَفْسُه
I am not holding you accountable	أَنَا مِش بَحَاسْبكُم
Reckoning is done by the God of reckoning	الحِسَابْ عَنْد رَب الحِسَاب
I mourn the way the squandered your life on filth and waste	أَنَا مِسْتَخْسَرْكُم فِي الضَّيَاع والنَّجَاسَة
You are today and tomorrow's hope	إِنْتُو الأَمَل بِتَاع النَّهَارْدَة وبُكْرَة

Allah's ire and wrath is on you	غَضَب الله وسُخْطُه عَلِيكُم
Our breaths are numbered, and no one knows when the end will come	والنَّفَس مَعْدُود وماحَدِّش عَارِف الأَجَل إمْتَى
You will die whilst committing a sin	تِمُوت عَالمَعْصِية
He is wailing (literally, 'crying sharply')	يَبْكِي بُكَاءً حَادًا
It's over for me; I am totally doomed ('doomed' is expressed by saying 'lost' twice, an Arabic way of stressing a word)	أَنَا خَلَاص ضَايِع ضَايِع
I did a lot of crimes and it's too late to save me	أَنَ عَمَلْت بَلَاوِي كِتِير وفَاتْ الأَوَان
Let Allah guide you	اِسْتَهْدَى بَالله يَابْنِي
Rely on Allah and get married	اِتْوَكِّل عَلَى الله واتْجَوِّز
And complete the second half of your religion in the Lord's lawful manner	وِكَمِّل نُص دِينَك فِي حَلَال رَبِّنَا وِبِالحَلَال
Say that again! It's music to my ears! I like the sound of that (in Arabic, 'may your mouth be saved')	يِسْلَم بُقَّك يَاحَاج
Our Lord made our encounter possible	رَبِّنَا يَسَرك فِي طَرِيقِي
So I can feel that there is still hope in me	عَشَان أَحِسْ إنْ لِسَّه فِي أَمَل فِيَا
Let's go to the mosque to perform absolution and pray 2raqah	يَالًّا بِينَا عَالجَامِع نِتْوَضَّأ ونْصَلِّي رَكْعتِين
Repent and regret, and keep your promise with God	تُوبَة ونَدَم وصِدْق العَهْد مَع الله
And stop tempting young men and entrapping them	وتْبَطَّل تِغْوِي الشَّبَاب وتوَقَّعْهُم
You will fall into a bottomless fire	وتُقَع فِي نَار مَالْهَاش قَرَار
Your youth will be marked against you	شَبَابك مَحْسُوب عَلِيك

It's possible to die the death of a dog	وَمُمْكِنْ تِمُوتْ مُوتة الكِلاَبْ
Or you'll fall into the hands of merciless thug	وَالا تُقَعْ في اِيد بَلْطَجِي مَابِيرْحَمْش
And then there'll be no life on earth or hereafter (i.e. the person will enjoy neither lives because of his sins: the way he dies will be gruesome, and he will be punished in the afterlife too)	ويْبْقَى لَادُنْيَا ولاَآخْرَة
I beg Allah for forgiveness and I repent to Him	أَسْتَغْفِرُ الله وَأَتُوب اِليه

أسئلة:

1. What is the name of the street where this scene takes place? In which city?
2. According to the gay man, what is the most attractive feature of the man approaching?
3. Is the gay man's friend also gay?
4. What is the person who gets upset with the gay men do for a living?
5. Is this gay person familiar to him?

| Morphological Scale | الميزان الصرفي |

Historical background

Almizan al sarfy, which means the morphological scale, was established by an ascetic and devout Arab Imam of Arabic language and literature, al-Farāhīdī (718-786), his researches and studies were motivated by his the desire to communicate and teach the Arabic language and Koran , which were prompted by the spread of Islam and the encountering of new culture and way of life of the new Muslims and the urgency of introducing the new language to them in a systematic and logical way and to ease their adoption of the Arabic language for those who wish to do so.

Language can be both functional and aesthetic. It is functional when you express a desire for something, or if you are exchanging greetings, or if you are giving orders, and so on. There is a purpose to this use of language. Language can also be aesthetic. This occurs most commonly in works of literature, where descriptive passages and metaphors are created for the readers' pleasure.

His search led him to surveying of Arabic language of which he found that most of its verbs consists of three letters, that carry similar vowels and the vowels can play a rule in the general meaning of each verb

He also notice that words larger numbers of letters are also derived from these three letters after augmented by other letters, which he also isolated and identified.

he also saw a pattern: how that "enlarged" words that has some of these ten letter follow certain patterns in the starting with similar letters, and carry similar vowel marks, and has similar meanings.

These findings were great for several reasons:

there will be no need for introducing new non-Arabic word into the language , since Arabic ability to accommodate the new meaning was one of the utmost importance of this finding which help keeping the language pure from foreign words that untimely can reshape it

Correct pronunciation of both old and new words

The ability to trace the origin of new words and build upon the old for new words,

Since Arabs historically known as the best poets, a method similar to prosody were invented to help in applying this method.

Therefore, he invented the scale; the word scale also means prosody and meter. So the words in question should match/rhyme with/has the same weight as something that can be compared to. And since they are comparing words, it should be a word. He choose a word that has the meaning of "doing", see فَعَلَ above, which is considered perfect choice, for the following reasons:

1. These letters constitute the word "doing" which a suitable reference to a verb, also the Arabic word for verb is spelled using these three letters.
2. The points of articulation of these three letters utilize the three main parts of the mouth, the back for ع , the lips/ the front for the ف , and the middle for the ل .
3. These three letters are not one of what is called "weak letters" in Arabic, and they are alif, waaw and yaa, since they can changed into different letters when they are subject to certain grammar condition.
4. They are three letters, which match the three letter verbs that are the most prevalent in the Arabic language.

Each letter of the word in question should match that of the reference word, see below

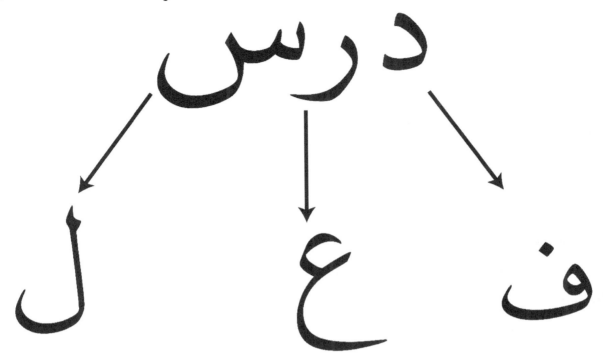

The simplest form of trilateral verbs in Arabic consists of three letters and the pattern of these three letters is "fa3ala".

As you can see, the "ف" in the pattern refers to the first letter of the verb, the ع refers to the middle letter of the verb and the "ل" refers to the last letter of the verb, and this holds for any simple trilateral verb.

The first letter will be called the "ف" of the verb, the second letter will be called the "ع" of the verb and the last letter will be the "ل" of the verb. The "ف", in other words, refers to the first letter of any trilateral verb. So, for the verb "kataba" (to write/he wrote), Arabs will not refer to the first letter as a "kaaf", but as the "ف" of the verb. When you refer to the last letter in the verb "kataba", you will call it the "ل" of the verb. So, if you were to say "place a dumma on the 'ف' of the verb", you will place a dumma on the first letter of whatever verb you are dealing with.

Arabic language does not have two letters verbs, only three or four.

Building وزن pattern when all letters are original in a trilateral verbs.

It is easy to build a pattern when all letters are original; you simply match the actual letters with the pattern letters فعل as you saw previously. First, match the letter, then the vowel. Letters of the verb that match the pattern's ف , ع , and ل , should all be original letters

Question:

Please write the وزن of each of following verbs:

كَرُمَ	سَمِعَ	نَصَرَ

Letters of increase:

Letters of increase are called in Arabic "hourouf al ziada" حُرُوفُ الزِّيَادَةِ.

They are ten letters. See them below.

These letters could be part of the letters that constitute a word along with its original letters.

A noun can have up to four extra letters of increase, a trilateral verb can have up to three, and quad literal verb can have up to two.

Letters of increase can occur anywhere in a noun, affixed or prefixed in verbs.

Why is it called letters of increase حُرُوْفُ الْزِيَاْدَةِ ?

Increase refers to increase in meanings; it is believed that the more letters added to the basic trilateral verb, the more meanings, in addition to its original meaning, the new verb carry.

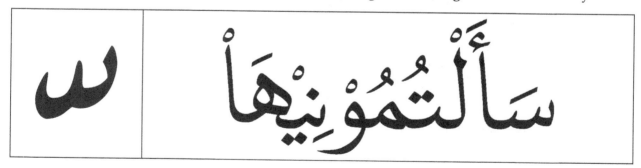

The literal meaning of the phrase above is, 'you asked me about it'.

السين والهمزة واللام والتاء والميم والواو والنون والياء والهاء والألف

The above word combines the ten "letters of increase" حُرُوْفُ الْزِيَأْدَةِ that could be inserted before or inside the trilateral verb to build verbal forms and new words on form I. This word means, "'you asked me about it'" (sa'altumuniha). Please notice that the whole phrase is written as one word. This phrase was invented to assist in memorizing the ten "letters of increase".

Building وزن **a pattern when some of letters are hourouf al ziada** حُرُوْفُ الْزِيَأْدَةِ.

These letters should be placed in the pattern of the orginal letters in the order they occur in the word with the same vowels mark as in the word, not the pattern, they also should pronounced as they are, i.e. miim as a miim, unlike when replacing original letters of verbs with ف, ع and ل. The letters of increase cause specific changes to root words. In order to build a pattern of a word that has taken on letters of increase, first determine where the 'faa', '3yn' and 'laam' of the original word are.

This is the basic trilateral form I pattern. Then look at the longer word – determine again where the three original letters are and highlight the letters of increase. The letters of increase and their positioning on the root letters will show you how the pattern has been built from the original letters. Remember to use the 'faa', '3yn' and 'laam' with the letters of increase when you build this pattern.

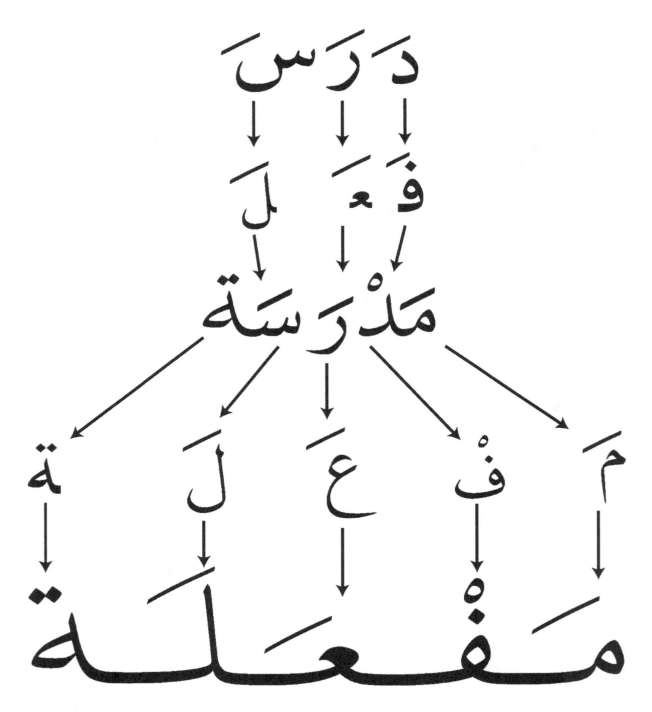

Below, you will see a number of words in the first row and their pattern below in a table. You will see that what all patterns have in common is that they contain the original pattern of the trilateral verb of each word and the rest are letters of increase. Notice that not all the words in the first row are verbs. Some are verbal nouns and others are regular nouns. It is very easy to deduce from these words the original trilateral verb by removing the letters of increase. If you know the meaning of the original trilateral root and have learned the way letters of increase effect this original meaning, you will be able to surmise the meaning of new words by being

462

able to identify the "ف", the "ع" and the "ل" of the verb as well as being able to recognize the pattern the word takes.

أفعل	تفعّل	افتعل	انفعل	استفعل	إفعال	افتعال	انفعال	استفعال	مفعال
أحسن	تفضّل	أقتطع	إنهزم	استغفر	إحسان	اختطاف	انكسار	استغفار	مصباح

Question:

Please write the وزن of each of following verbs:

	انْفَتَحَ		افْتَتَحَ		تَفَاتَحَ	تَفَتَّحَ	
	انْفَهَمَ		افْتَهَمَ		تَفَاهَمَ	تَفَهَّمَ	
	انْخَلَطَ		اخْتَلَطَ		تَخَالَطَ	تَخَلَّطَ	
	انْحَفَظَ		احْتَفَظَ		تَحَافَظَ	تَحَفَّظَ	
	انْأَمَرَ		ائْتَمَرَ		تَآمَرَ	تَأَمَّرَ	
	انْقَتَلَ		اقْتَتَلَ		تَقَاتَلَ	تَقَتَّلَ	
	انْرَفَعَ		ارْتَفَعَ		تَرَافَعَ	تَرَفَّعَ	
	انْبَعَدَ		ابْتَعَدَ		تَبَاعَدَ	تَبَعَّدَ	
	انْسَبَقَ		اسْتَبَقَ		تَسَابَقَ	تَسَبَّقَ	
	انْعَفَنَ		اعْتَفَنَ		تَعَافَنَ	تَعَفَّنَ	

Adding one or more of these letters to a verb will give it a new meaning.

TuDعeef تَضْعِيْف

These ten letters are not the only way to give a verb different meaning. Shaddah will also have an effect on expanding the meaning of a word; it is called in Arabic TuDعeef تضعيف, which literally means doubling, and it refers to placing a shaddah on one of the original letters of the verb. All letters of the Arabic alphabet can carry a shaddah except the letter alif.

Giving a new meaning to a verb is not the only purpose of adding these letters to a verb, some are added are for phonetic reasons, as to give a long vowel sounds to certain word, notice that the three long vowel letters alif, waaw and yaa are part of the letters of increase. Another reason is to using them as a replacement for a letter that has been elided because it is one of the weak letters, again alif, waaw and yaa.

463

When a سَأَلْتُمُونِيْها letter should be consider a letter of increase and when it should not

The ten letters combine in the word سَأَلْتُمُونِيْها should not always be considered a letter of increase and be remove or insert in a pattern:

1. All letters that denote a present tense verb, alif, nuun, yaa, and taa, despite being listed in the letters of increase group, are not considered letters of increase when they are parts of a verb conjugated in the present tense.

2. All letters that carry a meaning of their own, (part of the letters with meaning) are not considered letters of increase, for example: the letter nuun when it comes as a pronoun i.e. النساء ذهبن the women are gone, there nuun is a pronoun and it used as the subject of these sentences, and therefore should not be considered a letter of increase.

3. In addition, there are verbs that consists entirely of the letters of increase, i.e. the verb "he asked" سأل, this does not mean that the verb does not exist. Therefore, when you remove the letters of increase form a word there should be at least three or four letters remaining.

Rules of determining when a letter in the word سألتمونيها will be considered a letter of increase:

In order to determine when a letter will be a letter of increase you need to understand first when a letter will not be, i.e. original.

Original letters

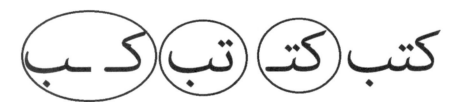

Original letters are letters that are essential to the meaning of a word, removing any will render a word meaningless, and affect its grammatical function. Here you see the verb kataba (he wrote); taking out any letter will making it meaningless from its intended meaning. You will find these original letters in all of their derived forms and in their original order. It is easier for an Arab to determine which letter is a letter of increase due to his vast knowledge of vocabulary and his knowledge of the ten letters of increase. These are grouped into the word سألتمونيها He will remove the suspicious letter(s); if the word still has meaning then this letter is extra. As you build your vocabulary, you will gradually adopt this method.

> A verb that has all of its letters as original is called in Arabic "al-fa3lu al-mujarradu", which means the stripped verb, which comprises verbs that have no less than 3 and no more than 5 letters. All original. "Al-fa3l al-mazeed", which means the increased verb, is a verb that has letter (s) of increased.

Letters of increase can be affixed to a word to 'increase' its meaning. The ten letters of increase are original letters in their own right as well as letters of increase. How do you recognize that a letter is a letter of increase? In this part, I will develop an understanding of these letters of increase. In the table below, the letters of increase are listed with a brief description of it. Each letter of increase comes with an example of the letter in context.

Letter of increase	Examples
Hamza is considered a letter of increase under this condition: when it comes only at the beginning of a word and is followed by three original letters. Please note that Hamza comes at the beginning of a word, always comes with an alif.	أعرِج، أفضل، أذهبُ، أقرِئُ.
Hamza is considered a letter of increase when it comes at the end of the word and is preceded by a vowelless alif and three original letters. (A vowelless alif is called a long vowel alif in Arabic when a letter with a fatHa precedes it.)	علماءُ، أنبياءُ، قُرُفصاءُ.
Hamza is considered an original letter in the words on the right.	أكْل، أمسْ، أمان، ماء، وفاء.
Alif, whether it is a long vowel alif, or alif maqsuarah, is considered a letter of increase when it comes in a word with three or more original letters.	قائل، قاتل، سحاب، حُبلى، قرطاس، انطلاق.
Alif maqsuarah comes as the seventh letter in a noun will be considered a letter of increase. If an alif comes in a word with just two original letters, it should be considered a replacement for a weak letter waaw or yaa.	أربُعاوى) قال، دعا، باب، ناب.
Waaw will never be considered a letter of increase when it comes at the beginning of a word. If it comes in the middle of a word with more than two original letters, it should be considered a letter of increase.	جدول، عجوز، ترقوة، عنفوان، قلنسوة، دولاب.
Yaa will be considered a letter of increase when it is in a word with more than two original letters.	يضرب، سيطر، رغيف، رفاهية، مغناطيس.
Yaa is an original letter in the word on the right.	يوم، ليلة، بيع، رمي.
Taa is considered a letter of increase when it comes as a verb conjugated in the present tense and in verb forms, you will be studying shortly, and which are easily identifiable. These form verbal nouns denoting intensiveness as you see in the last word on the right.	تكتب تخاصموا، احتربوا تكسَّر فعَّل تَسْيار.
Taa is considered a letter of increase when there is a feminine word ending, intensiveness, or plural. It is also considered a letter of increase when it is in a relational adjective word. Taa is	قائمة قامتْ داهية المغاربة

also considered a letter of increase as you see on the right, and forms verbal nouns.	الشافعية الحنفية.
Taa also conceded a letter of increase in forms on the right and their verbal nouns,	افتعل، استفعل
Taa is considered a letter of increase in the words on the right.	التِمْثَالُ، مَلَكُوْت، عَنْكَبُوْت
Siin is considered a letter of increase when it comes in form X.	اِستفعل
Laam is considered a letter of increase in the demonstrative pronouns shown on the right.	ذلك، تلك، هنالك
Miim will never be considered a letter of increase when it comes in a verb. It will be considered a letter of increase in nouns, verbal nouns starting with miim, Active Participle, Passive Participle, adverbs of time and place, and names of instruments. Here are examples of this grammatical rule on the right.	مَأْتَ المَجْلَس مَعْرَض – مَوْقِع مُقَأتِل – مُحْسِن-مُشَرِّع مُسْتَقْبَل – مَحْبُوْب -مُثَقَف مَدْرَسَةٌ مُسْتَشَارٌ مَوْعِدٌ مَطَأرٌ مِنْشَأرٌ
Nuun is considered a letter of increase when it is the first letter of a verb conjugated in the first person present tense, and in the pattern shown on the right. In addition, when it comes at the end of a word that has three original letters it is considered a letter of increase, as seen on the right.	نكتب انكسر، فَعَنْلَل سكران، عثمان، شبعان، عفّان.
If the situations above do not occur, nuun will be an original letter.	أمان عنقود
In certain words that are not allowed to have tanween, as you see on the right, the nuun is considered a letter of increase.	حسّان عفّان
haa is considered a letter of increase when it is added for the purpose of vowel placement and is the last letter articulated. See examples shown on the right. This type of haa is called the silent haa or vowelless haa. It is an extra haa added to the word for the purpose of protecting the last vowel mark from not being pronounced.	لمه؟ عمه؟ (أُم) أُمهات

Advantages of the morphological scale and of understanding verb patterns

1. Increase the ability to look up words in an Arabic dictionary. Words are listed by their original letters regardless of what letter the word starts with, i.e., school-madrasah should be listed under daal – darasa and not miim.

2. Distinguish between original letters and letters of increase in a word. This helps your deducing of derivative words such as the subject and the object of verbal sentence.

3. being able to correctly vocalize words according to their wazn.

4. Precision: choosing one verb form over the other that may have the same definition according to forms meanings. Example is the word earn; كَسَبَ, and اِكْتَسَبَ, both have the same meaning, the last one is earning with effort.

5. Ability to generate new words to fit modern times: washing machine, computers etc.

6. Brevity is the main advantage of this system. The main purpose of this system is to be able to use fewer words or even one word where without it you may need two or more words. An example is the word astghaferu Allah, asking Him for forgiveness.

7. Know exactly the true meaning of a word by belonging to certain forms.

8. Using the scale will reveal what is called in Arabic letter misplacement or placement reversal; where a letter in a singular word is not in the same order as it is expected, the scale will reveal that. I.e., the three letters ف , ع , and ل should come in that order; when they do not – ل ف and ع ; for example, it means that the out of order letter was subject to placement reversal.

9. Distinguish between trilateral, quadrilateral, and quintet verbs and nouns

10. Save time, since you do not have to list thousands of verbs or nouns individually, you can just refers to them by their patterns or forms. For example, in grammar books, types of plural are explained using the patterns of certain nouns; i.e. whenever you have a singular noun that has the pattern of فعلاء and its masculine has pattern of أفعل its plural will be فُعْل.

11. Great help for a speedy acquisition of vocabulary. Understanding verb patterns is of the utmost importance in learning Arabic. In addition, you will learn in you Arabic grammar study that places where the verb is performed, doer of the verb; for example, a player or a butcher are derived from their respective verbs: to play and to slaughter.

12. Expandable vocabulary that will not need the invention of new word to suit modern times. This expandability seems indefinite.

13. Know exactly the true meaning of a word by having the features of certain forms.

The meaning of verbs patterns

Each verb form in Arabic can give meanings in accordance with the patterns changes seen between forms. In the table below you will see the different meanings that verb forms can carry. There is, as expected, no one verb form contains all these different meanings; but two verb forms or more can give rise to the same meaning. Quite often, there is only one verb form that gives the relevant and precise meaning.

Form System

The most famous meanings of the increased forms of the trilateral verb

Arabic verbs are classified into ten different patters (there are more patterns, but these are seldom used). Each pattern we will call a "form", so we will have, (form I) form II form III, etc. Usually denoted with Roman numerals. Form one is the most basic form and contains only the three consonants of the root. The first consonant will have a fatHa, the last will have a fatHa, and the middle consonant may have fatHa, a dumma or a kasra. Forms II- X will give you a word that will have a different meaning, but one that is still related to form I.

No basic verb comprises all ten forms because sometimes, what would be there will not make sense in relation to the primordial meaning of the root found in the first form.

It is possible to find form one, the origin of all forms, is no longer in use, while the derived forms are. تكلم he talked.

Below, you will see the ten verb forms/patters for trilateral verbs.

	فَعِلَ / فَعُلَ /فَعَلَ
# Form I	
يَفْعَلُ أو يَفْعِلُ أو يَفْعُلُ	

This verb form can have any of the vowels on the medial consonant. In Arabic, we do not call it the medial letter. Arabs will usually call it the "ع" of the verb, by which they mean the second letter. This is because the second letter in the verb "fa3al- فعل" is "ع".

Also, please note that when this verb is conjugated in the present tense, the vowel mark on the medial consonant will remain the same.

Form I can appear in three different versions. The ع of the verb can carry any vowels; the ف and the ل of the verb will always have a fatHa.

Most of the meanings attributed to this verb are dictated by the vowel placed on the ع of the verb. When you have a dumma on the ع of the verb, the meaning will most likely refer to a feature or an attribution of the subject of the verb.

When a dumma is on the ع of the verb, the verb must be intransitive: it must therefore refer to a feature of the subject. For example, "the man shrunk / grew" or "the woman became prettier". This sounds long-winded – and not particularly pertaining to verbs – but these Arabic verbs contain the implications carried in English in adjectives.

When the fatHa is on the ع of the verb, the verb could be transitive or intransitive. This is the most common type of form I.

When the kasra is on the ع of the verb the verb could be transitive or intransitive, although more often the verb will be intransitive. Most meanings related to this type of verb are related to sickness and sad feelings and their opposites (joy, elation, etc.).

Form I denotes that the verb has happened one time. It gives the basic meaning of the verb and is done by someone, such as "Adam *studied* his lessons today". It also expresses the activity of the root or the general verbal meaning. For example, "he wrote" (kataba).

Form examples

Adam studied his lessons today.	دَرَسَ ادمُ دروسَ اليومِ.	دَرَسَ
Tom left the room.	خَرَجَ توم من الغرفةِ.	خَرَجَ

Mazen collected his toys off the ground.	جَمَعَ مازنٌ لُعَبَهُ من الأرضِ.	جَمَعَ
Allah helped the believers (in this context, this means that God made the believers victorious)	نَصَرَ اللَّهُ الْمُؤْمِنِينَ.	نَصَرَ
The teacher read the lesson.	قَرَأَ المُعَلِمُ الدرسَ.	قَرَأَ
The father sat on the chair.	جَلَسَ الأبُ على الكرسي.	جَلَسَ
The mask fell from the face of the traitor.	سَقَطَ القناع عن وجه العميل.	سَقَطَ

نَظَرَ	نَقَلَ	شَكَرَ	سَمَحَ	قَطَعَ	رَسَمَ	سَمَحَ	كَتَبَ	هَرَبَ

The translation of the verbs above goes from right to left: To escape, to write, to allow, to cut, to draw, to think, to transport, to look. Please note that all these are Arabic verbs in form I which have a fatHa over the medial letter and conjugated in the third person masculine singular "he" (هو).

Next, you will see the second two versions of form I where the medial letter carries a kasra or a dumma.

بَرِحَ	طَرِبَ	مَرِضَ	شَهِدَ	سَلِمَ	نَدِمَ	حَزِنَ	فَرِحَ	ضَحِكَ

Above you will see verbs in form I with a kasra under the second letter translated as follows from right to left: To laugh, to accept, to become sad, to regret, to be saved, to witness, to hear, to be elated (this verb means that someone becomes elated, but is usually connected to listening to music or singing), to leave.

$$\text{فَعُلَ}$$

حَدُبَ	بَلُغَ	شَرُفَ	قَرُبَ	بَؤُسَ	حَسُنَ	صَعُبَ	عَظُمَ	كَمُلَ

Above, you will see verbs in form I with a dumma over the second letter. The verbs are translated from right to left: To be completed, to become great, to be/become difficult, to be/become strong, to improve, to be/become near, to be honored, to reach/arrive (a destination), to provide sympathy/compassion.

$$\text{يَفْعَلُ أُو يَفْعِلُ أُو يَفْعُلُ}$$

يَقْطَعُ	يَسِمُ	يَنْثُرُ	يَرْسُمُ	يَسْقَطُ	يَجْلِسُ	يَقْرَأُ	يَجْمَعُ	يَخْرَجُ	يَدْرُسُ

The verbs above are conjugated in the present tense and are translated from right to left. To study, to leave, to collect, to read, to sit, to fall, to go, to disperse, to speak/write in prose, to allow, to cut.

Instances where form I is rarely used:

Form I usually denotes the origin or root form of a verb. So whenever you have a verb form different to form I, you can trace it back to its origin in form I. However, some verbs are rarely seen in form I. In the examples below, rare form I verbs are given, while the verbs on the right denote the form that is frequently used for that verb.

دَاهَمَ -------------------- دَهَمَ --------------- دَاهَمَ الجَيشُ حُصُونَ العَدو

The army stormed the enemy's fortified areas.

شَاغَبَ ------------- شَغَبَ ----------------- شَاغَبَ الوَلَدُ أَثْنَاءَ الدَّرس

The boy caused a disturbance during the lesson.

تَوَرَّطَ ------------- وَرَطَ ------------------ تَوَرَّطَ مُحَمَد فِي تَلْبِيَةِ طَلَبِ أَبِيهِ

Mohammed became involved in answering his father's requests.

لَفَّقَ --------------- لَفَقَ ------------------ لَفَّقَ الرَّجُلُ لِصَدِيقِهِ تُهْمَةً

The man fabricated an accusation against his friend.

سَهَمَ --------- سَاهَمَ ------------------- سَاهَمَ أَهْلُ الخَيرِ في عِلاجِ الطِّفْلَةِ

Kind people participated in the treatment of the female child.

شَرَكَ --------- شَارَكَ ------------------- شَارَكَ التَّلامِيذُ في تَزيينِ الصَّفِ

The students participated in decorating their classroom.

بَغَتَ ------- بَاغَتَ ------------------- بَاغَتَنِي خَالد بِسُؤَالِهِ

Khalid surprised me with his question.

سَرَعَ ----- أَسْرَعَ ------------------- أَسْرَعَ الطِّفْلُ الَى أُمِّهِ

The child went quickly to his mother.

سَفَرَ ----- سَافَرَ ------------------- سَافَرَت عُلا الَى أَمريكَا

Alaa travelled to America.

نَهَزَ ----- انْتَهَزَ ------------------- انْتَهَزَ أَحْمَدٌ الفُرْصَة

Ahmed took the opportunity.

دَخَرَ ---- ادَّخَرَ ------------------- ادَّخَرَ عُمَرٌ مَصْرُوفَهُ

Omar saved his stipend.

نَزَهَ ----- تَنَزَّهَ ------------------- تَنَزَّهَ طَارق في الحَدِيقَةِ

Tarek took a walk in the park.

| وَقَف | نَصَبَ | وَصَلَ | وَعَدَ | سَلِمَ | قَدِمَ | كَرُمَ | حَطَمَ | عَلِمَ | I |
| وَقَّف | نَصَّب | وَصَّل | وَعَّد | سلَّم | قَدَّم | كرَّم | حطَّم | علَّم | II |

Form II is distinguished from form I by a shaddah being placed on the ع of the verb. In the Arabic language, shaddah is associated with plurality: when a shaddah appears on a verb, it carries the connotations that the action of the verb is repeated. This is why the shaddah is used when you name professions. For example, take the verb 'najara', meaning 'to carve'. A carpenter ('najjar') carves repeatedly (it is his profession) and so in Arabic a shaddah is marked on the 'jiim'. The same rule applies to a painter ('rassam' from 'rasama', to paint), or someone who works in stationery ('warraq').

| وَرَّاق | رَسَّام | نَجَّار |

Further example of verbs changing their meaning to a professional or something being done repeatedly: 'to steal' is 'saraqa'. Someone who steals once is called a 'sareq'; placing a shaddah on the 'raa' changes the meaning to 'professional thief' – or someone who often steals – ('sarraq'), because he steals repeatedly. سَرَّاق/سَأرِق

Therefore, placing a shaddah on the ف of the verb indicates that verb is performed repeatedly – this is contrasted with form I, which is always done once. For example, 'qatar3' means 'to cut' (once); 'qatta3' means 'to shred' or cut repeatedly.

The second feature of form II is how it changes intransitive verbs into transitive verbs, and transitive verbs into double intransitive. For example:

| The one who passed the exam was happy. / I made the one who passed the exam happy. | فَرَّحْتُ اَلنَّاجِحَ. | فَرِحَ اَلنَّاجِحُ. |

| قَطَّعَ سَارَة اللَّحْمَ | قَشَّرَ آدَمَ التُّفَّاحَ |

Form II: means that the verb is frequently done, repeatedly done, or expresses intensiveness. When you try to compare the meanings of this verb form with the English translations, you will find that they do not quite match. For example, when you say, "Adam peeled the apple" or "Sara cut the meat into small pieces", there will be the impression that this verb has been done

473

repeatedly, not just a single peel action nor a single slice. If Sara cut the meat once, you would use form I, but when you cut it into small pieces, it is implied that there is repetition of the same action. In English, the translation of these verbs may not give the impression that the subject is doing the verb frequently, repeatedly, or with intensiveness. However, in Arabic, when you say for instance that "he peeled some fruit", you will use form II, because the person, when he peels the fruit, will have done the verb multiple times. Note: do not confuse this form with the English progressive or continuous aspect: this Arabic form specifies repetition, whereas the English progressive aspect denotes action happening at the time of speaking or writing.

Another example of form II is "the teacher divided the students into groups". In English, when you say, "divided", there is the impression that the verb is done once. Whenever an Arab is trying to find a verb to express an action that was done repeatedly, he will naturally choose form II.

Another meaning of form II is 'nesba'. This is when, for example, a judge deems a testimony false; or when people declare 'zaid' (infidel). This is when someone is thought to be an atheist. Form II also carries the meaning of 'removal'. You will encounter this when you remove the peel from fruit.

Removal: In the example you will see, 'I removed the ambiguity from the book.' (Removing the ambiguity from the book means that the letters requiring dots have been dotted.)	أَعْجَمْتُ اَلْكِتَابَ

This form can also be used when you talk about travel and directions: if you are headed / bound for somewhere. For example, 'sharraqa' شَرَّقَ means he went east and 'gharraba' غَرَّبَ means he went west. This is mainly used in the intransitive mode.
Another important facet of this form is its capacity to replace long phrases. The Islamic declaration of faith, "La ilaha illallah", can be replaced simply by 'hallal'; "Subḥana'llāh" by saying 'sabbaHa'.

These truncated words	means
هَلَّلَ	لا إله الا الله
سَبَّحَ	سُبْحان الله
To praise, glorify, extol, laud, eulogize Allah	
كَبَّرَ	اللهُ أكبر
لَبَّى	لَبَّيْكَ
Here I am! At your service	
أَمَّن	آمين
Amen	

فَعَّلَ

Adam **peeled** the apple.	قَشَّرَ ادمُ التفاحةَ.	قَشَّرَ
Sara **cut** the meat into small pieces.	قَطَّعَتْ سارةُ اللحمَ قطعاً صغيرةً.	قَطَّعَ
The teacher **divided** the pupils into groups.	قَسَّمَ المعلمُ التلاميذَ الى مجموعاتٍ.	قَسَّمَ
The judge **did not believe** your testimony.	كَذَّبَ القاضي شهادتَك.	كَذَّبَ
The mother **nursed** her sick son.	مَرَّضَت الأمُ ابنها المريضَ.	مَرَّضَ

In the sentence, "The judge did not believe your testimony", we use form II that has been derived from form I of the verb "to lie". You may ask yourself why form II (which we explained means something done repeatedly) is used, when form I means to lie. Does this mean that the verb given here should translate into "he lies repeatedly"?

According to the rules, it should indeed mean, "he lies repeatedly". When you change the verb 'kazaba' (to lie) into form II, the meaning changes to "accuse somebody of lying". When you accuse somebody of lying, you have the counter effect of lying; i.e. you belie the lie. For example, if Mark lies when he says, "I gave you fifty dollars," you (in effect) lie to the lie to come to the truth. "No, I didn't," would accuse Mark of lying – belying his lie.

You will encounter some form II verbs that look similar to form I verbs, but have the opposite meaning. This sounds strange in English but is how form II of 'kazaba' is created in Arabic!
To recap, form II can be split into two types of verbs: verbs that have their form I counterpart, and means it is done repeatedly; and verbs that have the opposite meaning of their form I counterparts due to negating a negative verb.

Many verbs come under this latter category. We will give you the paradigm of this apparently contradictory meaning. The final example in the box above is, "the mother nursed her sick son". Can you think why form II of the verb "to be sick" is used here to mean "to nurse"? In the above example, the negative verb "lie" was countered and the meaning "accuse" or "disbelieve" arose. Here the negative verb "be sick" is countered and the positive meaning "nurse" is produced. The mother is being sick to her son's illness, you could say.

This is could be difficult for non-Arabic speakers to understand because there is no equivalent in English. Another way to think of this verb group is the 'double negative' rule in English – 'I haven't got no money' means 'I have got some money'.

هَلَّلَ	كَسَّرَ	صَعَّبَ	صَمَّمَ	صَدَّقَ

$$يُفَعِّلُ$$

يُكَذِّبُ	يُقَشِّرُ	يُمَرِّضُ	يُهَلِّلُ	يُقَسِّمُ	يُكَسِّرُ	يُقَطِّعُ	يُصَعِّبُ	يُصَمِّمُ	يُصَدِّقُ

Timing. When you use a noun relating to time, change it into a verb by using this pattern. This is different to the verbs of transformation above. Examples are, 'a man entered into midday' and 'the traveler entered into the morning'. The words morning, midday, night, afternoon, evening, etc. can be changed into verbs. These verbs are directly related to timing, where the transformation verbs have the incidental effect of timing.	فعَّل: هجَّر الرجل. صبَّح المسافر.

Form II: when you place a shaddah on the ع the verb, it will have several meanings that we will explain in detail below.

1. Doing the verb repeatedly / frequently, as you see in the examples below.

The pilgrim circled the Kabba repeatedly.	طوَّف المعتمر حول الكعبة.
I roamed the (entire) city (for hours).	جوَّلتُ في المدينة.
Death is spread among the camels / Camels died in large numbers.	موتتْ الإبل.

Verbs in form II could refer to doing the verb repeatedly or for a longer time, and also the effect could be on the subject rather than the verb. In the first two examples, the verbs 'circled' and 'roamed' are the words that are repeated. In third example, the death of the camels is widespread - death occurs repeatedly. The camels are not active in their performance of the verb, but nonetheless, the verb occurs repeatedly.

In the two examples below, you will see that the effect of the form II verb strengthens the verb. So the first example, rather than being 'the door was locked', is rather, 'the door was double-locked (you are sure they are locked well).' The second example means 'the clothes were shredded / cut into small pieces'.	
قطَّعتُ الأثواب.	غلَّقتُ الأبواب.

Not all verbs in form II are verbs that are done repeatedly or exaggeratedly. As you see in the next examples, from right to left: to make someone happy, honor someone, to teach someone, to brand someone something.

وسَّم	علَّم	كرَّم	فرَّح

Form II can also indicate transitivity: it can make an intransitive verb transitive. You can see on the second column form I is an intransitive verb; in column three (on the right), the verb has become transitive. Transitive verbs take a direct object whilst intransitive verbs do not.

The one who passed the exam was happy. / I made the one who passed the exam happy.	فرِحَ الناجح.	فرّحتُ الناجح.
The guest sat down. / I made the guest sit down (offered him a seat).	جلس الضيف.	جلّستُ الضيف.
The neglected one stood up. / I made the neglected one stand up (admonish him).	قام المهمل	قوّمتُ المهمل.
The child fell asleep. / I got the child to fall asleep.	نام الطفل.	نوّمتُ الطفل.

By stressing the ع of the verb, a transitive verb with an object can be changed to take two objects. Form II cannot take three objects (form IV can take three objects)

Below you will see examples of form I verbs changing to form II, which are transitive to two objects.

لَبَسَ الطفْل الثَوْب	ألبَسْتَهُ الثَوْب	لبّستُ الطفل الثوب
The child wore the garment.	I dressed him in a garment.	I dressed the child in a garment.
فهم الدارس المسألة	أفْهَمْتَهُ المَسألة	وفهّمتُ الدارس المسألة
The student understood the question.	I made him understand the question.	I explained to the student the question.
عَلِمَ الطفل المشي	أعَلَمْته المشي	عَلّمتَهُ المشي
The child learned how to walk	I taught him how to walk.	I taught him how to walk
أكَلَ الطائر الحب	أأكلته الحب	أكّلت الطائر الحَبَّ
The bird ate the seed.	I fed him the seed.	I fed the bird the seed.

If I declare a person as an infidel, or I declare a woman as a cheater, we malign or tarnish them. In Arabic, the verb 'to become an infidel' exists instead. This verb is in form II. Literally this would crudely translate as, 'I infidelise you', as in a charge. This is important because the person charging is the subject and the charged person is the object. The process of attributing or ascribing something to somebody is called 'nisba', 'accusing (somebody)'.

You will see that in this format for 'nisba' the object of the sentence is attributed to the root of the verb.

I attributed the man to debauchery. / I called him a debaucher.	فسَّقت الرجل.
I ascribed someone infidelity. / I called him an infidel.	كفَّرت فلانا.
I attributed the woman to cheating. / I called her a cheater.	خوَّنت المرأة.

Praying for or against the object.

May Allah amputate you	جدعك الله.	جدعته.
May Allah injure you	عقرك الله.	عقرته.
May Allah provide the man with water	سقيا لك.	سقيت الرجل.
May Allah take care of you	رعاك الله.	رعيته.

Form II can also express removal of something from something else.

The butcher skinned the sheep	جلَّد الجزار الشاة.
The shepherd removed the tick from the camel	قرَّد الراعي البعير.
I peeled the fruit	قشَّرت الفاكهة.
I clipped the nails	قلَّمت الأظافر.

Form II can also indicate transformation similar to a derivative form of the root of the verb.

The man was hunched over (in Arabic it is literally 'bowed', as in the gesture in Western societies)	قوَّس الرجل.
The place has become like garden: it is now much-frequented (in Arabic gardens are known to be popular places)	روَّ المكان.
The mortar / clay solidifies (in Arabic we use the word 'hajjar' which means to harden to a rock in form II; it is derived from the word for rock)	حجَّر الطين.
The woman became old ('become old' in Arabic has the same meaning as being incapable of)	عجزَّت المرأة.

Going to a certain destination: this is created by changing (for example) the noun Kufa into the verb 'going to Kufa' (as it is in Arabic) by applying the pattern of form 2 verbs. The sentences on the right are: 'the immigrants went to Korfa', 'student went to Egypt', 'the soldier went to Yemen', 'the traveler went east', ' the bird went west' and 'the train went west'.	كوَّف المهاجر مصَّر الطالب يمَّن الجنود شرَّق الرّحالة غرَّب الطائر غرَّب القطار

Form II can also mean performing certain tasks in the time frame derived from the verb.

| The man travelled at midday | هجَّر الرجل. |
| The traveler moved in the morning | صبَّح المسافر. |

Form II verbs denote subjects becoming the original noun meaning of the verb

This first verb means 'became leafy', in form II. By removing the vowels, you can change it into a noun. This noun means leaf. Form II verbs tells you that the subject of the sentence now has leaves. Thus, these verbs show a change in the state of the subject to the original noun meaning of the verbs. The original noun meaning of 'became rotten' is mold - therefore the bread turns moldy.

Below you will see the verb and how it has been derived from the noun:

ورق	ورَّق
عفن	عفَّن
قيح	قيَّح

The tree became leafy	ورَّق الشجر.
The bread became rotten	عفَّن الخبز.
The wound had puss emanating	قيَّح الجرح.

Acceptance. Form II can also indicate acceptance of something.

| I accepted Mohammed intercession | شفَّعتُ محمدًا. |
| I accepted Khalid's mediation | وسَّطتُ خالدًا. |

Truncate phrases: You can also use form II to truncate phrases into single words. A Christina example is the word 'Hallelujah', derived from the Hebrew phrase meaning 'Praise the Lord'.

The imam said, "Allah is the greatest."	الله أكبر.	كبَّر الإمام.
The man who was praying said, "Glory to Allah."	سبحان الله.	سبَّح المصلي.
The Haj said, "I answer your call, Allah."	لبيك.	لبَّى الحاج.
The people said, "There is no God but Allah."	لا إله إلا الله.	هلَّل القوم.
The people who were praying said, "Amen."	آمين.	أمَّن المصلون.

In English we often use the word 'said' in narrative. The Arabic equivalent is modified to suit what is said. Sometimes an entire phrase that is uttered can be turned into a verb. In English, if someone says, 'I ask for help,' this would be reported as, 'he asked for help', rather than 'he said, "I ask for help."' In a similar way, when Arabs say, 'Allah is the greatest', there is a single verb that literally means 'I said Allah is the greatest'.

Sometime a different verb must be used. For example, 'the people said, "There is no God but Allah."' Here you say the verb, 'hail'. The idea here is to truncate the sentence into one word. 'Hail' literally means, 'saying there is no God but Allah' in Arabic

Causation

I gathered the students	جمّعت الطلاب.
The man made the meal heavy	دسم الرجل الطعام.

Verb form III is mainly used in relation to the participation between the subject of the verb and its object.

Form III is formed by inserting an alif after the 'ف' of the verb. In form I above you can see that the '3yn' of the verb can take any vowel. To make form III you must choose a verb from form I which has a fatHa over the '3yn'.

سمح	وعد	وصل	نزل	باع	منع	شرك	ضرب	قتل
سامح	واعد	واصل	نازل	بايع	مانع	شارك	ضارب	قاتل

Form III can have several meanings. The subject and the direct object both participate in the activity of the verb. For example, two people are corresponding with each other: "John corresponded with Tom." 'Corresponded' will be form III: John is doing the action with Tom. Another example is when two people are fighting.

In the above examples, participation is clear. However, when you start translating it into English misunderstandings and mistranslations arise.

For example, if somebody watched a movie. We use form III here. Why? The movie was made to be watched, so there is a participatory relationship between 'somebody' and the movie: the watcher and the watched. Another example of verbs that do not seem as if there are two people participating, but there are according to this form, is somebody punishing another: "a father punished his son." Of course, the son is not participating in the punishment against himself, but he participates in the action of the verb "punished" by having misbehaved (or whatever he had done). This is his role in the participatory act. Therefore, a passive participant may have initiated the action of the verb by causing the subject to carry out that action: the action is warranted.

Mazin corresponded with his friend Tom in America.	رَاسَلَ مازنٌ صَدِيقَه توم في أمريكا.	رَاسَلَ
Amir sat with his guest (entertained his guest).	جَالَسَ أميرٌ ضيفَه.	جَالَسَ
Tom watched a new movie.	شَاهَدَ توم فيلماً جديداً.	شَاهَدَ
The father punished his son.	عَاقَبَ الأبُ ولدَه.	عَاقَبَ
Amir helped the old man.	سَاعَدَ أميرٌ الرجلَ العجوزَ.	سَاعَدَ
Ahmed travelled to Khartoum.	سَافَرَ أحْمَدُ إلْ الْخَرْطُوْم	سَافَرَ

Translations for form III verbs below (right to left): to support, to participate, to contribute, to forgive, to fight (in a battle), to wage war.

حَارَبَ	قَاتَلَ	سَامَحَ	سَاهَمَ	سَانَدَ

يُفَاعِلْ

يُحَارِبْ	يُقَاتِلْ	يُسَامِحْ	يُسَاهِمْ	يُسَانِدْ	يُسَاعِدْ	يُعَاقَبْ	يُشَاهِدْ	يُجَالِسْ	يُرَاسِلْ

The translations of present tense form III verbs above are: to fight in a war, to fight, to forgive, to participate, to contribute, to help, to punish, to watch, to sit with, to correspond with.

This verb indicates participation between two or more parties. Please note that being the subject does not mean that he is the one who started the action. Both parties are equally involved in the action; they are equal participants in giving and receiving the action of the verb(s).

Ahmed and Mohammed are fighting	صارع أحمد محمدًا
The army and the enemy are fighting	قاتل الجيش العدو
Ali and Khalid are boxing / hitting each other	لاكم عليّ خالدا
Majid and his brother are hitting each other	ضارب ماجد أخاه

Adding an alif to form I makes it form III. This makes an intransitive transitive verb. Below you will see two examples. On the right is 'to arrive'; on the example in the corner next to it is added an alif. This changes the meaning to 'continue'. The verb has adopted an object. The verb next to it means 'sit down'. By adding an alif, the meaning changes 'to sit with / entertain' and the verb is intransitive.

To arrive / the man continues his trip	واصل الرجل سفره.	وصل
To sit down / Mohammed sits down / provides company to his friend	وجالس محمد صديقه.	جلس

جاذب اللاعب خصمه الحبل	جذب اللاعب الحبل
In form III verbs, the player participates in the pulling of the cord with his competitor. We have inserted the word 'competitor' as the second object; the subject becomes the first object and both participate in the pulling.	The player pulled the cord. Player = subject, cord = object. The cord cannot participate with the player in pulling. This is a form I verb.
Form III verbs are transitive verbs concerned with participation. When a form I verb is changed into form III, it requires an object which is a participant (if the original object is incapable of participation). A	

participating object must be added to the sentence in form III verb sentences if there is not one originally. This subject becomes the first object and the inserted object will participate with this.

Another feature of form III verbs is that the subject has an attribute that is indicative of the verb / derived from the verb. For example, the teacher punished the negligent child. The negligent child has an attribute that was indicated by the verb – the child is a negligent, punished child.

The teacher punished the negligent	عاقب المعلم المهمل.
Allah makes the patient recover	عافى الله المريض.
I rewarded the hard worker	كافأت المجتهد.
The man turned his face away in distain	صاعر الرجل خده.

Continuation of the verb without interruption.

I followed the work with interest	تابعت العمل باهتمام.
The man continued fasting	والى الرجل الصوم.
The patient continued fighting the disease	قاوم المريض المرض.

Exerting effort / doing something intensely or repeatedly

He doubled my effort.	ضاعف الجهد.
He surveyed the place.	عاين المكان.

This form also indicates difficulty in achievement – verbs which are not easy to do

The man travelled.	سافر الرجل.
The people emigrated.	هاجر الناس.

Form III verbs can carry the same meaning as form IV verbs.

May Allah give your health back.	عافاك الله. - أعفاك الله.
Lend us your ears.	راعِنا سمعَك - أرعِنا سمعَك.

	يُفْعِلُ	أَفْعَلَ

Form IV resembles what in English grammar we call causative verbs.

Form IV is formed by prefixing an alif to form I (this alif is actually 'hamzah al-qat3') and putting a sukuun on the 'ف' of the verb. The meaning is to cause the verb to happen to somebody else. The subject causes something to happen to the object. The translations of the examples given for this form sound unusual in English: "I made somebody sad", "I broke my fasting", "I made somebody understand a lesson", "I made somebody leave the room," or "I burned the food." In English when you say these phrases, more words are needed to express the sentiment. In Arabic, this form is just one word. You will see in a translation how this one word is used; it is more concise than its English counterpart is.

Study the following examples to see how form IV is used:

English	Arabic	Verb
Mazin seated his guest, so the guest sat down.	أَجْلَسَ مازنٌ ضيفَه فجلسَ.	أَجْلَسَ
The teacher made Tom leave the class. (Either Tom did something that was punished, or he was unable to leave on his own accord.)	أَخْرَجَ المعلمُ توم من الفصلِ.	أَخْرَجَ
John made the boy enter his house. (This can be as forceful as it comes across in English, or it can simply mean he let the boy in.)	أَدْخَلَ جون الولدَ الى منزلِه.	أَدْخَلَ
The teacher made the students understand the new lesson. (Again, this does not necessarily carry the forceful overtones of the English translation.)	أَفْهَمَ المعلمُ التلاميذَ الدرسَ الجديدَ.	أَفْهَمَ
The person who was fasting broke his fast at sunset.	أَفْطَرَ الصائمُ عندَ المغربِ.	أَفْطَرَ

Form IV can also be used with the following verbs: to burn (something), to do justice (to somebody), to be charitable (to something/one), to neglect (something/one) and to participate.

أَفْعَلَ

أَسْهَمَ	أَهْمَلَ	أَحْسَنَ	أَنْصَفَ	أَحْرَقَ

يُفْعِلُ

يُسْهِمُ	يُهْمِلُ	يُحْسِنُ	يُنْصِفُ	يُحْرِقُ	يُفْطِرُ	يُدْخِلُ	يُفْهِمُ	يُخْرِجُ	يُجْلِسُ

Above you can see form IV in the present tense. The translation from right to left: to make someone sit down, to make someone leave, to make someone understand (to explain), to let someone in, to offer someone breakfast, to cause something to burn, to be charitable to someone, to neglect, to participate.

Form IV can be transitive or intransitive. Please note that the alif prefixed to form IV is the only 'hamzatu-l'qaT3' in all ten forms.

There are several traits to verbs in this form. Changing verbs from form I to form IV will cause them to take an indirect object: in Arabic, we call this changing from transitive (form I) to double intransitive (form IV). Double intransitive simply means having two objects. For example, "Ahmed understood the lesson." The verb understood is 'fahama' (form I) and is transitive: it takes one object. To take this verb and change it to form IV would make it double intransitive: "Ahmed explained the lesson to Mustafa." The two objects here are now 'lesson' and 'Mustafa'. 'Afhama' is form IV.

Another feature of form IV is agreement: the recipient accepts the action of the verb. For example, in form II the sentence 'the man offered breakfast to the faster' (the man who is fasting) changes to 'the man broke his fast' in form IV.

Form IV verbs might also have the capacity to change transitive verbs into intransitive. For example, 'the man defeated his friend' changes to 'his friend was defeated'; 'I burned the food' to 'the food was burned'. Note: do not confuse this with active and passive voices in English. Another feature is removal: this can be the direct removal of, say, dust from your eye, or it can be used more abstractly. This could be the removal of ambiguity from a text, or removing an unjustness that was levelled at a suspect.

Also expressed by form IV verbs is causation. If you make somebody enter / exit a building, make somebody the owner of something or make someone a fugitive you use form IV verbs.

Form IV verbs can also express the condition of somebody. For example, if you find somebody praiseworthy or dishonest upon getting to know them.

Transformation, such as a bare tree becoming leafy, or a plant coming into fruition, also employs form IV verbs.

Another feature of form IV verbs is reaching a destination. For example, 'masr' (Egypt) can be changed in form IV to 'amsara' – he reached Egypt. 3raq (Iraq) changes to 'a3raqa' to mean 'he reached Iraq'. 'Masaa' (evening) changes to 'amsaa' to mean 'he reached evening' or 'something happened in the evening'. You can also use this form with numbers to mean, 'he reached [the number]'. For example, 'thalathah' means three, so 'athalatha' means 'he reached three'.

An unusual feature expressed by verbs in this form is that one verb can have the exact opposite meaning to itself: 'asrratu' could mean either 'divulged [a secret]' or 'hid [a secret]'.

Prefixing a Hamza to intransitive form I verbs makes it transitive. If the original verb is transitive, adding a Hamza means it takes two objects. If it is transitive to two objects, it will become transitive to three.

Two tables below you will see examples of these. On the table below, you will see the example numbers of the number of objects the transitive verbs take.

Intransitive	1 4
Transitive to one verb	2 3 5 7 8 9
Transitive to two verbs	10 11 12 13 14 15
Transitive to three verbs	16 17 18

The man is gone	1. ذهب الرجل.
Allah took away his vision	2. أذهب الله بصره
Praise be to Allah who made our grief go away	3. الحمد لله الذي أذهب عنا الحزن
The student left the school	4. خرج الطلاب من المدرسة.
The teacher let the students out of school	5. أخرج المعلم الطلاب من المدرسة
And He who grows pasture	6. والذي أخرج المرعى
The man wore abaya	7. لبس الرجل العباءة.
The boy memorized the lesson	8. حفظ الولد الدرس.
The child drank the milk	9. شرب الطفل اللبن.
The mother dressed the child in the garment	10. ألبستْ الأم الطفل الثوب.
The teacher oversaw the children memorizing the anthem	11. أحفظ المعلم التلميذ النشيد.
I made him drink the milk	12. أشربته اللبن.
I learned that Khalid is travelling	13. علمت خالدا مسافرا.
I realized honesty is a virtue	14. رأيت الأمانة فضيلة.
I was informed that Mohammed is coming	15. بلغت محمدا قادما
I let my father know that Khalid is travelling	16. أعلمت والدي خالدا مسافرا.
I made Ali realize that honesty is a virtue	17. أرأيت عليا الأمانة فضيلة
I informed / let the teacher know that Mohammed is coming	18. أبلغت المعلم محمدا قادما

Offering: this means offering an object to be lent, for example, offering someone a book. This is also used in the context of pawning items, or offering something for sale.	أبَعْتُ العقار. أبَعْتُ البيت أرهن الرجل سَاعته أرهن الرجل المتاع. أعرت الكتاب.

These verbs are ones that suggest transformation, where the subject has become an altered state related to the verb. For example, 'the sun has risen' ('risen' in Arabic is a derivative of 'east' – the direction of the sun rising), 'the woman became a mother', 'the garden has bloomed', 'the fruit has ripened', 'the female camel became itchy', 'the sky became dusty' and 'the female sheep became fat'. This attribute can also be related to time and space. This is regarding transformation from one time to another. In Arabic, the verb 'become' is expressed in the context of time of day – when, for instance, you say, 'the man became sick', in Arabic you say, 'in the morning' too. When you talk about somebody fasting, you say that they are 'starting the month (of fasting)'. Another example is, 'the sailor sailed': the verb 'to sail' is created with a hamzah before the noun 'sea'. The literal meaning is 'the sailor entered the sea'. Further, 'the traveler went to Iraq'. We use a verb form that consists of a hamzah plus the noun 'Iraq'. This will create the meaning, 'the traveler entered Iraq'. Be careful as there is a similar form carrying a different meaning: the present form indicates that the person has arrived at his destination, the other that the person is going to his destination. A different attribute of this present form is a certain relationship with numbers. The above notion of becoming an altered state is replicated: 'the number has reached three', 'the fetus has reached nine (months)', 'the children have become five' (if four kids are joined by a fifth) or 'the people in the meeting reached ten'.	ألحمثُ الشاة. وأطفلتُ الأم أينع الثمر. أزهرت الحديقة. أجربت الناقة. أشرقت الشمس. أغبرت السماء أصبح الرجل أمسى المسافر. أشهر الصائم. أبحر الملاح. أعرق الرحالة. أثلث العدد أتسع الجنين أخمس الأولاد. أعشر المجتمعون

Condition that the subject find the object in, you find that a sheep fat, or found Khalid generous. There is two cases in this category, to find the subject in a condition or to the object in a condition, these conditions matches the verb, for example the sheep gained weight, in Arabic gaining weight is a verb and it will come before the noun, the sheep, when you place the verb gaining weight in form number three, you basically saying that YOU found the sheep gained weight, the thing that gained weight is the subject of the action, gaining weight, and you find the it as the doer of the gaining of the weight,

Verb form IV could indicate the condition that you find something in. These verbs act like adjectives derived from verbs. See examples below.

I found the sheep fat.	سمينة	أسمنت الشاة
I found Mohammed generous.	كريما	أكرمت محمدا

Also in this verb form, you can see the object has the condition of the root of the verb. In Arabic, there is just one verb used to state '… found [him] praiseworthy.' In form I, the root meaning is 'I praise.' By changing it to form III, you change the meaning to 'I found [him] praiseworthy.' Thus, the condition of being praiseworthy is derived from the root (praise) of the verb. Read the examples below.

I found Khalid praiseworthy.	محمود	أحمدت خالدا
I found the traitor dispraised.	مذموم	أذممت الخائن
I found the hater subdued.	مقهور	أقهرت الحاقد

Removal of the meaning of the verb. In form I, the verb 'complain' is used ('the student complained'). In form IV, the complaint is reversed – 'Somebody removed the source of the student's complaint. You remove the meaning of verb from the object.

I removed the source of the depressed person's complaint.	أشكيت المهموم
I clarified the book – i.e. I removed the source of its ambiguity.	أعجمت الكتاب
I straightened the piece of iron.	أعوجت الحديد

The next attribute to these verbs denotes a certain time when the subject deserves to achieve a certain state.

The crops are ready to be harvested.	أحصد الزرع
The girl is ready for marriage. (i.e. she is at a certain age)	أزوجت الفتاة

This attribute indicates multitude For example:

The place has lots of trees.	أشجر المكان
Spring brings out many flowers.	أزهر الربيع
The valley has plenty of antelopes.	أظبأ الوادي

The next attribute concerns 'enabling:'

I enabled him to dig the well.	حفرته البئر

I enabled him to fill the vat		أملأته الزير

Praying is used by way of this verb form.

I prayed for Muhammad to have water, Praying for someone to be provided with water for his crops is a common prayer in an environment historically known for drought. This is changing now, as, for some reason, the area is inundated with water and flooding.	أسقيت محمدًا.

تَفَعَّلَ	يَتَفَعَّلُ	Form V				
ت	+	Form II				

Form V is formed by prefixing form I with a 'te', stressing the ع of the verb and placing a shaddah on the verb. These verbs can be both transitive and intransitive.

توسَّط	تأخَّر	تقدَّم	تفهَّم	توصَّل	تسلَّم	تكرَّم	تعلَّمَ
تلوَّن	تكسَّر	تحيَّر	تجشَّم	توسَّم	تنقَّل	تغيَّر	تعجَّل
	تكلَّف	توعَّد	تقوَّم	تقلَّص	تنبَّه	تجوَّل	تحوَّل

Form V can have several meanings. One of them is a reflexive version of form II. For example, when you say that somebody is in pain or that someone is talking. Also, sometimes, it is an intensive version of Form I.

Realization: The main feature of this form is how its verbs denote that an intended action is completed. 'I taught you a lesson, so you learnt.' 'I broke the cup and it was damaged.'

Transformation: Another feature of verbs with this form is transformation. This could be somebody becoming a Jew or a Christian or Shia.

This attribute occurs when verbs suggest someone has to endure a situation he may not want to be part of. Others would say to him, 'be brave' or 'hold out till the end'.

'Be patient', 'be tough' and 'be aware' are examples of this form in use.

Verbs in this form may share some characteristics with verbs in form X.

See below to see more examples of how to use these verbs.

Sometimes an intensive version of a form 1 verb

The main feature of this form is how its verbs denote that an intended action is completed. 'I taught you a lesson, so you learnt.' 'I broke the cup and it was damaged.' In short, you get your just deserts!

To translate the table below:

English	Arabic	Verb
I taught Khalid how to swim, so he learned.	عَلمتُ خالدَ السباحةَ فتَعَلَّم	تَعَلَّم
I delivered the package to the man, so he received it.	سلمتُ الرجلَ الطردَ فتَسَلَّمَ.	تَسَلَّمَ
I beat the boy, so he was in pain.	ضربتُ الولدَ فتَأَلَّمَ.	تَأَلَّمَ
The boy was in pain because of the severity of the beating.	تَأَلَّمَ الولدُ من شدةِ الضربِ.	تَأَلَّمَ
The man talked a lot.	تَكَلَّمَ الرجلُ كثيراً.	تَكَلَّمَ
Ahmed did a gracious act by donating to the organization.	تَفَضَّلَ أحمدُ بالتبرع للمؤسسةِ.	تَفَضَّلَ

Form V is built on form II by adding a 'taa' before the 'ف' of the verb and placing a shaddah on the '3yn' of the verb. These verbs are reflexive forms of verb form II. One of the meanings of form V verbs expresses the result of the action of the verb, for example: "The teacher taught me, so I learnt." You will see how "taught" is form I; "learnt" is therefore form V. If you say simply, "I learnt from my teacher", form I does not need to be mentioned. This is because the cause the learning is expressed .

Sometimes the meaning in form V changes. This change sometimes can be seen as an intensification to Arabic speakers. For example, the verb 'to favor'. This is 'fadala' in form I in Arabic. If you change this to form V ('tefadala'), the meaning changes to 'do a favor for (somebody)' or 'be gracious enough (to do something)': "Ahmed was gracious enough to donate to the organization ".

Another example of this meaning changing is somebody is talking: "The man talked." When you choose the Arabic word for 'talked', you will see that it came from the verb in form I, 'kalema'. The meaning of this word is totally different in form I to form V; you must use form V to have the understanding that the man is talking with other people .

Because of the changes in meaning between forms, it is not always helpful to trace the verb to its root (form I)

تَأَمَّلَ	تَكَتَّمَ	تَمَسَّكَ	تَعَجَّلَ	تَهَشَّمَ

يَتَفَعَّلُ

يَتَكَتَّمُ	يَتَمَسَّكُ	يَتَعَجَّلُ	يَتَهَشَّمُ	يَتَفَضَّلُ	يَتَكَلَّمُ	يَتَأَلَّمُ	يَتَسَلَّمُ	يَتَعَلَّمُ

Form V in the present tense: to learn, to receive, to be in pain, to talk, to be kind enough, to crumble, to hurry, to be unyielding, to be reticent.

Example of a transitive verb	
Student learned the lesson	تعلم الطالب الدرس.
The man received the letter	تسلم الرجل الرسالة.
I promised (warned, threatened) the negligent man (with) a punishment	وتوعدت المهمل.
Example of an intransitive verb	
The army advanced	تقدم الجيش.
The visitors were delayed	تأخر الزائرون.
I wandered in the city	تجولت في المدينة.

One of the meanings of form V verbs is realizing the intention of form II verbs.

I broke the glass	تكسّر	كسّرت الزجاج.
I shattered the wood	تحطم	حطمت الخشب.
I demolished the building	تهدم	هدمت البناء.
I helped the student improve.	تأدّبَ	أدبت الطالب.
I alerted the man	تنبه	نبهت الرجل.
I provide him with religious jurisprudence	تفقه	فقهته في الدين.

Adoption: In Arabic, you can take an object and make it into a verb. This verb means that the object is being used as the origin of the verb. For example, if you sit on a rock, in Arabic we say that you 'chair' the rock. In this sense, you sit on a camel's hump when you ride it. Therefore, in Arabic you 'hump' the camel (although it is a double entendre in English). This meaning is transferred across to 'riding glory': an oft-used expression is, 'riding the crest of a wave' in a metaphorical sense.

The man accepted the place (as a house / دار)	تدير الرجل المكان.
Ali humped the glory (this clause uses the same verb as 'riding' atop a camel's hump / سنام)	تسنم عليّ المجد.
Mohammed used his garments as a pillow وسادة	توسد محمد الثوب.

Exert yourself to achieve a better result / quality (Assuming)

The translation of verbs below, from right to left, read: to honour, to endure, to be patient, to be prudent, to be brave. These qualities are ones a person aspires to achieve.

تنوه	تكرم	تجلد	تصبر	تحلم	تشجع

The adventurer strove to be braver		تشجّع المغامر.

The man wanted became prudent		تحلّم الرجل.
The injured man tried to become patient		تصبر المصاب.

Form V verbs denotes avoidance, which realizes the intention of form II.

Mohammed avoids embarrassment.	ترك الحرج.	تحرّج محمد.
I helped Mohammed avoid his embarrassment.	جنبته لحرج.	حرجت محمدا،
The man avoided committing sins.	ترك الإثم.	وتأثم الرجل.
I helped the man avoid committing sins.	جنبته الإثم.	اثمت الرجل
The man avoids sleeping at night.	ترك الهجود.	تهجد الرجل.
I helped the man avoid sleep at night.	جنبته الهجود	هجدت الرجل

To make gradual progress, to advance, to take a sip after another, to touch something repeatedly ,

This includes repetitive work within a deadline. It will be done to generally have a great benefit, and perform the act repeatedly.

Look at these examples and notice that some are physical and others are immaterial or abstract. These repetitive verbs that the form represents could be physical, as in taking medicine, or abstract, as in making someone aware of circumstances or teaching them.

I asked the patient to sip the medicine gradually, one sip after another.	فتجرعه	جرعت المريض الدواء.
I made the man touch the money repeatedly.	فتحسسه	حسسته المال

I taught the student the problem so learned. ('Teaching' someone in Arabic is a repetitive process, done over and again(	علمت التلميذ المسألة. فتعلمها
I made Mohammed aware of the situation, so he knew about it.	بصرت محمدا الأمر. فتبصر
I made him understand the situation, so he understood it.	فهمته الوضع. فتفهم

Verb form five تفعّل can also has the same meaning of asking , requesting or believing as in form ten in استفعل, in the table below you will see form five verbs and under it form ten verbs, both of them has the same meaning written in the middle row.

Form V تفعّل can also have the same meaning as form X استفعل when it means that you ask someone to accomplish something. For example, when somebody believes that he is an important person.

تعلّى	تبصر	تأمل	تفهم	تعظمته	تنجزته
He acted in haughty way.	He looked attentively at, he became aware.	He contemplated	He understood	I thought he was great	Asked him to accomplish something
استعلى	استبصر	استأمل	استفهم	استعظمته	استنجزته

Other meaning of form five تفعّل is being similar to the meanings of form one فَعَلَ

He was not fair to me	ظلمني	تظلمني
He scowled at me	جهمني	تجهمني

تفعل Can also be the reflexives/ realizing of intention of form two فعّل

I established his origin, so his origin was established.	فتأصل	أصلته
I gathered them together, so they were together.	تألب	ألبته
I prepared him so he became qualified.	تأهل	أهلته

تفعل Can also be the reflexives/ realizing of intention of form two فعّل

Form V can also show the realization of intention. This means that the object has become the origin of the verb: 'the grape becomes a raisin' - in Arabic the object becomes a verb, i.e. 'the grape raisinized.' The subject of the verb becomes the object. Another example is, 'I crowned the thing'. This does not necessarily mean that the thing literally has a crown now, but that it saw success. The thing becomes crowned. (Here subject and object are switched.)

The grape becomes a raisin.	تزبب العنب.
The thing was crowned with a garland.	تكلل الشيء.

## Form VI	يَتَفَاعَلُ	تَفَاعَلَ

تساءل	تراحم	تلاءم	تعانق	تشارك	تصارع	تقاتل	تخاصم	تعاظم

Form VI is made by prefixing form III with a 'taa' that carries a fatHa.

Form VI is similar to form III where two people are engaged in an action. Form VI expresses greater intensity. For example, if two people are competing against each other, you could express this competition using form III. However, if the competition is very intense, use form VI.

Two boxers fought with all their might.	تَقَاتَلَ الملاكمان بقوةٍ.	تَقَاتَلَ
The contender competed in a race.	تَنَافَسَ المتسابقون في السباقِ.	تَنَافَسَ
The beads of a necklace scattered all over the floor.	تَنَاثَرَتْ حباتُ العقدِ على الأرضِ.	تَنَاثَرَ
The two children quarreled over the sweet.	تَنَازَعَ الطفلان على الحلوى.	تَنَازَعَ
The two children divided a piece of candy.	تَقَاسَمَ الطفلان قطعةَ الحلوى.	تَقَاسَمَ

This is not the only meaning for form VI. For certain meanings, form VI verbs are the best choice and do not always denote intensity. An example of this other use of form VI verbs is when discussing equality in a game: a football match ending in a draw, for instance. This may have a relationship with other verbs that imply impartiality, neutrality or equality. As you can see, the intensifying relationship is not always there, but there is a relationship suggesting equality.

تَصَالَحَ	تَخَاصَمَ	تَنَاصَحَ	تَعَادَلَ	تَسَابَقَ

The verbs above are from right to left: to race, to draw, to consult, to quarrel, and to reconcile.

يَتَصَالَحُ	يَتَخَاصَمُ	يَتَنَاصَحُ	يَتَعَادَلُ	يَتَسَابَقُ	يَتَقَاسَمُ	يَتَنَازَعُ	يَتَنَاثَرُ	يَتَنَافَسُ	يَتَقَاتَلُ

The above are the form VI present tense, translations of the above: to fight, to compete, to scatter, to struggle, to divide, to race, to draw, to consult, to quarrel, to reconcile

These examples will lead you think carefully about the best choice of verb form.

Verbs in form VI are most likely to be encountered in the intransitive mode (but can be transitive) and share some characteristics with verbs in form III and V, especially when it comes to realization of an endeavor. The letter taa that you are prefixing to form IV is called 'realization of endeavor taa'. In Arabic, this is called 'taa almuTaw3ah'. When you say, for example, 'I pushed him away so he kept his distance'; 'I handed over something and he took it'. See further examples below.

بَعُدَ	تباعد	باعدته

	عَلَّمْتُهُ الرماية	I taught him archery
	فَهَّمْتُهُ المسالة	I explained the question to him.
انعدل	عدّلت الحديد	I straighten the (crocked) iron, it was straighten
انثنى	ثنيته	I bend it, it was bend

Participation is a feature of verbs in this form, which is also a feature of verbs in form III. The difference between them is that in form VI the two participants are subjects in the sentence as opposed to a subject and an object. So in form III you could have, 'Mohammed wrote to Omar'. This will change in form VI to 'Mohammed and Omar wrote to each other'. See how the subject becomes more than one.

Muhammad, Ahmad, and Khalid Quarreled.	تخاصم محمد، وأحمد، وخالد.
The guest and the host hugged	تعانق الضيف والمضيف.
So and so involved in the work.	تشارك فلان وفلان في العمل.

Examples for when the verb is transitive:

Sharing, and fought, and exchanges, and exchange.	تقاسم، وتنازع، وتراشق، وتبادل.
The heirs divided the money.	تقاسم الورثة المال.
Fought Muhammad Ali home.	تنازع محمد وعليّ المنزل.
The protestors of the Intifada and the Jews threw stones at each other.	تراشق المنتفضون واليهود الحجارة.
The participants exchanged accusations.	تبادل المجتمعون الاتهامات.

تشارك	تلاكم	تنازل	تقاتل	تصارع	تبارز

Muhammad and Ali duel	تبارز محمد وعلي
Khalid, Ahmad, and Ibrahim fought each other.	تصارع خالد وأحمد وإبراهيم

تمازحا	تشاركا	تقاتلا
They poke fun at each other	They (two) participate	They fought

496

In the case of double transitive verbs (a phrase that has two objects) that we find in form III, form VI uses a transitive construction: Form III would state, 'Mohammed fought Ahmed over the car.' Mohammed is the subject, Ahmed is the direct object and the car is the indirect object. In form VI, the sentence changes to, 'Mohammed and Ahmed fought over the car.' The car becomes the sole object of the sentence.

تنازعنا البيت.	نازعت جاري البيت.
We fought over the house.	I fought with my neighbor over the house.
تجاذب محمد وخالد الكرة.	جاذب محمد خالدا الكرة.
Mohammed and Khalid were pulling the ball from each other.	Mohammed pulled the ball from Khalid.

تضارب محمد وعلي	ضارب محمد عليا.
Mohammed and Ali exchanged punches.	Mohammed was punching Ali.
تخاصم يوسف وخالد	خاصم يوسف خالدا.
Yousef and Mohammed quarreled.	Yousef quarreled with Mohammed.

Another trait of form VI verbs is delusion / deception. You will find this in sentences that have a figure pretending he is something he is not: "Khalil pretended he was not paying attention." You may recall from form V that you affect a quality for a short period. This is not the same here, as form V deals specifically with affectation over a short period.

تمارضت	تخاذلت	تناومت	تعاميت	تكاسلت	تغافلت
To feign illness.	To lose strength or power.	To pretend to be sleeping.	To pretend not to see.	To exhibit laziness.	To feign inattention.

I ignored the situation	تجاهلت الأمر

Form four can also indicates gradual increase or realization of the subject,

The flood is increasing	تزايد السيل.
The money grows	تنامى المال.
The news kept coming	تواردت الأخبار.
The bees reproduced	تكاثر النحل.

Form I	+	انْ

Form VII is formed by adding an alif (hamzat al-waṣl) and 'nuun'. These letters are prefixed to form I.

This verb form is similar to the English passive voice. The object of the sentence becomes the subject: in English, the passive voice in the sentence "Tarek rides the bicycle" is "The bicycle is ridden [by Tarek]".

Form VII present tense translations from right to left: to dart, to leave, to cut, to break, to spill, to break out, to blow up, to pour, to submerge, to turn over.

يَنْقَلِبُ	يَنْغَمِرُ	يَنْهَمِرُ	يَنْفَجِرُ	يَنْدَلِعُ	يَنْسَكِبُ	يَنْكَسِرُ	يَنْقَطِعُ	يَنْصَرِفُ	يَنْطَلِقُ

The driver drove the car quickly.	انْطَلَقَ قائدُ السيارةِ مسرعاً.	انْطَلَقَ
Ahmed returned to the house.	انْصَرَفَ أحمدُ عائداً الى منزله.	انْصَرَفَ
The rope was cut.	انْقَطَعَ الحبلُ.	انْقَطَعَ
The glass cup was broken.	انْكَسَرَ الكوبُ الزجاجيُّ.	انْكَسَرَ
The water was spilled on the floor.	انْسَكَبَ الماءُ على الأرضِ.	انْسَكَبَ

This form is heavily concerned with realization of intention, which we have seen before: the subject is the initiator of an action that is carried out and completed. You will see that sometimes the recipient of your action cannot affect the action. For example, 'I cut the rope so the rope was cut.' The rope in this instance has no participation in the cutting action. 'Tarek broke the glass, so the glass was broken.' (Literally this would translate as, 'Tarek broke the glass, so the glass broke.') For form VII verbs, the clause must therefore be intransitive. Remember we are concentrating on the latter clauses of the examples given here.

He achieve victory by himself, made himself victorious	انتصر تعني نصر نفسه
It was broken by itself,	انكسر كسر نفسه

انحنى	انداح	انصهر انبلج	انجبر	اندحر	انعصر
To bend	To spread out	To melt / To shine	To be mended	To be defeated	To be squeezed
انقضى	انذبح	انفك	انقاد	انقلب	انحاز	انجلى
To elapse	To be slaughtered	To unravel	To be led	To flip over	He side with	To be clear

The mujahidin won	انتصر المجاهدون
The glass was broken.	انكسر الزجاج
The enemy was defeated	اندحر العدو

We have seen that the realization of action can be accomplished by using several forms, such as the current form VII, form VIII and form IV. As you progress with your studies, you will find that there is only one form will accurately communicate your meaning. This is (as you can tell) difficult to accomplish given the amount of overlap between forms, and especially at the level of Arabic, we are currently working at.

I broke it so it was broken	كسرته فانكسر
I smashed it so it was smashed	حطمته فانحطم
I straightened it so it was straightened.	عدلته فانعدل
I pulled it so it was pulled	جذبته فانجذب

Form VII verbs, aside from representing realization of intention, can also represent intransitive verbs, such as the verbs below.

انكمشت	انجردت	مضى	ذهب
shrunk	Stripped of	passed	gone

Form VIII | اِفْتَعَلَ يَفْتَعِلُ

Prefixed with hamzatu alwasl, and taa is place after its ف. This verb can be both intransitive and transitive, such as:

| اِحْتَقَرَ | اِحْتَقَنَ | اِقْتَصَرَ | اِحْتَبَسَ | اِحْتَمَلَ | اِحْتَرَفَ | اِخْتَتَمَ | اِكْتَسَبَ | اِعْتَذَرَ | اِحْتَرَقَ |

The verbs above for form VIII are translated as: burns, apologizes, acquires, concludes, becomes a professional, bears, is trapped, is limited, is congested, despises.

| اتزن | اتخذ | افترش | افتتح | ارتقى | ارتزق | ارتبك |
| التحف | اتقى | انتقم | اتسع | افترج | التأم | اصطبر |

Form VIII verbs have several features, one of which is the realization of intention. Realization of intention can be transitive or double transitive. Transitive sentences in form VIII can be stated like this: 'I moved the item, so the item was moved' or 'I burned something, so it was burned.' Double transitive verbs here are written thus: 'Mohammed dressed the man with a shirt.' The intention has been realized because the man is wearing the shirt. There are two objects, the shirt and the man, so it is double transitive. We will use form VIII to make the object of the sentence singular: 'the man wore the shirt'.

You should be aware that realization of intention could be an attribute of many verb forms. This is because every verb that you do is anticipated to be achieved, or carried through

The second facet of this form is the idea of acquisition. In English, if you grow a beard, it could be said that you 'adopt' a beard; if someone accepts a bribe, or apologizes, or turns professional – all these examples are expressed using form VIII. You acquire money when you accept a bribe, acquire a pardon when you apologize, acquire a better lifestyle or living when you turn professional.

Related to this aspect of form VIII verbs, these verbs are also used to express the struggle to acquire something – striving for possession. The key verb here is 'kasaba', which in form I means to gain, acquire or earn. This will most likely denote that you have not suffered, e.g. winning the lotto. However, in form VIII, the derived verb is 'iktasaba'. This has a similar meaning but gives the distinct impression of striving for something.

The food was burned.	اِحْتَرَقَ الطعامُ.	اِحْتَرَقَ
The boy apologized to his friend.	اِعْتَذَرَ الولدُ لصديقه.	اِعْتَذَرَ
The team scored a [new] goal.	اِكْتَسَبَ الفريقُ هدفاً جديداً.	اِكْتَسَبَ

The manager concluded.	اخْتَتَمَ المديرُ كلمتَه.	اخْتَتَمَ
The potter turned professional.	احْتَرَفَ الصانعُ صناعةَ الخزفِ.	احْتَرَفَ

The verb pattern here means that you achieve results with great effort. For example, you can earn money or work or be able to do something – but it was not that difficult. You can alter the meaning of these verbs by changing their pattern to stress that earning money was difficult, working was very hard to do, being able to do something was very difficult to achieve. The emphasis for these verbs is on striving. 'I am totally capable of executing this job', 'the students studied hard'.	اكتسب. اكتسبت المال. اقتدر. اقتدرت على العمل. اجتهد. اجتهد الطالب.

يَفْتَعِلُ

يَحْتَقِرُ	يَحْتَقِنُ	يَقْتَصِرُ	يَحْتَبِسُ	يَحْتَمِلُ	يَحْتَرِفُ	يَخْتَتِمُ	يَكْتَسِبُ	يَعْتَذِرُ	يَحْتَرِقُ

Form VIII verbs can be transitive or intransitive modes. An example of intransitive form VIII verbs is, 'the house burned down' ('iHtaraqa al-bait'). 'iHtaraqa' is the verb, and al-Bait is the house. An example of a transitive verb is, 'Ahmed bought a car' ('ishtaraa Ahmed sayaartan').

Example of intransitive	
The speaker improvised the sermon.	ارتجل الخطيب الخطبة.
The director open the ceremony	افتتح المدير الحفل.
The sleeper lie down on the ground.	افترش النائم الأرض.
Example of a transitive	
The speaker were Embarrassed.	ارتبك المتكلم.
The wound was healed.	التأم الجرح.
The breach was widened.	اتسع الخرق.

501

The most common attribute of form VI is the realization of the intention of form I when it has a fatHa on the ع of the verb. This realization of intention is like cause-and-effect. The cause of something happening is your action, and the effect is that something has happened. There is a slight change according to different verb forms, when the verb is relating to something physical or to learning / thinking.

When you do something, it is written in form I; when that has been realized, or achieved, it is in form VIII. This is cause-and-effect. When you do something, it is written in form I; when that has been realized, or achieved, it is in form VIII.

This is the realization of intention of form I when it has a fatHa on the ع of the verb.

I collected / gathered something, so it is collected / gathered. 'I collected / gathered' is form I; 'so it is collected / gathered' is form VIII.	جمعته فاجتمع
I straightened it up, so it is straightened.	وعدلته فاعتدل
I elevated something, so it is elevated.	رفعته فارتفع
I extracted something, so it is extracted.	نزعته فانتزع
I distressed him, so he is distressed.	غممته فاغتم

Physical (action) verbs can are subject to the condition of cause-and-effect (or realization of intention). Verbs that are not physical are not subject to realization of intention. Examples of physical verbs are, from right to left, to hit, to cut, to drag, to pull, to break, and to smash.

التحطيم	التكسير	الجذب	السحب	القطع	الضرب

Examples of non-physical (inactive) verbs are to teach, to let him know or to think: these do not have cause-and-effect, so they do not follow this course of action.	الظن	العلم

Cause-and-effect occurs when the verb is form IV أفعل .

I was just to him, so he felt fairly treated. (Notice this second clause is expressed by the same word in Arabic as the first clause, 'just'.)	أنصفته فانتصف
I made him listen, so he listened.	أسمعته فاستمع
I prohibited him, so he was prohibited.	أنهيته فانتهى

Form VIII can also have verbs that evince realization of intention of verbs from form II فعَّل

I bring something to me, so it is closer.	قربته فاقترب
I levelled it, so it is level.	سويته فاستوى
I soldered it, so it is soldered.	لحمته فالتحم

I organized it, so it is organized.	نظمته فانتظم

Acquisition Examples using as adoption

When you are acquiring the service or the benefit of something, whether that of being served food, sitting on a saddled horse, or eating grilled food, form VIII is used in Arabic, which will be a derivative of the item in question.

There are similarities in English, for example when you use a horse for transportation, you say, 'I mount / saddle the horse'; when you want to obtain grilled meat, 'I grilled the meat', and so forth. However, when you want to employ the service of a waiter, you cannot say, 'I servicized myself', but this how you would use the verb in Arabic.

I 'servicized' myself (i.e. I acquired the service of a servant)	اختدم الرجل
The knight mounted the horse (meaning the knight made the horse his seat - this verb is used solely for animals that you can mount)	امتطى الفارس الجواد
The cook grilled the meat (you could use a different verb form - form I for example - to express this sentence, but form VIII clarifies that the cook grilled the meat to serve himself; the connotations of these verbs is that you do it for yourself)	اشتوى الطاهي اللحم

It has the same participation meaning as form six; تفاعل

The boys fought each other.	تقاتلا	اقتتل الولدان
Mohammed and Mustafa quarreled.	تخاصما	اختصم محمد وخالد
Mustafa and Amr had a dispute.	تخالفا	اختلف مصطفى وعمر
The two guests sat next to each other.	تجاورا	اجتور الضيفان

To struggle to acquire something – striving for possession

اجتهد	اقتدر	اكتسب

I worked hard to earn as much as I could.	اكتسبت المال
I was totally able and capable of performing the job.	اقتدرت على العمل
The student worked so hard to acquire the knowledge.	اجتهد الطالب في تحصيل العلم.
This is a verse from the Koran meaning, 'for every soul there is what it has acquired, and against every soul there is what it has strived to acquire.' (God is merciful, so any good deed, however	لها ما كسبت وعليها ما اكتسبت

small, is a good deed nonetheless; yet only those bad deeds that have been calculated and worked hard to do will be considered bad deeds – not petty ones.)		

Form VIII can have the same meaning as form I verbs.فَعَلَ

I read	اقترأتُ	قرأتُ
I seized	اختطفت	خطفت

Form VIII verbs can also indicate appearance or exhibition.

The man apologized (he is exhibiting a plea)	اعتذر الرجل
The man raged (he showed anger)	اغتضب الرجل
The leader excelled / triumphed / gloried (showed greatness)	اعتظم القائد

Form IX	يَفْعَلَّ	افْعَلَّ
Form I	+	ا

Form IX is formed by adding an alif (hamzat al-waşl) before form I, and adding a sukuun on the 'ف', a fatHa on the '3yn' and a shaddah with a fatHa to the 'ل' of the verb.

The most common attribute of form IX is its color or a physical deformity.

These verbs are used with colors. The color stated is what the subject of the sentence turns into. For example, "my skin turned red". In Arabic, change the color ('aHmar') into a verb form XI by placing the above markings on 'aHmmar'.

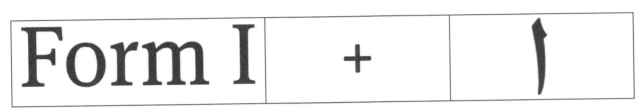

| اعْوَجَّ | احْوَلَّ | ازْرَقَّ | اخْضَرَّ | اسْوَدَّ | احْمَرَّ | ابْيَضَّ | اصْفَرَّ |

Translations from right to left: becomes yellow, becomes white, red, black, green, hue, cross-eyed, and crooked.

Another meaning for form IX is to denote a defect, such as "turning cross-eyed" or "to be crooked".

Ahmed's face turned yellow because of the disease.	اصْفَرَّ وجهُ أحمدٍ من المرضِ.	اصْفَرَّ
My teeth turned white because of the new toothpaste.	ابْيَضَّتْ أسناني ... تعمالِ المعجونِ الجديدِ.	ابْيَضَّ
Linda's face turned red due to shyness. [Blushed]	احْمَرَّ وجهُ ليندا من خجلِ.	احْمَرَّ
The banana turned black after I peeled it and forgot about it.	اسْوَدَّ الموزُ بعدَ أن قشّرتُهُ ... تُه.	اسْوَدَّ
My leg became crooked and it hurts me a lot.	اعْوَجَّت ساقِي وتؤلمني كثيرا.	اعْوَجَّ

يَفْعَلُّ

| يَعْوَجّ | يَحْوَلّ | يَزرّ | يَخْضَرَّ | يَسْوَدَّ | يَحْمَرَّ | يَبْيَضّ | يَصْفَرّ |

The dates turned red	احمرَّ البلح
The grapes turned black	اسودَّ العنب
The grass turned green	اخضرَّ العشب
The man became one-eyed	اعورَّ الرجل
The child became limp	اعرجَّ الطفل

Form X | يَسْتَفْعِلُ استَفْعَلَ

Form X is built on form I by adding alif (hamzat al-waṣl), 'siin' with a sukuun and a 'taa' with a fatHa; the 'ف' of the verb takes a sukuun.

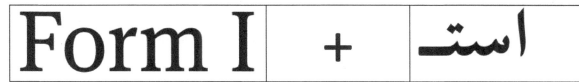

| Form I | + | است |

Please note the hamza in the beginning is the connecting hamza, its purpose is to be able to pronounce the vowelless siin that comes after it. The siin and the taa that follow it denoting a request,

Examples:

the buyer enquires about the price	اسْتَعْلَمَ المشتري عن السِعْرِ.
Ahmed considers the bag heavy, so he left it	اسْتَثْقَلَ أحمدُ الحقيبة فتركَها.
my father invested some money	اسْتَثْمَرَ والدي بعضَ المالِ.
the patient enquired about his condition	اسْتَفْسَرَ المريضُ عن حالتِه.
my brother used my pen	اسْتَعْمَلَ أخي قلمِي

This form is considered by Arabic linguists to be the most brilliant of forms for its ability to replace several words with just one. It is built from stripped, trilateral الفعل المجرد, transitive المتعدي and intransitive اللازم form I verbs. 'Ista3lama' إستعلم means 'to enquire'. It is from '3alema', عَلِمَ 'to know', a form I verb.

Examples of transitive verbs	
The patient used the medicine	استعمل المريض الدواء.
The believer asked Allah for forgiveness	استغفر المؤمن ربه.
Mohammed sought to clarify the matter	استجلى محمد الأمر.
The man took some water out of the well	استخرج الرجل الماء من البئر.
Examples of intransitive verbs	
The enemy surrendered	استسلم العدو.
The mud hardened like a stone	استحجر الطين.

The shadow straightened	استقام الظل.
He regarded the matter as tremendous	استعظم الأمر.

There are several features of this form. One is to perceive someone has certain characteristics. For example, 'istakramtuhu' استكرمته means 'I perceive generosity in him'.

This verb group can also be used to ask for something; for example, to ask somebody to give you a gift or to ask somebody for forgiveness. This can be confusing, for if you say, 'I used the pen' أستعملت القلم you actually put the verb 'used' in form X. This literally translates as asking the pen to work for you.

Also evinced in verbs in this form is transformation, specifically metaphors. For example, if someone acts like a lion; أستأسدَ.

Form X is how you perceive form I. Thus, form X 'to enquire' is derived from form I 'to know': I got the knowledge by enquiring. Form X 'I consider the bag is heavy' is derived from form I 'to make the bag heavy': I consider it heavy because I saw you putting more things in it .

The definition of form X we have given is by no means conclusive. There will always be a relationship between form I and form X, perhaps not as direct as we have suggested above.

Whenever you have a verb derived from another, in most cases there will be a relationship between the two.

اسْتَفْعَلَ

اسْتَكَ	اسْتَصْغَرَ	اسْتَعْمَلَ	اسْتَفْسَرَ	اسْتَثْمَرَ	اسْتَثْقَ	اسْتَشْهَدَ	اسْتَعْلَمَ	اسْتَعْجَلَ	اسْتَعْظَ

To consider it great, to become a martyr, to hurry, to enquire, to consider it heavy, to invest, to ask for clarification / enquire, to use, to consider it small / belittle, to regard as great.

يَسْتَفْعِلُ

يَسْتَعْجِلُ	يَسْتَشْهِدُ	يَسْتَعْظِمُ	يَسْتَكُ	يَسْتَصْغِرُ	يَسْتَعْمِ	يَسْتَفْسِرُ	يَسْتَثْمِرُ	يَسْتَثْقِلُ	يَسْتَعْلِمُ

Form X will often be used in the context of asking. This can be asking God for forgiveness or a generous person to give you charity. Sometime this asking is metaphorical: you can use form X to say that, for example, oil is being extracted from the earth, or if you are a poet and you are looking for an inspiration. In these cases, you are not asking directly for these things, but metaphorically: it suggests that the process was not easy.	استكتبت البائع استعطيت الكريم استغفرت ربي استخرجت النفط من البئر

The translations on the right are: I asked the salesman to write, I asked the generous person for charity, I asked god for forgiveness, I extracted the oil from the well, I seek inspiration for speech, I seek guidance for the novel.	استلهمت القول استوحيت القصة

The condition or quality that you find someone in: 'I found him to be boring', 'I thought he was fat'. The subject of the verb should have the characteristic of the verb. 'I believe his speech was perfect', 'I believe Mohammed was generous', 'I think the water is sweet', 'I find the food salty' or 'I found him unpunctual'. Another attribute of these verbs is how they describe somebody's characteristics: in Arabic, rather than simply using (for example) the adjective 'arrogant', you can use a clause with a verb of this type to state that somebody is acting pompously or pretentiously.	استحسنت كلامه. استكرمت محمداً. استعذبت الماء. استملحت الطعام. استعظمته تكبر الرجل . تفهم واستفهم. تأمل واستأمل . تبصر واستبصر. تعلّى واستعلى.

Question:

Please write the verbs that correspondent to form pattern meaning next to them.

Form I Depending on the medial vowel, the verb could refer to an attribute of the subject of a verb, express the general verbal meaning of the root in question, or refer to emotions and its opposites. Denotes that the verb has happened one time.	فَعِلَ

Form II
  1. Participation
  2. Intransitivity
  3. Repetition
  4. Timing
  5. Nisba, the object has an attribute of the verb
  6. Continuation of action
  7. Praying for or against
  8. Transformation related to the verb
  9. Heading into direction
  10. Timing, verb is performed in certain time
  11. Acceptance to act on your behalf
  12. Truncating a phrase
	فَعَّل

13. Causation 14. Truncating phrases 15. Removal	

Form III
  1. Participation
  2. Becoming, having an attribute indicated by the verb
  3. Continuation of action
  4. Intensiveness in performing the verb
  5. Enduring hardship while performing the verb
	فَاعَلَ

Form IV
  1. Transitivity
  2. Timing
  3. Direction
  4. Reaching a number
  5. Removal
  6. Becoming, having an attribute indicated by the verb
  7. Object has the attribute of a verb
  8. Due for action
  9. Indicate plentitude
 10. Enabling someone perform the verb
 11. Praying
	أَفْعَلَ

Form V
  1. Realization of intention, reflexive
  2. Intensification
  3. transitivity
  4. adoption
  5. Assuming a quality or an attribute
  6. Avoidance
  7. Gradual repetition of action
  8. Requesting, similar to form ten
	تَفَعَّلَ

Form VI
  1. Participation with intensity
  2. Intransitivity
  3. Deception, delusion
  4. Gradual increase
	تَفَاعَلَ

FormVII
  1. This form is heavily concerned with realization of intention
  2. Transitivity
	إِنْفَعَلَ

Form VIII
  1. Realization of intention, reflexive of several verb forms.
  2. Participation
  3. Exerting effort
  4. Intensiveness
  5. Acquisition/adoption
  6. Showing emotions
	إِفْتَعَلَ

Form IX 1. Intensity of color 2. Expressing physical deformity	اِفْعَلَّ
Form X 1. Requesting 2. Perceiving, believing 3. Transformation of characteristics	اِسْتَفْعَلَ

A different way of studying verb forms

Studying the meanings of different verb forms by their numerical verb form is a European concept, originating in the nineteenth century. In Arab academia, and in some Western grammar books, this topic is explained differently. It is taught by dividing trilateral verbs (or any other verb that has all original letters, such as quadrilateral verbs) into those that increase by one letter, and those increased by two letters, and those increased by three letters. The reason this is done is that a verb form cannot be limited to certain meanings, as you see from the above: the meanings overlap and are duplicitous; therefore, it will be arduous to give form numbers to verbs and assign numbers to it.

Here you can see the other method:

You can see trilateral verbs that increase by one letter. This one letter could be a hamzah, could be an alif after the 'faa' of the verb, and also could be a shaddah placed on the 3yn of the verb. Next, you will find a trilateral verb that has been increased by two letters. You will see verbs that are prefixed by an alif and a nuun (the alif is actually hamzah-tunwasl); a verb that increases by an alif and a 'taa'; a verb that increases by a 'taa' and an alif; a verb that increases by a 'taa' and a shaddah. You will also see the trilateral verbs that increase by three letters. These are verbs preceded by an alif-siin and a 'taa'.

Trilateral verb that increased by one letter	الفعل الثلاثي المزيد بحرف واحد
Trilateral verb that increased by two letters	الفعل الثلاثي المزيد بحرفين
Trilateral verb that increased by three letters	الفعل الثلاثي المزيد بثلاثة أحرف

أولا: الفعل الثلاثي المزيد بحرف واحد

Increase by a shaddah		Increased by an alif after the faa of the verb		Increase by a hamzah		Trilateral Basic verb
pattern	Verb after the increase	pattern	Verb after the increase	patterns	Verb after the increase	

فَعَّل	خَرَّج	فَاعَل	خَارِج	أَفْعَل	أَخْرَج	خَرَج
فَعَّل	قَبَّل	فَاعَل	قَابَل	أَفْعَل	أَقْبَل	قَبل
فَعَّل	نَطَّق	فَاعَل	نَاطَق	أَفْعَل	أَنْطَق	نَطَق
فَعَّل	كَرَّم	فَاعَل	كَارَم	أَفْعَل	أَكْرَم	كرم
فَعَّل	صَلَّح	فَاعَل	صَالَح	أَفْعَل	أَصْلَح	صَلُح
فَعَّل	كَثَّرَ	فَاعَل	كَاثَرَ	أَفْعَل	أَكْثَرَ	كَثُرَ
فَعَّل	غَلَّب	فَاعَل	غَالَب	أَفْعَل	أَغْلَب	غَلَب
فَعَّل	شَرَّك	فَاعَل	شَارَك	أَفْعَل	أَشْرَك	شرك
فَعَّل	قَضَّى	فَاعَل	قَاضى	أَفْعَل	أَقْضى	قَضى
فَعَّل	حَكَّم	فَاعَل	حَاكَم	أَفْعَل	أَحْكَم	حَكَم
فَعَّل	نَصَّف	فَاعَل	نَاصَف	أَفْعَل	أَنْصَف	نَصَف
فَعَّل	قَسَّم	فَاعَل	قَاسَم	أَفْعَل	أَقْسَم	قَسَم

ثانيا: الفعل الثلاثي المزيد بحرفين:

المزيد بالتاء والتضعيف		المزيد بالتاء والألف		المزيد بالالف والتاء		المزيد بالألف والنون		الفعل
وزنه	الفعل بعد الزيادة	وزنه	الفعل بعد الزيادة	وزنه	الفعل بعد الزيادة	وزنه	الفعل بعد الزيادة	
تَفَعَّل	تَفَتَّح	تَفَاعَل	تَفَاتَح	افْتَعَل	افْتَتَح	انْفَعَل	انْفَتَح	فَتَح
تَفَعَّل	تَفَهَّم	تَفَاعَل	تَفَاهَم	افْتَعَل	افْتَهَم	انْفَعَل	انْفَهَم	فَهِم
تَفَعَّل	تَخَلَّط	تَفَاعَل	تَخَالَط	افْتَعَل	اخْتَلَط	انْفَعَل	انْخَلَط	خَلَطَ
تَفَعَّل	تَحَفَّظ	تَفَاعَل	تَحَافَظ	افْتَعَل	احْتَفَظ	انْفَعَل	انْحَفظ	حَفِظَ
تَفَعَّل	تَأَمَّر	تَفَاعَل	تآمَرَ	افْتَعَل	ائْتَمَرَ	انْفَعَل	انْأَمَرَ	أَمَرَ
تَفَعَّل	تَقَتَّل	تَفَاعَل	تَقَاتَل	افْتَعَل	اقْتَتَل	انْفَعَل	انْقَتَل	قَتَلَ
تَفَعَّل	تَرَفَّع	تَفَاعَل	تَرَافَع	افْتَعَل	ارْتَفَع	انْفَعَل	انْرَفَع	رَفَعَ
تَفَعَّل	تَبَعَّد	تَفَاعَل	تَبَاعَدَ	افْتَعَل	ابْتَعَدَ	انْفَعَل	انْبَعَدَ	بَعُدَ
تَفَعَّل	تَسَبَّق	تَفَاعَل	تَسَابَقَ	افْتَعَل	اسْتَبَق	انْفَعَل	انْسَبَق	سَبَقَ

| تَفَعَّلَ | تَعَفَّنَ | تَفَاعَلَ | تَعَافَنَ | افْتَعَلَ | اعْتَفَنَ | انْفَعَلَ | انْعَفَنَ | عَفِنَ |
| تَفَعَّلَ | تَسَلَّمَ | تَفَاعَلَ | تَسَالَمَ | افْتَعَلَ | اسْتَلَمَ | انْفَعَلَ | انْسَلَمَ | سَلِمَ |

ثالثا: الفعل الثلاثي المزيد بثلاثة أحرف:

الوزن	الفعل بعد الزيادة	الفعل
اسْتَفْعَلَ	اسْتَمَدَّ	مَدَّ (وأصله مَدْدَ)
اسْتَفْعَلَ	اسْتَعَادَ	عَادَ
اسْتَفْعَلَ	اسْتَخْرَجَ	خَرَجَ
اسْتَفْعَلَ	اسْتَكْثَرَ	كَبُرَ
اسْتَفْعَلَ	اسْتَلْقَى	لَقَى
اسْتَفْعَلَ	اسْتَغْفَرَ	غَفَرَ
اسْتَفْعَلَ	اسْتَعْمَرَ	عَمَرَ
اسْتَفْعَلَ	اسْتَنْهَضَ	نَهَضَ
اسْتَفْعَلَ	اسْتَقَامَ	قَامَ
اسْتَفْعَلَ	اسْتَرْضَى	رَضِيَ
اسْتَفْعَلَ	اسْتَفْهَمَ	فَهِمَ
اسْتَفْعَلَ	اسْتَوْثَقَ	وَثَقَ
اسْتَفْعَلَ	اسْتَكْتَبَ	كَتَبَ
اسْتَفْعَلَ	اسْتَعْمَلَ	عَمِلَ
اسْتَفْعَلَ	اسْتَنْفَعَ	نَفَعَ
اسْتَفْعَلَ	اسْتَنْطَقَ	نَطَقَ
اسْتَفْعَلَ	اسْتَزَادَ	زَادَ
اسْتَفْعَلَ	اسْتَقْرَأَ	قَرَأَ
اسْتَفْعَلَ	اسْتَشْعَرَ	شَعَرَ
اسْتَفْعَلَ	اسْتَمَعَ	سَمِعَ

To be far	بَعُدَ
to increase, grow, augment, intensify heighten, to be(come) more great(er) large(r)	زَادَ
to write, pen, write down, to compose, draw up, draft	كَتَبَ
To find, to meet	لَقِى
To be fair	نَصَف
To be content	رَضِيَ
oath	قَسَم
to accept (to), agree (to), consent (to), assent (to), approve (of), to settle for	قَبِلَ
to be good, right, to be virtuous, righteous, to be fit, suitable, to suit, fit, to serve (for) , to be serviceable, useful	صَلُحَ
to be sure of, certain of	وَثَقَ
to be useful, helpful, beneficial , profitable, to help, benefit , avail, serve	نَفَعَ
to be(come) great(er) big(ger) large(r) to grow increase augment	كَبُرَ
to carry out, accomplish, achieve, finish, to do, perform, fulfill, discharge	قَضَى
to defeat, beat, triumph over get the better of, overcome	غَلَبَ
to do; make, to act, to perform; carry out, to produce , to work, to toil, labor, to function; operate, run	عَمِلَ
to escape danger, to be safe; secure, to be sound , intact	سَلِمَ
to feel; sense, to perceive, notice, to be(come) conscious of	شَعَرَ
to forgive , pardon , excuse , condone , remit , absolve	غَفَرَ
to go out, come out, emerge, to walk out, exit, to leave	خَرَجَ
to hear, accept, answer, grant, fulfill	سَمِعَ
to honor, to ennoble, exalt, dignify, to entertain, welcome	كرم
to increase grow multiply to abound to be(come) numerous abundant plentiful ample	كَثُرَ
to keep, preserve, protect, (safe)guard, to maintain, to save, conserve , to observe, comply with, abide by	حَفِظَ
to kill; slay; murder	قَتَلَ
to live long; to build, construct, erect	عَمَرَ

to mix, mingle, blend, commingle, combine	خَلَطَ
to open, unlock, unfasten	فَتَحَ
to order, command , instruct	أَمَرَ
to precede, antecede, forego, to antedate, predate, to outstrip, outdistance, overtake, pass, go past	سَبَقَ
to pronounce, utter, say, to speak , talk	نَطَقَ
to raise, lift (up), uplift, hoist (up), elevate, to raise, increase, step up, hike, to heighten, enhance, to raise, erect, set up, put up, build, construct, to remove, take away , eliminate, to lift	رَفَعَ
to read, to recite	قَرَأَ
to return, come back, go back, to recur, reoccur, to go back to	عَادَ
to rise, get up, stand up, to set out	قَامَ
to rise, get up, to raise, lift, carry, to uplift	نَهَضَ
to rot, decay, decompose, putrefy, spoil, to mold	عَفِنَ
to rule, reign, to govern, manage, direct, run	حَكَمَ
to understand, grasp, comprehend, realize, see	فَهِمَ
Trap, snare, net	شَرَك